Social Cyber Engineering and Advanced Security Algorithms

This book takes readers on a captivating journey through the history of social engineering, tracing its evolution from the mechanical marvels of the clockwork era and the rise of automata to the modern age of artificial intelligence and the looming dawn of quantum computing. It explores how social engineering tactics have adapted alongside technological advancements, exploiting human psychology and vulnerabilities across every era.

Social Cyber Engineering and Advanced Security Algorithms delves into the intricate connections between human behavior, evolving technology, and the ever-changing landscape of cybersecurity. It examines how personal and psychological factors can be exploited in cyberattacks, providing real-world examples and case studies to illustrate these vulnerabilities. Beyond highlighting the challenges, the book offers proactive strategies and potential solutions for organizations and policymakers to navigate this complex terrain. It emphasizes the importance of algorithmic resilience in employee categorization and training and explores the transformative potential of quantum computing in bridging mental health and cybersecurity.

This book serves as a guide for computer scientists, engineers, and professionals interested in understanding the intricate relationship between human behavior, technology, and security in the digital age. It offers a unique perspective on the past, present, and future of social engineering, providing valuable insights for anyone seeking to build a more secure and resilient digital world.

Social Cyber Engineering and Advanced Security Algorithms

Soorena Merat and Wahab Almuhtadi

CRC Press
Taylor & Francis Group
Boca Raton London New York

CRC Press is an imprint of the
Taylor & Francis Group, an **informa** business

Designed cover image: Shutterstock

First edition published 2025
by CRC Press
6000 Broken Sound Parkway NW, Suite 300, Boca Raton, FL 33487-2742

and by CRC Press
4 Park Square, Milton Park, Abingdon, Oxon, OX14 4RN

CRC Press is an imprint of Taylor & Francis Group, LLC

ISBN: 978-1-032-81644-9 (hbk)
ISBN: 978-1-032-81643-2 (pbk)
ISBN: 978-1-003-50069-8 (ebk)

DOI: 10.1201/9781003500698

Typeset in Times
by KnowledgeWorks Global Ltd.

Contents

About the Authors

Soorena Merat is the Chief Cyber Security Officer at Silkatech Consulting Engineers Inc. With over three decades of experience in the technology industry, Dr. Merat brings unwavering commitment and a deep understanding of the ever-shifting cybersecurity landscape. His research focuses on the fascinating intersection of bioneural systems, artificial intelligence, and social cyber engineering. Dr. Merat's work delves into the intricate dynamics of human behavior within technological environments, exploring how vulnerabilities emerge and how they can be proactively addressed. He is particularly interested in developing predictive models that identify potential weaknesses in systems and generating actionable recommendations for enhanced security controls. This research combines insights from neuroscience, cognitive psychology, and computer science to create a more holistic approach to cybersecurity. Driven by a passion for innovation and a commitment to excellence, Dr. Merat's journey in the tech industry is marked by a continuous pursuit of knowledge. He remains at the forefront of advancements in the field, ensuring that his expertise and insights contribute to a safer and more secure digital world.

Dr. Wahab Almuhtadi has over 33 years of industry experience, concurrently over 27 years of university teaching experience. He is Professor/Coordinator of "Optical Systems and Sensors" Program, Algonquin College/Carleton University, Canada. He is Research Council Member, Digital Research Alliance of Canada. Previously, he was Senior System Engineer at Nortel, Optical Solutions R&D. With his professional background, he demonstrated outstanding leadership establishing Applied Research with $10.5M fund that fostered Algonquin College to become Polytechnic Institution. He is the founder of the $6 million cutting-edge Optophotonics Lab (Optical Communications Network) 200Gbps. He is one of the founders of Ontario's Centre of Excellence in Next Generation Networks (CENGN) with $65 million in funding. His expertise is in photonics, optical systems and sensors, optical communications, and wireless. He has published several technical papers and books. He received several awards from IEEE, academia, and industry, e.g., 2010 IEEE Leadership Award, 2015 IEEE Canada W.R. Service Award, 2009 Laurent Isabelle Teaching Excellence, 2006 NISOD Award, and 2015 Canadian Pacific Railway Engineering Medal, Engineering Institute of Canada-EIC. He is P.Eng. and EIC Fellow. Dr. Almuhtadi is actively involved in IEEE for over 29 years serving in many executive level posts across IEEE. He is also currently the President-Elect/Director-Elect (2024–2025) of IEEE Canada/Region 7. IEEE President of IEEE Consumer Technology Society (CTSoc).

Preface

A JOURNEY THROUGH THE DIGITAL LABYRINTH

In the golden light of an autumn afternoon in 2020, our team began a deep look into the vast troves of knowledge housed within the University of Toronto's online library. We sought to understand the explosive advancements in neural networks and AI, recognizing their power to reimagine our world. However, it was not just the technology that intrigued us but how it reshaped the most fundamental aspects of our existence – from the subtle ways, we connect digitally to the unseen vulnerabilities that leave us open to manipulation.

We realized that the "everyday life" of the digital era, with its emotional complexities and behavior patterns, was often overlooked in technical analyses. There was a disconnect between these systems' theoretical capabilities and the average user's lived experience. Our research aimed to bridge that gap, exploring how technology erodes authenticity and how the patterns we form online make us more susceptible to social engineering and vulnerable to manipulation. Additionally, we cast our gaze further, anticipating the revolutionary power of quantum computing and how AI algorithms running on these systems could further reshape our world.

To capture the human element, we developed a unique experimental model that analyzed how users interacted with systems and the emotions behind those interactions. We saw how even simple tasks, made needlessly complex through poor design, create frustration that opens the door for social engineers. This model highlighted the disconnect between those creating technology and those who must use it. Our studies extended beyond the purely theoretical. We conducted social engineering simulations where participants were not merely tested but became sources of insight into their hopes, anxieties, and how these manifest in a digital environment. It became clear that factors as seemingly irrelevant as a night of poor sleep made them far more likely to fall for attacks. Our bodies and our digital lives were more intertwined than we had expected.

We saw that each user's tech journey is shaped by their unique history and adapting our engagement strategies to be relatable dramatically improved results. Humor, surprisingly, became a countermeasure to manipulation.

Like the clockwork wonders of centuries past, today's technological marvels provoke excitement and unease. The automata of the past forced society to examine the nature of the human soul – today's algorithms make us question what it means to have an authentic identity. On the horizon, the enigmatic power of quantum computing hints at a future where AI might possess capabilities that challenge our current understanding of manipulation and social engineering.

As our work progressed, the enigma of how digital systems reshape us became less a question of if and more of how much. This book, therefore, is our attempt to make sense of it all. It guides those seeking to understand the social engineering dangers of this transformation and how we might shape a more secure and healthy digital future by learning from past mistakes.

Since we began this project, the pace of change has only accelerated. However, human nature remains constant. This book seeks to illuminate that duality: how ancient social dynamics manifest in new ways due to technology. We invite readers to observe this transformation and actively participate in shaping a future where we are masters of technology, not its unwitting victims.

A CALL TO ACTION: SECURING THE FUTURE

The potential of quantum computing, with its ability to crack current encryption methods and potentially revolutionize AI capabilities, adds another layer of complexity to the social engineering landscape. Like any emerging technology, the potential for misuse demands early attention.

While this book looks into quantum mechanics and its potential impact on cybersecurity, it is essential to note that this is not a comprehensive catalogue of quantum algorithms or their immediate applications. Instead, the focus lies on charting a visionary path forward, highlighting the strategic implications and need for out-of-the-box thinking in cybersecurity. By analyzing the unique properties of quantum systems and exploring the potential of quantum-inspired logic, the aim is to spark innovation and encourage future thinkers to embrace these concepts. The goal is to foster new approaches beyond traditional cybersecurity defense mechanisms. Let this book serve as a catalyst, inspiring cybersecurity strategies designed to meet the challenges of a future shaped by both the threats and opportunities presented by quantum technology.

We can confidently navigate the digital labyrinth, not just through technical mastery, but by fostering a broad public awareness that transcends the lines of code and technology textbooks. This awareness must be rooted in lessons from history, showcasing how societies throughout time have grappled with, and ultimately learned to navigate, the opportunities and challenges of technological advancement. This book seeks to bridge the gap between the societal and technological, reminding us that our greatest innovations are intertwined with our deepest vulnerabilities. While the link between these two realms may seem captivatingly strange and non-linear, understanding it is crucial for our digital future. We encourage you, the reader, to journey through these pages with an eye on the present – seeking out current examples of social engineering in the news and publications – and prepare for a thought-provoking exploration. We have peppered this text with real-world examples to guide you, but ultimately, it's up to each of us to equip ourselves for the intricate dance between humanity and technology.

NOTE TO READERS

This book is your guide to understanding how technology shapes our social and virtual lives, empowering you to make informed choices in an increasingly digital world. It's not a technical manual, but rather a journey through the evolution of technology and its impact on human behavior. We'll explore historical examples and offer practical takeaways to help you navigate the complex landscape of cybersecurity.

While some technical concepts will be touched upon, this book primarily focuses on fostering awareness and inspiring behavioral change. To fully grasp the real-world implications, readers are encouraged to supplement their reading with insights from cybersecurity experts and stay abreast of current events in the field. Prepare to embark on a thought-provoking exploration of the intricate relationship between technology and society, where the past illuminates the present, and proactive awareness becomes your most potent defense.

Section Two

EXPLORING THE INTRICACIES OF HUMAN BEHAVIOR AND SOCIAL CYBER ENGINEERING THREATS: TACKLING THE TECHNOLOGICAL CHALLENGES IN IDENTIFYING COMPLEX SOCIAL ISSUES

Beyond the Code: Deciphering the Human Element in Social Engineering

While cybersecurity often focuses on technical vulnerabilities, the most effective social engineering attacks exploit far more than flaws in software. They target the intricate workings of the human mind – our biases, emotions, and social instincts. To safeguard against these threats, we must venture beyond purely technological solutions. A deep understanding of human behavior is essential, as social engineers manipulate trust, fear, and desire to bypass even the most robust technical defenses. Identifying the subtle cues of social engineering amid the vast and dynamic tapestry of online interactions presents a formidable challenge. Traditional analysis methods often fall short when faced with human communication and persuasion nuances. This necessitates a multipronged approach, drawing insights from:

Psychology: Understanding cognitive biases, persuasion techniques, and the emotional triggers that social engineers exploit.

Behavioral Science: Analyzing how individuals interact and make decisions in digital environments reveals patterns attackers can manipulate.

Social Sciences: Examining the broader social and cultural contexts that shape online trust, vulnerability, and the spread of misinformation.

There are good examples and case studies that examine the weaponizing features of the social engineering aspects of human nature with the technological innovations, this section reviews the skills and knowledge that is needed to detect increasingly sophisticated attacks.

NOTE TO READERS

This section explores the intersection of societal vulnerabilities and social engineering in the context of emerging technologies. We will examine specific cases such as personal mental health challenges, substance abuse, and societal emergencies, illustrating how these can be exploited in increasingly sophisticated social engineering attacks.

The aim is not to alarm, but to empower. By understanding the tactics employed by malicious actors, who are often highly intelligent and well-versed in technology, readers can develop a heightened awareness and cultivate strategies for personal resilience.

As you navigate this section, pay close attention not only to the nature of each vulnerability, but to the potential for its exploitation within social engineering scenarios. This section encouraging readers to actively engage with the evolving technological landscape and understand its impact on their lives, both online and offline. Remember, knowledge is your first line of defense.

Section Three

SECURING TOMORROW: LEVERAGING ADVANCED TECHNOLOGY TO COUNTERACT COMPLEX SOCIAL ENGINEERING AND CYBERSECURITY THREATS

Securing Tomorrow: Beyond Conventional Defenses

Section Three of this book focuses on a specific type of quantum algorithm and quantum application that lends itself to simulation on classical computers or specialized digital hardware. This means that a physical quantum computer is not essential; however, these simulations might demand a combination of circuit depth, coherence time, or connectivity that currently exceeds the capabilities of available physical quantum computers. As the threat of social engineering attacks escalates, we must look toward security solutions that are as adaptable as the tactics themselves. The power of AI and machine learning offers exciting potential for rapid evolution and response. However, maximizing the effectiveness of these tools requires moving beyond technical solutions alone. Successfully combating social engineering demands a holistic approach, where cutting-edge technology seamlessly integrates with a deep understanding of the psychological vulnerabilities that such attacks exploit.

Figure 0.1 represents a miniature quantum computer undergoing testing. Today's data protection concept, such as saving encrypted data for decryption once powerful quantum computers become commonplace, highlights the quantum revolution's long-term implications. This strategy, often termed "Save Now, Decrypt Later," acknowledges that encryption methods considered secure today may become vulnerable to future quantum algorithms. By preserving sensitive information – such as top-secret government documents or other valuable data – organizations are essentially betting that powerful commercial quantum computers will one day unlock what is currently unbreakable. Another inherent nature of quantum computation also poses a significant challenge for commercialization. Unlike classical computers,

FIGURE 0.1 An example of testing quantum computers. (Image courtesy of Australian Broadcasting Corporation.)

which yield a single, definitive answer, quantum computers operate on the principle of superposition. This means that multiple states representing potential solutions exist simultaneously. The true power of quantum computers lies in their ability to process numerous possibilities in parallel. However, collapsing the system into a single, usable answer is essential to translate this superposition of states into real-world applications. Developing reliable, repeatable mechanisms to achieve this delicate balance – extracting the desired solution while preserving the system's delicate coherence – is a critical hurdle to the widespread adoption of quantum computing.

Figure 0.2 conceptualizes the delicate manipulation of quantum superposition states, a fundamental principle underlying quantum computing. Some sections of this book offer practical, low-tech solutions for human interaction. While these methods may not be high-tech, they effectively contribute to the overall "quantum intent" of the chosen solution. In other words, these simple strategies, when implemented, can nudge outcomes in a positive direction, aligning with the desired

FIGURE 0.2 A symbolic view of controlling quantum superposition for computing purposes.

goals. This approach underscores the disruptive potential of quantum computing and emphasizes the need for ongoing vigilance in the field of cryptography. It serves as a reminder of the far-reaching consequences of emerging technology and raises questions about the enduring value of information in the face of evolving computational power. As another example, let us look at The National Security Agency (NSA), which has painted a sobering picture of the potential impact of quantum computing on current cryptographic systems. They acknowledge the immense potential benefits of this technology but also emphasize the significant risks it poses to national security and economic well-being. The primary concern lies in the ability of quantum computers to break widely used public-key cryptography, potentially jeopardizing the confidentiality and integrity of sensitive communications, financial transactions, and critical infrastructure control systems.

The NSA has stressed the urgency of proactive measures. They advocate for a multi-pronged approach, including prioritizing developing and implementing quantum-resistant cryptographic algorithms well before the threat becomes imminent. Collaboration between government agencies, industry leaders, and academic researchers is crucial to ensure a smooth transition to a post-quantum cryptographic landscape. By acknowledging the threat posed by quantum computing and taking decisive steps toward mitigation, the NSA aims to safeguard classified information, protect critical infrastructure, and maintain stability in the digital age.

This highlights the need for a global conversation about the responsible development and deployment of quantum computing. While technology holds immense promise, neglecting the security risks could have far-reaching consequences. By fostering international collaboration and prioritizing the development of quantum-resistant cryptography, we can ensure that quantum computing ushers in an era of innovation without compromising security.

While quantum mechanics is extraordinarily successful in the physical concepts, its unique properties hold potential applications in strengthening cybersecurity defenses, particularly against social engineering attacks. The field of quantum logic seeks to translate the counterintuitive principles of quantum mechanics into logical frameworks. This has several potential cybersecurity applications:

Detecting Deception: Quantum logic could help analyze communication patterns or behavioral data to identify anomalies that signal deception attempts, a core tactic in social engineering.

Secure Communication: The principles of quantum entanglement and superposition could inspire new cryptographic protocols or methods for verifying the authenticity of communications, making it harder for social engineers to impersonate legitimate sources.

Human Behavior Modeling: Quantum logic might offer new ways to model and understand human decision-making processes. This could help predict vulnerabilities to social engineering manipulation and design more effective countermeasures.

Important Considerations

In the early stages of development, it's crucial to establish a strong foundation through effective communication and teamwork. Collaboration is key, as it fosters creativity and innovation while ensuring that diverse perspectives are integrated into the process.

Early Stage of Development: Quantum logic applied to cybersecurity is mainly theoretical. Extensive research and development are needed to translate these concepts into practical defense mechanisms.

Collaboration Is Key: Integrating the principles of quantum logic into cybersecurity will likely require collaboration between experts in quantum physics, computer science, logic, and social engineering tactics.

Here is how we begin; we will further look into some of the following areas:

The AI Arms Race: Can algorithms be trained to "think" like a social engineer, anticipating their next move?

Proactive Defense: Can we analyze user behavior to identify those increasingly susceptible to manipulation?

A New Kind of Cybersecurity Expert: Will we need specialists trained in threat detection and behavioral psychology?

The notion of training AI algorithms to mimic the tactics of social engineers presents a compelling prospect in the ongoing battle against cybercrime. By understanding the psychology behind social engineering and the techniques employed by attackers, could we empower AI to anticipate their next moves and ultimately thwart their attempts? This concept raises intriguing possibilities. With its vast data processing capabilities, AI could analyze communication patterns and behavioral cues to identify red flags that signal social engineering attempts. It could then intervene in real-time, alerting potential victims or disrupting the attack flow. However, significant challenges remain. Social engineering relies heavily on human interaction, often adapting tactics based on the target's emotional state and responses. Can AI truly replicate the nuanced understanding of human psychology that fuels successful social engineering scams?

Additionally, the ethical implications of creating AI that excels at deception require careful consideration. Whether AI can "think" like a social engineer may be less relevant than its ability to augment human defenses. Perhaps the most promising path lies in fostering a collaborative approach, where AI identifies potential threats while human expertise guides the response. By combining human intuition and judgment with the analytical power of AI, we could create a more robust defense network against the ever-evolving tactics of social engineers.

NOTE TO READERS

This section is dedicated to fostering public awareness about the versatility and complexity of emerging technologies. We explore potential social engineering scenarios to illustrate the attack vectors these technologies may present. Please note that this is not a technical deep-dive into these technologies or their inherent flaws. Rather, the goal is to raise awareness, deepen understanding, and empower readers to proactively adapt their behaviors in the face of an increasingly complex technological landscape.

1 Personal Security in the Era of Mechanical Marvels

A Historical Perspective

The clockwork and mechanical era offer a broad lens through which to view the evolution of security. The same precision that drove industry also reshaped how we thought about protecting ourselves. This chapter examines how advancements in mechanical marvels, automaton, clockmaking, and the changing social landscape have led to the innovation of new technologies and security measures.

In the early 1700s, while the age of complex automatons was dawning, personal security remained firmly rooted in communal and self-governed measures. For example, the night watchmen and community patrols served as the linchpins of public safety, while an individual's protection relied on means of mechanical advancements and physical barriers like locks, bolts, and personal arms. The specter of automaton, a machine with the potential for independent action, hinted at a future where safeguarding oneself might not be purely a matter of brute force.

As the century progressed and urban centers expanded, the need for more organized protection systems became clear. However, even with the advent of formal police services like the "Bobbies" of London near the century's end, personal vigilance and community solidarity remained paramount. This period highlights a tension that still resonates today: the reliance on external protectors versus the ingrained understanding that safety was fundamentally an individual responsibility. Subtly, the rise of automatons, with their intricate systems of control and potential for exceeding their intended function, mirrored anxieties about whether these emerging policing models could indeed guarantee safety or whether they introduced new vulnerabilities for those meant to be protected.

MECHANICAL ERA SHARED LIMITATIONS AND MODERN TECH ANXIETIES

The limitations of traditional night security guards, hampered by darkness, limited workforce, and the potential for corruption or exhaustion, created a persistent sense of vulnerability despite a system focused on protection. Similarly, while promising precision and tireless vigilance, the concept of automatons carried an underlying unease regarding the potential corruption of their mechanisms and the unintended consequences of their actions. This historical perspective mirrors our contemporary mixed feelings toward technology-driven security solutions. At the same time,

DOI: 10.1201/9781003500698-1

cameras and surveillance AI offer unparalleled oversight, and they simultaneously raise concerns about privacy and the potential for these systems to turn against those they are meant to protect.

The shift from collective security to reliance on institutions and technology carries significant implications. Community bonds, born from necessity, fostered a sense of shared responsibility for protection. The transition to formal policing altered this dynamics, making protection an external service and potentially reducing individual agencies in safeguarding oneself and neighbors. Furthermore, the concept of automatons hinted at a future where machines held responsibility for safety, a potentially empowering tool, yet also a step toward dependence on systems beyond individual control. This evolution resonates with contemporary debates on smart homes and internet privacy, where convenience often demands outsourcing vigilance to algorithms and corporations, leading us to question whether we have traded a sense of community for a false perception of technological security.

The rise of automation did not directly cause changes in personal security practices. However, they embodied a fundamental shift in thinking: the possibility that protection could come from engineered systems, not just human effort. This sparked anxieties and forced a re-evaluation of traditional safeguards – questions we continue to grapple with today. The following section of this chapter expands the groundwork for understanding by offering a range of exercises to cater to different learning styles and levels of understanding. We encourage you to approach these exercises with an open mind and apply your own imagination to create scenarios relevant to your personal life and professional experiences. Feel free to draw inspiration from outside industry sources, current events, or your own observations. This personalized approach will deepen your engagement with the material and enhance your ability to apply these concepts in the real world.

THE MECHANICAL ERA EXAMPLE, MASTER CRAFTSMAN'S VAULT, COMBINATION OF MECHANISMS

Imagine a renowned 18th-century clockmaker whose workshop houses valuable tools, materials, and intricate plans for groundbreaking timepieces. While the workshop utilizes the standard physical security of the time (strong locks, barred windows), the clockmaker, inspired and perhaps unsettled by the automata he sees at exhibitions, devises an additional layer of protection:

The Hidden Mechanism: He installs a complex sequence of hidden gears and levers within a seemingly ordinary grandfather clock. Only a specific, non-obvious series of actions – winding the clock at a particular time, subtly repositioning the hands – will disengage the actual vault's locking mechanism.

Exploiting the Uncanny: Rumors circulate that the clock is "haunted," subtly deterring casual theft. The clockmaker understands that the fear of the seemingly autonomous machine might be a better deterrent than additional bolts.

Control through Obscurity: This multi-step security measure reflects the automaton's era. It relies on specialized knowledge and precise action, mirroring the fear that a machine could be turned against its creator if its inner workings became known to the wrong person.

THE PLAUSIBILITY OF THIS EXAMPLE SCENARIO (WHY THIS COULD HAPPEN)

Ingenuity of the Age: The 18th century was a time of mechanical marvels, where the value of intellectual property – plans and prototypes – was as precious as physical goods. Individuals skilled in building automatons had the unique mindset to design security measures exceeding the ordinary, recognizing that standard locks could be picked. They understood that a system demanding specific knowledge was a more robust defense. Furthermore, capitalizing on the emerging fear surrounding the notion of a machine with a will of its own provided an extra layer of *psychological* protection.

MODERN ERA CONNECTIONS, DRAWS PARALLELS TO CONTEMPORARY SECURITY PRACTICES

Security through Obscurity: While not a primary defense, some systems still rely on complex, non-intuitive steps to deter casual attackers.

- **Fear as a Feature:** Alarm systems often emphasize the potential for swift response and apprehension, playing on the intruder's anxieties.
- **Multi-Layered Approach:** Just as the clockmaker combined physical and procedural security, modern systems often utilize multiple factors (locks, passwords, biometrics).

Let us speculate how *psychological* protection such as fear and fascination with automatons might have sparked unique security measures for wealthy merchants and inventors in the 18th and early 19th centuries.

OTHER MECHANICAL ERA EXAMPLE, THE MERCHANT'S LABYRINTHINE STORAGE

The Individual: A successful merchant dealing in rare spices and textiles possesses a fortune that easily attracts unwanted attention. Their home incorporates a seemingly ordinary warehouse, yet within lies a hidden security system inspired by the movement of automatons.

Deception and Misdirection: The warehouse floor is partially made of pressure-sensitive tiles. Stepping on the wrong sequence triggers seemingly innocuous events: tapestry shifts, revealing a hidden crawlspace; shelves rotate, obscuring passages. The correct path relies on subtle cues and memorization, not obvious physical obstacles.

Psychological Defense: Rumors are spread that the warehouse is "cursed." Mechanical sounds (creaking gears, chimes) are strategically triggered, fostering the idea that space is reacting to the intruder, echoing the fear of an automaton veering from its intended function.

OTHER MECHANICAL ERA EXAMPLE, THE INVENTOR'S PUZZLE BOX VAULT

The Individual: A brilliant but reclusive inventor safeguards prototypes and notebooks filled with revolutionary designs. Their dwelling boasts a dedicated workshop with a vault disguised as an oversized armoire.

Multi-Step Access: The armoire "unlocks" not with a single key but by manipulating seemingly decorative elements (carvings, inlays) in a specific order. Only the inventor knows the correct combination of rotations and subtle pressure points – similar to how one programs an elaborate automaton.

Fail-Safes with a Twist: Should the sequence be entered incorrectly, harmless but startling effects occur: a puff of colored smoke, a jarring musical tone. This creates sensory overload, disorienting a would-be thief and echoing fears of an automaton acting unpredictably when its purpose is thwarted.

Obscuring the obvious with vaults and reinforced rooms was a standard security practice, yet the era's excitement with mechanical ingenuity demanded more. Non-obvious security measures embodied the same specialized knowledge as the period's automatons, creating a sense of control for their owners amid uncertain times. These security systems, like the showy automatons, also held a theatrical element, transforming protection into a form of psychological warfare designed to impress and intimidate. With insights from previous examples in mind, let's explore further discussions.

OTHER MECHANICAL ERA EXAMPLE, THE NOBLEWOMAN'S TRAVELING DEFENSE

The Challenge: A noblewoman frequently journeys with her collection of priceless jewels. Carriages were vulnerable to highwaymen, and inns could not be fully trusted. Her solution draws inspiration from the deceptive simplicity of certain musical automatons.

- **The Jewelry Box with a Hidden Tune:** A seemingly unremarkable jewelry box possesses a series of hidden clasps and sliding panels. Only a specific sequence of subtle pressures, like playing a silent melody on a keyboard, will reveal the storage compartments.
- **Lightweight Deterrents:** Inside, select jewels have delicate threads secretly attached, connected to tiny bells within the box's lining. Disturbing the jewels creates a jarring chime, alerting the noblewoman even if the box's complex opening sequence has been compromised.
- **The Threat Evolves (Age of Mass Production):** As intricate mechanisms become less exclusive, our inventors and merchants must avoid would-be thieves who might acquire knowledge of common automaton-inspired security tricks.
- **Increased Randomization:** Systems based on fixed sequences become vulnerable. Devices might incorporate interchangeable parts (gears with differing numbers of teeth), allowing owners to reset their secret "combinations periodically."

- **The Decoy Principle:** Automatons often possess hidden compartments. Similarly, vaults might have false treasure caches designed to misdirect and buy time compartments filled with fool's gold or triggering non-harmful but attention-grabbing effects.
- **Imperfect Replication as a Tool:** Mass production lowers costs and introduces subtle variation. A lock with mass-produced tumblers might have unintended quirks in its operation – turning the key slightly to the side before upward – which the owner exploits as an extra security layer.

Multi-factor authentication, with its reliance on passwords and device-sent codes, mirrors the multi-step security of the past. Cybersecurity utilizes "Honey Pots" – fake servers with enticing data to study attackers, much like decoy treasure compartments were once used. However, the human factor remains constant, for overconfidence in technology has always been a risk. As with modern security, these systems are most effective when combined with vigilance and adaptability against evolving threats.

- **The Nobleman Heightened Vulnerability and Deception:** The noblewoman, aware that her unusual jewelry box might attract attention, devises an additional layer of deception.
  - **Extra Layer of Security, Sheet Music as Code:** She selects a visually complex but straightforward piece of music. The placement of notes on the staff corresponds to the pressure points on her box's hidden clasps. The final note sequence is required to open the final compartment containing her most valuable gems. The sheet music can be openly displayed as part of her belongings. Should the box be stolen, the thief is unlikely to suspect the sheet music holds the key to accessing its contents (literally). She can periodically change the "cipher" by selecting new sheet music, maintaining security on her travels.
  - **Extra Layer of Security, Electrifying the Vault:** Our inventor now resides in an age where early electrical wiring is possible but still an expensive novelty. They decide to harness this cutting-edge technology to enhance their workshop security. The vault's doorframe and surrounding walls have hidden, seemingly decorative metallic inlays. These are subtly wired to a battery system, creating a low-voltage circuit. The electricity circuit breakers are specific points on these inlays and serve as contacts. The "access key" is not a physical object but a conductive rod that completes the circuit in the correct sequence, disengaging the locking mechanism. So circuit breaker acts as the physical key, which provides an Auditory Illusion. A faint hum while the "key" is in use reinforces the feeling of manipulating something akin to a temperamental machine, playing on fears common to the era about the unpredictability of electricity.

The specialized knowledge required to understand electrical circuits provided a more robust defense than the increasingly widespread understanding of purely mechanical systems. The air of mystery and potential danger surrounding electricity also created a psychological deterrent for would-be intruders. With its gestural component, the noblewoman's system resembles a complex passphrase – an increasingly common security element today. The inventor's sensitivity to the system's "voice" serves as a primitive form of behavioral biometrics, a precursor to modern systems that analyze unique individual characteristics like typing patterns or gait for authentication.

ASSET PROTECTION DURING THE MECHANICAL AND CLOCKWORK ERA

Asset protection during this period was a tangible affair. Wealth was predominantly held in physical forms such as land, buildings, and gold; thus, safeguarding one's assets meant securing these items against theft or damage. However, alongside this focus on tangible security, the specter of the automaton lingered. Could machines, seemingly capable of independent action, one day become tools for circumventing traditional safeguards? Strongboxes and safes were not merely symbols of wealth preservation; their intricate locking mechanisms reflected an excitement with the same clockwork ingenuity embodied in the era's automatons. Locks became as much a testament to man's mastery over the potential of machines as they were a practical necessity.

The concept of insurance also began to take a more structured form, with the famed Lloyd's of London initially focused on maritime ventures before expanding into other areas. This risk pooling hinted at a growing awareness that traditional, individualistic protection might be insufficient against forces beyond one's control. It echoed, even subtly, the fear that even the most well-engineered automaton might malfunction with devastating consequences.

As the 1800s dawned, the Industrial Revolution saw the rise of banks and more sophisticated financial institutions. These offered safer alternatives for asset protection, promising the security of physical vaults and the intricate systems of ledgers and accounting. However, there was an undercurrent of unease; was this shift toward storing wealth as intangible entries, trusting in institutions rather than the gold in one's hand, an echo of the same trust one might place in a complex automaton, hoping its actions remained predictable and beneficial?

The excitement with automatons faded as the intricacies of the mechanical gave way to the new marvels of the digital age. However, the legacy of figures like Grimshaw and Vance lingers. The locksmith once focused on tangible protection now finds echoes of his craft in the domain of encryption, where unbreakable codes and hidden backdoors become the new fortresses and the new fields of battle. The spirit of Vance, the master of exploiting unseen flaws, lives on in security analysts and whistleblowers, striving to outsmart systems that have grown ever more complex and prone to concealed dangers.

Automaton, a metaphor of its time, reminds us of a timeless truth: the tools we build for our protection can harbor vulnerabilities. Systems designed for stability can be turned toward exploitation, wielded by those attuned to their hidden workings. Brilliance walks a knife's edge between creation and disruption. This tension is not confined to the domain of clockwork gears and thievery. We see it played out on a grander scale as algorithms shape our world, their inner logic as opaque and potentially dangerous as any automaton of the past.

However, there is a counterpoint, a thread of hope amid the unease. Perhaps the true legacy lies in a shift of mindset inspired by those who dared to look beyond the obvious. As Grimshaw might have learned, proper security may not lie in ever-increasing complexity, but in a relentless pursuit of understanding the weaknesses inherent in any system we devise. By fostering creators and thinkers akin to Vance's students, society might yet find a way to harness innovation without becoming enslaved by it. Much like decoding Vance's cryptic manifestos, the challenge is one we continue to decipher, each generation anew.

The excitement with automatons might have waned, their intricacy overtaken by new technological wonders. However, the echoes of Grimshaw and Vance persist as more than mere historical footnotes. Once focused on safeguarding the tangible, the locksmith sees his legacy reborn in the guardians of our digital world. They strive for elegant security, where transparency builds trust, not obscurity. Furthermore, the influence of Vance, the trespasser into hidden mechanisms, lives on in those who challenge the illusion of the unbreakable. They treat every system, no matter how benevolent its purpose, with the critical eye it deserves.

Automaton, a marvel of its era, is a timeless reminder that our creations often mirror our brilliance, flaws, and capacity for harm and healing. The struggle between those who would exploit systems and those who tirelessly illuminate their vulnerabilities is ongoing. However, there is a subtle shift born of hard lessons learned.

The true legacy lies not just in exploiting the gaps or crafting ever-more unassailable fortresses. It is in the awareness that no system is infallible, and no individual is beyond scrutiny. Proper protection emerges from collaboration, where Grimshaw's genius meets Vance's insights not in rivalry but in service to designing systems that prioritize the human element they were built to serve.

This new era of security is built on understanding, not blind faith. It is a world where complex codes are explained in children's books, where the very institutions meant to protect us are open to reasoned questioning, and where a new generation, inspired by the cautionary tales of the past, become both the architects and the vigilant guardians of the systems we depend on. The challenge remains as intricate as any clockwork mechanism, but hope becomes part of the design this time. The age of the automaton, with its wonder and unease, lingers as a powerful metaphor. Out of the struggles we witnessed – Grimshaw's obsession with invulnerability, Vance's destructive yet revelatory brilliance – a new approach to systems design has emerged. It is a future where resilience is not achieved by armoring ourselves in complexity but by embracing an enlightened vigilance mindset.

COMMON IMPROVEMENT CONCEPTS OF MECHANICAL TO MODERN ERA

Education as User Empowerment, from a young age, the principles of system analysis are woven into the fabric of learning. Students do not just consume information; they deconstruct its delivery mechanisms. Algorithms behind social feeds are dissected in classrooms, revealing how well-meaning design can be subverted.

Transparency as the New Security: Companies built on public trust make the inner workings of their decision-making processes accessible and engaging to understand. Visualizations and simplified explanations replace inscrutable legalese, fostering trust through comprehension, not blind acceptance.

The Rise of Ethical "Vances": Society lionizes not those who merely find the cracks but those who dedicate their talents to preemptively identifying and addressing potential points of failure. They work within governing bodies, consulting on everything from election security to the design of social safety nets.

Power in Decentralization: Inspired by the vulnerabilities inherent in any centralized system, new forms of decentralized governance emerge. Once associated with shadowy transactions, blockchain technology evolved into a tool for secure record-keeping and auditable decision-making, diffusing power across networks rather than concentrating it in the hands of a few.

This is not a utopia free of conflict. The battle to outsmart those who would seek to exploit will always continue. However, armed with the knowledge of past struggles, this future is one where innovation and vigilance go hand-in-hand. The automaton echoes in the tireless drive for improvement, but instead of fearing our creations, we learn to design with transparency and adaptability – systems that mirror our potential for both good and ill and give us the tools to consistently tip the balance toward a more equitable and secure world for all.

THE MECHANICAL MARVEL AND CLOCKWORK INFLUENCE INTO MODERN TECH ERA

The excitement surrounding mechanical marvels has certainly persisted into our modern age of technology. The intricate workings and elegant solutions of these early inventions continue to echo in our digital wonders, inspiring awe and fueling innovation. This section explores this enduring legacy, examining how the principles of gears, levers, and automatons shaped the very foundations of modern computing. We will trace the ingenuity of clockmakers and inventors, their relentless drive for precision and automation, and discover how these qualities find new expressions in the algorithms and architectures that power our world today.

The influence of automaton thinking, with its emphasis on system analysis and proactive threat management, has been particularly profound. Early automatons, with their intricate mechanisms and precisely timed movements, instilled a deep appreciation for the importance of order, synchronization, and efficiency. These principles found their way into the design of early computing machines, where gears and levers were replaced by electrical circuits and logic gates, but the underlying concepts of precision and automation remained central.

The lessons learned from historical struggles to manage security threats proactively also played a crucial role in shaping the development of modern computing. As societies became increasingly reliant on technology, the need to protect sensitive information and critical infrastructure from malicious actors grew more pressing.

The ingenuity of early inventors, who devised clever mechanisms to secure their creations and prevent tampering, laid the groundwork for the sophisticated cybersecurity systems we rely on today.

The influence of mechanical marvels on personal security and asset protection was subtle yet profound. While these inventions brought order and synchronization to daily life, they also instilled a deeper awareness of time as a precious resource, demanding vigilant management for optimal protection. This awareness fostered a mindset that mirrored the precision of automatons, one focused on creating immediate defenses, analyzing potential threats, and developing proactive countermeasures.

This mindset, with its emphasis on proactive security and the efficient management of resources, has become deeply ingrained in the culture of modern computing. From the design of secure operating systems to the development of intrusion detection systems and encryption algorithms, the principles of automation, system analysis, and proactive threat management continue to guide our efforts to safeguard our digital world.

In conclusion, the legacy of mechanical marvels extends far beyond their physical manifestations. The ingenuity, precision, and automation that characterized these early inventions have shaped the very foundations of modern computing, influencing our approach to system design, security, and the management of time and resources. As we continue to push the boundaries of technology, the lessons learned from the past will continue to guide us, ensuring that our digital creations are not only powerful and efficient but also secure and resilient in the face of evolving threats.

THE ENDURING POWER OF PHYSICS AND MODERN TECH ERA

The principles of physics and mechanical ingenuity, the very forces that powered the era's clockwork wonders, form the bedrock upon which robust security measures are built. A deep understanding of forces, motion, and the properties of materials allows for the crafting of barriers, deterrents, and alarms that can withstand the test of time and the relentless efforts of those seeking to breach them.

Locks, those seemingly simple devices that have secured our belongings for centuries, are a testament to the clever application of physics principles. The intricate interplay of levers, springs, and bolts, carefully calibrated to resist unauthorized access, exemplifies the elegant fusion of physics and engineering in the service of security.

Optics and wave mechanics, the sciences of light and sound, empower surveillance systems to become tireless guardians of our homes and businesses. Cameras, strategically placed and equipped with advanced lenses, capture and transmit images, transforming light into a vigilant observer. Motion sensors, harnessing the Doppler effect, detect the slightest disturbances in the surrounding environment, turning sound waves into silent alarms.

Moreover, the careful study of material properties ensures that our defenses can withstand the relentless assaults of those seeking to compromise them. The selection of robust materials, resistant to cutting, drilling, and other forms of physical intrusion, is crucial for the integrity of physical security measures. The understanding of material fatigue and the impact of environmental factors ensures that our defenses remain effective over time.

Physics, in this context, transcends its theoretical realm and becomes an active participant in safeguarding our most valued assets. It is the unyielding shield protecting our homes, our businesses, and our communities from those who would seek to do us harm. The principles of physics, combined with human ingenuity and engineering prowess, empower us to create a world where security is not just a concept but a tangible reality, woven into the very fabric of our built environment.

INTELLIGENCE AS THE INVISIBLE FORTRESS

The instinct for self-preservation is primordial, and as threats evolve, so must our defenses. Physical barriers alone are insufficient in a world where dangers can be as subtle as a cyber-attack or as brazen as a physical assault. Proper security lies in a proactive approach – the very mindset that drove the creation of intricate automatons. By embracing analysis and intelligent anticipation, we can identify, assess, and mitigate risks before they strike.

Staying informed about societal shifts, technological vulnerabilities, and the changing tactics of those seeking to exploit are all facets of modern security intelligence. This could involve monitoring local crime trends, maintaining vigilance about our digital footprint, or understanding the latest security innovations. It often leads to collaboration, neighborhood watch programs become networks for threat analysis, and private security services complement law enforcement. The modern individual embraces knowledge as a powerful form of self-defense.

THE CLOCKWORK INFLUENCE INTO MODERN TECH ERA: THREATS DRIVE INNOVATION

History teaches us that the quest for security propels technological advancement. From World War II to the Cold War, periods of conflict showcase this acutely. The Allies' efforts to defeat the Enigma encryption were driven by the need to protect lives, assets, and nations. The development of early detection methods, from acoustic horns to radar, exemplifies how necessity fuels the creation of security solutions. In espionage, we see the relentless pursuit of information supremacy, a battleground where personal skills and covert technologies intertwine, with the safety of individuals and the stability of entire societies at stake.

SECURITY AS AN EVOLVING ECOSYSTEM

The concept of security protection has grown increasingly complex, reflecting the need to adapt to an ever-shifting landscape of threats. While echoes of ancient methods remain (locks and bolts still have their place), modern security encompasses advanced digital safeguards and a focus on analyzing information to predict and prevent harm before it occurs. An understanding of systems of how seemingly secure structures can possess hidden flaws – this mindset, born from the automaton era – is now essential for those dedicated to maintaining security in the 21st century.

The Unseen Enemy: Unlike physical security, the adversaries in the cyber domain are often faceless and can strike from anywhere in the world. They do not need to break down doors or scale walls; they exploit software, systems, and human behavior vulnerabilities. This immateriality adds a layer of unease reminiscent of the automaton era, where the fear stemmed from what *could not* be directly observed.

The New Arsenal: The tools of cybersecurity are equally abstract. Firewalls and encryption protocols have become the digital equivalent of reinforced walls and complex locks. Security experts are the new locksmiths, analyzing vast datasets for patterns that might reveal hidden "backdoors" into our digital lives. Vulnerability scans mirror Vance's methodical search for flaws but on an exponentially larger scale.

A Mindset Shift: The rise of cybersecurity demands a fundamental change in our approach to security. We can no longer rely on the illusion of what we can physically see and touch. Instead, we must become detectives of the digital domain, fostering a healthy skepticism about the interacting systems. Passwords transform from mere inconveniences into the front-line soldiers of our security. Updates and patches are less annoying and more akin to reinforcing weak spots discovered in our defenses.

Knowledge Is Power: Staying informed about the latest cyber threats and understanding how common attacks work (phishing, ransomware) is essential. This echoes the automaton era's focus on analysis, but the information landscape is vaster and more ever-changing. Trusted sources become crucial allies, making reputable publications and security specialists our modern-day guides against the dangers lurking in the digital landscape.

The Eternal Struggle: Cybersecurity is an ongoing arms race. As defenses evolve, so do the tactics of those seeking to bypass them. This echoes the core lesson learned from figures like Grimshaw and Vance: no system is ever unbreakable. Constant vigilance, proactive analysis, and a willingness to adapt are the only ways to stay ahead in a world where security is constantly redefined.

THE MODERN-DAY AUTOMATONS FOR DEFENSE (KEY FACTORS)

The battleground of cybersecurity is shifting rapidly. As hackers and malicious actors employ increasingly sophisticated, automated tactics, the defenders turn to a powerful new weapon: artificial intelligence. AI-powered cybersecurity systems can:

Analyze massive datasets in real time, detecting patterns and anomalies that would elude human analysts.

Adapt their defenses on the fly, learning from past attacks and preemptively blocking new ones.

Run simulations to uncover potential vulnerabilities before they can be exploited, acting like a digital "Vance" searching for flaws within the system it protects.

The benefits of adopting modern technology and algorithmic advancements are clearly undeniable. However, with this power comes a subtle yet familiar unease. Let's look at some key factors:

Loss of Direct Control: Traditional security often relied on tangible actions or clear rules (strong passwords, timely updates). AI systems operate with a degree of autonomy; their decision-making processes are not easily comprehensible to the average user. Are we merely shifting trust from human experts to complex algorithms?

False Sense of Security: The success of AI defenses can breed complacency. Just as some felt Grimshaw's creations were infallible, the public could view AI as the ultimate shield, neglecting basic cyber-hygiene habits that are still essential.

Evolving Vulnerabilities of AI: AI systems themselves are not immune to manipulation. Could attackers learn how to "trick" the AI into misclassifying threats, opening a digital backdoor? This forces us to analyze the analyzers, adding a dizzying layer of complexity.

The Question of Bias: AI learns from what it has fed. Could unintentional biases in the data used to train these systems lead to unjust profiling, mirroring real-world concerns about surveillance? Where is the line when security becomes discriminatory instead of protective?

THE MODERN TECH UNEASE, UNINTENDED ECHO OF THE AUTOMATON

The core anxiety of the automaton age was that creations intended for good could be subverted or malfunction in ways their makers did not anticipate. We could witness a similar phenomenon with AI-based security:

Weaponization of Defense: Could the same techniques refined to protect systems be retooled by bad actors to design even more potent cyberattacks? Just like Vance's Knowledge, the AI tool itself becomes a vulnerability.

"**Black Box" Miscalculation:** What if a complex AI flags a legitimate activity as a threat, leading to disrupted services or unjust consequences for the individual? Challenging a machine's decision becomes far more fraught than appealing to a human's judgment.

Mitigating these anxieties requires a nuanced approach born from the hard-fought lessons of the automaton era:

Transparency, Not Obscurity: Companies employing AI security must prioritize transparent methods wherever possible, explaining (in plain language) the AI's logic. This builds trust, even when full technical intricacies are not grasped.

Humans in the Loop: AI should augment, not replace, human security analysts. This collaboration, similar to the uneasy but necessary alliance of Grimshaw and Vance, creates checks and balances.

Constant Vigilance: Proactive education about how AI can be manipulated becomes crucial. As we teach about phishing, we must develop "AI skepticism" – awareness that even the most brilliant defense is not a substitute for our critical thinking.

The rise of AI in cybersecurity presents a double-edged sword. Its immense potential for protection is undeniable, but the opacity of its decision-making processes fuels anxieties reminiscent of the automaton era. However, a new subfield of security innovation is emerging – Deliberately Explainable AI (DEAI) – specifically designed to address these anxieties by prioritizing transparency in AI-powered security systems.

WHY EXPLAINABILITY MATTERS WHEN ADAPTING MODERN TECHNOLOGY

In a future where artificial intelligence safeguards our digital lives, imagine an AI security system diligently monitoring your online banking transactions. It flags a recent payment as potentially fraudulent, swiftly freezing your account to prevent further damage. While such vigilance might seem ideal, the lack of explanation for this sudden interruption creates a wave of frustration and distrust. Was it a genuine anomaly, a sophisticated cyberattack, or simply a glitch in the AI itself? This uncertainty underscores the crucial need for explainable AI (DEAI) in cybersecurity.

DEAI aims to bridge this gap by making the reasoning behind AI's decisions comprehensible to humans. Instead of a black box that spits out verdicts without justification, DEAI provides insights into the factors that triggered the alert. Perhaps the AI detected an unusual spending pattern, a login attempt from an unfamiliar location, or a suspicious recipient account. By providing this transparency, DEAI empowers users to understand the situation, assess the risk, and take appropriate action.

Moreover, DEAI fosters a sense of control and trust in AI systems. When users understand how AI arrives at its decisions, they are more likely to trust its judgment and accept its interventions. This trust is crucial for the widespread adoption and effectiveness of AI security systems. Without it, users might dismiss alerts as false positives or disable security features altogether, leaving themselves vulnerable to cyberattacks.

DEAI also promotes accountability and ethical considerations in AI development. By providing insights into the decision-making process, DEAI allows for the identification of potential biases or discriminatory patterns in the AI's algorithms. This transparency enables developers to address these issues, ensuring that AI systems are fair, unbiased, and respect human rights and values.

In conclusion, DEAI is not merely a technical advancement; it is a crucial step toward building a future where AI and humans can coexist and collaborate effectively. By making AI's reasoning comprehensible, DEAI fosters trust, promotes accountability, and empowers individuals to make informed decisions about their digital security. As AI becomes increasingly integrated into our lives, DEAI will play a vital role in ensuring that these technologies serve humanity in a responsible and ethical manner.

BENEFITS OF DEAI IN SECURITY (KEY FACTORS)

Building Trust: Transparency allows users to understand the logic behind AI's actions. This fosters a collaborative environment where humans and machines work together, promoting a sense of ownership and shared responsibility for security.

Human Oversight: By deciphering the AI's thought process, security analysts can identify potential biases or weaknesses in the system's training data, allowing them to fine-tune the AI's response and prevent false positives.

Identifying Malicious Actors: Decoded AI reasoning might reveal vulnerabilities previously unknown. Hackers who attempt to manipulate AI's decision-making can be identified, and their techniques can be countered more effectively.

Standardization and Regulation: DEAI paves the way for establishing industry standards for explainability in security AI. This ensures responsible development and deployment of these powerful tools, potentially leading to regulations that mandate transparency in AI-driven security systems.

CHALLENGES AND CONSIDERATIONS OF ADAPTING MODERN TECHNOLOGY

Developing robust DEAI solutions is no easy feat:

Balancing Security and Transparency: Striking the right balance is crucial. Overly detailed explanations might inadvertently reveal the inner workings of the security system, potentially aiding attackers in exploiting vulnerabilities.

The Limits of Explanation: Not all aspects of AI decision-making can be easily translated into understandable human terms. The complex neural networks at the heart of AI may offer only statistical probabilities, not clear-cut cause-and-effect relationships.

User Comprehension: Even with simplified explanations, there is a risk that users might not possess the technical background to grasp the complexities of AI reasoning fully. Effective communication strategies become crucial.

Shifting throughout history, the emphasis on security has mirrored the most valuable assets of time. In ancient civilizations, physical security was paramount. Fortifications like walls, moats, and gates were erected to protect resources and people, deterring invading forces. Even then, the seeds of cybersecurity were sown – symbols, ciphers, and basic codes were used to safeguard communications from adversaries.

Security evolved in tandem as societies advanced into the Middle Ages and Renaissance. The focus extended to protecting individuals, as evidenced by castles boasting intricate defenses and hidden routes. Alongside this, information security matured. Complex ciphers, like the Caesar cipher famously employed by Julius Caesar, became the tools to protect sensitive military strategies. Today, we have witnessed a renaissance of social cybersecurity. Our

most precious assets are often our digital identities and the flow of information across networks. The battleground has shifted, but the core principles remain to defend what is valuable and outmaneuver those seeking to exploit it.

Our understanding of security has always been intricately tied to the most valuable assets of a given era. Let us look into this historical parallel, exploring how physical security in the past laid the groundwork for the social cybersecurity renaissance we are experiencing today.

Physical Security as King: In the earliest civilizations, the primary concern was protecting tangible resources and people. Walls, moats, and imposing gates became the defining features of towns and cities. These fortifications served as a physical deterrent, designed to delay or repel invading armies seeking to plunder resources or conquer populations.

Early Seeds of Cybersecurity: Even in this era, the need to safeguard communication channels arose. Simple codes, ciphers, and symbols served as rudimentary tools for information security. This practice aimed to ensure sensitive messages reached only their intended recipients – a practice that directly translates to the encryption technologies used in today's digital world.

Securing Individuals: As societies transitioned into the Middle Ages and Renaissance, security broadened beyond protecting settlements. The rise of influential figures and ongoing conflicts created a need for personal safety. This era witnessed the construction of castles – elaborate structures boasting intricate defensive features like thick walls, strategically placed towers, and even hidden passageways. These features served a similar purpose to modern-day security systems and access controls, safeguarding individuals and valuables within the castle walls.

Information Security Takes Shape: The need to protect sensitive information also saw significant advancements. More complex ciphers emerged, replacing the rudimentary methods of the past. The Caesar cipher, famously used by Julius Caesar himself, is a prime example. It employed a simple substitution method to scramble messages, making them unreadable to anyone unfamiliar with the key. This concept laid the groundwork for the sophisticated encryption algorithms safeguarding our online transmissions today.

THE SOCIAL CYBERSECURITY RENAISSANCE (KEY FACTORS)

Fast forward to today, and we find ourselves in a digital age where our most valuable assets often reside online. Our digital identities, financial information, and social lives are intricately woven into the fabric of the internet. This digital landscape has necessitated a renaissance of cybersecurity practices, but the core principles remain the same:

Defending What Is Valuable: Just as physical security protected people and resources in the past, social cybersecurity focuses on safeguarding our online identities and information. The attack methods have evolved from physical invasions to cyberattacks and social engineering. We counter these threats with firewalls, intrusion detection systems, and best practices in online behavior.

The social aspect of cybersecurity highlights the importance of human behavior as a critical line of defense. Spreading awareness of online threats, fostering responsible digital citizenship, and promoting healthy skepticism toward online interactions are all vital aspects of this renaissance.

In essence, the history of security is a story of continuous adaptation. While the battlegrounds have shifted from physical landscapes to the digital domain, the fundamental principles of safeguarding what is valuable and outsmarting those who seek to exploit it remain constant. This understanding fosters a deeper appreciation for the evolution of security and empowers us to participate in the ongoing social cybersecurity renaissance.

Let's highlight a few critical parallel factors between the social physical security evolution and cybersecurity renaissance:

Defense in Layers: Castles employed multiple physical barriers. Today, a robust cybersecurity posture also uses layered defenses (firewalls, software, user awareness).

Deterrence vs. Delay: Ancient walls aimed to deter or delay invaders, buying time for a defense. Modern cybersecurity practices often have a similar goal: slowing down hackers and giving time for countermeasures.

The Human Factor: Human error could lead to breaches even with solid castles. The same holds for cybersecurity – phishing attacks and social engineering often exploit human vulnerabilities.

Adaptation Is Survival: As attackers evolved, so did defenses. Security today is a constant cycle of learning, adapting, and overthinking cyber threats.

Understanding the evolution of security increases the gain more than just historical insight. It emphasizes the following example key points for ease of topic navigation or what we need to protect most shapes our security strategies. Keep in mind that there is a perpetual dance between those who protect and those who seek to exploit and the goals of defense, deterrence, and access control transcend time, even if the methods change drastically. With insights from previous examples in mind, let's explore further discussions:

EXPLORING THE CYBERSECURITY RENAISSANCE BY CONCEPT OF DEFENSE IN LAYERS

Defense in layers is an ancient concept that has given new life and relevance to cybersecurity.

ANCIENT ROOTS

The enduring image of a medieval castle with its imposing outer walls, concentric defensive layers, fortified keeps, and vigilant guards offers a timeless analogy for robust security. Just as a castle was not defined solely by its outermost defenses, modern security strategies demand a multifaceted approach. The redundancy principle, as seen in secret passageways and layered protection for valuables, translates directly into the concept of "defense in depth" employed in cybersecurity.

However, just as imposing walls crumble without watchful sentries and trained defenders, the most sophisticated technological safeguards are undermined without a crucial element: the human factor. Educated users, trained to recognize threats and act as an additional layer of defense, are indispensable. This echoes the castle, where guards keenly watched for signs of intrusion. Security principles are timeless, whether defending a physical stronghold or our digital lives, multiple barriers, vigilance, and the human element remain essential components of a resilient defense.

Building a robust defense in the digital age relies on layers, just as a medieval castle did. Firewalls form the outer perimeter, filtering traffic like a moat and drawbridge. Segmentation divides networks into smaller zones, limiting damage like the inner walls of a fortress. Intrusion detection and prevention systems act as guards, sounding the alarm and responding to suspicious behavior. Encryption is our safety, safeguarding the most precious data even if adversaries slip inside.

However, the strongest castle stands little chance against a traitor inside. User awareness is the critical final layer. Education on phishing scams, secure passwords, and spotting social engineering tactics empowers individuals to become the last, and often most vital, line of defense. This multifaceted approach, combining technical safeguards with a vigilant human element, offers the best chance of building digital fortresses capable of withstanding the ever-evolving attacks of the cyber domain.

THE LAYER ARRANGEMENTS; WHY THIS MATTERS (KEY FACTORS)

No Single Point of Failure: A layered approach means breaches are likely contained to a smaller area, buying time for mitigation and response.

Flexibility: Security needs to change rapidly. Layering allows new technologies or practices to be added/removed without rebuilding the defense system.

Human-Technological Blend: Layers reflect that technology alone is not enough. User awareness bridges the gaps that technology cannot.

ONGOING EVOLUTION

The concept of defense in layers is alive and evolving in cybersecurity

Zero Trust Architecture: Moving away from the traditional "castle and moat" model toward assuming no user or device is inherently trustworthy, even within the network perimeter.

Micro-Segmentation: Taking network segmentation to a finer level, isolating individual applications or workloads to minimize the spread of attacks.

Behavior-Based Detection: Advanced systems use AI and machine learning to analyze typical user or network behavior, flagging deviations that might indicate a breach.

Even as the battlefield shifts to cyberspace, the principles of security remain. Layered defenses, adaptability, and recognizing the human element are timeless strategies for safeguarding what matters most. While documented evaluations of historical security measures are not as readily available as we might like, we can explore a compelling case historical study to compete the comparison cycle.

THE 1666 GREAT FIRE OF LONDON AND THE SUBSEQUENT REBUILDING EFFORTS UNDER KING CHARLES II

This event offers a glimpse into how a historical disaster led to reevaluating fire safety measures in London.

BEFORE THE FIRE: A CITY VULNERABLE

The architectural landscape of 17th-century London, with its densely packed timber-framed buildings and thatched roofs, was a tinderbox waiting for a spark. Limited firefighting techniques – reliant on buckets, hand pumps, and hastily created firebreaks – offered little defense against a rapidly spreading blaze. The lack of building codes or fire safety regulations fostered a haphazard urban environment where structures were erected quickly and cheaply, disregarding the inherent dangers. These factors converged to create a perpetually risky city where a single stray ember could ignite an inferno that would consume entire neighborhoods. This underscores the complex interplay between urban planning, technology, and regulation in determining a city's vulnerability to disaster.

THE DEVASTATING IMPACT

The Great Fire of London, raging for four days in September 1666, became a stark reminder of the city's vulnerability. It destroyed over 13,000 homes and displaced an estimated 70,000 to 80,000 residents. The devastation forced a re-evaluation of London's fire safety measures.

KING CHARLES II'S RESPONSE: A NEW APPROACH TO SECURITY

The Rebuilding Act of 1666 mandated the use of fire-resistant materials like brick and stone for rebuilding efforts. Timber could only be used for internal structures, significantly reducing the overall flammability of new buildings.

Wider Streets: The act also called for wider streets to create firebreaks and allow for more effortless movement of firefighting equipment.

Improved Firefighting Infrastructure: The act led to a more organized firefighting force and the establishing of fire stations strategically placed throughout the city.

EVALUATING THE NEW MEASURES

While formal "security evaluations" in the modern sense were not conducted, the effectiveness of the new measures became evident over time. The Great Fire of London remains the last major fire disaster to engulf the city, and the city has assessed the impacts of the implemented changes. Let's take a look at the key factors:

Reduced Fire Risk: Replacing timber with brick and stone significantly lessened the risk of rapid-fire spread.
Improved Response: Wider streets and a more organized firefighting force allowed faster response times and better containment efforts.
Long-Term Impact: The rebuilding efforts and safety regulations laid the groundwork for a more fire-resistant London for centuries.

LIMITATIONS OF THE CITY ASSESSMENTS (KEY FACTORS)

Focus on Rebuilding: The measures taken after the Great Fire were primarily reactive, a response to a devastating event. Modern security evaluations are often more proactive, seeking to identify vulnerabilities before a disaster strikes.
Lack of Data: Quantifiable data on the effectiveness of the rebuilding efforts are scarce. Modern security evaluations rely heavily on data analysis to assess the impact of implemented changes.
Learning from Failure: Despite limitations, the Great Fire serves as a reminder of how historical evaluations, even when informal, can lead to significant improvements in security measures. This parallels how modern security evaluations, based on past breaches or security incidents, inform future strategies.

The story of the Great Fire of London and the subsequent rebuilding efforts offers valuable insights into how historical societies evaluated and improved their security measures. While the methods differed from today's data-driven approach, the core principles of identifying vulnerabilities, implementing changes, and learning from experience remain constant.

The relentless advancement of technology has transformed our lives, granting us connectivity and conveniences unthinkable to those who came before. However, this digital landscape is haunted by surveillance, threatening the erosion of our privacy. Surprisingly, the seeds of this modern dilemma were sown in the 19th century – an era marked by the rise of new communication technologies and shifting societal perspectives on information control.

This chapter looks into the striking parallels between the cybersecurity challenges of today and those faced over a century ago. We will examine how the telegraph exposed vulnerabilities, sparking debates about correspondence's sanctity that mirror our data security anxieties. By exploring these historical echoes, we gain crucial insights into the changing nature of privacy expectations, strategies for protecting information, and the timeless conflict between individual liberty and the pursuit of security.

THE HISTORIC EVOLUTION OF CONTROLS: POLICING AND ORDER TO COMMUNITY (KEY FACTORS)

The focus on reason, social contract theory, and the systematic organization of society set a foundation for rethinking security and order. The Industrial Revolution further fueled this transformation with dense urban centers, complex social problems, and the rise of centralized nation-states. These shifts created a pressing need for formalized systems of public safety and information gathering, giving birth to the concepts of modern policing and intelligence agencies.

Policing Evolves: Localized security guards and informal community security gave way to the first professional police forces. This shift emphasized proactive prevention rather than simply reacting to crime. Uniforms, hierarchies, and mandated training aimed to increase professionalism and accountability.

The Rise of Espionage: Nations created dedicated intelligence agencies to gather strategic information on adversaries and protect against counterintelligence efforts. Cryptography advanced rapidly throughout this period, with increasingly sophisticated ciphers demanding innovation from the codebreakers determined to pierce them.

THE MODERN TECH INFLUENCES ON POLICING, THE INVENTION OF TELEGRAPH (KEY FACTORS)

The invention of the telegraph profoundly impacted the development of policing.

Centralized Control and Rapid Response: Near-instant communication over vast distances enabled centralized dispatch, coordination during significant incidents, and mobilizing resources efficiently based on real-time information.

Data Sharing and Pattern Identification: Police headquarters could now receive updates from various jurisdictions, allowing them to spot trends in criminal activity and predict potential hotspots for targeted responses.

Catching Fugitives on the Run: Descriptions and identifying details of suspects could be transmitted rapidly across borders, significantly increasing the chances of apprehension for those fleeing justice.

A Foreshadowing of Challenges: The telegraph, while revolutionary, was a one-way communication tool, and its transmissions could be intercepted. This highlighted the ongoing tension between technological advancement and security vulnerabilities, a theme relevant even in today's cybercrime and digital surveillance era.

The 20th century witnessed ongoing transformations in policing philosophies. While technology undoubtedly shaped advancements, a decisive shift emerged with the rise of the community policing model, emphasizing collaboration and proactive approaches. Community policing recognizes that effective law enforcement depends on strong partnerships between police and the communities they serve. Foot patrols, community meetings, and data-driven problem-solving are hallmarks of this approach, fostering more excellent responsiveness to local concerns and aiming to prevent crime at its source.

Crucially, community policing extends beyond traditional enforcement. Successful models often involve collaborations with diverse agencies like healthcare providers and social services. This underscores a vital truth: crime is often intertwined with complex social issues that policing alone cannot fully address.

However, the path toward widespread community policing is not without its hurdles. It can be resource-intensive, and genuine change requires commitment from police leadership and the community. Furthermore, success in this model cannot solely be measured by crime statistics. Indicators of community trust, police legitimacy, and the overall perception of safety are equally important.

Despite these challenges, community policing offers a compelling and necessary vision for the future. It is a model that moves beyond simple reaction, forging collaborative solutions, addressing root causes, and, ultimately, striving for safer and more just communities for all.

2 Individual Cybersecurity in the Era of Digital Computing and the Internet

In the digital age, a powerful force has emerged: socially engineered media. This chapter looks into the philosophy behind this phenomenon content deliberately crafted to manipulate us. We will explore its double-edged sword: fostering a shared digital culture while potentially isolating users from traditional forms of social interaction.

Digital culture isolation limits exposure to diverse perspectives and real-life social cues, hindering the development of crucial social skills, empathy, and critical thinking. This "intelligence gap" can make individuals more vulnerable to manipulation and deception online, increasing their susceptibility to social cyber engineering attacks.

In its earliest days, the internet held the promise of unfettered information flow and unconstrained expression. Social media was heralded as a new kind of agora, a virtual public square fostering dialogue and community. However, as these platforms matured, their capacity to reshape social interactions became starkly apparent. Content curation algorithms prioritize engagement, influencers sway public opinion, and targeted advertising manipulates consumer choices. The engineered nature of social media is a deliberate feature, not an accidental byproduct, designed to mold our digital environment and influence our behaviors within it.

A nuanced philosophical lens reveals how socially engineered media drives integration. These platforms foster a sense of belonging by tailoring content that aligns with individual biases. They become echo chambers in some ways, yet also form the basis of digital communities. In a sense, they emulate the ancient concept of the polis – a place where individuals come together to debate, share, and forge collective identities. Algorithmic manipulation, while problematic, can also facilitate genuine connections and foster a sense of solidarity among diverse groups.

The integration fostered by socially engineered media lies in its power to unite people around shared interests, causes, and stories. It challenges traditional gatekeeping structures, giving a global voice to those who mainstream media outlets might overlook. From this perspective, social media holds the potential to weave a more interconnected digital society.

It is vital to remember that this landscape is fraught with complexities. Algorithms can amplify misinformation or polarize groups, feeding division rather than cohesion. The influence of individuals with large platforms and the opaque force of

DOI: 10.1201/9781003500698-2

targeted advertising raises severe concerns about manipulation and erosion of individual autonomy.

Let us look into one of the complexities that have highlighted – the ethics of algorithmic content manipulation in social media.

THE ETHICS OF ALGORITHMIC MANIPULATION (KEY EXAMPLES AND FACTORS)

The Ethics of algorithmic manipulation examines how algorithms shape our online experiences, starting with the filter bubble phenomenon, which limits exposure to diverse viewpoints and fosters insularity. This environment affects critical thinking, as individuals become less inclined to challenge their beliefs. The resulting polarization and social division deepen societal rifts, with groups entrenched in their narratives. Ultimately, this creates the illusion of choice, where users think they are making informed decisions while their options are heavily restricted, highlighting the urgent need for ethical standards in digital platforms. The following definitions provide more clarification:

The Filter Bubble Phenomenon: Algorithms designed to maximize engagement often prioritize content that aligns with a user's existing beliefs or interests. This can create "filter bubbles" or "echo chambers," where individuals are exposed to a narrow range of ideas, reinforcing biases and limiting exposure to opposing viewpoints.

Impact on Critical Thinking: Filter bubbles can hinder the development of critical thinking skills. If individuals primarily encounter information that confirms their beliefs, they may become less likely to question those beliefs or engage thoughtfully with differing perspectives.

Polarization and Social Division: Algorithmic reinforcement of biases can exacerbate polarization. Users trapped in filter bubbles might develop increasingly extreme views, leading to social fragmentation and a reduced ability to find common ground for compromise or respectful dialogue.

The Illusion of Choice: While users may feel they have control over what they see, algorithmic curation limits the scope of available information. The illusion of choice can obscure how platforms subtly shape the digital information landscape.

ARGUMENTS IN FAVOR OF ALGORITHMIC CURATION (KEY FACTORS)

Personalization Enhances User Experience: Content aligned with users' interests can make social media more engaging and enjoyable. It reduces the need to sift through irrelevant information, potentially improving the user experience.

Discovery of Niche Communities: Algorithms can help users discover like-minded communities they might not have found organically. This is especially beneficial for those with niche interests or marginalized viewpoints seeking connection with others.

Reducing Information Overload: The sheer volume of content online is overwhelming. Content curation algorithms can help individuals focus by filtering out potential noise and tailoring a personalized feed. The use of algorithms to curate content walks a fine ethical line. It highlights a few key questions:

- **Where Does Responsibility Lie?** Do platform creators bear responsibility for the societal effects of their algorithms, or does the onus fall on the user to be a discerning consumer of information?
- **The Line between Curation and Manipulation:** At what point does personalization become manipulation? When does filtering information move from helpful to harmful?
- **Transparency and User Control:** How much transparency should users have in the algorithms' workings? To what extent should they be given control to override algorithmic choices?

There is no easy solution to this ethical dilemma. Here are some potential approaches:

Ethical Algorithm Design: Incorporating ethical considerations into the very design of algorithms, prioritizing exposure to diverse perspectives and actively countering the formation of filter bubbles.

Increased Transparency: Greater transparency about how algorithms function, empowering users to make informed choices about navigating their social media feeds.

Media Literacy Education: Encouraging critical thinking skills and fostering awareness of how social media platforms attempt to shape online experiences.

Social media's promise of connection carries a haunting counterpoint exile. The algorithms crafting personalized content can become walls of an echo chamber, isolating users within feedback loops of their own beliefs. This exile is not about banishment from the digital world but rather from the vast marketplace of diverse ideas and perspectives.

In pursuit of heightened engagement, socially engineered media often amplifies content that triggers strong emotional reactions. This fuels polarization, pushing individuals further into ideological trenches. Nuanced discourse gives way to tribalism and a shared sense of reality fractures within the mosaic of these self-reinforcing bubbles.

Ultimately, socially engineered media exists at a philosophical tipping point. Does it ultimately connect or isolate us? Critical questions arise about individual autonomy in a landscape that shapes our choices. How do we retain agency? Can true community exist alongside a relentlessly personalized feed, or does it require exposure to the challenging and the unfamiliar?

Understanding this tension demands acknowledgment of the responsibilities of both sides:

Platform Creators: The ethical burden falls on developers to design social media platforms that value healthy public discourse over pure engagement metrics. This might necessitate algorithms promoting diverse viewpoints and environments where respectful disagreement is possible, not silenced.

Users: We must be vigilant consumers of digital content. Understanding the manipulative forces in social media, actively seeking out contrasting perspectives, and remembering the irreplaceable value of offline interactions are crucial countermeasures against the isolating effects.

Erosion of Trust: Echo chambers breeding intense tribalism erode the ability to evaluate information sources critically. This makes us susceptible to disinformation campaigns, where we are more likely to trust content that aligns with existing beliefs without verifying its origin or legitimacy.

Authority vs Authenticity: The rise of influencers, where popularity can supersede expertise, muddies the waters of credible information sources. This paves the way for social engineers to impersonate authoritative figures or manipulate audience perceptions to gain trust.

Emotional Exploitation: Socially engineered content often aims for viral spread by tapping into solid emotions – fear, outrage, or a sense of urgency. This can bypass our rational defenses and lead to hasty actions (clicking suspicious links, sharing unverified information) that attackers can exploit.

THE USERS SELF-DEFENSE: AWARENESS AND CRITICAL THINKING

The key to combating the pervasive threats of social engineering and manipulative tactics in our media-saturated world lies in cultivating a critical and discerning mindset. We must foster a healthy skepticism toward the information that bombards us online, recognizing that not all sources are created equal and that the digital landscape is rife with misinformation, disinformation, and carefully crafted narratives designed to exploit our vulnerabilities.

This requires a proactive approach to information consumption, a willingness to step outside our echo chambers and engage with diverse perspectives. We must cultivate the habit of verifying sources, cross-checking information, and seeking evidence-based perspectives before we accept, act upon, or amplify content further.

Developing resilience against social engineering tactics also necessitates an understanding of the underlying mechanics of social media platforms. We must recognize how algorithms shape our online experiences, how filter bubbles can limit our exposure to diverse viewpoints, and how our own cognitive biases can make us susceptible to manipulation.

By fostering media literacy and critical thinking skills, we can empower individuals to navigate the digital landscape with greater discernment, to identify manipulative tactics, and to resist the allure of emotionally charged or sensationalized content. We must encourage a culture of healthy skepticism, where individuals question the information they encounter, seek out reliable sources, and engage in thoughtful dialogue with those who hold differing perspectives.

In essence, combating the threats of social engineering and media manipulation requires a shift in mindset, from passive consumers of information to active and critical engagers. By cultivating a discerning eye, a questioning mind, and a willingness to step outside our comfort zones, we can build a more resilient and informed society, one where individuals are empowered to navigate the digital landscape with confidence and contribute to a more truthful and trustworthy online environment.

BUILDING INDIVIDUAL RESILIENCE

The best defense against manipulation lies in fostering a mindset of critical engagement with online content and social interactions. This encompasses several key components:

Awareness: The Foundation

Understanding the Mechanics: Recognize how algorithms shape your feeds. Be aware of filter bubbles, the pursuit of engagement, and how these can be exploited.

Social Engineering Primer: Familiarize yourself with common social engineering tactics: phishing, pretexting (impersonation of authority figures), baiting (offers that seem too good to be confirmed), and emotional manipulation techniques.

Your Digital Footprint: Reflect on what personal information you share online and how this can be aggregated and potentially used against you.

CULTIVATING HEALTHY SKEPTICISM

Question Everything: Approach information discerningly, especially content that triggers solid emotions or promises outlandish rewards.

Verify: Before sharing, clicking on links, or making decisions based on online information, fact-check using reputable sources. Investigate the origin of the content and cross-reference.

Slow Down: Social engineers often rely on creating a sense of urgency. Pause before engaging with content that feels manipulative. Reflect, investigate, and then decide.

Beware of Oversharing: Limit the personal information you reveal on social media. Consider minimizing "real" details for online profiles where appropriate.

Trust, but Carefully: Be cautious of unsolicited friend requests or messages, even if they seem to come from known contacts (accounts can be compromised).

There must be constant user practice to develop a proactive security habit and to develop trust in user intuition. If an online interaction seems suspicious, disengage, even if you cannot pinpoint the exact reason. Here are a few key factors for proactive security habits development:

Solid and Unique Passwords: Use strong passwords and change them regularly. Enable two-factor authentication wherever possible.

Software Updates: Keep operating systems and software patched, as updates often fix critical security vulnerabilities.

Antivirus and Anti-Malware: Use reputable security software and keep it current.

The concept of "social media literacy" is vital and educational initiatives must focus on the journey of navigating the digital world demands a critical toolkit. By teaching students to recognize filter bubbles, emotional manipulation disguised as content, and the red flags of social engineering, we begin to empower them. This includes developing strong source evaluation skills helping them assess the credibility, reliability, and potential biases of the information they encounter. Fostering a healthy online skepticism – where not everything is instantly believed simply due to appearance or popularity – is crucial for combatting misinformation.

Furthermore, it is essential to emphasize the value of offline connection. Strong, real-world communities and face-to-face interactions are vital counterweights to the potential isolation and manipulation of purely online social environments. With insights from previous examples in mind, let's explore further discussions:

MANIPULATIVE ATTACK TECHNIQUES: EMOTIONAL EXPLOITATION

It reveals how emotions are weaponized for control and delves into the art of using human emotions as tools for manipulation. The initial hook captures attention, while the fear evokes a sense of danger. The outrage stirs strong reactions, and the urgency pushes quick decisions. Also, validation and belonging exploit social connections, highlighting the profound impact of emotional manipulation.

The Hook: Social engineering attacks and heavily biased online content often aim to trigger strong emotional reactions – fear, anger, outrage, a sense of urgency, or even feelings of validation or belonging. These serve to short-circuit our rational thinking.

Fear: Preying on our fears is a powerful tactic. Fake security alerts about hacked accounts, threats of financial loss, or alarming news headlines with exaggerated risks all aim to make us act impulsively without careful consideration.

Outrage: Content engineered to cause offence or spark intense anger floods social media. Social engineers can exploit this outrage to incite users – encouraging them to like, comment, and share inflammatory material, amplifying its reach without regard for its veracity.

Urgency: Manipulators create a false sense of urgency. This might involve limited-time offers and warnings that you must "act now" to claim a prize or help someone in dire need. The goal is to bypass rational decision-making and tap into our "fight or flight" instincts.

Validation and Belonging: Feeling included and validated are powerful emotional drivers. Disinformation campaigns can leverage this by creating content that confirms firmly held beliefs and provides a sense of group identity. This discourages critical analysis and fosters a sense of us vs. them.

ETHICAL DESIGN CAN COUNTERMEASURE THE EMOTIONAL EXPLOITATION

A platform can be designed to mitigate these manipulative techniques. Here are a few potential strategies and key thinking factors:

Disrupting Emotion-Driven Virality: Algorithms could be tweaked to slow down the spread of content designed primarily to incite strong emotions. Introducing a slight delay before sharing or commenting could promote reflection.

Friction for Outrage: Platforms could make it slightly more challenging to engage with outrage-inducing content. A simple prompt, "Are you sure you want to share this?" could break the impulsive action loop and provide a split second for reconsideration.

Nudges for Verification: Design subtle cues highlighting when content lacks credible sources or independent verification. Visual indicators or warnings could encourage a more critical evaluation before sharing or believing the information.

Diversifying the Feed: Actively work against filter bubble formation by suggesting content that introduces slightly different perspectives. This does not imply heavy-handed censorship but promotes exposure to ideas outside our comfort zone.

Transparency and Control: Give users more insights into how algorithms influence their feeds. Offer granular controls for customization, allowing users to opt for settings that prioritize verified sources or focus on diversity of viewpoints.

The tension between freedom of speech and the danger of online manipulation underscores the need for a nuanced approach to ethical design in the digital domain. Finding ways to combat harmful disinformation and trust erosion without outright censorship is vital. Ultimately, a healthy digital ecosystem depends on users and platform design. Individuals cannot absolve themselves of responsibility; they must cultivate healthy skepticism and equip themselves with critical thinking skills. These ethical interventions serve as tools to assist in this process, not to replace individual vigilance.

Notably, the battle against social engineering must be considered ongoing and adaptable. Just as social engineers evolve their tactics, so too must ethically design. This demands proactive vigilance, constantly reassessing how manipulative actors exploit digital platforms and seeking innovative ways to counter those tactics. The rise of immersive virtual environments introduces an additional layer of complexity into the landscape of trust and vulnerability, demanding further research and discussion. At the core of this issue lies the fundamental nature of human psychology. We are wired for social interactions; trust is often essential for collaboration. It is precisely this fundamental human characteristic that social engineers prey upon. Understanding this philosophical tension between the positive and manipulative sides of trust is critical as we navigate the ever-evolving complexities of the digital age.

TRUST ISSUES IN THE VIRTUAL MANIPULATIVE DOMAIN: VR, AR, AND VCHAT

Virtual reality (VR), augmented reality (AR), and platforms like VChat are indeed transformative technologies, pushing the boundaries of digital interaction and redefining our relationship with both the digital and physical realms. They offer immersive experiences that transcend the limitations of traditional screens and keyboards, allowing us to step into virtual worlds, overlay digital information onto our physical surroundings, and connect with others in ways that blur the lines between the real and the virtual.

However, as we increasingly inhabit these digitally mediated spaces, a complex interplay emerges between human psychology and the fundamental building blocks of trust. The very nature of these technologies, with their ability to create convincing illusions and manipulate our perceptions, raises questions about authenticity, identity, and the nature of trust itself.

In virtual worlds, we can embody avatars, digital representations of ourselves that can take on any form we desire. This freedom of self-expression can be liberating, allowing us to explore different identities and connect with others in novel ways. However, it also raises questions about authenticity and deception. Can we truly trust someone we meet in a virtual world, where their appearance and identity can be easily manipulated?

AR overlays digital information onto our physical surroundings, enhancing our perception of the world and creating new possibilities for interaction. This technology has the potential to revolutionize fields like education, healthcare, and manufacturing. However, it also raises concerns about privacy, surveillance, and the potential for manipulation. Can we trust the information presented to us through AR interfaces, or could it be used to influence our decisions or track our movements?

Platforms like VChat, which enable real-time video communication and virtual interactions, have become increasingly popular for social connection and remote collaboration. However, these platforms also raise questions about the authenticity of online interactions and the potential for deepfakes and other forms of digital deception. Can we truly trust the people we interact with online, or could their appearance and voice be manipulated to deceive us?

As we navigate these emerging technologies and the blurred boundaries between the physical and digital worlds, the need for critical thinking and media literacy becomes paramount. We must develop the skills to discern truth from falsehood, to evaluate information critically, and to build trust in a world where appearances can be deceiving.

The future of our relationship with technology hinges on our ability to understand the psychological and social implications of these immersive experiences. By fostering awareness, promoting ethical development, and cultivating critical engagement with these technologies, we can ensure that they enhance our lives and strengthen our connections with each other, rather than eroding the foundations of trust and authenticity.

Presence and the Illusion of Reality

The core of VR and AR lies in "presence" – the potent feeling of existing within the simulated world. This immersion has profound implications for trust. It amplifies positive connections; virtual interactions *feel* genuine, increasing their emotional impact. However, this illusion can also be weaponized. Our usual cues for evaluating trustworthiness become less reliable, leaving us potentially more susceptible to social engineering tactics.

Navigating Avatars and Anonymity

Avatars, our digital representatives, have become central to virtual communication. Subtle avatar behaviors, eye contact, gestures, proximity – tap into the nonverbal communication we instinctively interpret to gauge trust in the real world. However, the fact that these cues can be simulated or manipulated creates uncertainty.

Anonymity offers both freedom and risk. It can foster a sense of liberation, encouraging honesty and open exchange without fear of real-world prejudice. However, the absence of verifiable identity makes it inherently challenging to discern intentions. Platforms like VChat often attempt to establish community norms for building trust, but the inherent fluidity of digital identities remains a challenge. Trust in immersive technologies raises essential questions:

Impact on Trust Formation: How does manipulating presence and identity in VR/AR shape our ability to form and maintain genuine trust in these environments?

Redefining Authenticity: How do we assess authenticity and trustworthiness when customizable avatars embody individuals in spaces where real-world identity can be fluid or obscured?

Platform Responsibility: What role should VR, AR, and VChat environment creators play in designing features and facilitating community norms that promote healthy trust dynamics?

Ethical Considerations: What are the ethical implications of building trust in deeply immersive spaces where simulations can become indistinguishable from offline reality? What safeguards should be in place against deceptive use?

THE REMEDIATION PATH FORWARD: USER AWARENESS AND TECHNOLOGY ADAPTATION

Navigating trust in an immersive digital domain requires critical awareness. It is a dance between embracing the potential of these technologies and understanding how they might rewire our perceptions and instincts. We must develop new forms of digital literacy that prioritize critical evaluation of virtual interactions alongside traditional cybersecurity practices to discuss manipulative social engineering tactics that might become particularly potent within immersive environments due to the sense of presence and difficulty verifying identity. Here are some key examples:

Psychology of Avatars: Analyze research about how avatar design and behavior influence trust perception – in both positive and potentially manipulative ways.

Design for Trust: Brainstorm potential technical features or community guidelines for VR/AR/VChat platforms that could increase transparency, promote accountability, and enhance user agency in trust decisions. Let us look into specific design features and potential community guidelines within VR/AR/VChat platforms that could bolster trust dynamics.

Verifiable Identity Cues: While complete anonymity might not be feasible, some platforms could explore optional, two-factor authentication schemes that allow users to signal their real-world identity. This could involve linking verified social media profiles or email addresses to avatars.

Avatar Reputation Systems: Consider implementing reputation systems based on user interactions and community feedback. Positive contributions could boost an avatar's reputation score, while negative behavior might lead to temporary limitations or require participation in educational modules on responsible VR/AR conduct.

Transparency Tools: Platforms could provide users with tools to look closer into an avatar's profile and past interactions. This could include a history of user reviews, participation statistics in different virtual communities, or flagging mechanisms for suspicious behavior.

Nonverbal Cues with Nuance: Developers could refine avatar animation capabilities for more subtle and expressive nonverbal communication. This could enhance trust by mirroring the richness of real-world interactions where slight nuances in body language can speak volumes.

"Safety Zones" and Trusted Spaces: Consider incorporating designated spaces within VR/AR environments where anonymity is still possible, but primary identity verification is required for entry. These "safety zones" could be designated for sensitive discussions or vulnerable user groups.

COMMUNITY GUIDELINES REMEDIES AND CODES OF CONDUCT

Platforms could establish clear guidelines regarding acceptable avatar behavior and communication norms. This could encompass rules against harassment, impersonation, and manipulative tactics designed to exploit trust within the virtual space.

Prioritizing Transparency: Community guidelines should encourage users to be upfront about their intentions and the limitations of their avatars. Avatars may not perfectly reflect real-world identities, but fostering transparency about this limitation can help build trust.

Bystander Intervention Tools: Platforms could create mechanisms for users to report suspicious activity or intervene in situations where they witness social engineering tactics being used to exploit trust.

Educational Resources: Platforms can provide educational resources within VR/AR environments to teach users about healthy trust dynamics in these spaces. This could involve interactive tutorials or simulations highlighting potential manipulation techniques and strategies for building genuine trust with others.

User Control and Customization: Give users control over their trust environments. This could allow them to filter avatar interactions based on reputation scores, limit unsolicited communication, or interact only with verified users within designated areas.

Striking a balance between promoting positive aspects of anonymity (like open dialogue) and ensuring accountability for actions within VR/AR spaces will be crucial.

Standardization across Platforms: The design features and community guidelines would ideally be adopted across different VR/AR/VChat platforms to create a more consistent user experience and trust ecosystem.

Evolving Threats: Social engineering tactics will likely adapt to new features. Constant vigilance and ongoing development of new safeguards will be necessary.

Building trust in the virtual world is an ongoing challenge. By thoughtfully integrating technical features, fostering healthy community norms, and educating users, VR/AR/VChat platforms can become spaces where genuine connections and collaboration can flourish alongside a healthy dose of skepticism and critical thinking.

Within the burgeoning digital landscapes of VR, AR, and VChat platforms, unwritten social rules – social contracts – organically emerge, shaping user behavior and expectations. These contracts provide a framework for establishing trust and fostering community cohesion. They encompass interaction etiquette community norms and delineate acceptable and unacceptable behaviors.

THE EVOLUTION OF GOVERNANCE

Developing and maintaining robust social contracts requires a delicate balance between technical solutions and human-centered governance. Moderation tools and behavior tracking aid in identifying breaches of trust, but actual community ownership often necessitates participatory governance models. This ongoing negotiation seeks to protect user freedom while prioritizing community safety, a balance vital for cultivating a trustworthy environment. The immersive nature of VR and AR holds the power to profoundly shape our emotions, cognitions, and subsequent actions – both within the virtual world and potentially extending beyond it. The ability to experience the world from another's viewpoint can ignite powerful empathy, forging connections and laying the groundwork for trust across perceived differences.

However, There Is a Crucial Caveat: This intensity raises concerns about psychological well-being. Desensitization, the blurring of boundaries between real and virtual behavior, and the potential for manipulative tactics demand careful attention as we seek to design environments where trust remains paramount.

As virtual environments become more complex, so will the mechanisms for promoting and safeguarding trust. Key areas of focus may include these key factors:

Robust Identity Systems: Exploring advanced identity verification that balances the benefits of anonymity with the need to counter anonymity-fueled deception.

Community-Driven Governance: Empowering users to shape and uphold the social contracts that make these virtual worlds function.

Psychological Research: Understanding the long-term effects of immersive technologies on user well-being is crucial. Designers must prioritize ethical, psychologically informed environments.

Intelligent Safeguards: Harnessing AI and machine learning to detect patterns that threaten trust (harassment, fraud) while safeguarding user privacy and autonomy.

Navigating trust amid the complex psychological impacts of VR, AR, and VChat is an ever-evolving challenge. It demands collaboration between developers, users, and researchers. By recognizing the nuances of trust in virtual landscapes, we can shape immersive experiences marked not only by innovation but also by psychological safety and the growth of genuine, hard-earned trust in communities that transcend the purely physical.

A FURTHER REMEDIATION ANALYSIS WOULD REEMPHASIZE ON THE FOLLOWING KEY FACTORS

Community Governance Models: Analyze potential models (e.g., representative systems, direct voting), discussing their strengths and weaknesses within virtual world contexts.

Psychology of Avatars: Explore how avatar design choices (realism, anthropomorphism) can influence empathy, trust, and the risk of deception with examples.

Ethical AI: Discuss the potential for AI-powered trust systems and the ethical pitfalls to avoid (bias, over-surveillance, reducing individual user agency). Let us embark on a multi-pronged exploration of community governance models, the psychology of avatars, and the ethical considerations surrounding AI-powered trust systems.

Pros: Efficient decision-making potential for specialized expertise among those in governance roles.

Cons: Risk of disengagement from the general user base, potential for power concentration in the hands of a few.

There should be an virtual model, where users within a virtual community elect or appoint members to represent their interests in rulemaking and moderation decisions. This mirrors real-world representative democracies.

Direct Voting: Decisions regarding platform rules and moderation might be made through direct voting that is accessible to all users.

Pros: Maximizes democratic participation and offers users a sense of direct agency.

Cons: Time-consuming, can be susceptible to "mob rule" if passionate minorities consistently outvote a more apathetic majority.

Hybrid Models: Blending aspects of representation with mechanisms enabling direct user input on critical issues. This could involve community-elected bodies responsible for drafting proposals, but with those proposals subject to a public vote before implementation.

Pros: Leverages efficiency of representative systems with the participatory nature of direct democracy.

Cons: It can increase the complexity of governance structures and requires careful processes to manage conflicting interests.

THERE ARE CHALLENGES SPECIFIC TO VIRTUAL ENVIRONMENTS (KEY CHALLENGES)

Authentic User Verification: Ensuring only legitimate community members participate in governance votes is crucial, especially with anonymity features.

Maintaining Engagement: Incentivizing ongoing participation in governance and combating apathy is necessary for the health of these models.

DEEPER CHALLENGES OF THE VIRTUAL ENVIRONMENT, PSYCHOLOGY OF AVATARS

Should avatars strive for high visual fidelity, mirroring the user's natural appearance, or embrace more abstract, stylized forms?

Realism: This can promote familiarity and self-identification, potentially enhancing initial trust. However, the "uncanny valley" effect (where nearly realistic representations evoke unease) must be considered.

Abstraction: Allows for greater freedom of self-expression, reduces judgment based on physical appearance, potentially fostering trust centered on shared interests rather than superficial traits.

Anthropomorphism: To what extent should avatars mimic human features and behavior? This is a very challenging topic and needs further understanding:

Advantages: Instinctual understanding of non-verbal cues based on human norms can build initial trust.

Risks: Excessively anthropomorphized avatars designed to deceive might exploit these innate responses, blurring the line between humans and artificial agents.

Platforms like VRChat showcase the vast spectrum of avatar design. Analyzing user experiences within these communities could shed light on how avatar aesthetics and behavioral capabilities influence trust formation. There are essential and ethical questions regarding such a platform.

ETHICAL AI AND TRUST ISSUES ASSOCIATED WITH VRCHAT (KEY FACTORS)

Pattern Recognition: AI can detect subtle behavioral patterns in interactions, flagging potential instances of harassment, impersonation, or fraud.

Anomaly Detection: Systems can learn to identify deviations from established social norms within communities, alerting moderators to potential emerging issues.

- **Bias:** AI systems are only as unbiased as the data on which they are trained. Ensuring that these trust systems do not perpetuate existing societal prejudices is crucial.
- **Over-Surveillance:** A panopticon-like virtual environment where users feel constantly monitored erodes the trust necessary for genuine interactions.
- **Erosion of User Agency:** Over-reliance on AI for trust and moderation decisions can reduce users' sense of responsibility for their actions, potentially weakening accountability.

The future of virtual world governance and trust systems will undoubtedly involve a nuanced interplay of these human and technological aspects. Let me know if you would like to brainstorm how to mitigate the ethical risks of AI or explore real-world examples of community governance from online gaming. Let us emphasize the interplay between authority, social norms, information dynamics, and the ethical dilemmas inherent in security within socially engineered environments.

Within socially engineered environments, the human instinct to defer to authority can be a potent tool for protection and manipulation. We are socially conditioned to seek guidance from those perceived as knowledgeable or in positions of power. However, this inclination can be exploited to induce undue compliance, bypassing our critical faculties that should be the foundation of solid security decisions.

Security is not merely a technical problem. How we perceive threats and respond to protective measures is deeply intertwined with social constructs and narratives. Popular media can amplify fear, blurring the lines between real and exaggerated risks. Alternatively, cultural messages that downplay dangers can leave individuals ill-prepared. This highlights the need to acknowledge the role of social influence in shaping our security mindset.

At the other hand, information is a potent currency in socially engineered environments: personal and technical knowledge grants power. However, the act of gathering and using information also opens up vulnerabilities. Understanding the context of information – who holds it, how they use it, and whose behavior it might seek to shape – is essential for robust security strategies that balance effectiveness with privacy and individual autonomy.

THE ETHICS OF INFLUENCE AND PROTECTION IN A PLATFORM LIKE VRCHAT

Security within environments designed to influence our behavior raises profound ethical questions. Where does legitimate persuasion for security-conscious choices end, and manipulative erosion of autonomy begin? Security philosophies must grapple with these complexities. Transparency about the design of security interventions, empowering users with knowledge, and fostering individual resilience against coercion are vital considerations in any ethical approach. Security in socially engineered environments demands constant vigilance. It requires:

Critical Thinking: Challenging our instincts to defer to authority and questioning alarmist and overly reassuring narratives about security threats.

Media Literacy: Discerning how security is presented in popular culture, recognizing how it might exaggerate or minimize risks for dramatic purposes.

Information Sensitivity: Understanding the potential value of our personal information and technical details about the systems we use, recognizing that their disclosure can create vulnerabilities.

Ethical Advocacy: Demanding transparency about the "why" behind security measures and pushing back against those who subtly seek to manipulate behavior rather than empower informed choices.

There are real world case studies, where social engineering tactics exploited the illusion of authority or manipulated the public perception of security risks. Here are a few examples.

CASE STUDY 1: PHISHING ATTACKS IMPERSONATING AUTHORITY

Phishing emails or fake websites are designed to appear as if they originate from a legitimate, trustworthy entity like a bank, government agency, or well-known company. These attacks leverage people's inherent trust in these institutions.

Official-looking logos, convincing language, and urgent requests for personal or financial information are calculated to bypass critical thinking. An email claiming to be from the IRS, warning about an overdue tax payment and threatening legal action. Clicking embedded links leads to a fake IRS website designed to capture sensitive data.

CASE STUDY 2: TECH SUPPORT SCAMS

Scammers contact victims claiming to be from a reputable tech company (like Microsoft or Apple). They fabricate software problems or security issues to incite fear. The scammer manipulates the victim by creating a false sense of urgency and using technical jargon to appear knowledgeable. They often pressure the victim into buying expensive "repairs" or granting remote device access. A pop-up window or phone call claiming a virus has been detected on the victim's computer. The scammer "walks" the victim through several steps, ultimately installing malware or extracting payment for unnecessary security software.

CASE STUDY 3: SOCIAL MEDIA AND THE SPREAD OF MISINFORMATION

False or misleading news articles, memes, or social media posts designed to appear legitimate. They use sensational headlines fabricated quotes from "experts," often appealing to strong emotions. The proliferation of misinformation and inflammatory content skews public understanding of security threats. This can involve exaggerating risks for political gain or downplaying dangers to minimize financial or reputational harm. Fake news stories about outbreaks of violence attributed to minority groups during an election cycle, designed to provoke fear and division. Alternatively, a chemical plant downplays a toxic leak's dangers to avoid negative press and potential legal repercussions.

The key learning points from above case studies are listed as follows:

The Power of Impersonation: Social engineers are adept at mimicking legitimate authority's visual and linguistic markers to trick victims.

Emotional Manipulation: Fear, urgency, or the desire for a quick "fix" are all exploited to override rational security behaviors.

Broader Societal Impact: When public understanding of risks is distorted, it can lead to poor decision-making on an individual level and hinder the development of effective security policies on a larger scale.

Addressing these threats requires a multi-pronged approach:

Technical Safeguards: Robust spam filtering, malware detection, and tools for verifying website authenticity.

Education and Awareness: Teaching people to recognize common social engineering tactics and the red flags associated with phishing, scams, and fake news.

Healthy Skepticism: Encouraging a critical mindset where individuals question the source and motivations of urgent security prompts or claims of authority.

There are attacks based on psychological scams, such as the notorious "romance scam" as a prime example of how social engineers exploit a wide range of psychological vulnerabilities for manipulation and financial gain. Let's look at its key factors.

ROMANCE SCAMS: THE ANATOMY OF MANIPULATION

Romance scams operate as a carefully orchestrated manipulation of human desires and insecurities. The scammer systematically identifies susceptible individuals, often those seeking connection or recently experiencing hardship, and preys upon the inherent need for belonging. They fabricate an idealized persona, a perfect mirror image reflecting the victim's deepest desires for love, admiration, and support. A web of trust is swiftly built through relentless communication and manufactured intimacy, replacing skepticism with the intoxicating belief that one has found a soulmate. This trust, however, lays the foundation for exploitation. The scammer gradually isolates the victim, subtly discouraging other connections while painting themselves as the only person who truly cares. When the emotional trap is firmly sprung, fabricated emergencies are introduced. These crises, coupled with a carefully cultivated sense of obligation, shame, and fear of losing the illusion of love, drive the victim to send money or aid. Romance scams are not just about financial loss; they inflict deep emotional wounds. Victims are left grappling with betrayal, self-blame, and the shattered belief in their judgment. These scams highlight the chilling reality that in the digital age, those who prey on our most fundamental human needs can cause devastating harm while hiding behind a mask of affection.

KEY PSYCHOLOGICAL FACTORS THAT LEVERS AT ALGORITHM DESIGN

The Key Psychological Factors Are as Follows:

Loneliness and Need for Belonging: Humans are inherently social. Romance scams offer a counterfeit but compelling antidote to isolation.

Confirmation Bias: The scammer's persona validates the victim's hopes and desires. We overlook inconsistencies that do not fit the ideal we want to believe in.

Sunk Cost Fallacy: The emotional investment the victim has already made makes them more reluctant to walk away, even when doubts arise.

Altruism as Vulnerability: The desire to help someone in need is admirable but can be turned into a tool for manipulation.

Romance scams cause not only devastating financial losses but also profound emotional trauma. Victims often experience shame, self-blame, and a deep sense of betrayal that can hinder their ability to form trusting relationships in the future.

KEY FACTORS FOR COMBATTING ROMANCE SCAMS

The following key elements are vital for effectively combating romance scams:

Awareness: Educating potential targets about the common tactics and red flags (requests for money, avoidance of face-to-face meetings, excessively idealized online persona) is crucial.
Breaking the Isolation: Encouraging victims to speak to trusted friends or family can help break the psychological hold of the scammer.
Reducing Stigma: Creating an environment where victims feel safe to report these crimes without judgment is vital for enabling prosecution and preventing others from falling prey.

The scourge of romance scams necessitates a multi-pronged approach, and technology, while not a panacea, can play a crucial role. Exploring tools that aid in verifying identities or detecting patterns in the language scammers frequently employ is essential. Reverse image searches integrated into platforms could unmask stolen photos, while AI-powered language analysis might flag inconsistencies or typical sentimental manipulation tactics. While still a developing field, investigating secure and optional verification systems could bolster user confidence. These systems need to prioritize user privacy.

Beyond the individual user, the role of social media platforms is critical. These platforms must address their responsibility in combating romance scams. This includes proactive moderation, easy reporting mechanisms, and potential warning systems when detecting suspicious patterns.

Lastly, we cannot ignore the devastating impact on victims. Support systems are essential – not only for financial recovery but also to address the emotional trauma these scams inflict. Resources like counseling, peer support groups, and educational materials tailored for those who have been exploited can play a significant role in rebuilding lives and preventing future victimization.

While technology plays a crucial role in combating romance scams, it is essential to acknowledge its limitations. Scammers are relentlessly adaptable; even the most sophisticated AI algorithms can reflect biases in their underlying training data. Thus, a comprehensive approach goes beyond technical solutions, emphasizing public awareness and education alongside proactive action by social media platforms.

Extensive verification measures, while potentially helpful, also raise privacy concerns. It is essential to strike a balance between security and individual privacy. Users should retain control over the information they share and understand how it will be used. Transparency and responsible data handling by platforms are paramount.

Social media platforms have a moral and ethical responsibility to fight romance scams more assertively. Algorithms designed to detect suspicious patterns, combined with easily accessible reporting tools and explicit warnings about common red flags, can empower users to be the first line of defense. Additionally, platforms should build robust partnerships with law enforcement agencies, sharing information and facilitating investigations to bring these criminals to justice.

Successfully battling romance scams in the digital age requires a multi-pronged approach. Technology is a vital tool but cannot replace human vigilance, education, and proactive measures by the platforms themselves. By fostering a culture of awareness, collaboration, and respect for individual privacy, we can reduce the heartbreak and financial devastation caused by these manipulative schemes.

We can dismantle the intricate web of manipulation employed in romance scams by implementing technological interventions, social media platform accountability, and robust support structures for victims. Let us emphasize the importance of adaptive security strategies, the interplay between technical and human-centric approaches, and the role of encryption within a comprehensive security toolbox.

The rapidly evolving nature of socially engineered environments demands a security philosophy prioritizing flexibility and continuous improvement. Traditional, static security models are insufficient when facing attackers constantly refining their tactics to exploit technological flaws and human psychology. Adequate security in this domain is characterized by:

Constant Vigilance: Ongoing monitoring of emerging threats, social trends, and technological advancements is needed to identify potential new vulnerabilities.

Adaptable Design: Security systems must be built with agility in mind. This involves modular components that can be updated in response to new threats without significant overhauls.

User-Centric Focus: Cultivating a security mindset among all users is essential. Education, awareness campaigns, and user-friendly tools empower individuals to become active participants in maintaining a secure environment.

Proper security in socially engineered environments transcends rigid technological solutions. Understanding the interplay between human behavior and technical defenses is paramount. A single careless user can undermine robust security protocols. A holistic approach necessitates:

Awareness Campaigns: Educating users about social engineering tactics (phishing, impersonation, emotional manipulation) cultivates a healthy skepticism that counteracts manipulative techniques.

Behavior-Based Security Tools: Technical solutions that analyze user behavior patterns to detect anomalies can flag potential insider threats or compromised accounts.

Human-Centered Design: Security systems that are intuitive and seamlessly integrated into workflows are more likely to be adopted and used correctly by the human element of the equation.

THE ROLE OF ENCRYPTION WITHIN A SECURE ECOSYSTEM

The role of encryption within a secure digital ecosystem is undeniable. Its ability to transform sensitive information into an unreadable form, protect its integrity, and ensure only authorized parties have access makes encryption a cornerstone of modern cybersecurity. However, a comprehensive approach is crucial.

While encryption shares specific goals with techniques like steganography, obfuscation, and hashing, each has unique strengths. Steganography complements encryption by concealing the very existence of sensitive data. Obfuscation adds a layer of complexity but does not offer the same level of protection. Hashing is vital for ensuring data integrity but does not prevent unauthorized access itself. Similarly, while access controls are essential to limit who can access data, they provide little protection if a system is breached, or data are in transit. Ultimately, encryption is a powerful weapon in the cybersecurity arsenal. However, it must be deployed thoughtfully alongside other protective measures to achieve proper security. A successful security strategy requires a multi-layered approach, recognizing the complementary roles of data obfuscation, access controls, secure transmission protocols, and continuous monitoring. By understanding encryption's essential role within this larger framework, we can construct digital environments that better safeguard our most valuable information. The security philosophy in socially engineered environments recognizes that no solution is foolproof. An adaptive, multi-layered approach that combines technical measures, behavioral awareness, and a focus on the human-technology interface is critical. It is a continuous dance between anticipating threats, educating users, and deploying robust safeguards – like encryption – within a security design focused on resilience and adaptability.

There are concerns about deep engineered cases that even encryption is not so efficient with. The world of social engineering is constantly evolving, with attackers crafting ever-more sophisticated tactics to exploit human vulnerabilities. Here is a glimpse into some concerning trends:

Deepfakes and Synthetic Media: The rise of deepfakes and hyper-realistic videos manipulated to place someone in a situation they never experienced presents a significant threat. Imagine a CEO announcing a company meltdown in a fabricated video or a political candidate delivering a doctored speech that sways public opinion. These deepfakes can erode trust in legitimate information and sow discord.

Social Engineering via AI Chatbots: AI chatbots are becoming adept at mimicking human conversation. Malicious actors could leverage these to impersonate customer service representatives, tricking victims into divulging personal information or clicking on malicious links.

Spear Phishing 2.0: Hyper-Personalization: Phishing attacks are becoming more targeted and sophisticated. Attackers are harvesting vast amounts of personal data through social media breaches. They can then craft highly personalized phishing emails that appear to come from a trusted source (friend, colleague, boss), increasing the likelihood of a successful attack.

Weaponizing Social Causes: Social engineering tactics are increasingly weaving into hot-button social issues. Attackers might pose as supporters of a cause, exploiting people's emotions and desire to help manipulate them into donating to fake charities or spreading misinformation.

Gamification of Scams: Attackers incorporate game mechanics like points, leaderboards, and rewards into scams. This can be particularly enticing to younger demographics, blurring the line between entertainment and manipulation.

These emerging threats highlight the necessity for ongoing security awareness training and the development of robust detection tools that can identify suspicious patterns in communication and user behavior. Here are some good examples of deep engineered attacks.

THE TWITTER HACK OF 2020

The Breach: In July 2020, a coordinated social engineering attack compromised the Twitter accounts of high-profile individuals, including celebrities, politicians, and tech giants. Attackers gained access by targeting Twitter employees with a vishing (voice phishing) scam. The attackers tricked employees into divulging login credentials, granting them access to internal systems and the ability to hijack prominent Twitter accounts.

Human Factor: The success of this attack hinged on exploiting human error. The vishing scam relied on social engineering tactics to bypass security protocols. Employees caught off guard and pressured to act quickly fell victim to manipulation.

Technical Considerations: While Twitter undoubtedly had technical security measures in place, this breach underscores the importance of employee training in recognizing social engineering tactics. Multi-factor authentication could have also added an extra layer of protection.

Lessons Learned: This case study highlights the critical role of human vigilance in a robust security posture. Even the most sophisticated technical defenses can be compromised by human error. Regular security awareness training and a culture of skepticism toward unexpected requests are essential.

THE EQUIFAX DATA BREACH OF 2017

The Breach: In 2017, a massive data breach at Equifax, a credit reporting agency, exposed the personal information of nearly 150 million Americans. Attackers exploited a vulnerability in a website used for online dispute resolution. This vulnerability allowed them to gain unauthorized access to a database containing sensitive information like Social Security numbers and birth dates.

Human Factor: While technical vulnerability was the initial point of entry, it is essential to consider the human factors that might have contributed. A lack of awareness about the importance of patching vulnerabilities or inadequate monitoring for suspicious activity could have played a role.

Technical Considerations: The vulnerability exploited in this breach was known, and a patch was made available. However, it appears this patch was not applied promptly. Additionally, it is possible that insufficient monitoring for unusual access attempts allowed the attackers to operate undetected for an extended period.

Lessons Learned: This case study emphasizes the importance of a layered security approach. Technical safeguards like vulnerability patching and regular security audits are crucial. However, fostering a culture of security awareness within an organization, where employees are vigilant and report suspicious activity, is equally important.

The fight against social engineering and human error within cybersecurity is a dynamic and ever-evolving battleground. It demands not only continuous technical innovation and a deep understanding of emerging threats but also a keen awareness of the recurring vulnerabilities that are exploited time and again. By meticulously scrutinizing past breaches, we gain invaluable insights into the tactics, techniques, and psychological manipulations employed by those who seek to undermine our security systems. This knowledge is not merely historical artifact; it is a crucial foundation for building defenses that are both robust and adaptable, capable of withstanding the relentless onslaught of social engineering attacks and human fallibility.

The road ahead is paved with the stones of continuous vigilance. It requires a multi-pronged approach that empowers users to become the first line of defense through heightened awareness and comprehensive education. By fostering a culture of cybersecurity consciousness, we equip individuals with the knowledge and skills to recognize and resist social engineering tactics, to question suspicious emails and links, and to protect their sensitive information from those who would seek to exploit it. Simultaneously, we must bolster our technological safeguards, fortifying our systems with robust firewalls, intrusion detection systems, and multi-factor authentication. We must invest in the development of advanced security technologies that can detect and mitigate emerging threats, such as artificial intelligence-powered systems that can identify and flag suspicious patterns of behavior. Through this synergistic combination of human understanding and technical fortification, we can strive toward a more resilient security posture – one that is less easily compromised by social engineering and human vulnerabilities. The human element, often seen as the weakest link in the cybersecurity chain, can also be our greatest strength. By empowering individuals with knowledge, awareness, and a sense of responsibility, we can transform them into vigilant guardians of our digital realm. The ongoing battle against social engineering and human error is not merely a technological challenge; it is a contest for the human mind, a struggle to outwit those who would exploit our trust, our emotions, and our inherent vulnerabilities. By fostering a culture of cybersecurity awareness, investing in robust technological safeguards, and recognizing the dynamic nature of this threat landscape, we can build a more secure and resilient digital future for all.

3 Individual Security in the Era of Algorithmic and Artificial Intelligence Advancements

In an era of AI and ever-evolving algorithms, the concept of personal cybersecurity has changed. No longer can we rely solely on firewalls and antivirus software. Understanding how these technologies shape our world is essential for staying safe. There is a delicate dance between trust and skepticism in the digital domain, where unseen forces sculpt and manipulate interactions. Encryption, the mathematical shield, stands as a constant companion, whispering assurances that data travels less vulnerable. However, its protection is one layer in this complex landscape where algorithms play an equally potent role in shaping social reality.

PROTECTING WITH ENCRYPTION: THE BEDROCK, NOT THE SUMMIT

Robust encryption is the bedrock upon which trust in socially engineered environments rests. It protects conversations, transactions, and traces digital existence. While vital, its role is limited. It secures the conduits of information but cannot dictate the content flowing within or how that content make feel and shapes my perceptions.

PROTECTING WITH ALGORITHMS: SHAPING REALITY FROM SHADOWS

Algorithms, the quiet orchestrators, curate a seemingly personalized experience based on clicks, likes, and scrolls. They can reinforce or challenge their worldview, amplifying certain voices while silencing others. These hidden rules nudge me toward behaviors, subtly manipulating user choices. The convenience of this tailored experience carries the tradeoff of a less nuanced and serendipitous digital journey. The user becomes both the actor and the acted upon.

The algorithmic curation and the security that engenders my participation feed an undercurrent of isolation. Authentic human connection – forged through the unfiltered, messy beauty of face-to-face interactions – contrasts my hyper-personalized digital life. Do these digital ties weaken the very bonds they were meant to facilitate?

 DOI: 10.1201/9781003500698-3

Today, and more so in the future, traversing socially engineered environments demands constant vigilance. It compels the understanding of how algorithms subtly shape reality while exercising the skepticism born from countless security breaches. It must be recognized how the trust inspired by encryption can be exploited by other forces, often out of direct sight.

This awareness journey is not only outward-focused but also inward. Understanding my biases, desire for affirmation, and susceptibility to tailored content is as vital as any technical safeguard. It calls for critical thinking even within spaces designed to distract. It embraces the benefits of a digitally connected, encrypted world, yet recognizing that algorithms and social engineering will forever reshape societal and individual interactions. The best path lies neither in absolute cynicism nor blind trust. Instead, it lies in cultivating a "digital mindfulness" and an informed awareness guiding me through this evolving terrain. It is a mindfulness of the cryptography that keeps my secrets, yes, but also of the hidden persuasions that seek to subtly shape my actions, thoughts, and relationships with the world. Let us embark on a multi-pronged exploration, analyzing potential solutions for algorithmic bias, examining the societal consequences of unfettered algorithmic manipulation, and debating the merits and challenges of both regulation and self-policing of social media platforms.

THE BATTLE AGAINST BIAS AND ALGORITHMIC MANIPULATION: REDESIGNING THE DIGITAL LANDSCAPE

Dataset Diversification and Auditing: Algorithms reflect the data on which they are trained. Proactive effort must be invested in creating diverse datasets in content and the individuals who provide that data. Regular auditing of these datasets, both internally and potentially by third parties, can help identify unintended bias creeping in. If users understand the basic logic behind why content is recommended, it demystifies the process. Platforms might provide options like, "You see this because you engaged with X post type." While total transparency of the algorithm is unlikely, even partial explainability combats the feeling of being mindlessly manipulated. Critical decisions should have human oversight even when assisted by algorithms. For example, if algorithm flags content as potentially harmful, having humans review the context provides a layer of safeguard against false positives or misinterpretation of nuanced language. Deliberately boosting the visibility of quality, well-researched content that challenges dominant narratives within a filter bubble can help users encounter alternative perspectives. However, this needs careful implementation to avoid the perception of forced "re-education" and further entrenchment in existing beliefs.

BEYOND THE INDIVIDUAL USERS: THE SOCIETAL RIPPLE EFFECT

Democratization of Information and Opinion Formation: When algorithms primarily optimize for engagement, polarizing or sensationalist content often wins. This undermines the idea of a shared public sphere, making reasoned debate difficult. It erodes trust in institutions and the perception of the shared reality upon which democracy depends. Biased algorithms can perpetuate systemic prejudices. This can have tangible consequences in areas like employment, housing, and even the justice system, where algorithms are increasingly being used for decisions with real-world impact. The hyper-personalization fueled by algorithms can limit exposure to ideas and experiences outside our established preferences. This diminishes the chance encounters that drive innovation and a deep understanding of those different from us.

REGULATION VS. SELF-POLICING: SEEKING ACCOUNTABILITY

The Emerging Cases for Regulation

Emerging Cases for Regulation Focus on Leveling the Playing Field, Enhancing Transparency, and Initiating Proactive Audits

Levelling the Playing Field: Rules that apply to all platforms create consistency and make it harder for companies to claim ignorance of harmful effects they can then ignore.

Enforcing Transparency: Legislation could mandate some degree of algorithmic transparency, making it harder to hide behind the "black box."

Proactive Auditing: Regulatory bodies could conduct audits, incentivizing companies to proactively mitigate bias and filter bubbles.

The Emerging Cases for Platform Responsibility and Self-Policing

The emerging cases in this area are primarily centered on:

Agility and Nuance: Platforms may be better positioned to respond quickly to emerging forms of algorithmic harm than legislation's slower pace.

Trust-Building: Demonstrating a commitment to fairness and transparency can build user trust, potentially averting the need for heavier regulation in the long run.

Sector-Led Standards: Collaboration between platforms could lead to industry-wide ethical standards for algorithms, creating a culture of accountability even with less direct government oversight.

The Challenges of Both Approaches (Key Factors)

Assessing the Challenges of Both Approaches Uncovers Crucial Factors Like Stifled Innovation, Enforcement Challenges, and Global Disconnects

Stifled Innovation: Overly strict regulation can hinder beneficial uses of algorithms. Striking the right balance is crucial.

Enforcement: Effectively monitoring compliance, particularly in complex algorithmic systems, is a significant hurdle.

Global Disconnects: Regulation is often national, while platforms are global. This creates loopholes and conflicting standards.

There is no simple answer moving forward. Addressing these issues will likely involve a hybrid approach:

Multi-Stakeholder Dialogue: Involving technologists, ethicists, policymakers, and the public in ongoing discussions.
Investment in Research: Fund interdisciplinary research into the societal impacts of algorithms and the development of bias-mitigating techniques.
User Empowerment: Digital literacy campaigns to help citizens understand how algorithms shape their online lives and advocate for their interests.

It is essential to recognize that even perfectly unbiased algorithms operating on neutral datasets can reproduce harmful societal patterns due to how platforms are utilized. This exposes the need for solutions encompassing technical fixes and understanding the human side of the equation. Here are some case examples:

CASE EXAMPLE 1: TOXICITY AMPLIFICATION THROUGH USER ENGAGEMENT

Issue: Even if a social media platform has no "bias" in its core recommendation algorithm, prioritizing engagement can systematically amplify toxic content. Hate speech, conspiracy theories, and inflammatory posts often generate strong reactions (even negative ones). The algorithm may promote them, not because it "endorses" the content but because it predicts high engagement that benefits the platform. The spread of misinformation related to elections or public health crises – content designed to be shocking often goes viral, even as users debunk it. Online extremism, where groups that promote violent or hateful ideologies exploit algorithmic mechanics to gain visibility that might exceed their actual numbers.
Why Technology Alone Cannot Fix This Issue: The problem is not the data but how engagement is measured. Promoting less reactive but more nuanced or educational content is hard when the algorithm is blind to such distinctions. This requires human input on what kind of engagement is beneficial vs. detrimental, a much trickier thing to code and scale effectively.

CASE EXAMPLE 2: RECOMMENDER SYSTEMS AND RADICALIZATION PATHWAYS

Issue: Platforms like YouTube have faced criticism for their recommendation algorithms unintentionally leading users down paths toward increasingly extreme content. A person watching videos with mild political views might be incrementally led toward conspiracy theories or radical content due to algorithmic suggestions. Research suggests this phenomenon contributed to the radicalization of individuals involved in far-right movements or acts of violence. It also operates in non-political contexts, such as health misinformation, where starting with mild diet tips can lead a user down a path to promoting dangerous pseudoscience.

Why Technology Alone Cannot Fix This Issue: No clear, universal definition of "harmful radicalization" exists. Algorithms struggle with nuance. Users may intentionally seek increasingly extreme content. Distinguishing this from the algorithm nudging them is difficult.

Limiting recommendations risks the perception of censorship, even when well-intentioned.

CASE EXAMPLE 3: BIAS IN SEEMINGLY OBJECTIVE TOOLS

Issue: Many AI-driven tools are billed as "objective" compared to human decision-making and thus fairer. The reality is more complex. Facial recognition systems trained on datasets with predominantly white faces perform worse on individuals with darker skin, leading to misidentifications with potentially severe consequences in law enforcement or security settings.

Job recruitment software might perpetuate gender biases by being trained on historical data where men dominated specific roles, subconsciously de-prioritizing resumes even from highly qualified women.

Why Technology Alone Can't Fix It: Even if the algorithm is unbiased, the "world" it is learning from is not. The tool reflects the data, not some idealized unbiased reality.

Detecting these biases is difficult, as the inner workings of these tools are often opaque, making accountability challenging.

KEY TAKEAWAYS OF ABOVE CASE EXAMPLES

Social Engineering Is Intertwined: Bad actors exploit these algorithmic dynamics, knowing incendiary content spreads more easily, intentionally gaming the system.

Human Judgment Is Still Essential: Algorithms lack the context to distinguish outrage bait from constructive debate or the intent behind certain content.

Focusing on Outcomes, Not Just Intentions: Algorithms can produce undesirable results even with good intentions. This necessitates a focus on real-world impact, not merely the technical neutrality of the code.

EXPLORING SOLUTIONS FURTHER

While important, the pursuit of accuracy in recommender algorithms must not become the sole guiding principle. Instead, we must ask ourselves the crucial question: is this algorithm truly enhancing the user experience, or does it risk causing harm? This requires adopting metrics that transcend mere performance indicators. We must assess fairness, examine societal implications, and prioritize digital well-being.

Furthermore, to build algorithms that genuinely serve the diverse needs of users, those who create these systems need to reflect that same diversity. Development teams and data scientists must represent various backgrounds, experiences, and perspectives. This will help anticipate unintended consequences and mitigate the risk of perpetuating biases through technology designed to enhance our experiences.

Finally, empowering users is crucial. Platforms should offer more granular controls for shaping recommendations, allowing individuals to opt out of specific content categories even if they promise high engagement. This empowers users to curate their own online experiences and fosters a sense of agency within these complex systems.

The concept of proactive intervention, where platforms cultivate a healthy online ecosystem not just through reaction but deliberate design choices, offers a compelling, albeit complex, avenue for mitigating the limitations of purely technological solutions.

IMPORTANCE OF PROACTIVE BEHAVIOR (KEY FACTORS)

Proactive behavior fosters positive interactions and critical thinking by encouraging individuals to seek diverse perspectives and engage meaningfully with community-building tools. It helps break filter bubbles and slows down the spread of misinformation by promoting careful content sharing and fact-checking. Additionally, reflective prompts and appreciation for friction enhance personal growth and adaptability, leading to a more informed and connected society. Overall, these elements work synergistically to create a more resilient and engaged community.

Promoting Positive Behaviors: Instead of focusing solely on removing "bad" content, this approach emphasizes incentivizing positive engagement and nudging users toward beneficial online habits:

Critical Thinking Boost: Fact-checker prompts reminders to consider source reliability integrated into the UI, not just as an afterthought to debunk something.

Source Diversity: Could platforms suggest content from reputable sources with opposing viewpoints when a user heavily interacts with a single perspective?

Community Building Tools: Features that promote civil discourse structured debate spaces to foster connection instead of just optimized posting for likes.

Beyond Raw Engagement: Algorithms could prioritize the quality of interaction – longer read times, positive comments, not just mindless clicks and scrolling.

Breaking Filter Bubbles: Purposely interjecting occasional content outside a user's established interests to encourage exploration and reduce the sense of an echo chamber.

Slowing Down Virality: Could limits on shares/re-tweets within a short timeframe reduce algorithmic amplification of unverified information?

Friction as a Feature: Introducing elements that slow users down, encouraging mindfulness over mindless reactions.

Fact-Checking Quizzes: Before sharing an article, a quick multiple-choice quiz about the content might make people think twice before spreading misinformation.

Reflective Prompts: Asking "Why do you want to share this?" before posting could encourage users to evaluate their motivations.

POTENTIAL BENEFITS OF PROMOTING PROACTIVE BEHAVIORS (KEY FACTORS)

Promoting proactive behavior leads to increased engagement, better critical thinking, and stronger community connections. It encourages individuals to seek diverse perspectives, reduces the spread of misinformation, and fosters a culture of reflection and growth. The following benefits contribute to a more informed, resilient, and collaborative society.

Addresses Root Causes: Focuses on user behavior, not just playing "whack-a-mole" with harmful content.

Preemptive, Not Reactive Behavior: This could mitigate the spread of misinformation by creating an environment where it is less likely to flourish in the first place.

Increased User Agency: These interventions empower users to make more informed choices about their online behavior.

Trust-Building: A proactive focus on healthy engagement signals that the platform values a positive user experience, potentially increasing long-term trust.

The potential of algorithmic interventions to shape positive online experiences is undeniable, as are the challenges accompanying their implementation. If executed poorly, they risk alienating users – being perceived as overbearing, restrictive, or futile against cynicism. It is crucial to strike the right balance between promoting well-being and retaining the elements of enjoyment that draw users to social media platforms in the first place.

Furthermore, users seeking to manipulate the system or circumvent limitations will adapt their behaviors, highlighting a fundamental "arms race" aspect. Interventions will require ongoing refinement and adjustment to remain effective. Lastly, defining what constitutes "positive" online behavior platforms should foster poses a significant question. Before algorithms can promote those behaviors, quantifiable metrics and robust data must be collected and analyzed. These challenges underscore that algorithmic interventions in social media are not a technological cure-all. Their success will rely on careful design, continuous adaptation, and recognition that pursuing healthier online experiences is an ongoing dialogue between platforms and their users.

Proactive intervention cannot be a series of blunt force tools thrust upon users. It demands focusing on a user-centric design, some of the key factors are as follows:

Transparency: Be upfront about how these interventions work, fostering trust and minimizing the feeling of arbitrary manipulation.
User Control: Granular settings allow users to adjust the levels of intervention they experience.
Feedback Loops: Mechanisms for users to report when an intervention feels misplaced or intrusive, informing platform developers.

FURTHER DISCUSSION POINTS ABOUT USER-CENTRIC BEHAVIOR

Further discussion points could delve into how user-centric design not only creates enjoyable features that encourage positive online behavior but also how education equips users to identify and resist manipulation.

The "Fun" Factor: Can you brainstorm ways to incorporate healthy practices into intrinsically enjoyable features, not just ones that feel like chores?
Gamification Upside and Downside: Can badges, leaderboards, etc., be used to incentivize positive online behavior, or does this risk introducing another unhealthy feedback loop?
The Role of Education: Should this go hand-in-hand with broad digital literacy campaigns outside the platforms, making users less susceptible to manipulation in the first place?

Proactive interventions and the broader idea of engineering platforms to reshape user behavior raise ethical questions. Let us analyze the most pressing concerns, as this concept treads a fine line between fostering a healthier online environment and potentially overstepping into paternalism or unintended manipulation. Where is the line between suggesting further content or nudging users toward beneficial behaviors and interfering with their freedom to engage with the platform? Heavy-handed interventions could infantilize users or make them feel like their choices are no longer truly their own. Even well-intentioned attempts to expose users to diverse viewpoints or "healthy" content can backfire. Who decides what constitutes a legitimate opposing view or what content is unhealthy? These platforms become curators of information, opening the door for their biases to seep into interventions. This potential for disguised paternalism necessitates vital transparency and oversight. Proactive interventions could slide into exploiting the same psychological techniques social engineering relies on. While potentially engaging, gamification of "good behavior" risks creating new feedback loops where users prioritize the metric over genuine engagement or develop an unhealthy obsession with curating their digital "good citizen" persona. It is impossible to predict how users might respond to changes in platform design. Trying to force specific outcomes can have ripple effects. Algorithms that promote constructive conversations might inadvertently incentivize users to employ more subtle ways to spread negativity or harmful ideas. The platform becomes a new battleground, potentially leading to unforeseen negative social dynamics. Where does it stop? If the aim is to engineer a less toxic online environment, platforms might feel justified in progressively stricter interventions over time. These risks turning them into highly controlled environments, losing the vibrant, even if sometimes chaotic, essence of the internet as a space for self-expression.

THE FOCUS TO ADDRESSING THE HUMAN ELEMENT

Tackling the root cause represents a paradigm shift in addressing cyberattacks, moving beyond mere technical defenses and delving into the heart of human behavior. This approach seeks to cultivate a more resilient mindset among users, empowering them to recognize and resist manipulation tactics, thereby reducing their susceptibility to cyberattacks and fostering a safer online environment. By promoting self-awareness, critical thinking, and ethical decision-making, we can empower users to become active guardians of their own security and that of their communities.

Empowering user interventions provide individuals with the tools and knowledge to proactively shape their online experiences and foster a healthier digital environment. This includes promoting digital literacy, educating users about online risks and best practices, and providing access to resources that support mental well-being and resilience. By fostering self-awareness and encouraging users to take ownership of their online interactions, we can create a culture of collective responsibility and mutual respect.

Shared accountability and empathy-focused features can play a crucial role in strengthening a sense of community and countering the isolating effects that often accompany online interactions. By fostering a sense of shared responsibility for online safety and encouraging users to empathize with the potential impact of their actions on others, we can create a more positive and supportive online environment. This, in turn, can contribute to a reduction in cyberattacks, as individuals become more mindful of their online behavior and less likely to engage in harmful or malicious activities.

In essence, these approaches represent a holistic vision for cybersecurity, one that recognizes the interconnectedness of technology, human behavior, and societal well-being. By addressing the root causes of cyberattacks, empowering users, and fostering a sense of shared responsibility, we can create a safer, more resilient, and more compassionate digital world.

KEY ETHICAL CONCERNS FOR ADDRESSING HUMAN ELEMENTS (KEY FACTORS)

Emotional Manipulation: Interventions to elicit specific emotions must avoid being overly exploitative or inadvertently insincere.

Performative Empathy: There is a risk of users' play-acting empathy to avoid social penalties or to appear virtuous online. This highlights the need for interventions to change behavior and genuinely influence attitudes.

Backlash and Gaming the System: Those determined to spread harmful content will find ways to circumvent these well-intentioned tools or turn them into a new form of harassment.

Surveillance Concerns: Collecting more nuanced data on emotional states or personal stories, even with good intentions, raises privacy issues and potential misuse.

FINDING BALANCE: ETHICS AND PRACTICALITY

The effectiveness and ethical soundness of human interventions hinge on some of the key factors.

These technological interventions' effectiveness and ethical implications depend on several crucial factors. Opt-in frameworks must be paramount, ensuring users maintain ultimate control over their participation. Any data collection for emotional analysis needs to prioritize privacy and transparent methodology. Ultimately, these tools should augment, not replace, human moderators with the nuance and judgment to navigate complex online situations. Crucially, user feedback should shape iterative design processes, ensuring that interventions remain effective and not become stale or easily bypassed. These considerations highlight the delicate balance between the potential benefits and ethical concerns surrounding using technology to combat social engineering. This leads us to question the often-covert nature of social engineering algorithms and the transformative power of AI in this ever-evolving battleground. Within the intricate web of socially engineered environments, where human behavior is subtly influenced and guided, algorithms operate as unseen conductors. This algorithmic governance shapes our digital experiences with an invisible hand. It analyzes our every click and scroll to personalize content, tailor recommendations, and curate our perceptions of the world.

The decision to design social engineering algorithms as dynamically undetectable serves several purposes and key factors:

Seamless User Experience: Invisible algorithms create frictionless user experiences. By blending seamlessly into the background, they avoid alerting users that their interactions are subtly steered. This promotes a perception of unfettered autonomy, even when it is, to an extent, an illusion.

Sustained Engagement: These algorithms maximize our time and attention on the platform. Transparent manipulation breeds resistance. Overt tactics could make users feel like lab rats in an experiment rather than valued participants in a vibrant community.

Competitive Edge: Finely tuned yet undetectable algorithms are the secret sauce that sets many platforms apart. By remaining hidden, companies make their work harder to replicate, helping them maintain their edge.

Walking the Ethical Tightrope: While the ideal is to improve user experience, the line between personalization and manipulation is often blurry. Opaque algorithms offer some plausible deniability ("The system suggested that, not us!"), helping platforms navigate public scrutiny and concerns about user autonomy and privacy.

THE RISE OF AI: A PARADIGM SHIFT IN HUMAN CENTRIC DESIGN

Artificial intelligence is poised to revolutionize the landscape of social engineering algorithms, introducing a new era of sophistication and adaptability that poses both unprecedented opportunities and significant challenges. The inherent strengths of AI, such as its capacity for hyper-adaptability, predictive analysis, and human-like conversational mimicry, can be harnessed to create highly effective social engineering tactics that are harder to detect and counter.

AI's hyper-adaptability stems from its ability to analyze massive, complex datasets in real time, dynamically adjusting its tactics based on the target's responses and behaviors. This surpasses the capabilities of manually coded rules, which are inherently static and predictable. AI-powered social engineering algorithms can evolve and adapt on the fly, making it exceedingly difficult for users to identify manipulation patterns or anticipate the next move.

Furthermore, AI algorithms excel at predicting human behavior, leveraging vast troves of data to anticipate what we will click on, watch, and buy, even before we consciously make those decisions. This predictive power enables social engineers to craft highly targeted and persuasive messages, leading users down specific content paths, triggering impulse purchases, or subtly shaping their opinions and beliefs.

The rise of AI chatbots adds another layer of complexity to the social engineering landscape. These chatbots, capable of mimicking human conversation with remarkable fidelity, can be deployed ethically to provide support and assistance. However, in the hands of unscrupulous actors, they can be used to create seemingly authentic, yet artificial bonds with users, fostering a sense of trust and loyalty that can be exploited to gather personal data or manipulate online behavior.

The implications of AI for social engineering are profound and far-reaching. As AI technology continues to advance, we can expect to see even more sophisticated and subtle forms of social engineering, blurring the lines between genuine human interaction and artificial manipulation. This underscores the need for increased awareness, critical thinking skills, and the development of robust countermeasures to protect individuals and communities from the evolving threat of AI-powered social engineering.

THE URGENT NEED FOR TRANSPARENCY AND OVERSIGHT ON HUMAN CENTRIC INTERFACES

The growing sophistication of AI-driven social engineering algorithms demands that we critically examine their impact on how we connect, consume information, and make decisions online. There is an urgent need to secure feature to support key factors such as explainability. Even partial insight into how these algorithms influence choices allows users to be more critical of what they are presented. Clear guidelines are needed to hold platforms responsible for both the positive and potentially manipulative outcomes their algorithms produce. Digital literacy efforts must teach the public about the hidden forces at play online. This informed skepticism leads to users reclaiming agencies.

The future of socially engineered environments hinges on striking the right balance between leveraging these powerful tools for personalization and user experience while respecting individual autonomy and protecting against manipulation. This necessitates a collaborative effort involving technologists, ethicists, lawmakers, and the public.

The relationship between AI and the amplification of filter bubbles is a complex and pressing issue. Let us dissect the mechanisms by which AI can exacerbate existing biases and then explore whether it might also hold potential solutions, even if those come with challenges.

The promise of AI to personalize our online experiences carries a potent but unsettling side effect: the reinforcement of filter bubbles. This phenomenon is a technical glitch and a complex web of interconnected factors. AI-powered recommendation systems, designed to optimize engagement, inadvertently prioritize content reinforcing pre-existing beliefs. They foster online communities rooted in shared views, isolating users from differing perspectives. Moreover, the very profitability of many platforms depends on AI's ability to show us emotionally charged material that keeps us hooked, often at the expense of nuance and critical thinking. This cycle gets further amplified by AI's chillingly accurate ability to predict our behavior, narrowing our exposure based on what it thinks we like, ultimately limiting our worldview.

Recognizing this interplay is crucial. The danger lies in viewing AI-driven filter bubbles as a passive occurrence rather than an actively reinforced process. If left unchallenged, we risk becoming trapped in increasingly narrow echo chambers where diverse opinions and critical thinking wither. Addressing this challenge will demand awareness and a critical re-evaluation of how we design AI algorithms, prioritize content, and reorient incentives from mere engagement to a system that fosters intellectual diversity and a well-informed citizenry.

COULD AI BE PART OF THE SOLUTION? CHALLENGES AND POTENTIAL

Paradoxically, while AI plays a significant role in creating filter bubbles, it may, under careful guidance, hold some potential (though not a silver bullet) for mitigating their effects. Algorithms could intentionally surface content that challenges a user's established viewpoint, not to "change their mind," but to introduce them to alternative perspectives they may otherwise never encounter due to their personalized feed. The challenge lies in defining this "diversity" in a way that feels constructive, not patronizing. AI could be trained to identify potentially harmful content that is likely to go viral due to triggering outrage. De-prioritizing this content in recommendations – even slightly – could potentially slow the spread of misinformation and inflammatory material that fuel filter bubbles. While full transparency of a recommendation algorithm's work is impractical, partial explanations could help users see beyond their bubble. For example: "We are showing you this because you often engage with posts about X topic." This promotes awareness without undermining the seamless user experience.

CRUCIAL CONSIDERATIONS (KEY FACTORS)

Defining "Harmful" Content: There is no universal agreement on this. This makes it hard to train AI for intervention without platform bias or accusations of censorship.

Backfire Potential: Clumsy attempts at bursting filter bubbles could make users feel manipulated, leading to mistrust and further entrenchment in their existing beliefs.

Individual vs. Societal Impact: Even if AI could somewhat reduce filter bubbles for individuals, the broader societal effects on polarization are complex.

Should users have granular control over the "bubble breaking" level in which their feed engages.

How can AI gently introduce different viewpoints without feeling like an attack on the user's worldview. AI is a tool. Social change also requires addressing the root causes of polarization: economic inequality and education gaps. Tech fixes alone are insufficient.

While technological solutions offer great potential, recognizing technology's inherent limitations is crucial when addressing complex societal problems like filter bubbles, polarization, and the spread of misinformation. Let us see why expecting technology to resolve these issues single-handedly is unrealistic and potentially harmful.

KEY TECHNOLOGY LIMITATIONS, FOCUSING INTO AI AND HUMAN INTERACTIONS (KEY FACTORS)

Technology Reflects Existing Biases: Algorithms and AI models are trained on real-world data, which reflects societal biases, prejudices, and blind spots. If the data are flawed, the technology built upon it will reproduce rather than correct these problems. For example, if an AI system is fed historical news articles for training, it may learn that certain minority voices are less represented and reproduce this marginalization in its outputs.

The Nuances of Human Interaction: Social platforms thrive on complex human dynamics – sarcasm, empathy, groupthink, and the desire for belonging. Technology struggles to understand the subtle cues and motivations behind online interactions. Platforms cannot effectively moderate discourse or promote healthy engagement by solely relying on algorithms to distinguish harmless banter from harmful bullying, for instance.

Adversarial Adaptation: Those who spread misinformation or exploit platforms for malicious purposes are highly adaptable. They will find ways to circumvent technological safeguards – manipulating language to avoid content filters or subtly tweaking tactics to fly under the radar of AI detection systems. This leads to a constant arms race, not a permanent solution.

The Illusion of Objectivity: The mere idea of using AI to "fix" societal problems carries the risk of assuming algorithms can achieve a level of objectivity that humans cannot. This ignores that algorithms are designed by people with their own inherent biases, which shape what the algorithm is trained on and how it interprets the world.

Focus on Symptoms, Not Causes: Often, technology is applied to deal with the surface-level manifestations of deeper societal problems. An algorithm that slows the spread of misinformation is practical, but it does not address why people are so susceptible to it in the first place. This lack of critical social analysis can lead to over-reliance on tech solutions, neglecting other potential interventions.

THE DANGERS OF TECHNO-SOLUTIONISM

Techno-solutionism is the belief that technology will solve all our problems. In the context of filter bubbles and social engineering, this carries several key risk factors:

Moral Abdication: Expecting platforms to "teach" their way out of ethical quandaries creates a sense of complacency. Companies may prioritize easily implementable algorithm tweaks over broader, harder-to-measure efforts like promoting critical thinking and respectful discourse among their users.

Eroding Responsibility: When the onus falls on the algorithm to "fix" things, it subtly absolves both users and platforms of their role in maintaining a healthy information ecosystem. Users are responsible for being critical information consumers; platforms have a responsibility to design environments that do not incentivize the most toxic content.

Missed Opportunities: Focusing exclusively on tech-based solutions stifles innovation in other crucial areas. Addressing societal polarization requires complex interventions like media literacy campaigns, educational reform, and supporting community-led initiatives that bridge divides.

TECHNOLOGY AS A TOOL, NOT A PANACEA: A DIFFERENT POINT OF VIEW

While technology plays an undeniably vital role in addressing the spread of harmful content online, it would be a mistake to view it as a cure-all. Lasting solutions demand a nuanced understanding of technology's power and limitations. Rather than seeing it as a panacea, technology must be viewed as a powerful tool that can be wielded for both good and ill.

Forging actual progress requires a genuinely holistic approach. While technical innovation is essential, it cannot be divorced from investments in education, thoughtful policymaking, and fostering a public equipped with critical thinking skills and empathy. Similarly, it is crucial to recognize the importance of human judgment and oversight. Algorithms can be powerful tools for moderation and content curation, but they should serve to augment human expertise, not outright replace it.

Finally, the battle against harmful content demands constant evolution. As perpetrators of online abuse and misinformation adapt their tactics, so must the technological and non-technological safeguards we employ. This means embracing a mindset of continuous learning, experimentation, and adaptation to stay ahead in this ever-shifting digital landscape. Ethical technology designs are inherently subjective and culturally influenced. What constitutes "fairness" or "healthy engagement" will be fiercely debated. This necessitates ongoing dialogue between stakeholders to establish broadly acceptable standards. Ethical considerations sometimes introduce trade-offs regarding raw algorithm efficiency or profit. Companies must demonstrate a genuine commitment to prioritize long-term societal well-being, even if it means slightly slower growth or less "optimized" engagement. Codes of ethics are well-intentioned, but without solid accountability mechanisms, they remain aspirational. This is where a potential role for regulatory bodies or independent certification programs emerges.

UNINTENDED CONSEQUENCES: THE COMPLEXITIES OF TECHNOLOGICAL SOCIAL INTERVENTION

Even with the best intentions, technological interventions to shape social behavior are prone to unintended, often unpredictable consequences. Completely deplatforming those who promote hateful or harmful ideology might offer temporary relief but risks the "forbidden fruit" effect, driving them to spaces with zero oversight where their views can solidify unchecked. Drawing the line between harmful content and merely unpopular opinions is complex. Overly broad suppression can lead to silencing legitimate dissent and creating mistrust in the platform itself. Even those promoting harmful views rarely identify as such. They evolve their language and tactics to become more challenging to detect automatically. This is a problem of improving the algorithm and recognizing that human ingenuity will constantly try to outwit the system. If suppressed content migrates to less-regulated platforms, it deepens fragmentation. The goal of a healthier information ecosystem is undermined as people exist in increasingly isolated social media bubbles. Instead of seeking to eliminate misinformation or hate, platforms embracing an ethical outlook might aim to make users less susceptible to manipulation. This means emphasizing critical thinking and healthy skepticism alongside content moderation. Rigid, single-solution thinking is dangerous when tackling complex social problems. Platforms need to be more transparent about conducting smaller-scale experiments, evaluating both positive and negative effects, before the widespread rollout of any significant social engineering algorithm change. Nudging users toward healthier behaviors is fine, but actual agency rests on choice. Platforms ensuring users have meaningful control over the algorithms shaping their experiences foster much-needed trust. Should there be specific legislation around bias audits or explainability requirements for algorithms used by platforms with significant social impact. How do we address ethical concerns when platforms are transnational, but values and laws vary wildly between countries.

Now, let us examine the crucial role of legislation in upholding algorithmic ethics and the complexities of establishing global standards in a world where definitions of "ethical" vary wildly.

The Case for Algorithmic Legislation

The argument for legislative intervention concerning the use of socially influential algorithms rests on several key points:

Setting Minimum Standards: While companies may have internal ethical guidelines, voluntary compliance often proves insufficient. Clear legislation establishes a baseline, ensuring that all platforms operating within a jurisdiction meet specific requirements on bias, transparency, and user protections, limiting the potential for the most harmful practices.

Protecting the Public Interest: Market forces do not always align with the public good. Legislation can address scenarios where the most profitable algorithm might also be the most socially harmful. Laws level the playing field, preventing companies from arguing that they had to use ethically dubious practices to remain competitive.

Encouraging Proactive Design: When ethical considerations are legally mandated, they are more likely to be incorporated into the design process from the start. This avoids costly retrofits or the need to abandon projects once they have been discovered to cause harm.

Addressing Power Imbalance: The average user has little leverage against complex, opaque algorithmic systems. Legislation empowers oversight bodies to act on the public's behalf, providing a mechanism for accountability that does not depend on individuals navigating complex legal battles.

The quest for effective AI oversight demands a multifaceted approach. Isolated technological solutions will not suffice. Successful oversight strategies must start with an interdisciplinary foundation, where technologists actively engage ethicists, sociologists, and representatives of the communities AI will affect. This collaboration should not be a one-off consultation but ingrained throughout the design and deployment of algorithms. Furthermore, oversight cannot be a static snapshot in time. Iterative assessments and regular audits are essential. Algorithms learn and evolve, and their societal impacts change alongside them. Finally, even with increasingly sophisticated AI, we must maintain the principle of "human-in-the-loop." Critical decisions with real-world impact should always have the element of human oversight, ensuring that an algorithm's recommendations are considered in context and potential nuances are carefully examined.

The Evolving Future of AI: Opportunities and Responsibilities

The future of AI holds vast potential across healthcare, transportation, environmental sustainability, and countless other sectors. It promises personalized medicine, safer and more efficient cities, and data-driven solutions for global problems. To fully realize this potential, will take a look into the kay factors:

The AI-Savvy Workforce: Focusing on reskilling and lifelong learning is essential as AI transforms jobs and skill demands.

Global Equity Considerations: Proactive efforts to ensure that AI benefits are distributed equitably across nations and socioeconomic groups, avoiding a further widening of digital and technological divides.

Human–AI Collaboration Redefined: The lines between what humans and algorithms do best will continuously shift. We must foster an environment where AI augments human strengths and creativity, not replaces them.

AI-driven social engineering is still in its early stages, but its potential impact is immense. By combining the power of AI with a commitment to human-centric design, transparency, and ethical governance, we can unlock a future where AI serves as a positive force, enhancing both digital experiences and the well-being of society as a whole.

The concept of a "Slow AI" movement is a compelling and much-needed counterbalance to the current dominant paradigm of optimizing solely for speed and efficiency. Let us look into its philosophy, potential benefits, and real-world applications.

THE PHILOSOPHY OF "SLOW AI"

Inspired by the Slow Food movement that values quality and sustainability, Slow AI proposes a deliberate shift in the design and use of artificial intelligence systems. It emphasizes:

Mindfulness over Mindless Optimization: Instead of focusing solely on maximizing speed, engagement, or profit, Slow AI encourages mindful consideration of both the intended and unintended consequences of algorithms on individuals and society.

Reflection and Human Judgment: Technology exists to serve us, not vice versa. Slow AI prioritizes space for reflection and conscious choice, ensuring human judgment remains at the helm, not merely as a fail-safe for the algorithm.

Serendipity and "Positive Friction": The over-personalization fueled by current algorithms can lead to insularity. Slow AI advocates reintroducing a degree of serendipity and "positive friction" that exposes users to ideas and perspectives outside their established comfort zones.

Algorithmic Explainability: Slow AI does not necessarily mean less sophisticated AI, but rather AI designed with explainability as a core value. Users should be able to understand, at least in broad terms, how and why the system presents them with specific content.

Focus on Long-Term Well-Being: Metrics for success should prioritize user well-being instead of short-term engagement boosts. This means platforms tracking things like time spent away from a device or indicators of healthy online social interactions, not just likes and clicks.

POTENTIAL BENEFITS OF SLOW AI (KEY FACTORS)

Combating Information Overload: The constant firehose of algorithmically optimized content can be overwhelming and contribute to anxiety. Slow AI systems could promote more mindful and less reactive consumption.

Fostering Healthy Skepticism: By nudging us to consider why we see particular content, Slow AI encourages a more critical approach to online information, potentially mitigating the spread of misinformation.

Mental Space and Creativity: Introducing pauses and moments for reflection could spark innovation and allow humans to connect the dots in ways an algorithm focused on immediate optimization might miss.

Breaking Filter Bubbles: Purposefully surfacing diverse viewpoints or content slightly outside our usual patterns can counterbalance the isolating effects of hyper-personalized feeds.

Trust and Agency: Algorithmic transparency and choice contribute to a sense of user agency. This fosters greater trust between humans and the technology they use.

PRACTICAL APPLICATIONS OF SLOW AI

"Reflection Prompts": Before serving inflammatory content, asking users, "Is reading this likely to make you feel more informed or upset?" could promote critical thinking.

"Breaking News Pause": Delaying the spread of unverified breaking news slightly to allow initial fact-checking could lessen the amplification of misinformation in the heat of the moment.

Anti-Recommendation Engines: A platform section specifically designed to show you things you probably will not like but might expose you to new ideas.

"Algorithmic Diet Mode": Users could opt into receiving less algorithmically curated content, with a greater emphasis on chronological feeds or human-selected highlights.

The Slow AI movement, while promising, is not without its challenges and considerations. For it to be genuinely transformative, several hurdles must be addressed. New metrics focused on genuine well-being, not just screen time, will be crucial for companies to develop and prioritize to evaluate success fairly. Slow AI systems may need to overcome an initial competitive disadvantage; will users embrace a slightly less addictive online experience in exchange for greater personal control? Companies championing these principles must clearly articulate their value to gain user support.

Furthermore, Slow AI features must avoid the "novelty trap." Simply presenting these elements as gimmicks undermines their ethical intent. Instead, they must demonstrate tangible benefits for user well-being. Realistically, we are likely to see hybrid models shortly. A complete rejection of AI-driven curation is impractical. A gradual approach with Slow AI features coexisting alongside traditional ones while emphasizing user choice is feasible and respects existing user behaviors. Expanding upon these challenges leads to thought-provoking discussions. Could the principles of Slow AI be integrated into digital literacy education, fostering healthy skepticism of algorithms alongside traditional media literacy? What if platforms offered a "Human Boost" feature, where users flag insightful content, creating a hybrid system driven by algorithms and direct community curation?

The Slow AI movement offers a powerful counterbalance to the relentless pursuit of attention and engagement. Its success hinges on a combination of innovation, clear communication of its benefits, and a willingness to embrace a more mindful approach to technology. It can redefine our relationship with the digital world, fostering healthier habits and a more fulfilling online experience.

Now, let us explore the dangers of manipulative algorithms and the critical need for transparency, regulation, ethical design, and user empowerment.

THE DARK SIDE OF SOCIAL ENGINEERING: MENTAL HEALTH MANIPULATION

The evolution of sophisticated social engineered algorithms has granted them the alarming power to manipulate our mental health. While often intended to improve user experience and provide personalized content, these algorithms can have unintended and detrimental consequences for our psychological well-being.

Hyper-personalization, a hallmark of modern social media platforms, can trap users in echo chambers where they are constantly exposed to information and perspectives that reinforce their existing beliefs. This constant validation can breed intolerance, heighten anxiety, and contribute to feelings of isolation, as users become increasingly detached from diverse viewpoints and the complexities of the real world.

Algorithms thrive on engagement, often prioritizing emotionally charged or outrage-inducing content to capture users' attention and keep them scrolling. This can create a toxic online environment where negativity and conflict are amplified, leading to increased stress and anxiety for users.

Furthermore, these algorithms fuel a culture of comparison, where users' self-worth becomes tied to the curated and often unrealistic representations they encounter on social media. This can adversely impact body image, self-esteem, and overall mental health, particularly for vulnerable individuals who are already struggling with self-doubt or body image issues.

The endless scroll of algorithmically sorted information can lead to information overload and a constant sense of urgency. This, coupled with the fear of missing out (FOMO), creates a state of perpetual anxiety that is detrimental to our well-being. We feel compelled to constantly check our phones, refresh our feeds, and stay connected, leading to disrupted sleep, strained relationships, and a diminished sense of presence in the real world.

Targeted ads, powered by sophisticated algorithms that track our online behavior and preferences, can prey on our insecurities and vulnerabilities. For those predisposed to addiction or compulsive behaviors, this manipulation can be particularly harmful, deepening these tendencies and leading to unhealthy consumption patterns.

The intermittent rewards of social media platforms, such as likes, comments, and notifications, are often engineered to mimic the brain's dopamine system, creating a cycle of anticipation and reward that can lead to addictive behaviors. This can disrupt sleep patterns, strain real-world relationships, and contribute to a decline in overall mental health.

In conclusion, the evolution of sophisticated social engineered algorithms has granted them the alarming power to manipulate our mental health. While these algorithms offer benefits in terms of personalization and convenience, they also pose significant risks to our psychological well-being. By understanding the mechanisms and consequences of these algorithms, we can take steps to mitigate their negative impacts, cultivate healthier online habits, and reclaim control over our digital lives.

THE URGENT NEED FOR SAFEGUARDS

We cannot stand by as algorithms subvert mental well-being. Here is some key factors on how we fight back, by:

Demanding Algorithmic Transparency: Users cannot protect themselves without understanding how they work. Regulations mandating explainability without compromising company secrets will foster awareness and healthier engagement.

Regulation with Teeth: Clear laws are needed on data use and how algorithms are allowed to target ads or curate content. This levels the playing field, preventing companies from exploiting user vulnerabilities for profit.

Ethical Design: Instead of prioritizing engagement at all costs, metrics should emphasize healthy usage patterns and user well-being. Features such as "intentional use" settings or reminders to take offline breaks are a start.

Empowering the User: Granular control over the kinds of content they see, the ability to opt out of hyper-personalization, and clear warnings on potentially triggering content shift the power imbalance.

Digital Mindfulness Education: From a young age, individuals must be taught to be critical consumers of online information. Teaching how algorithms work and encouraging healthy skepticism contributes to a less easily manipulated populace.

THE PATH TO RESPONSIBLE INNOVATION

The critical takeaway lies in recognizing that technology, in and of itself, is not inherently good or evil. It is a tool, a powerful extension of human ingenuity, capable of both extraordinary feats of creation and devastating acts of destruction. The real danger arises when the relentless pursuit of profit, the insatiable hunger for engagement, and the unyielding drive for market dominance fuel design choices that undermine our mental well-being and exploit our vulnerabilities.

However, there is a path forward, a way to reshape this landscape and reclaim our digital agency. It begins with ethical technologists, those who understand the profound impact of their creations on human lives, working from within to advocate for design practices that prioritize mental health alongside innovation. It requires regulators to step up, to establish and enforce clear boundaries, protecting users from unchecked exploitation and holding corporations accountable for the consequences of their design choices.

Educators play a vital role in this endeavor, fostering digital literacy and equipping individuals with the critical thinking skills and awareness needed to navigate the complex digital world. By empowering individuals to understand the persuasive tactics employed by social media platforms, the addictive nature of algorithms, and the subtle ways in which their attention and emotions are manipulated, we can create a more informed and resilient digital citizenry.

Ultimately, it is the users themselves who hold the power to shape the future of technology. By demanding better practices, holding corporations accountable, and consciously choosing where to direct their attention, users can influence the market and steer the evolution of socially engineered algorithms. The goal is not to abandon the undeniable benefits of connectivity and access but to achieve a balance, a digital ecosystem where design choices respect our cognitive limits and vulnerabilities, where mental health is valued as much as engagement metrics.

This is how we can harness technology's power for good, building a digital world that truly supports human flourishing, where innovation and well-being go hand in hand, and where the human spirit is not diminished but rather elevated by the tools we create.

4 Algorithmic Insights into the Nexus of Interpersonal Mental Challenges and Social Engineering

Algorithms designed to manipulate our behavior have a hidden cost: mental health. From social media to recommendation engines, these systems can worsen existing conditions and create new vulnerabilities. This chapter explores the dark side of engagement-driven design and the ethical imperative to build a more humane digital world.

THE HIDDEN DANGERS OF SOCIALLY ENGINEERED ALGORITHMS

Today's digital algorithms are not neutral – their designs can profoundly impact our emotional well-being. Here are some key factors to how they can harm mental health:

Feeding Negative Emotions: Algorithms learn our preferences and vulnerabilities. Someone feeling lonely might be bombarded with content reinforcing those feelings, creating a dangerous feedback loop.

The Burden of Information Overload: The endless torrent of news, updates, and ads can overwhelm our minds, leading to stress and anxiety. This is especially damaging for those already struggling with these conditions.

The Comparison Trap: Curated feeds presenting idealized lives make us compare ourselves unfavorably. This erodes our self-esteem and can worsen existing depression or body image issues.

Designed for Addiction: With its unpredictable rewards, the "like" and "share" system taps into our brain's dopamine circuits. This drives compulsive use that compromises mental health, sleep, and genuine social connections.

ETHICS AND THE NEED FOR CHANGE

The mental health impact of these algorithms demands a severe ethical discussion. Tech companies must prioritize well-being over pure profit. Here is where we need to focus:

Positive Content Promotion: Algorithms must be redesigned to highlight uplifting or supportive content.

DOI: 10.1201/9781003500698-4

User Empowerment: Give users better tools to manage their consumption, filter content, and limit online time.

Transparent Design: People must understand how algorithms personalize their feeds to make informed choices.

Research and Regulation: We must extensively research algorithm-driven platforms' long-term mental health effects. This must guide policy to ensure digital spaces work *for* our well-being.

The Bottom Line: Digital environments have vast power to shape our minds. It is time for companies, policymakers, and users to demand that technology be designed to protect and support our psychological health as a primary goal.

Throughout this chapter, we have explored the multifaceted nature of mental health. It is essential to remember that mental health is a state of well-being where individuals can cope with life's inevitable stresses, realize their potential, work productively, and contribute positively to their communities. This goes beyond the mere absence of mental illness.

Mental health encompasses a wide range of emotional, psychological, and social well-being. It shapes how we think, feel, act, relate to others, and make life choices. Crucially, mental health exists on the spectrum. Even individuals considered mentally healthy will experience moments of sadness, anger, and stress. Conversely, living with a mental illness does not mean a constant state of crisis. With the proper support and treatment, many people with mental health conditions lead fulfilling and productive lives. Let us work together to break down the stigma that surrounds mental health and build a society where everyone's mental well-being is valued and supported.

THE DOUBLE-EDGED SWORD OF TECHNOLOGY

Technology can have both positive and negative impacts on our mental health. Social media's highlight reels lead to unrealistic comparisons, feeding self-doubt, and "fear of missing out" (FOMO). Online harassment, threats, and humiliation can have devastating consequences, especially for young people. The relentless stream of news and updates can overwhelm our minds, increasing stress and anxiety. Blue light from devices suppresses melatonin, disrupting sleep patterns vital for mental well-being. Platform designs that leverage variable rewards (likes, comments) can trigger addictive behaviors, impacting our focus and real-world relationships. The influence of technology on mental health extends beyond challenges and risks. It also offers profound potential to enhance support, access, and self-understanding. Online communities foster connection and combat isolation for those with shared experiences, dissolving feelings of being alone. Teletherapy, self-help apps, and online resources improve access to mental health care, particularly for those in underserved areas or with limited in-person options. Through mood trackers and wearables, individuals gain greater awareness of their mental health patterns, identifying potential triggers and empowering them to take proactive steps toward well-being. Furthermore, digital tools provide avenues for creative expression and exploration of identity, promoting self-understanding and emotional growth. Finally, online platforms contribute to reducing the stigma surrounding mental health, fostering more open conversations, and encouraging individuals to seek the help they need. While technology is not a substitute for in-person mental health care, it can serve as a valuable supplement, extending support and empowering individuals to take ownership of their mental well-being. As technologies continue to evolve, so will the opportunities for positive change in mental health.

WHERE DOES THE BALANCE LIE

The impact of technology on mental health is highly individual and depends on several factors:

Pre-Existing Conditions: Those with anxiety or depression may be more susceptible to harmful impacts.

Usage Patterns: Passive scrolling vs. active engagement can make a big difference.

Content Type: Consuming negative news vs. supportive communities has vastly different effects.

Mitigating the risks and maximizing technology's benefits requires deliberate design approaches. Here are some key factors to ways forward:

Algorithms Promoting Well-Being: Introducing features that nudge users toward healthier social media habits and promote positive content.

Tools for Digital Wellness: Encouraging breaks, offering content filtering options, and providing time management tools.

Ethical Considerations over Profit-Driven Design: Companies must prioritize user mental health over engagement and monetization.

Transparency and User Control: Clear explanations of how algorithms work and giving users control over their data and personalized feeds.

Collaboration: Mental health professionals, researchers, and technologists must work together to create better digital environments.

HOW AN ALGORITHM CAN CONTRIBUTE TO MENTAL WELL BEING

An algorithm is a step-by-step procedure for solving a problem or performing a task. Much like a recipe guides you through baking a cake, an algorithm guides a computer through sorting data, calculating routes, or recommending content. Algorithms take inputs (data), process them according to a defined set of instructions, and produce outputs (results or solutions).

CRITICAL POSITIVE ELEMENTS IN ALGORITHM DESIGN (KEY FACTORS)

Correctness: The algorithm must produce the correct or expected output for all valid inputs.

Efficiency: The algorithm should solve the problem quickly and with as few resources (memory, processing power). This is where notions like time complexity and space complexity come in.
Clarity and Readability: A well-designed algorithm is easy to understand, implement, and modify.

The algorithm should handle different input sizes and complexities. There are numerous types of algorithms, each with its strengths and suitable applications:

Sorting Algorithms: Organize data into a specific order (e.g., Bubble Sort, Quick Sort, Merge Sort).
Search Algorithms: Find specific items within a dataset (e.g., Linear Search, Binary Search).
Graph Algorithms: Solve network problems (e.g., Dijkstra's Algorithm for the shortest path, Depth-First Search for traversal).
Dynamic Programming: Break complex problems into smaller, overlapping subproblems and store solutions for reuse.
Machine Learning Algorithms: Enable computers to learn patterns from data without explicit programming (e.g., Decision Trees, Neural Networks).

ALGORITHM ANALYSIS AND BIG O NOTATION

Algorithm analysis is a method of evaluating the efficiency and performance of algorithms, primarily in terms of time complexity (how the execution time grows with input size) and space complexity (how the memory requirement grows with input size). Big O notation is a mathematical notation used to describe the upper bound of an algorithm's time or space complexity.

Key concepts in algorithm analysis:

Time Complexity: Describes how an algorithm's runtime scales with input size. Big O notation (e.g., O(n), O(n^2), O(log n)) is used for this, allowing us to compare algorithm efficiency on a general scale.
Space Complexity: Describes how much memory an algorithm uses relative to its input size. It is also expressed with Big O notation.

Standard techniques for crafting algorithms include:

Divide and Conquer: Break the problem into smaller, similar subproblems, solve them individually, and combine solutions.
Recursion: An algorithm calls itself with smaller portions of the problem, creating a chain of solutions back to the original input.
Greedy Algorithms: Make locally optimal choices at each step to reach a global optimum (not always guaranteed).
Backtracking: Explore possible solutions, abandoning paths if they do not meet requirements.

Designing practical algorithms requires creativity, logical thinking, and an understanding of data structures. It is both an art (finding elegant solutions) and a science (analyzing their correctness and efficiency).

THE EVOLVING RELATIONSHIP BETWEEN ALGORITHM DESIGN AND MENTAL HEALTH

Historically, social media platforms and other engineered environments prioritized user engagement and data collection for ad revenue. This focus on metrics like time spent and clicks, while effective for business, often disregarded the toll on users' mental health. Features like infinite scroll and notifications fuel addictive behaviors, potentially worsening anxiety, depression, and attention issues.

The negative impact of these platforms on mental health has sparked increasing concern, fueled by research, public discourse, and mental health advocacy. Some tech companies now offer tools like screen time management, options to hide "likes" and mental health resources. While positive, these changes are often limited in scope. Individual experiences with mental health are diverse. Design that universally benefits everyone is complicated. We need clear, evidence-based standards for embedding mental health awareness into design processes. Business models dependent on engagement and data make prioritizing hard.

THE FUTURE: OPPORTUNITIES AND USER EMPOWERMENT

Human-Centered Design: Platforms MUST prioritize user well-being over metrics. Deep engagement with users, especially those with lived mental health experiences, is crucial to creating supportive spaces.

Interdisciplinary Teams: Psychologists, ethicists, users, and designers working together can create genuinely beneficial environments and anticipate unintended consequences.

Algorithmic Transparency and Control: Users need to understand how algorithms shape their feeds and have the power to adjust them for their personal needs.

Algorithms designed to detect or respond to users' mental states pose unique hurdles. Mental health is nuanced. Algorithms struggle to grasp their individual, dynamic nature accurately. Analyzing sensitive mental health data raises serious concerns about consent, potential misuse, and where the line between support and surveillance lies. Misinterpreting data could worsen a user's condition through unhelpful recommendations or interventions. Prioritizing well-being might mean rethinking profitable platform models, which is a difficult hurdle. This complex area has no transparent best practices for ethical, practical design. Actual progress demands collaboration. Direct feedback mechanisms, alongside these ideas, offer great potential:

User Feedback on Content Impact: Let users report how content makes them feel. Algorithms can use this data to tailor feeds more responsibly.

Community Moderation: Users, especially those with lived mental health experience, can augment algorithms in identifying and flagging potentially harmful content.

User-Driven Tools and Options: Work with user communities to design tools and settings that allow individual customization for improved mental health.

The Imperative for Change. While integrating mental health awareness into algorithm design is complex, the potential benefits for individuals and society are massive. This transformation is an ethical responsibility and an exciting path for technology to serve humans flourishing indeed.

Let us look into the exciting potential of user empowerment algorithms. Here is a breakdown of key concepts and how to implement them.

WHAT ARE USER EMPOWERMENT ALGORITHMS

Shifting the Power Balance: These algorithms put users at the center of their digital experience. They prioritize choice, autonomy, and understanding how these vast platforms work to support mental health and well-being.

Beyond Settings: Empowerment algorithms go beyond basic settings panels. They are designed with input from mental health experts and users, creating proactive, intelligent customization tools.

Algorithms offer simple summaries of why content is recommended (e.g., "Based on your interest in X" or "Similar to things you have liked before"). This promotes conscious scrolling, not just passive intake. Users can see what information the platform gathers and how it is used, and they have full agency to edit or delete it.

Personalized Content Control

Personalized content control algorithms analyze user data to deliver tailored recommendations using methods like mood-based filters, trigger warnings, and positive feed boosting. These approaches enhance user experience by aligning content with individual preferences and sensitivities.

Mood-Based Filters: Algorithms learn what makes a user feel overwhelmed and anxious and offer options like "Show only lighthearted content today" or "Avoid news for the next hour."

Trigger Warnings: Users can input specific topics or content types that are upsetting (e.g., body image content for eating disorder recovery). Algorithms help flag or filter this accordingly.

Positive Feed Boosting: Algorithms designed to prioritize content with known mental health benefits (e.g., nature videos, content from supportive communities).

Instead of generic screen-time warnings, algorithms help users set break patterns that work for them (e.g., 10 minutes off after every 45 minutes scrolling, with calming content suggested).

Friction for Compulsive Use: If algorithms detect unhealthy usage patterns, they can introduce pauses, require an extra tap to load more content, or suggest a mood check-in.

Active vs. Passive Use: Algorithms can highlight posts a user has commented on and interacted with, encouraging meaningful engagement over mindless scrolling.

UNDERSTANDING TWITTER'S CHALLENGES INTO PERSONAL HABITS FORMATION

Rapid-Fire Content: Twitter's feed moves incredibly fast, making mindless consumption easy. This can contribute to being overwhelmed and fueling negativity spirals.

Polarization: Algorithms often amplify divisive content that plays into anger and outrage, harming mental health on individual and societal levels.

Limited Context: Tweets' short format can lead to misinterpretations, lack of nuance, and a hostile conversational tone.

Doomscrolling: Trending topics and breaking news can be particularly anxiety-inducing for many users.

AREAS FOR ALGORITHMIC INTERVENTION TO PERSONAL HABITS DEVELOPMENT

Curbing Information Overload

Summarization Options: For dense threads or news articles, a "Summarize for me" button could give users a quick overview before diving in, promoting informed choice.

Content Density Controls: A slider where users set their desired "tweet intensity" – maybe they want a lighter, meme-filled feed some days, while others favor long-form discussions.

Proactive Breaks: Algorithms could recognize scrolling patterns indicative of overwhelm and suggest a pause with calming content.

PERSONALITY COMBATTING, AGAINST NEGATIVITY AND POLARIZATION (KEY FACTORS)

Emotional Tone Check: Before posting, an optional prompt could ask, "This seems emotionally charged… Want to take a moment before sharing?" This promotes self-reflection, not censorship.

Diversity Boost: Introduce a toggle to slightly favor tweets from accounts the user rarely interacts with. This helps burst filter bubbles.

Constructive Conversation Nudges: Identify threads with high potential for respectful debate. Algorithms could offer a "Discuss, do not attack" reminder, even suggesting resources for civil discourse.

PRIORITIZING MINDFUL CONSUMPTION

To empower users and foster a healthier relationship with Twitter, the platform could provide greater transparency and encourage more meaningful engagement. One way to achieve this is by offering a clear breakdown of why each tweet appears in a user's feed. This explanation could include factors like, "Followed by X," indicating that a tweet is from someone the user follows, or "Popular with people who liked Y," suggesting that a tweet is trending among users with similar interests. This transparency would give users a better understanding of how the algorithm curates their feed and empower them to make informed choices about the content they consume.

Furthermore, Twitter could shift its focus from tracking screen time to rewarding active engagement. This could involve promoting features that encourage thoughtful interactions, such as replying to tweets, participating in meaningful threads, and creating original content. By incentivizing these behaviors, Twitter could foster a more engaging and enriching experience for its users, promoting dialogue and discouraging passive consumption.

To further encourage self-reflection and mindful engagement, Twitter could periodically suggest "quality check" questions to its users. These questions could prompt users to consider the value of their interactions and the quality of the content they consume. For example, a question like, "Who are three people you enjoy interacting with? Catch up with their content," encourages users to actively seek out meaningful connections and engage with content that resonates with their interests and values.

By implementing these features, Twitter could empower its users to curate a more personalized and enriching experience, fostering a sense of agency and promoting a healthier relationship with the platform. This approach would not only benefit individual users but also contribute to a more vibrant and engaging Twitter community as a whole.

BEYOND THE ALGORITHM: ADDITIONAL PERSONAL EMPOWERMENT FEATURES

Let users filter out specific words, trends, or subjects for a period if needed. Users should be able to receive notifications *only* for mentions by select accounts or when specific keywords they choose are used. Twitter could collaborate with well-being apps, allowing users to set screen time limits or "emotional temperature" pauses enforced across both platforms.

THE IMPORTANCE OF PERSONAL ADVOCACY

These are just starting points; the user community will have the best ideas to start threads and polls asking what people want from the platform and tag Twitter executives. Amplify mental health advocates, designers, and ethicists already proposing solutions in this space. If Twitter remains stagnant, supporting smaller platforms that prioritize ethics can shift the market overall.

The push for a more empowering, less addictive Twitter experience cannot rest solely on the platform's creators. The user community itself must become a catalyst for change. Initiatives like open discussions, where users directly tag Twitter executives to voice desires for new features or address concerns, hold the potential to make a difference. Furthermore, amplifying the work of mental health advocates, designers, and ethicists who actively propose solutions helps shape a larger conversation that Twitter cannot ignore. Ultimately, if calls for change are met with inaction, users have the power to shift the market by supporting alternative platforms that place ethical design and user well-being at their core.

This chapter has focused on Twitter's algorithmic influence, but a broader context is crucial. Further research should compare how the algorithmic design choices of other major platforms – from video-sharing to search engines – impact user empowerment. Are there examples of platforms prioritizing transparency or offering greater control over what content surfaced? Identifying those models can fuel further advocacy and drive the broader social media landscape toward more ethical and human-centered design.

Let us explore how Twitter's algorithm focus could compare to other popular platforms regarding user empowerment.

PERSONAL EMPOWERMENT IN COMPARISON WITH OTHER SOCIAL MEDIA GIANTS

Instagram: Focus on Visuals

User empowerment algorithms here would prioritize control over the *types* of images and videos shown. This could include filters for overly edited body image content, the option to see less "perfect lifestyle" posts, and features highlighting diverse, realistic content. Instagram's visual nature makes mood or topic detection complex, but algorithms could analyze image captions and the emotional tone of comments.

Facebook: Connections and Groups

Empowerment here lies in giving users more control over what appears from friends, family, and groups. More granular "snooze" options ("Hide posts about politics from Aunt Mary for the next month") would be decisive. Algorithms could identify Groups that tend to be supportive vs. drama-fueled for a user, subtly promoting the positive ones.

TikTok: The Power of Short-Form Video

TikTok is already better than some at letting users say "Not interested" in content, leading to a curated feed. Expanding this is critical. "Emotional vibe" selectors could exist: "I am stressed, show me ONLY silly animal videos" vs. "Pumped up, give me motivational content." The addictive nature demands robust tools: Time limits per content type or algorithms pause if a user scrolls for hours without interacting.

A DEEPER LOOK INTO TWITTER'S UNIQUE ADVANTAGES AND DISADVANTAGES

Advantage: Text is Easier to Analyze: Algorithms can potentially understand the sentiment and topics of a Tweet more quickly than a photo. This allows for the nuanced features we discussed earlier.

Advantage: Real-Time Nature: Twitter's focus on current events allows empowerment tools to intervene before outdated or fear-mongering news goes viral.

Disadvantage: Hostile Conversation Potential: Twitter's infamously argumentative culture is a huge barrier. Empowerment algorithms need to walk a tightrope between safeguarding users and enabling essential debates.

Disadvantage: Speed Matters: With the feed moving so quickly, algorithm-based interventions must be near-instant, or they lose effectiveness. This adds development complexity.

THE USER EMPOWERMENT; NEED FOR CROSS-PLATFORM STANDARDS (KEY FACTORS)

Ideally, the best user empowerment ideas would be shared and adapted across platforms. Imagine if your "No political rants for now" setting on Twitter also filtered out similar content on Facebook! Here is the challenge:

Business Model Differences: Platforms monetize user attention in different ways. An ad-heavy platform may be less willing to embrace features that reduce screen time.

Feature Complexity vs. Accessibility: Powerful algorithms and granular settings risk overwhelming some users. A balance needs to be struck.

Regulation Might Be Needed: If companies do not prioritize well-being independently, legislation could set minimum standards for ethical design and transparency.

Let us look into the exciting domain of cross-platform standards for user empowerment in the digital world.

THE CASE FOR CROSS-PLATFORM STANDARDS

User-Centric Experience: Imagine if your preferences for content, break reminders, and privacy settings followed you across social media platforms and other algorithm-driven websites. This creates a sense of control and consistency in your online experience.

Combating Digital Fatigue: Being bombarded by the same types of negativity or overly curated content across multiple platforms contributes to burnout. Coordinated standards could offer relief.

Leveling the Playing Field: Smaller, ethically minded platforms should not have to reinvent the wheel. Established standards can make positive features accessible to all, not just tech giants.

Driving Industry Change: If regulations or widespread user demand favor platforms with specific standards, it incentivizes everyone to improve, not just the ones already leaning toward ethical design.

KEY AREAS WHERE STANDARDS COULD EMERGE TO IMPROVE USER EMPOWERMENT

Transparency and Explainability (Key Factors)

Common language and methods for disclosing how algorithms work, why users see specific content, and how their data are used. This empowers users to make informed choices regardless of the platform.

Content Moderation And Safety

Shared frameworks for defining harmful content (hate speech, misinformation, etc.), with clear guidelines for user reporting and platform response.

This combats the issue of one platform's lax rules allowing dangerous content to spread elsewhere.

Well-being Tools

Standardized "mental health check-in" features, time management tools, and options to curate feeds based on emotional impact. This ensures a baseline of support options on every central platform.

Data Portability and Control

Users can easily export their data, preferences, and friend lists between platforms.

This breaks down the "walled gardens" that lock users in and promotes competition based on features, not just network size.

CHALLENGES TO IMPLEMENTATION (KEY FACTORS)

Corporate Resistance: Big tech firms may fight standards that limit their data collection or profit-driven engagement methods.

Technical Complexity: Algorithms vary wildly between platforms, so standards must be adaptable without sacrificing effectiveness.

Global Considerations: Privacy laws, definitions of "harm" and cultural values differ worldwide. Standards must be flexible or regionally specific.

Enforcement and Evolution: Who would ensure compliance? How often would standards be updated to reflect evolving tech?

PATHWAYS TO STANDARDIZE THE EXISTING PLATFORMS

Grassroots advocacy can be a powerful catalyst for change, empowering individuals and communities to raise their voices and demand greater accountability from technology companies. User communities, passionate about reclaiming control over their digital experiences, can organize online and offline campaigns, circulate petitions, and engage in public discourse to raise awareness about the importance of algorithmic transparency and user well-being tools. Mental health organizations, recognizing the potential impact of technology on mental well-being, can lend their expertise and advocacy power to this movement, pushing for the development and implementation of features that prioritize user mental health and digital well-being.

Industry collaboration can also play a crucial role in driving change. Smaller tech companies, often more agile and innovative than their larger counterparts, can lead by example, developing and implementing user-centric features that prioritize transparency and well-being. Evolving ethicists and researchers, deeply invested in the ethical implications of technology, can contribute their expertise by developing open-source standards, guidelines, and toolkits that make it easier for companies of all sizes to adopt these features. This collaborative approach can foster a culture of responsible innovation, where technology companies work together to create a digital landscape that prioritizes user well-being and societal benefit.

If self-regulation and industry collaboration prove insufficient, government intervention may become necessary. Governments, acting in the best interests of their citizens, could mandate minimum standards for algorithmic transparency and user well-being tools. This could involve requiring companies to disclose how their algorithms work, providing users with greater control over their data and online experiences, and implementing features that promote digital well-being and mitigate the potential harms of technology. While government regulation should be approached with caution, it can serve as a powerful tool for ensuring that technology companies prioritize the well-being of their users and contribute to a more equitable and just digital society.

INSPIRATION TO STANDARD PLATFORMS AND MAXIMUM USER EMPOWERMENT (KEY FACTORS)

GDPR (General Data Protection Regulation): While focused on privacy, it sets a precedent for regulating how tech companies handle user data.

Web Accessibility Standards: These international standards ensure that websites are designed to be usable by people with disabilities. A similar approach could be taken for mental well-being.

Ethical AI Frameworks: Various organizations propose guidelines for responsible algorithm design. These could be expanded and codified into cross-platform standards.

Let us take a look at some existing ethical AI frameworks and identify the principles most relevant to empowering users in their interactions with algorithms:

AI AND STANDARD PLATFORMS, KEY ETHICAL FACTORS

The Montreal Declaration for Responsible Development of Artificial Intelligence stands as a comprehensive ethical framework, emphasizing the crucial role of democracy, well-being, equity, and sustainability in the design and deployment of AI systems. It calls for a human-centric approach to AI development, ensuring that these technologies serve to enhance human capabilities and promote societal well-being, rather than exacerbating inequalities or undermining democratic values. The declaration stresses the importance of inclusivity, transparency, and accountability in AI development, ensuring that these technologies are deployed in a manner that benefits all members of society.

The Partnership on AI's Tenets represents a collaborative effort by major tech companies and nonprofit organizations to establish ethical guidelines for AI development. It focuses on fairness, transparency, and accountability in AI systems, recognizing the potential for bias, discrimination, and unintended consequences if these principles are not upheld. The partnership aims to foster a sense of responsibility among AI developers, encouraging them to consider the societal impact of their creations and to prioritize the well-being of all stakeholders.

The Asilomar AI Principles, developed by a diverse group of experts in the field, provide a comprehensive set of guidelines to steer the development of beneficial AI. These principles emphasize safety, ensuring that AI systems are designed and deployed in a manner that minimizes risks and avoids unintended harm. They also stress the importance of privacy, recognizing the potential for AI to collect, analyze, and utilize vast amounts of personal data. The Asilomar Principles call for AI development that prioritizes social benefits, ensuring that these technologies are used to address pressing societal challenges and promote the well-being of humanity.

The OECD Principles on AI, adopted by numerous governments worldwide, focus on the responsible stewardship of trustworthy AI that benefits society. These principles emphasize the importance of human-centered values, fairness, transparency, and accountability in AI development. They also highlight the need for international cooperation and collaboration to ensure that AI technologies are developed and deployed in a manner that promotes global peace, security, and sustainable development.

These ethical frameworks and principles represent a growing recognition of the profound impact that AI is having and will continue to have on our societies. They underscore the importance of responsible AI development, ensuring that these technologies are used to enhance human capabilities, promote societal well-being, and safeguard the values that define our humanity.

AI FRAMEWORK ELEMENTS RELEVANT TO USER EMPOWERMENT

Key Issues Regarding AI Platforms Transparency and Explainability

Users should understand how AI systems work, why they see specific content, and how their data are used. Frameworks emphasize clear disclosure and the potential need for simplified explanations.

Frameworks promote user choice and meaningful control over how algorithms impact their experience. This aligns with our discussions about customizable feeds, content filters, and data rights.

Fairness and Non-discrimination

Frameworks recognize algorithmic bias and its potential to amplify existing societal inequalities.

Ensuring recommendations and content moderation do not unfairly disadvantage certain users is crucial for empowerment and mental well-being. While these frameworks offer valuable guidance, they must be translated into concrete, actionable standards for social media and similar platforms. This could include:

Standardized "Why Am I Seeing This?" Explanations: Common terminology across platforms to explain how content is selected.
Algorithmic Auditability: Independent review processes to assess algorithms for bias, potential harms, and adherence to well-being principles.
User Feedback Mechanisms: Formalized ways for users to report when algorithms negatively impact their mental health, contributing to continuous improvement.
Specificity: Broad ethical principles need detailed translation for the unique challenges of user-facing algorithms.
Enforcement: Who monitors compliance with standards? What repercussions exist for violating them?
Balancing Empowerment with Functionality: User control should not come at the cost of a platform's core purpose. Bridging the gap between broad ethical principles and the nitty-gritty of platform design is the most crucial and challenging part of ensuring algorithms truly serve user empowerment. Here is how we can approach this:

BREAKING DOWN THE USER EMPOWERMENT PROCESS (CONSIDERING ALL ABOVE FACTORS)

The journey from abstract principles like "fairness and non-discrimination" to their practical implementation on platforms like Twitter is a complex and ongoing challenge. These principles are essential guideposts shaping the kind of digital spaces we strive to create. However, translating these ideals into concrete features, algorithms, and moderation tools requires careful consideration and constant refinement. Consider the principle of fairness. This might manifest in algorithms designed to ensure posts from diverse users are given equal visibility or moderation systems that proactively seek out and remove harmful content aimed at marginalized groups. Non-discrimination, on the other hand, could influence how users are verified, the development of language detection tools that identify hate speech, and even the image recognition systems that help identify and crop profile photos.

However, the path from principle to application is rarely straightforward. Technology is both powerful and imperfect. Algorithms can perpetuate biases if not rigorously tested, and even with the best intentions, defining what is "fair" or constitutes "harm" can be deeply subjective. This demands an ongoing dialogue between technologists, ethicists, and users to constantly question assumptions and refine the tools to uphold these principles.

The goal is not a perfect, frictionless technological solution to deep human problems. Instead, the actual value lies in the pursuit – the willingness to wrestle with complex principles and strive to embed them, even imperfectly, into the fabric of our digital platforms. This ongoing commitment will create online spaces that are more equitable, inclusive, and ultimately safer for all users.

POSSIBLE USER EMPOWERING APPLICATIONS

The quest for online spaces that foster true diversity of thought and protect against the suppression of viewpoints requires a multifaceted approach. Algorithms have the potential to play a crucial role. By proactively surfacing diverse perspectives, they can counterbalance the echo chambers that often form online. Additionally, analyzing retweet patterns, we can understand whether certain accounts or ideas are systematically marginalized and suppressed. Furthermore, techniques like "blind" content moderation, where identifying details like usernames are concealed, can help reduce biases that often unconsciously influence decisions about what content is permissible.

While technological solutions hold promise, it is essential to remember that they are not a silver bullet. True inclusivity and protection of diverse voices demand an ongoing societal dialogue. Algorithms should be designed and deployed with transparency and accountability, subject to continued scrutiny and refinement to ensure they promote fairness rather than inadvertently perpetuating existing biases. Ultimately, they create online spaces that genuinely reflect the rich tapestry of human perspectives, which requires technological innovation and a sustained commitment to open dialogue and respect for all voices.

TECHNICAL FEASIBILITY VS. IDEAL CASES

The Real-World Intrudes: Perfect fairness is perhaps impossible, but what is realistically achievable with current technology?

Prioritization: Focus on the most significant potential harm areas or the features users are most loudly demanding.

Iterative Design: Start with a good-faith attempt, collect data on the outcome, and improve continuously.

FROM USER NEEDS TO CODING APPLICATIONS

This chapter explored the journey from raw user needs to the lines of code underpinning digital solutions. The example of a user feeling overwhelmed by negativity online highlights the importance of this process when tackling sensitive areas like mental health. Real progress in this domain requires a deep understanding of technology, human psychology, and emotional well-being.

These demands bridge the gap between disciplines. Mental health professionals are crucial in articulating the ideal user experience and promoting positive mental states, while UX designers and engineers bring the technical expertise to translate those outcomes into workable tools and features. It is a translation effort, recognizing that mental health expertise does not directly produce code, but it guides the creation of digital environments that genuinely address the root of user needs. This collaborative, human-centered approach is essential for developing solutions that do not merely patch the surface but offer meaningful mental and emotional well-being support in the digital age.

TOOLS AND APPROACHES FOR SUCCESSFUL APPLICATION PROJECT (KEY SOCIETY FACTORS)

Design Workshops: Gather interdisciplinary teams to brainstorm how one principle could manifest in multiple feature ideas.

User Testing and Feedback: At every stage, real users (especially those with diverse backgrounds and lived experiences) are involved.

Algorithmic Audits: Hire independent experts or form an "ethics committee" to check if the tools are aligned with the principles regularly.

Scenario Planning: Imagine the WORST ways a feature could be abused or cause harm, and then design safeguards.

Transparency as Default: Explain the limitations and aims of the tech openly to users. These builds trust even when things are not perfect.

ALGORITHMIC BIAS AS HIDDEN ISSUES (KEY FACTOR EXAMPLES)

Algorithmic bias arises from factors like dataset diversity, human–algorithm collaboration, and the need for "explain yourself" features. Underrepresentation in datasets can lead to discrimination, while overreliance on algorithms can perpetuate biases. Explainable AI enhances transparency, allowing users to understand and question decisions, fostering trust and accountability. Addressing these issues is essential for creating fairer AI systems.

Dataset Diversity: Data used to train mental health detection algorithms MUST represent a wide range of experiences, reducing the potential to misinterpret cues from marginalized groups.

Human–Algorithm Collaboration: Combine algorithmic insights with trained moderators for nuanced situations.

"Explain Yourself" Feature for Algorithms: If an intervention is triggered, let the user see the data points leading to it, allowing them to dispute if needed.

IDEAL APPROACH: EMPOWERING USERS AT EVERY STAGE (KEY FACTORS)

Empowering users at every stage involves several key factors that enhance their experience, engagement, and satisfaction. Here's an ideal approach:

Design: Include users with lived mental health experience in ideation workshops, not just focus groups.

Data Donation: Frame it as an empowering choice, with clear breakdowns of the benefits and risks.

Advocacy: Platforms should amplify user-led initiatives and provide spaces for respectful debate on these topics.

The importance of a holistic approach:

Algorithms Are Not Therapists: On-screen reminders that they are tools and easy access to crisis support.

Education and Self-Awareness: Platform features that teach users about the psychology behind how algorithms work, encouraging conscious interaction.

Corporate Responsibility: Tech companies should invest in internal ethics teams working proactively alongside engineers.

HOLISTIC DATA LABELING AND ANNOTATION, FURTHER USER EMPOWERING

In building responsible and unbiased AI models, it is imperative to prioritize ethical and inclusive practices during the data labeling and annotation phase. Ensuring that your labeling teams reflect the diversity present in your datasets can help mitigate unconscious bias and lead to more representative outcomes. Additionally, utilizing blind labeling strategies, where possible, can further reduce the influence of preconceived notions by shielding labelers from potentially sensitive information like demographics. This encourages focusing solely on the objective features of the data.

Notably, the process should not stop at the initial labeling. Regular reviews and refinements of your labeled data are crucial for identifying and correcting systematic biases that may have crept in. Adopting an iterative approach and consistently scrutinizing your labeled data can pave the way for the development of fairer and more equitable AI systems. Let these principles serve as a compass guiding your data labeling and annotation journey, ensuring that the AI models built upon this foundation genuinely reflect the values of inclusivity and responsibility.

TRANSPARENCY AND EXPLAINABILITY, FURTHER USER EMPOWERMENT

Documenting Data Collection Methods: Be transparent about how and from whom data is collected, allowing for public scrutiny and trust-building.

Sharing Datasets for Independent Research: Partner with academic institutions or independent researchers to encourage broader analysis and verification of findings.

Explainable AI Techniques: When using complex algorithms, strive to explain how they arrived at specific conclusions based on the data.

CHALLENGES AND CONSIDERATIONS

Organizations today face a growing challenge in balancing the need for data security with the ethical imperative of protecting user privacy. This balancing act requires significant investment in robust encryption technologies, the development of transparent data usage policies, and a commitment to adapting to the evolving landscape of digital threats. Privacy concerns are paramount in today's data-driven world. Organizations must adhere to strict ethical guidelines and implement robust privacy protections to ensure that user data is collected, stored, and utilized responsibly. This includes obtaining informed consent, minimizing data collection, and implementing strong security measures to prevent unauthorized access and data breaches. The challenge of anonymity adds another layer of complexity. While protecting user identities is crucial, organizations also need some contextual information to fully understand the data and derive meaningful insights. Striking the right balance between anonymity and context is essential for conducting responsible research and analysis while respecting user privacy. Furthermore, building inclusive datasets that accurately reflect the diversity of human experiences requires a significant investment of time, effort, and collaboration. Traditional data collection methods often perpetuate biases and exclude marginalized communities. Organizations must actively seek out diverse perspectives and engage in collaborative partnerships to ensure that their datasets are representative and inclusive. As digital threats continue to evolve, organizations must remain vigilant and adaptable to maintain user trust and uphold ethical practices. This includes staying abreast of emerging cybersecurity threats, investing in advanced security technologies, and regularly reviewing and updating data privacy policies. In conclusion, navigating the complex landscape of data privacy and security requires a multifaceted approach that prioritizes ethical considerations, transparency, and user trust. By embracing these principles, organizations can harness the power of data while safeguarding individual privacy and promoting a more equitable and inclusive digital world.

THE ROAD TO A MORE EQUITABLE FUTURE

By prioritizing inclusivity in data collection and actively mitigating bias, we can create datasets that accurately reflect the vast spectrum of human experiences when it comes to mental health. This will lead to more effective algorithms supporting a more comprehensive range of users and less likely to perpetuate existing inequalities.

NAVIGATING THE PSYCHOLOGICAL IMPACTS OF SURVEILLANCE (NEGATIVE EMPOWERMENT)

The intersection of convenience, social engineering, and increasingly pervasive surveillance threatens both individual mental health and societal well-being. Here is why we must act urgently:

Privacy Erosion = Anxiety: The constant feeling of being watched, even when "opting in" to services, breeds anxiety and erodes our sense of personal autonomy.

Decision Overload: Algorithmic attempts to personalize *everything* can overwhelm our decision-making, leaving us paralyzed by too many tailored choices.

The Illusion of Control: While we are told data collection empowers us, the reality is that few understand how these data are used, fostering distrust and a sense of helplessness.

Navigating the Psychological Impacts of AI Surveillance: The Next Frontiers

AI-powered surveillance takes these risks to a terrifying new level. Here is how algorithms could violate our inner lives:

The Mood from Biometrics: Facial expressions, voice patterns, and even walking can be analyzed for signs of depression, anxiety, and more.

Mental Health from Behavior: What we post, buy, and search, along with data from wearables, can be used to create psychological profiles.

The Danger of "Help": The goal of this may be early intervention, but the danger is misdiagnosis, stigma, and the erosion of the boundary between private thought and public surveillance.

PROTECTING OUR MENTAL HEALTH IN THE AGE OF SURVEILLANCE

The relentless march of AI-powered surveillance poses a growing threat to our mental health and well-being. Unfortunately, our legal frameworks remain woefully behind the pace of this technological revolution. Too often, consent is treated as a checkbox formality, masking the long-term consequences of having our behaviors, emotions, and even thoughts relentlessly tracked and analyzed. Worse, algorithms often carry hidden biases, amplifying inequalities and discrimination.

The impact, however, goes beyond the issue of personal data privacy. The chilling realization that our most intimate thoughts might be exposed, judged, and potentially used against us strikes at the core of self-expression and freedom. When constantly observed, we might hesitate to explore new ideas, engage in dissent, or access help for mental health struggles.

It is time to move beyond a narrow focus on consent and technical safeguards. We must demand comprehensive regulations that address the unique risks AI surveillance poses to our mental well-being. This includes ensuring algorithms are transparent and free from bias, mandating clear limitations on collecting and using mental health data and recognizing the insidious impact of constant surveillance on our freedom of thought and expression. Let us advocate for a future where technology serves human flourishing, not as a tool for undermining the foundations of a healthy mind.

Examples of parallels to AI surveillance:

Medical Advancements: The development of X-rays, genetic testing, and potent pharmaceuticals all raised questions about bodily autonomy, consent, and the potential for misuse of information.

Lessons for AI: The slow evolution of medical ethics shows the need for constant adaptation. What is acceptable today in mental health data may be horrifying a decade from now. Regulations must be designed for flexibility.

National ID Systems: Many countries have these in some form to prevent fraud or ensure access to services. However, they can become tools of mass surveillance.

Lessons for AI: The "slippery slope" is natural. Even with good intentions, seemingly limited data collection can be expanded and used in ways never originally intended. Safeguards must be structural, not just promises from those in power.

Censorship for the "Greater Good": Throughout history, governments have sought to control information to prevent unrest or promote certain ideologies. This always conflicts with individuals' right to free expression.

Lessons for AI: AI filtering of content or flagging risk individuals based on their online activity is akin to censorship, even if done to prevent harm. Determining who gets to set the standards of what is "harmful" is crucial for preventing abuse.

It is important to note that NONE of these historical examples are perfect analogies. They offer insights, not a ready-made blueprint:

CRITICAL TAKEAWAYS FOR FINDING BALANCE TO EMPOWER USERS

Ensuring ethical AI demands a fundamental shift in mindset. There is no single solution, no magic switch that, once flipped, renders AI forever harmless or beneficial. Instead, we must approach this challenge as an ongoing process, recognizing the need for constant vigilance and adaptation as technology evolves. Just as vigorous debates about potential hazards shaped the early medical ethics field while those technologies were still nascent, we need to foster that same robust public discourse around AI now.

This debate cannot be confined to the tech companies themselves. It is imperative to have independent oversight involving diverse stakeholders – ethicists, social scientists, legal experts, and the public – to establish ethical guidelines and hold those developing and deploying AI accountable. These guidelines should address issues such as bias in algorithms, data privacy, transparency in decision-making, and the potential impact of AI on employment and social structures.

Additionally, as AI surveillance tools become increasingly tempting for those claiming to act in the interest of the public good, we must shift the burden of proof. Those advocating for such technologies must demonstrate their effectiveness and provide concrete evidence of safeguards to protect privacy, mitigate bias, and ensure they do not cause more harm than they solve. This includes rigorous testing, independent audits, and transparent reporting on the use and impact of these technologies.

The stakes are too high to approach ethical AI in a passive or reactionary manner. The potential consequences of inaction – from widespread discrimination and social unrest to the erosion of privacy and autonomy – are too grave to ignore. This conclusion is a call for ongoing public discourse, independent scrutiny, and proactive measures to ensure that the development and use of AI align with the values we hold dear: privacy, fairness, and the protection of individual rights in an increasingly complex technological landscape. Only through such vigilance and proactive engagement can we harness the transformative power of AI while safeguarding the ethical foundations of our society.

5 Quantum Breakthrough

Revolutionizing the Historical Challenge of Social Cyber Engineering

Analog computers have a rich history and have been used for centuries to solve complex problems. Unlike digital computers, they operate on continuous data. This unique approach is found in everything from early mechanical calculators to specialized encryption devices. The core idea is to split a significant problem into smaller, independent tasks that can be solved simultaneously by multiple processors/cores. Think of it as many cooks in a kitchen working on different dishes for a meal.

TYPES OF PARALLELISM

Data Parallelism: The same operation is performed on different parts of a large dataset (e.g., processing pixels in an image)

Task Parallelism: Entirely different tasks are assigned to different processors (e.g., one processor calculates physics, another handles graphics rendering). Idea use cases are such as scientific simulations, machine learning model training, extensive data analysis – anything where the work is naturally divisible.

"Mainstream" Computing on the other hand is tricky to define, as it changes over time! Right now, it includes:

Sequential Processing: Most consumer software is still largely sequential – instructions executed one after the other. Even multi-core devices often run sequential programs simultaneously rather than actual parallel processing.

Distributed Computing: This is distinct from parallel. Tasks are spread across multiple computers over a network (e.g., the SETI project). It is helpful for problems that are too large for one machine but adds communication overhead.

Cloud Computing: Increasingly common. We rent time on vast server farms as needed and are often used for computation without buying dedicated hardware. It can be either parallel or sequential, depending on the task.

One of the key differences between parallel and sequential computing lies in the approach to problem-solving. Parallel computing demands a more strategic mindset, requiring you to carefully consider how a problem can be broken down into smaller,

DOI: 10.1201/9781003500698-5

independent tasks that can be executed simultaneously. In contrast, sequential programming often allows for a more linear approach, where code can be written without explicitly planning for simultaneous execution. Furthermore, true parallel computing often thrives on specialized processor architectures, such as Graphics Processing Units (GPUs), which are designed to handle the massive parallelism required for tasks like image rendering and scientific simulations. However, most consumer devices, like laptops and smartphones, rely on general-purpose CPUs, which may limit the potential gains of parallelism. Another crucial difference lies in the programmer's skillset. While tools and libraries for parallel programming exist, the majority of programmers are primarily trained in sequential programming paradigms. This lack of widespread expertise in parallel programming restricts its adoption, even on devices that are theoretically capable of handling parallel tasks. In essence, parallel computing represents a paradigm shift in how we approach computation, demanding a more strategic, hardware-aware, and specialized skillset. While it offers significant potential for performance gains, its adoption is hindered by the limitations of current hardware and the need for more widespread training in parallel programming techniques.

On the Other Hand, modern CPUs have features for processing several data items with a single instruction (but not the complete flexibility of true parallelism). The web is inherently distributed, when you load a page, your browser fetches bits from many servers distributed computing even if the tasks on each server are not parallel. Cloud farms are used for tasks like AI training, bringing enormous computational power without specialized local hardware.

WHY DOES THIS DISTINCTION MATTER

Understanding performance limits, investment value, and the shift to parallel processing is essential for optimizing resources and managing costs. This knowledge helps make informed decisions that enhance efficiency in hardware and software development.

Performance Limits: Sequential thinking will hit a performance wall, as single cores cannot get much faster. Unlocking the next leap often requires parallel approaches.

Understanding What You Pay for Cloud services may advertise "cores," but how well that translates to performance depends heavily on whether your software can exploit them in parallel.

The Future Is More Parallel: To keep devices getting faster, everyday software may need to become more parallel-aware and ready for quantum computing data revolution.

REDEFINING EFFICIENCY

Superposition for Speed: With qubits existing as 0 and 1 simultaneously, quantum computers can explore multiple solutions simultaneously. This is fundamentally different from classical computers checking options one by one.

Data Explosion Tamed: Tasks taking years on supercomputers (like analyzing massive medical datasets) could be tackled in vastly reduced timescales with quantum tech.

NEW TYPES OF STORAGE POSSIBILITIES

Beyond Bits: Qubits' complex states could allow information storage at densities far beyond what we achieve with binary data.
Quantum Memory: Research into this could lead to "locking" data with quantum properties, potentially creating unbackable storage with standard methods.

Imagine searching instantly through the entire Library of Congress, not just getting a list of relevant books. This has both positive and (for those in power) scary implications.

If quantum tech decentralizes (like the early internet), it could become more complex for any entity (government or corporation) to control huge data pools. This cuts both ways – it could empower individuals and make tracking harmful content more difficult.

THE PRIVACY PARADOX OF QUANTUM POWER

The Privacy Paradox of Quantum Power reveals how advancing quantum technologies threaten traditional encryption while sparking a race for new methods. As quantum surveillance grows, privacy risks becoming a luxury, highlighting the tension between security and oversight.

Encryption Under Threat: Many current encryption methods rely on math that quantum computers could break trivially. Banking, secure communications, etc., are vulnerable in the long run.
The Race for New Encryption: We will need quantum-resistant standards, but this task is enormous. The transition period could be chaotic, with bad actors likely to exploit it.
Quantum Surveillance: If governments master quantum tech first, the tools they could build to "see through" encrypted citizen data are terrifying.
Privacy as a Luxury: It is possible that access to quantum-resistant encryption is expensive and available only to the wealthy and powerful.

BEYOND THE TECHNICAL: THE NEED FOR QUANTUM ETHICS

Who decides the rules when developing quantum computing; that should not just be left to technologists. We urgently need public forums debating its potential social impact *before* the tech becomes widespread.

Equity of Access: If quantum power is concentrated in the hands of a few, the inequalities it could create will dwarf what we have seen with the digital age so far.

Preparing Society: Most people do not grasp the basics of current tech, let alone quantum principles. We need mass education efforts to ensure that fear or hype does not dominate public debates about quantum.

Further Discussion Starter Topics

Do you see the potential benefits of quantum computing outweighing the privacy risks? Or vice versa?

Beyond encryption, how else might quantum computers upend how we think about data ownership and control?

What role, if any, should governments play in regulating quantum tech development, given both its potential for good and ill?

Let us look closer into the chilling potential of quantum surveillance and how we can prepare society for the ethical complexities of this powerful technology.

THE LOOMING SHADOW OF QUANTUM SURVEILLANCE

Imagine a world where communications are all encrypted and emails, messages, and even phone calls become easily decipherable by governments (or anyone with access to quantum computers).

Secure banking systems could be cracked, allowing for large-scale theft or manipulation of financial data. Susceptible medical data could be accessed without authorization, potentially leading to discrimination or extortion. These are just a few frightening scenarios if quantum computers fall into the wrong hands. Scenarios are like when the current encryption relies on factoring large numbers or the difficulty of finding discrete logarithms. Quantum algorithms can solve these problems exponentially faster. New encryption standards are being developed but are still in their infancy. There is a transition period where much of the data will be vulnerable. The nation, corporation, or criminal organization that gets quantum computing operational first will have a significant advantage in surveillance capabilities.

PREPARING SOCIETY FOR THE QUANTUM AGE

It is not all doom and gloom. There are certain steps we can take to mitigate the risks and maximize the benefits:

Open Discussions and Public Education: We need to move beyond technical jargon and have frank conversations about the ethical implications of quantum computing. Everyone, from lawmakers to ordinary citizens, must be aware of the issues.

International Cooperation: No single nation can develop robust quantum-resistant encryption standards alone. Global agreements are needed to ensure all countries have access to these tools.

Focus on Quantum Ethics: Embedding ethical considerations into the research and development of quantum technology is paramount.

Promoting Transparency: Governments and tech companies must be transparent about their quantum computing initiatives, fostering public trust and reducing fears of a "quantum surveillance state." There is a risk of a quantum arms race, with nations developing quantum tech primarily for offensive cyber capabilities. Efforts are needed to redirect resources toward peaceful applications.

Rethinking Data Privacy Laws: Privacy laws from the pre-quantum era may need a complete overhaul. The "informed consent" concept takes on a new meaning when data cannot be genuinely anonymized.

Empowering Users with Quantum Knowledge: As quantum tech becomes more integrated into society, individuals need the tools to understand how it works and how to protect their data.

Further Discussion Prompts

Who bears the responsibility for mitigating the risks of quantum surveillance? Is it solely governments, or do corporations and individuals also have a role to play?

How can we balance the need for national security with the right to privacy in the quantum age? Should there be international treaties banning the use of quantum computers for offensive cyber operations?

By fostering open dialogue, international cooperation, and ethical considerations, we can harness the power of quantum computing for good while safeguarding privacy and security in this exciting new era. Let's take a look at all the actors and roles.

GOVERNMENTS

They have the power to regulate, set research priorities, and potentially use this technology themselves. They have to protect citizens, even when that hampers national security efforts.

Secrecy vs. Transparency: It is a delicate balance. Too much secrecy breeds distrust, but some level is needed to avoid giving adversaries an edge. Oversight bodies can help but cannot be perfect.

Global Leadership: Wealthy nations must not just develop quantum defenses for themselves but aid in making these tools accessible to less powerful countries or risk worsening global inequality.

CORPORATIONS

Private companies, often with government funding, are at the forefront of building quantum hardware and algorithms. They have ethical duties alongside the pursuit of profit.

Collaboration Is Key: Reluctance to share information, even when there is a common threat like quantum-cracking encryption, can be harmful. Governments might need to incentivize this.

Corporate Espionage Factor: The same tech that protects banks from a quantum-enabled hacker could be used by one corporation to spy on another. Regulations must anticipate this.

INDIVIDUALS

The average person cannot build quantum tech or change policy alone. Their responsibilities are more about staying informed and making choices.

Informed Consent 2.0: Understanding how much data you surrender to a company when using their new quantum-backed service will be crucial, but the terms will be hard to comprehend.

Pressure from the Bottom: Consumer backlash, boycotts, etc., can influence corporate behavior even when government regulation is slow. This requires mass awareness.

ADDITIONAL CONSIDERATIONS

Criminal groups, hacktivists, etc., will potentially gain access to quantum tools. This makes enforcement of any agreements that much more challenging.

Education Is Vital: We need to invest in educating the public about quantum risks so they can put pressure on governments and businesses to prioritize ethical development.

Unintended Consequences: Even well-meaning quantum-resistant encryption schemes could accidentally empower authoritarian regimes by making *all* citizen data harder to access.

FURTHER DISCUSSION POINTS

Are there historical examples (environmental tech, medical research, etc.) where a balance was found between corporate responsibility and government regulation? Could those provide a model?

How might a "quantum privacy score" for businesses look? What would consumers need to know to make it effective?

Who is responsible for educating the public about quantum threats? Schools? Media? Tech companies themselves?

History, while imperfect, can offer valuable insights into models where a degree of balance was achieved between corporate responsibility and government oversight. Let us examine a few examples:

CASES ASSOCIATED WITH ENVIRONMENTAL TECHNOLOGY

Case Study: Catalytic Converters: Mandated by the Clean Air Act in the US dramatically reduced vehicle emissions. Automakers initially resisted, but competition and innovation led to breakthroughs. Strict goals spurred tech development. Companies dragged their feet but ultimately found compliance could be profitable.

LESSONS FOR QUANTUM

Government-set standards are essential, even if the tech does not exist yet to meet them. International standards are more challenging but vital for issues with global impact. Consumer pressure can be as powerful a market force as regulation.

CASES ASSOCIATED WITH MEDICAL RESEARCH

Case Study: Pharmaceutical Regulation: Drug approval processes (FDA) were toughened after tragedies like Thalidomide. Companies cannot bring products to market based solely on their say-so. Independent review of safety data is non-negotiable. The public must trust the process, or even good drugs/tech are rejected.

LESSONS FOR QUANTUM

The mindset of "Move fast and break things" will not fly with tech impacting privacy.

Regulation should not stifle ALL risk-taking, but those risks must be calculated, not recklessly imposed on the public.

CASES ASSOCIATED WITH NUCLEAR POWER (A CAUTIONARY TALE)

Case Study: The Complex Case: Immense potential but catastrophic risks. Regulation varies wildly worldwide, with accidents shaping perception as much as a science. When the worst-case scenario is horrific, oversight cannot just be about profit, even if that hampers development.

Public trust is quickly shattered and almost impossible to regain once lost.

LESSONS FOR QUANTUM

The surveillance potential is less "apocalyptic" than nukes but hits closer to home for many. Encryption failures could destroy faith in digital systems. None of these are perfect parallels to quantum computing. However, they highlight principles to guide us.

Companies often innovate in surprising ways when the alternative is being shut down. The right balance depends on the specific risks and benefits of the technology. People will not support what they do not understand, making them more vulnerable to fearmongering OR overconfidence.

ADAPTING TODAY'S MODELS TO QUANTUM COMPUTING

Adapting models to quantum computing faces global challenges, but a tech-savvy public offers opportunities. The unknown factor is the speed of these adaptations.

Challenge: Global Nature: One nation's strong quantum privacy laws mean little if others become havens for surveillance.

Opportunity: Tech-Savvy Public: People know more about data and hacking than when environmental regulation was new. This can be leveraged.

The Unknown Factor: We may not grasp the FULL impact of quantum-enabled surveillance until it is too late to roll it back completely. Precautions must be baked into the system.

TOPICS FOR FURTHER THINKING

The questions posed at the end of this chapter invite us to consider the complex interplay between regulation, public perception, and technological development within the quantum domain. There seems to be a disparity in how urgency is perceived; data privacy, with its immediate personal impact, might incite greater public demand for control and regulation than the seemingly distant threat of climate change. Understanding these nuances is crucial for determining effective strategies to motivate timely action.

Additionally, the potential for companies to gain a competitive advantage through robust self-regulation presents an intriguing possibility. Could this proactive approach outpace typically slower government regulation, shaping industry standards while building public trust? Furthermore, the role of investigative journalism is vital. Journalists can hold stakeholders accountable by shining a light on the development and implications of quantum technologies, fostering transparency and empowering a more informed public.

These are not questions with straightforward, definitive answers. They demand continuous dialogue engagement between policymakers, industry leaders, scientists, and journalists. Only by grappling with these complexities can we ensure that the immense potential of quantum technology is harnessed responsibly and serves the greater good.

QUANTUM COMPUTING'S IMPACT ON PRIVACY: POWER AND PROTECTION

Quantum computing could revolutionize privacy with unbreakable encryption, but it also threatens current encryption methods and disrupts blockchain security, necessitating new protective measures in a quantum era.

The Unbreakable Encryption Promise: Quantum key distribution could offer secure communications; even the most powerful computer could not crack them. As we know, this has vast implications for data privacy.

The Current Encryption Threat: In contrast, quantum computers could break the most current encryption (financial transactions, private messages, etc.). We urgently need quantum-resistant replacements to avoid a security freefall.

Blockchain Disrupted: Even the seemingly tamper-proof world of cryptocurrencies is at risk if quantum machines can solve their algorithms. The entire concept of decentralized digital trust might need to be rethought.

THE ETHICS OF THE QUANTUM AGE

The potential for quantum computing to simultaneously strengthen and decimate privacy raises urgent questions:

The New Digital Divide: Will access to quantum tech be fair, or will it worsen existing inequalities? Those who cannot afford quantum-resistant tools will be completely exposed.

Surveillance Beyond Imagination: If governments master quantum computing's offensive side first, will there be any way for citizens to maintain privacy?

Global Standards Are the Only Solution: Much like early nuclear technology, and this is hard to enforce when rogue actors do not want to play by the rules.

DARK LINES OF QUANTUM DOMINATION: LESSONS FROM STALINISM

Oddly, the pre-digital totalitarianism of Stalin's regime offers a chilling reference point for understanding the dangers of unchecked quantum surveillance power:

Privacy as a Weapon: Under Stalin, the mere suspicion of private thoughts that did not align with the state was a crime. This shows how the end of privacy is not just about knowing your secrets but controlling what you dare to think.

From Humans to Algorithms: Stalinist surveillance required vast bureaucracies of informants. Quantum tech could make surveillance vastly more powerful and impersonal, potentially alienating citizens from the concept of a private life.

The Cost of Fear: Even when most people were "innocent," the constant knowledge of being watched bred distrust, harming society beyond the direct victims of the regime.

The quantum revolution is not just about faster computers. It forces us to rethink the line between the personal and the public and the tools those in power have to cross that line. History shows that it is tough to regain once privacy is lost.

Further Discussion Starter Topics

Is it naive to hope for ethical self-regulation from those developing quantum computers, or does the track record of past tech booms make this an unlikely path?

Beyond encryption: How might quantum computing change the online right to be forgotten? Could it make it genuinely impossible to erase past data?

Could the need to make EVERYTHING quantum-resistant lead to unintended consequences, like slowing innovation, due to the focus on security?

Let us look into how quantum computing could shake the foundations of the "right to be forgotten" online and explore the feasibility (and potential drawbacks) of making everything quantum resistant.

THE "RIGHT TO BE FORGOTTEN" IN THE QUANTUM AGE

The European Union's "right to be forgotten" (RTBF) allows individuals to request the removal of personal data from search engines and other online platforms. However, quantum computing throws a significant wrench into this concept:

Un-Deleting the Undeleted: Current deletion practices often mark data as inaccessible rather than truly erasing it. Quantum computers, with their ability to potentially recover even "deleted" data, could render this practice useless.

Data Resurrection: Scary as it sounds, algorithms designed to exploit the unique properties of qubits might allow for reconstructing data previously thought to be permanently deleted. This could have severe ramifications for RTBF requests.

The Decentralized Dilemma: With its distributed data storage, Blockchain technology poses a further challenge. Even if an individual successfully erases data from one node in a blockchain, it might still exist elsewhere in the network, potentially retrievable with quantum computing power.

THE QUANTUM-RESISTANT ARMS RACE

While making everything quantum-resistant seems like the logical solution, the path toward this goal is challenging. The costs associated with upgrading infrastructure and software will be significant and potentially pose hurdles for smaller businesses and individual users. Furthermore, a single-minded focus on quantum resistance could paradoxically stifle innovation in other vital areas of cryptography. Perhaps most importantly, we must acknowledge that the battle against quantum cryptanalysis will likely be unending. It is a perpetual arms race, where even our best quantum-resistant defenses could be rendered obsolete by future advancements in quantum computing power and associated attack methods. This highlights the ongoing and demanding nature of maintaining security in the ever-evolving digital landscape.

Finding the Right Balance

There is no easy solution, but here are some potential approaches:

Prioritization Is Key: Focus on protecting the most critical data first (e.g., healthcare records, financial transactions) while acknowledging that some less sensitive information might be more vulnerable.

Hybrid Solutions: Combining quantum-resistant algorithms and other security measures (like access controls and data anonymization) might offer a more sustainable approach.

Regulation and Collaboration: Open international discussions are crucial to ensure everyone can access quantum-resistant solutions, preventing a situation where only powerful nations have truly secure data.

Discussion Prompts

Should the "right to be forgotten" online be re-evaluated in light of the limitation's quantum computing poses? If so, how?

Who should bear the financial burden of making systems quantum-resistant – individuals, governments, or tech companies?

How can we balance the need for robust security with fostering an innovation environment in cryptography?

By acknowledging the challenges and working together, we can develop strategies to protect privacy and security while harnessing the immense potential of quantum computing.

Let us move from the theoretical to the practical, exploring real-world strategies being developed to balance the benefits of quantum computing with protecting privacy and security:

Strategies in Development, Post-Quantum Cryptography (PQC)

The selection of four post-quantum cryptography algorithms by NIST in July 2022 marks a watershed moment in the evolution of cybersecurity. This underscores the urgent need for cryptographic systems resilient against the computational power promised by quantum computers. The fact that three of these standardized algorithms rely on the complexities of mathematical lattices highlights the importance of this specific mathematical structure within the domain of quantum-resistant cryptography. Additionally, selecting an algorithm rooted in vector spaces and tensor grids demonstrates that diverse mathematical approaches hold promise in securing our digital world against future threats. These momentous decisions by NIST pave the way for the widespread adoption of post-quantum cryptography, ensuring the protection of sensitive data even as quantum computing capabilities continue to advance.

The Core Idea: Develop encryption algorithms that are believed to be secure against attacks even from quantum computers.

Real-World Example: The National Institute of Standards and Technology (NIST) is running a competition to select PQC standards. Promising candidates include lattice-based cryptography and code-based cryptography.

How It Helps: If standardized and widely adopted, PQC would allow us to encrypt data and communicate securely online, even in the era of widespread quantum computing.

QUANTUM KEY DISTRIBUTION (QKD) (KEY FACTORS)

The Core Idea: Using photons and their quantum properties to securely transmit encryption keys, making eavesdropping theoretically impossible to carry out undetected.

Real-World Example: Several countries, such as China and Switzerland, have established QKD networks for secure communication, primarily for government and financial sectors.

How It Helps: QKD could provide an ultra-secure foundation for encrypting sensitive data exchanges.

HOMOMORPHIC ENCRYPTION (KEY FACTORS)

The Core Idea: Allows computations to be performed directly on encrypted data without decrypting it first.

Real-World Example: Limited implementations exist. They have the potential to protect privacy in cloud computing, where users can have their data processed without revealing it to the cloud provider.

How It Helps: This could revolutionize how we use sensitive data for research (medical, etc.) with strong privacy guarantees.

HYBRID APPROACHES AND QUANTUM RISK MANAGEMENT (KEY FACTORS)

Hybrid quantum risk management combines classical and quantum methods for improved decision-making, using quantum algorithms for faster portfolio optimization and better risk assessments.

The Core Idea: Recognizing that a blanket "quantum-proof everything" might be impossible. Combine PQC, traditional encryption, and physical security measures tailored to the protected data.

Real-World Example: A financial institution may use PQC for the most critical transactions, strong traditional encryption for less sensitive data, and physical vaults for long-term archival data storage with a low risk of being targeted by quantum adversaries.

How It Helps: A nuanced approach makes the best use of resources and allows for adaptation as quantum threats evolve.

CHALLENGES AND CONSIDERATIONS

Implementing new systems can be complex and requires careful integration. Trust is crucial, as stakeholders need confidence in the system's reliability. Global standards are necessary for consistency and interoperability across regions.

Implementation Complexity: Rolling out these strategies is not just a software update. It may involve hardware changes, new protocols, and major overhauls to existing systems.

The Question of Trust: QKD, for example, relies on the inherent physics of quantum mechanics. Will the public trust this, or are systems that are at least somewhat hackable "more acceptable" because they are understood?

Global Standards: Fragmentation is the enemy here. Nations and industries must agree on the methods used, or even secure systems cannot "talk" to each other.

Let us look into those discussion prompts, exploring the challenges and opportunities surrounding quantum-resistant strategies.

IDENTIFYING INDUSTRIES AS EARLY QUANTUM COMPUTING ADOPTERS

Early adopters of quantum computing include healthcare for advanced data analysis, research for enhanced problem-solving, and critical infrastructure for improved security.

Healthcare: With highly personal medical records often shared across institutions, healthcare is a prime target for bad actors. Here, the benefits of homomorphic encryption (data analysis without revealing content) could be huge, alongside strong PQC for transmitting records.

Research and Intellectual Property: Companies and universities pour resources into data that, if leaked, could benefit competitors immensely. Quantum threats add urgency to already existing privacy needs. PQC and secure cloud solutions using homomorphic encryption would be heavily utilized.

Critical Infrastructure: Power grid transportation systems increasingly rely on networked devices. Sabotage enabled by quantum decryption is not just a spy movie plot. Hybrid approaches, where the most vital systems get QKD-level protection, are likely.

Educating Without Alarmism or Complacency

Educating on Quantum Key Distribution (QKD) needs clear analogies to balance transparency and avoid fearmongering, fostering informed engagement.

Analogies Matter: Most people do not grasp the technicalities of encryption, but they understand physical security. Liken PQC to "stronger locks," emphasizing that bad actors need vastly more time and resources to break in, not guaranteeing perfection.

Transparency vs. Fearmongering: Be honest; quantum tech is evolving rapidly, so we will always play catch-up. Focus on how these new methods make privacy harder to violate, not impossible, to avoid a "why bother?" attitude in public.

Demystifying QKD: "Unbackable" communication sounds too good to be true. Explain the physics in plain terms and explain that its real-world use often involves QKD passing traditional keys, which then get updated frequently for ongoing security.

BALANCING QUANTUM READINESS WITH "EVERYDAY" CYBERCRIME

Balancing quantum readiness with everyday cybercrime shows that advancements don't reduce risks. New skills and compliance are essential to address both threats.

The Zero-Sum Fallacy: It would be shortsighted to assume resources put into quantum defense must be taken from combating current threats. More robust baseline security benefits everyone, whether the attacker uses a supercomputer or a phishing scam.

New Skills Needed: Cryptographers who understand classical and post-quantum methods will be in high demand. This requires investment in education alongside updating the tech itself.

The Compliance Factor: Regulations pushing for quantum readiness may have a ripple effect, forcing companies that otherwise wouldn't prioritize security to meet the new basic standards. This can have a positive impact on the broader cybersecurity landscape.

Let us examine these two avenues of how the quantum computing revolution could shape the cybersecurity landscape.

HOW QUANTUM READINESS CREATES NEW CYBERSECURITY OPPORTUNITIES

Quantum readiness is driving the need for post-quantum cryptographers to develop new security schemes, requiring both technical skills and the ability to communicate with non-experts to tackle emerging quantum threats.

The Rise of Post-Quantum Cryptographers (Key Factors)

Need: Developing, testing, and implementing PQC algorithms requires specialized expertise in bridging mathematics, cryptography, and computer science.

Roles Include researchers designing new PQC schemes, engineers optimizing them for real-world performance, and security analysts auditing their integration into systems.

Skills Beyond the Technical: Strong communication is needed, translating quantum security to non-expert stakeholders and advocating for adoption.

NEED FOR HYBRID SECURITY SPECIALISTS

Understanding the interplay of classical encryption, PQC, and physical security for that nuanced risk-based approach will be highly valued. Security consultants advising organizations on tailored protection plans, developers creating hybrid solutions, and system administrators managing these complex setups. Assessing an organization's specific data needs and balancing them against the cost/complexity of quantum-resistant versus traditional methods.

QUANTUM SECURITY AUDITORS AND ETHICAL HACKERS

As with all new techs, someone needs to find the flaws before bad actors do. Pentesters specializing in quantum systems will be in demand. "Red teams" simulate attacks, helping companies improve defenses. Also, researchers proactively worked to break PQC candidates to find weaknesses early. The mindset of an attacker, but also strong ethics. Those with this talent can make the system safer or exploit it for personal gain.

Beyond Pure Tech: Policy analysts who understand the implications of quantum tech for law and governance, risk communicators explaining it to the public…the cybersecurity ecosystem will become even more diverse.

Education Is Key: Universities need to develop courses in this area quickly. Also, re-training programs for existing security professionals to upskill.

INTERNATIONAL REGULATORY BODIES AND QUANTUM STANDARDS

Fragmentation is dangerous here. Global cooperation is needed, from algorithm choices to how quantum networks are governed.

EXISTING PLAYERS (MIGHT TAKE THE LEAD)

NIST (US standards body): They are already influential due to their role in traditional encryption standards.

International Telecommunication Union (ITU): Sets global telecom standards that have the potential to expand into quantum-secure comms.

ISO (International Organization for Standardization): Has broad standards-setting experience that could be applicable here.

Balancing national security interests with global cooperation and finding the right level of detail is the key challenge. Standards must be specific enough to ensure compatibility but not overly prescriptive to stifle innovation. Key players in the International Standards Arena have their own specific challenges, let's take a look at them,

NIST (National Institute of Standards and Technology)

Advantage: Proven track record in traditional cryptography, running the current high-stakes PQC competition. Their selections will likely be widely adopted.

Challenge: Balancing purely technical expertise with the need to win global buy-in for their chosen standards. They are seen as US-centric by some.

ITU (International Telecommunication Union)

Advantage: Truly a global body representing many nations and expertise in setting standards that allow diverse systems to interoperate.
Challenge: Traditionally focused on telecom infrastructure. We will need to build up specific expertise in quantum security.

ISO (International Organization for Standardization)

Advantage: Vast experience in non-technical standard-setting (management, quality control, etc.). It could help set broader standards around how PQC is implemented, audited, etc., not just the algorithms themselves.
Challenge: Limited prior work on cutting-edge cryptography may mean they partner with other bodies for the core technical content.

OTHER ORGANIZATIONS TO WATCH

ETSI (European Telecommunications Standards Institute) could play a role in harmonizing standards specifically for Europe, even if they do not become the sole global standard-setter.

Industry Consortiums and tech companies may attempt to create their standards. Ideally, these get integrated into broader regulations to avoid fragmentation.

BALANCING INTERESTS: KEY ISSUES FACING THESE BODIES

International bodies face key issues like balancing national security with transparency, ensuring smaller nations have a voice, and the need for adaptability to respond to changing global dynamics.

National Security vs. Openness: How much detail is made public about the reasoning behind choosing one PQC algorithm over another? Nations will want some secrecy, but too much sow's distrust.
Inclusion of Smaller Nations: It is not just about the standards but providing funding and technical assistance so all countries can implement them. This is vital for proper security.
Adaptability Is Key: Standards bodies cannot be slow-moving behemoths in this domain. There needs to be a built-in process of updates as new attacks and PQC candidates emerge.

Future undercover new issues that lead to the new standards needed for quantum devices' physical security, to prevent theft/tampering.

LESSONS LEARNED FROM EARLY DEVELOPMENT

Lessons learned from developing early internet standards, examining potential parallels for international cooperation in quantum security provide a unique learning opportunity.

Meaning that, even with security concerns, involving a wide range of countries will improve buy-in. Nations left out are the ones most likely to use rogue systems.

Also, setting basic, adaptable PQC standards quickly may matter more than spending years choosing the absolute "best" one. This allows industry and governments to start the transition.

A mechanism for non-government experts to review standards (while respecting some secrecy) is vital. This builds public confidence that choices are being made on sound technical grounds.

We cannot ignore that companies stand to profit immensely from quantum tech. Standard bodies must have strong conflict-of-interest policies to avoid being captured by industry players.

Let us examine where a modern "RFC"-style process might fit into quantum security standards development and the areas where it has limitations.

WHERE AN "RFC"-INSPIRED APPROACH MIGHT WORK

An "RFC"-inspired approach can improve algorithm refinement, share implementation best practices, and enable quick reporting of emerging threats.

Algorithm Refinement and Feedback: As new PQC candidates emerge, a process akin to RFCs could allow cryptographers to Publish their proposed algorithms for open review, Receive feedback on strengths, weaknesses, and potential attack surfaces, and Iterate on their designs in response to this global peer-review process.

Implementation Best Practices: Once core PQC algorithms are standardized, we will need guidance on using them safely in the real world. RFC-like documents could outline:

Secure ways to roll out new encryption keys as PQC becomes integrated.

System architectures optimizing for a hybrid of classical and post-quantum methods.

Performance optimization tips for specific hardware platforms.

Emerging Threat Reporting: As attacks against PQC or new vulnerabilities are discovered, a rapid, open mechanism for information sharing is needed. This is where an RFC system shines, making knowledge public outside of slow-moving official channels.

WHERE RFCS FALL SHORT FOR QUANTUM

RFCs fall short for quantum technology by lacking robust standards, overlooking physical security, and prioritizing speed over due diligence, risking security and integrity.

The Core Standardization Choice: The actual selection of "winner" PQC algorithms likely cannot be fully transparent. National security agencies will demand input; some based on classified data the public cannot see. An RFC process might inform this decision but not be the sole decider.

Physical Security of Quantum Devices: Standards around preventing tampering with quantum hardware probably need a different approach. This resembles engineering standards, with less room for open, bottom-up development.

Speed vs. Due Diligence: The RFC process favors thoroughness, which can be slow. For urgent quantum security needs, there may need to be a "fast track" parallel system for publishing critical warnings or baseline standards, even if not fully polished.

THE QUANTUM ALGORITHMS AGE: RETHINKING SECURITY AND PRIVACY

Quantum computing, with its potential to break classical encryption, poses a formidable challenge to securing digital communications and private data. This era brings the fear of unprecedented computational power undermining the foundations of privacy and echoing surveillance under totalitarian regimes but through fundamentally different technological means. The quantum era's threat comes not from direct human agents but from abstract computational power. The ability to decrypt previously secure communication could expose individuals to new levels of surveillance, potentially at the hands of state actors or malicious entities. However, unlike in Stalinist times, this power is wielded through technology rather than brute force or networks of informants.

The quantum leap in computing introduces a dual-edged sword in areas such as *Quantum Cryptography*, where techniques like quantum key distribution (QKD) could establish unbreakable secure communication channels, revolutionizing data privacy. In addition, issues such as *Breaking Today's Encryption* Algorithms like Shor's threatens to undermine widely used encryption schemes (RSA, ECC). Malicious actors might even harvest encrypted data now, waiting for the day quantum computers can decrypt it.

THE MOST IMPORTANT ISSUE, "PLANNING THE TRANSITION"

Moving into the quantum-secure world demands proactive measures. Planning to enter this phase must include issues such as *Post-Quantum Cryptography,* for developing and standardizing new encryption methods to withstand quantum attacks. *Education is Key*, educating stakeholders, from governments to individuals, about the shifts ahead will promote a smoother transition. *Ethics and Regulation* Balancing the benefits of quantum-enhanced security with the potential for misuse and ensuring fair use of these technologies.

The rise of quantum algorithms signals a seismic shift with far-reaching security implications. While harnessing this power has the potential to unlock incredible advancements, it also necessitates a proactive and multifaceted re-evaluation of security across diverse domains.

First, we must consider how quantum technology might reshape market structures. Its high costs and complexity could create barriers to entry, potentially leading to monopolies. Antitrust regulations must evolve alongside these technologies to ensure a level playing field and protect against the harmful effects of limited competition.

Second, public trust in digital systems is paramount. As quantum computing renders current encryption methods vulnerable, we must redefine our understanding of digital security. Ensuring trust in new quantum-resistant solutions will require extensive public education, transparency around their implementation, and robust safeguards.

Third, we have an ethical imperative to prevent the widening of the digital divide. Quantum capabilities must not become a tool for entrenching existing inequalities. Investing in research, education, and policies that promote widespread access to and understanding of quantum-resistant security protocols is crucial.

The era of quantum algorithms demands technological solutions and a holistic response that considers its economic, societal, and ethical dimensions. Through collaboration, proactive regulation, and a commitment to individual security and the broader public good, we can navigate this transformative period and ensure an innovative and secure digital future for all.

There are other fundamental issues to be addressed in the early planning phase. Issues such as Quantum Computing and Antitrust. Current antitrust frameworks focus on price-fixing and predatory behavior within a mature market. Quantum tech is so new that the landscape could shift rapidly and unpredictably. A company might gain dominance not through crushing competitors directly but by being the first to leverage quantum optimization in its non-tech sector (logistics, drug design, etc.). Can other countries even enforce antitrust concepts if one nation gains a large lead in practical quantum tech? Treaties might be unenforceable if the power disparity is too great. When discussing monopolization, we think of Google. However, what if a smaller entity patents a key post-quantum algorithm? They could become the "gatekeeper" for entire industries without the resources to develop their own.

Quantum's impact on trust breaks down into the user issues of people do not grasp how encryption works now, let alone the nuances of quantum-resistant methods. Will the public trust systems they do not understand, especially in the wake of tech scandals? QKD gets touted as secure due to physics. However, everyday use often involves mixing it with vulnerable classical encryption. Explaining these nuances so people do not fall into either blind faith or total cynicism is a communications challenge unlike any other. If state secrets are no longer safe due to quantum decryption, will this erode trust in the government? Paranoia could grow even if most individuals are never directly targeted.

Those groups that are left behind the quantum technology will eventually understand how to use quantum-safe systems and affording them become the new mark of privilege. This could leave a vast population vulnerable not just to crime but to exploitation by those who *do* control this knowledge. Most discussions in technology forums assume a playing field of wealthy nations. What if the first breakthroughs come from the developing world? This could upend existing power structures, but it also risks exploitation if they lack the internal infrastructure to use their discovery wisely. Quantum security awareness must be baked into essential digital literacy education efforts. We cannot wait until the crisis hits, as the gap will be too wide to close.

Let us dissect how the quantum computing revolution could force a significant restructuring of antitrust regulation.

THE UNIQUE CHALLENGES OF QUANTUM MONOPOLIES

In traditional tech, even giants face disruption by startups. The first to achieve certain milestones with quantum computing could gain an insurmountable lead. Imagine one company that can optimize supply chains with a power no competitor can match for a decade.

It is not just about who can build the most qubits. The specialized talent pool is small. A company that attracts top quantum scientists, even with less powerful hardware, might outpace a better-funded competitor with mediocre staff. This makes it harder to use just capital investment as a regulatory lever. What if a university lab, not seeking market dominance, makes the critical post-quantum crypto breakthrough? They would then be pressured to license it – will the terms be fair, or will fear of quantum hacking create a bidding war that excludes all but the most significant players? If a government heavily subsidizes domestic quantum development, does that count as unfair competition internationally? Nations may claim that any attempt to regulate them attacks their sovereignty.

While there is no perfect parallel to the unique challenges of regulating quantum monopolies, the early days of the biotechnology industry offer some valuable insights and potential lessons,

BIOTECH BEGINNINGS

Biotech started with key scientific breakthroughs and strong university–industry partnerships, leading to the rise of biotech giants that transformed medicine and agriculture.

The Scientific Breakthrough: In the 1970s, the development of recombinant DNA technology revolutionized biology, allowing scientists to manipulate genes with unprecedented precision. This breakthrough had massive potential for medicine, agriculture, and beyond.

University–Industry Nexus: Much like quantum computing, early biotech was driven by academic research. Discoveries often happen in university labs, prompting the need to commercialize them and bring potential treatments to market.

The Rise of Biotech Giants: Companies like Genentech emerged as industry leaders by licensing discoveries from universities, scaling up production, and navigating the complex regulatory landscape. While fostering innovation, this also raised concerns about the concentration of power and potential monopolies.

BIOTECH EARLY DAYS REGULATORY RESPONSES AND LESSONS FOR QUANTUM

In biotech's early days, proactive regulatory measures were vital for ensuring safety while fostering innovation. Balancing incentives and oversight is crucial, with public funding supporting development. Traditional antitrust approaches may struggle to address the unique challenges posed by rapidly evolving technologies like quantum.

The Importance of Early Action: Recognizing the field's potential, the NIH (National Institutes of Health) established guidelines for recombinant DNA research in the 1970s. This early intervention helped address initial safety concerns and set ethical ground rules, even if it did not directly tackle monopolies. Similarly, proactive dialogue about quantum antitrust needs to start now.

Balancing Incentives and Oversight: Patent law played a crucial role in encouraging biotech investment, but the Bayh-Dole Act (1980) allowed universities to retain patent rights on federally funded research, fueling industry partnerships. However, this also potentially gave early players an advantage. Finding ways to reward quantum innovators without entrenching long-term monopolies is critical.

The Role of Public Funding: Significant government funding spurred biotech but came with strings attached. Recipients sometimes had to agree to "reasonable pricing" clauses to ensure treatments were not out of reach for ordinary people. Could similar stipulations be placed on quantum grants, making it harder to gain a stranglehold on a critical technology?

Limits of Traditional Antitrust: Biotech has fallen under existing antitrust laws over time. However, the process has sometimes been slow and reactive. With quantum computing, the need to think about competition from the outset and potentially design new regulatory tools is clear.

While the implications of quantum technology for both human advancement and societal disruption cannot be overstated, it is vital to recognize that this field does not exist in a vacuum. Some caveats and crucial considerations must be acknowledged. First, unlike the "winner takes all" scenarios often seen in software, the multifaceted nature of biotechnology allows multiple companies to succeed. Regulators must diligently identify those areas within the quantum landscape where monopolies are most likely to emerge and create mechanisms to foster a competitive and innovative environment.

Second, the global factor presents a unique challenge. While intellectual property in biotechnology is generally respected globally, national security concerns might lead countries to circumvent or disregard international regulations in the quantum arena. This adds a layer of complexity to governance, demanding new forms of international negotiation and collaboration.

Finally, the uncertain timeline of pivotal quantum breakthroughs poses a significant challenge. In contrast to the more predictable trajectories often seen in biotechnology, quantum's "eureka moments" could drastically alter the regulatory landscape overnight. This demands an unprecedented level of flexibility and foresight from oversight bodies. They must be prepared to rewrite the rules on the fly in response to breakthroughs, ensuring the technology is steered toward progress and not peril.

REGULATORY ACTS HAVE IMPLICATIONS BEYOND THE TECHNICAL

Our current notions of data privacy may be rendered obsolete by quantum decryption. Will we redefine what it means to have "secrets" in a world where our past activities could be laid bare, or will we find even stronger technological countermeasures? Who controls access to quantum cybersecurity tools? If this becomes the new divide between the protected and the vulnerable, it could worsen social tensions and make specific populations targets for exploitation. Quantum hacking will not respect borders. Treaties and ethical norms on using this tech are urgently needed, yet more challenging than ever to achieve in a geopolitically fragmented world. Could we see a race to exploit quantum powers outweighing efforts to manage them responsibly?

The dawn of the quantum security era demands urgent actions to protect the delicate systems and information we increasingly rely on. Our path forward must prioritize proactive investment in post-quantum cryptography, the development of flexible yet robust regulatory frameworks, and comprehensive public education. Delay means vulnerability; we cannot afford to wait for devastating breaches to force us into action.

Regulation, inevitably, will lag behind technology's rapid pace. We need adaptable legal structures that allow swift responses to emerging quantum-powered threats without stifling innovation that can benefit society. Moreover, widespread public education is essential. When individuals understand the potential impact of quantum technologies on their lives, they become a powerful force driving businesses and governments toward prioritizing security.

As we enter this new technological era, the stakes could not be higher. Our choices about deploying and regulating quantum algorithms will profoundly shape global power dynamics, the future of privacy, and the very nature of trust citizens place in digital systems and the institutions that govern them. Let us seize this moment to chart a responsible course, building a future where the power of quantum technologies is harnessed for good, protected from exploitation, and built a more secure world for everyone.

6 Influence of Multitasking on the Rise of Social Engineering Attacks

THE MULTITASKING TRAP: HOW DIGITAL HABITS WORSEN CYBER THREATS

In today's hyper-connected world, where the digital realm seamlessly intertwines with our daily lives, multitasking has become the norm, a badge of efficiency and productivity in an age of constant demands on our attention. However, this relentless pursuit of doing multiple things at once comes at a hidden cost, a vulnerability that cyber attackers are increasingly exploiting: the erosion of our focus and the degradation of our decision-making abilities.

Despite the illusion of multitasking, humans are not wired to truly handle multiple tasks simultaneously. Instead, we rapidly switch between tasks, diverting our attention from one to another, creating a fragmented mental landscape where focus becomes a fleeting commodity. This cognitive switching comes at a price, as our brains struggle to maintain the vigilance and critical thinking required to navigate the complex digital landscape safely.

The consequences of this fragmented attention are particularly evident in the realm of cybersecurity. When our minds are scattered across multiple tasks, we become more susceptible to the subtle manipulations of cyber attackers. We are more likely to miss the telltale signs of a phishing attempt, to overlook security warnings, and to generally make riskier choices online.

Verizon's Data Breach Investigations Report, a comprehensive analysis of cybersecurity incidents, consistently highlights the human factor as the weakest link in the majority of cyberattacks. Even with extensive training and awareness campaigns, well-crafted phishing scams continue to succeed at alarming rates, preying on our distracted minds and exploiting our vulnerabilities.

The illusion of multitasking, coupled with the ever-increasing complexity of the digital world, creates a perfect storm for cyberattacks. As we juggle emails, social media notifications, and work tasks, our ability to maintain focus and make sound decisions diminishes, leaving us susceptible to the cunning tactics of those who seek to exploit our vulnerabilities.

MEDIA MULTITASKING, AMPLIFYING THE PROBLEM

The challenges faced by individuals juggling multiple tasks are significantly amplified in today's media-saturated world. We are constantly bombarded with information, notifications, and stimuli from a multitude of sources, vying for our attention and

DOI: 10.1201/9781003500698-6

fragmenting our focus. This constant state of partial attention makes us more susceptible to errors, oversights, and vulnerabilities, particularly in the realm of cybersecurity.

Research by Hadlington and Murphy highlights the detrimental effects of media multitasking on our cognitive abilities. Constantly switching between platforms, such as social media, email, and messaging apps, depletes our attentional resources, making it more difficult to concentrate on individual tasks and increasing the likelihood of errors. This fragmented attention makes us more susceptible to falling prey to phishing scams, using weak passwords, and oversharing personal information online.

In this hyper-connected world, where distractions are abundant and our attention is constantly divided, there is no single panacea for the challenges of multitasking. Instead, a multifaceted approach that combines various tactics is crucial for mitigating risks and enhancing our cognitive resilience.

One key factor is cultivating mindfulness, the ability to be fully present in the moment and focus on the task at hand. By practicing mindfulness techniques, such as meditation or deep breathing exercises, we can train our minds to resist distractions and maintain focus, reducing the likelihood of errors and enhancing our ability to make sound decisions.

Another crucial aspect is developing effective time management and organizational skills. By prioritizing tasks, setting realistic goals, and utilizing productivity tools, we can streamline our workflow, reduce stress, and minimize the need for constant multitasking.

Furthermore, fostering a culture of cybersecurity awareness is essential. By educating ourselves about the risks of phishing scams, the importance of strong passwords, and the dangers of oversharing personal information, we can empower ourselves to make informed choices and protect our digital well-being.

In conclusion, the challenges of multitasking in a media-saturated world demand a multifaceted approach that combines mindfulness, effective time management, and cybersecurity awareness. By cultivating these skills and adopting a proactive approach to digital well-being, we can navigate the complexities of the digital landscape and mitigate the risks associated with fragmented attention and constant distractions.

Tech Tools Matter but Are Not Enough: Anti-phishing software helps but will not catch everything. We need safety nets at multiple levels.

Mindfulness over Multitasking: Promoting a work culture where single-tasking is encouraged, at least for critical activities. This might initially be unpopular, but the long-term security payoff is worth it.

Training in the Age of Distraction: Security awareness must acknowledge how our brains work against us. Traditional training that assumes perfect focus is unrealistic in the modern workplace.

Design That Helps, Not Hinders: Warnings should catch the eye even for the overloaded user. Security should not be an afterthought in the design of apps and websites.

Individual Responsibility + Systemic Change: Both matter. Blaming "dumb" users lets companies off the hook for designing systems that exploit our cognitive weaknesses.

GAMIFICATION: TURNING SECURITY AWARENESS INTO A REFLEX

Instead of relying on dry, lecture-based cybersecurity training that often falls on deaf ears, consider transforming security awareness into an engaging and interactive game. By framing cybersecurity as a dynamic challenge where quick pattern recognition and the ability to spot anomalies earn points and rewards, we can tap into the very wiring of our brains that makes us so susceptible to the addictive nature of social media.

This approach leverages the power of gamification, transforming mundane security lessons into fast-paced, reward-driven activities that capture attention and foster a proactive security mindset. Imagine a cybersecurity training program that resembles a popular mobile game, complete with levels, challenges, and leaderboards. Users could earn points for correctly identifying phishing emails, spotting suspicious links, or recognizing social engineering tactics.

By incorporating elements of game design, such as immediate feedback, progress indicators, and rewards for achievements, we can create a learning experience that is not only informative but also intrinsically motivating. This approach aligns with how our brains are wired to respond to challenges, rewards, and the satisfaction of mastering new skills.

Furthermore, by tapping into the same psychological mechanisms that social media platforms exploit, we can redirect users' attention toward a more productive and protective purpose. Instead of passively scrolling through feeds and consuming information, users can actively engage in cybersecurity challenges, honing their skills and developing a proactive security mindset.

This gamified approach to cybersecurity training has the potential to transform how we educate individuals about online threats and empower them to protect themselves in the digital world. By making security awareness engaging, interactive, and rewarding, we can cultivate a generation of cyber-savvy individuals who are not only aware of the risks but also equipped with the skills and motivation to mitigate them.

Benefits of this concept are such as meeting people on their level – acknowledges multitasking is the norm. Builds muscle memory for what "feels wrong," potentially catching threats our conscious mind would miss. And it can be competitive, which taps into many people's motivations.

But there are challenges of this concept implementation simply because it requires skillful design to be engaging, not gimmicky. To stay relevant, new "attack patterns" must be regularly updated. Could backfire if people prioritize "winning" over real-world security habits.

HOLDING COMPANIES ACCOUNTABLE FOR "UNSAFE" DESIGN

If a product search takes five clicks, we call it bad design. However, when that difficulty leads to users turning off security features out of frustration, whose fault is it? Companies should be held to a standard of not making secure behavior unreasonably burdensome.

The future of design responsibility in cybersecurity presents two potential paths: proactive regulation or reactive lawsuits. The first path envisions new agencies or empowered existing bodies establishing clear UI security guidelines. These guidelines would set minimum standards for incorporating security into user interfaces, similar to building codes ensuring physical safety in structures. This approach offers the benefit of standardization and proactive prevention but could stifle innovation if overly restrictive.

The alternative path involves the evolution of case law, where legal precedents are set through lawsuits holding companies accountable when demonstrable negligence in UI design directly leads to a security breach. This path, while potentially slower to take hold, appears more likely in the short term, given the current regulatory landscape. It allows for flexibility and adaptation to emerging technologies but relies on the costly and time-consuming process of litigation to drive change.

Both paths have their merits and drawbacks. Proactive regulation offers the potential for standardization and widespread adoption of secure design practices, but it risks stifling innovation if not carefully crafted. Reactive lawsuits, while potentially slower to effect change, allow for flexibility and adaptation to emerging technologies, but they rely on the costly and time-consuming process of litigation to drive progress.

The ideal approach may involve a combination of both paths, with regulatory bodies providing high-level guidance and legal precedents establishing specific standards of accountability. This would create a dynamic and responsive framework that encourages innovation while ensuring that companies prioritize cybersecurity in their design practices.

Ultimately, the responsibility for secure design lies with the companies that create and deploy these technologies. By prioritizing user safety and incorporating cybersecurity considerations into every stage of the design process, companies can build trust, mitigate risks, and contribute to a safer and more secure digital world.

SECURITY EDUCATION FOR THE NEXT SOCIETY GENERATION

Children growing up in today's hyper-connected world face a unique set of challenges when it comes to cybersecurity awareness and online safety. Unlike older generations who had the opportunity to develop "good" digital habits gradually, today's kids are immersed in a digital environment from a very young age. Their baseline is multitasking, with constant exposure to social media, online games, and a barrage of digital stimuli competing for their attention. This constant state of distraction and fragmented attention makes them particularly vulnerable to online manipulation and social engineering tactics.

Teaching children about cybersecurity requires a comprehensive approach that goes beyond simply identifying phishing URLs or recognizing suspicious emails. It must address the deeper psychological and emotional aspects of online interaction, educating them about the dangers of oversharing personal information, the manipulative tactics used by malicious actors to exploit emotions, and the importance of critical thinking and skepticism in the digital realm.

Parents, often overwhelmed by the rapid pace of technological change, may find themselves ill-equipped to guide their children through the complexities of online safety. This highlights the need for community programs, libraries, and educational institutions to step up and fill the gap, providing children with the knowledge and skills they need to navigate the digital world safely and responsibly.

These programs should go beyond technical instruction, incorporating age-appropriate lessons on digital citizenship, online ethics, and the importance of critical thinking and media literacy. By empowering children with the tools and knowledge to recognize and resist online manipulation, we can help them develop healthy digital habits and cultivate a resilient mindset in the face of ever-evolving cyber threats.

CHALLENGES

Security changes fast – what is taught could be outdated quickly. Competing with the "fun" kids experience elsewhere online is hard and Risks exacerbating the digital divide, as well-supported schools will have an edge. Sadly, there is no easy solution upon which everyone will readily agree. Fund gamified security training in a few workplaces or schools to rigorously measure results vs. traditional methods. Success breeds adoption. Security researchers should start publicly shaming breaches and the UI choices that contributed to them. This builds pressure on companies.

Instead of demanding just "screen time" limits, make tech companies hear that they want tools and settings designed to make safe usage easier for families.

Amplified by our media-rich digital landscape, the multitasking mindset has inadvertently opened the door to a new era of cyber threats. While traditional technical defenses remain vital, they are no longer enough. The battleground has shifted into our brains, where the struggle for focus and attention is critical to staying safe online.

Addressing this crisis demands a shift in how we think about cybersecurity. Blaming individuals for falling victim to attacks designed to exploit their natural wiring is a dead end. Gamified awareness training, stronger design accountability, and security education that starts in childhood offer pathways forward. This will not be easy. Companies profit from keeping us engaged, not from keeping us safe. Habits are hard to break in ourselves and the systems around us. However, the stakes are too high to ignore. Our privacy, the integrity of our institutions, and perhaps even our sense of self may depend on finding ways to reconcile our digital world with the limitations of the human mind.

7 Influence of Surveillance on the Rise of Social Engineering Attacks

WHEN SURVEILLANCE BACKFIRES: INCREASED SECURITY RISKS IN THE WORKPLACE

Implementing workplace surveillance with the best intentions can create unintended cybersecurity vulnerabilities. Employees who feel constantly watched may become resentful and disengaged. This erodes the trust vital for a strong security culture. They may be less likely to report mistakes (like falling for a phishing scam) out of fear, allowing threats to spread unchecked. Surveillance also creates a high-pressure environment where anxiety is common. Stressed people make poor choices – the kind social engineers exploit. A panicked employee bypassing security protocols to "fix" something they fear getting in trouble for poses a severe risk. The money spent on surveillance tech is *not* spent on training users or hardening systems. An imbalance in the security approach is dangerous. Hackers love backdoors. Complex monitoring tools, often hastily implemented, can create new ways *into* a company's network. Privacy laws are complex. Employers may think they are covered, only to face costly lawsuits later. This distraction weakens their overall security posture.

Imagine a heavily monitored office. Employees know every keystroke is logged and web traffic tracked. This was meant to boost productivity, but the feeling is more like being treated as a suspect, not a valued team member. A phishing email, seemingly from the CEO, demands sensitive data by the end of the day, or someone will be fired. In a healthier work environment, this would raise red flags. However, between the stress and a culture of fear, clicking that malicious link starts to look like the less risky option.

It is a mistake to think surveillance *is* security. Organizations need a holistic approach to security awareness training should be empowering, not threatening. Open communication channels help people feel safe reporting incidents. Strong firewalls and up-to-date software matter more than most fancy monitoring tools. Clear guidelines on what monitoring, if any, is done and why can ease employee concerns and protect the company legally.

SECURITY AND A HEALTHY WORKPLACE ARE NOT IN CONFLICT – THEY GO HAND IN HAND

In the realm of cybersecurity, where the protection of sensitive data and the prevention of malicious attacks are paramount, the conventional approach often leans toward stringent controls, surveillance, and a culture of distrust. However, a growing

DOI: 10.1201/9781003500698-7

body of evidence suggests that a more effective strategy lies in fostering a culture of trust and empowering employees to become active participants in the cybersecurity ecosystem.

Let us examine how building trust, rather than fostering paranoia, can be the cornerstone of a robust cybersecurity strategy. When employees feel micromanaged and constantly monitored through intrusive surveillance systems, a sense of distrust permeates the workplace. This erosion of trust not only destroys morale but also ironically leads to employees doing the bare minimum, ultimately hurting the very productivity that surveillance was intended to increase.

Moreover, the best tech workers, those with the skills and expertise to navigate the complex landscape of cybersecurity, are highly sought after and have options. Overly surveilled workplaces will struggle to attract and retain these top talents, who value freedom, autonomy, and a workplace culture built on respect and trust.

When fear becomes the primary motivator in a cybersecurity strategy, mistakes are more likely to be hidden rather than fixed. This creates a false sense of security for management, while minor breaches and vulnerabilities fester, potentially escalating into major security incidents.

Furthermore, severely distrustful environments can breed resentment and disengagement among employees. A disgruntled employee with access to sensitive information and systems poses a far greater threat than an outside hacker, especially if they possess the knowledge and skills to circumvent the surveillance measures designed to catch them.

In contrast, a workplace culture built on trust and transparency fosters a sense of shared responsibility for cybersecurity. When employees feel valued, respected, and empowered, they are more likely to become proactive partners in protecting the organization's digital assets. Open communication channels, where employees feel comfortable reporting potential vulnerabilities or security incidents without fear of reprisal, are essential for creating a robust cybersecurity posture.

Investing in cybersecurity training and awareness programs that educate employees about cyber threats and best practices can further empower them to become active participants in the organization's defense strategy. By fostering a culture of trust, transparency, and shared responsibility, organizations can create a more secure and resilient cybersecurity environment, where employees are not merely subjects of surveillance but rather valued partners in the ongoing effort to protect sensitive data and mitigate cyber risks.

HOW TRUST CREATES A SECURITY CULTURE

Cybersecurity training that truly empowers goes beyond simply dictating rules and regulations. It focuses on fostering a sense of shared responsibility, transforming users from potential liabilities into active partners in safeguarding digital assets. By emphasizing the "why" behind security protocols and the potential consequences of noncompliance, organizations can cultivate a culture of cybersecurity awareness.

When individuals understand the nature of cyber threats and the importance of their role in maintaining a secure digital environment, they become more invested in behaving safely. This proactive engagement is strengthened by establishing clear channels for reporting suspicious activity. For example, a dedicated email address or online form for reporting phishing attempts or suspicious websites can encourage employees to take action without fear of reprisal.

In today's tech-savvy workforce, attempting to implement covert monitoring strategies is not only ethically questionable but also likely to backfire. If limited monitoring is necessary, transparency is key. Organizations should clearly communicate the rationale behind the monitoring, involve employees in crafting the policy, and ensure responsible data handling.

Furthermore, celebrating employees who actively contribute to cybersecurity efforts can have a powerful impact. Publicly acknowledging those who thwart phishing attempts or identify vulnerabilities reinforces positive behavior and fosters a sense of collective responsibility.

Effective cybersecurity training is not just about imparting knowledge; it's about cultivating a culture of awareness, responsibility, and trust. By empowering individuals, fostering open communication, and recognizing contributions, organizations can create a cybersecurity ecosystem where everyone plays a vital role in safeguarding digital assets. This requires a multifaceted approach, including interactive training modules, regular communication updates, and positive reinforcement mechanisms, to ensure that cybersecurity becomes an integral part of the organizational culture.

DATA VERIFICATION AND REVIEWS, TOPICS FOR FURTHER CONVERSATION

The purpose of this section is to create an excitement line for further reading/conversation. You cannot go from surveillance-heavy to complete trust overnight. It must move in small steps that are critical, such as showing employees that the change and shifting paradigm is genuine. People handling sensitive critical data should have different monitoring capabilities than a social media manager. Transparency means explaining this distinction, not hiding it. If the C-suite breaks security rules, no amount of training for lower-level staff will fix things. The trust-based approach has to start at the top and while it is difficult to find companies willing to go on record admitting their past reliance on surveillance, there are some examples we can look to and trends that suggest this mindset is changing. Unfortunately, a common trigger for change is a significant security incident due to human error. So, resilience factors such as investigation might reveal that a culture of fear made things worse. We are unlikely to get a company saying this publicly, but security consultants who advise in these situations could offer anonymized examples. Some tech-forward companies, especially smaller ones, prioritize attracting top developers, etc. These workplaces are often more focused on output than logging every keystroke. While they will not frame it as a past mistake, their security model might be instructive. Are there sectors (healthcare, perhaps, with its privacy focus) where we see a move *away* from heavy surveillance alongside strong security outcomes? This suggests a correlation between trust and robust defenses, even without named cases.

Decreased incident reports might mean people are better at hiding things, not that risk is lower. Looking for the following cases/questions where the metrics go beyond "rule breaking" caught; is very crucial for further understanding,

Did the behavior shift come with a rebranding of security as "protecting our team, not spying on it"? Glassdoor reviews do not tell the whole story, but a sudden uptick in mentions of feeling "trusted" around the same time security tools changed is a clue worth exploring. Are there security experts, either consultants or academics, known for advocating a human-centric, less surveillance-focused approach? Check their blogs, conference talks, etc. They might have general examples, even if they do not name companies. Instead of searching "surveillance to trust," look for companies touting meagre incident rates, fast response times, etc. Then, dig into their HR materials – do they emphasize respect for employees alongside their security narrative? This might hint at the approach. Did a significant security framework (NIST, etc.) shift its language on user behavior in the last few years? If so, case studies accompanying new guidelines might provide before/after examples of how this plays out in the real world. Pick a field where BOTH security and employee privacy are top concerns. Look at smaller companies where they are less likely to have entrenched surveillance practices and more willing to tout their positive culture to attract talent. Do not just attend vendor-heavy mega-events. Seek out smaller security conferences with tracks like "Security Culture" or "The Psychology of Cybersecurity." Speakers here are more likely to grapple with the nuances of the trust issue. Publications on organizational psychology or change management might discuss security shifts as part of broader workplace trends. Do not limit your search to tech-only sources.

Do you know anyone who works in cybersecurity or at a company with a reputation for being both secure AND a great workplace? Even off-the-record conversations can reveal if the trust-based approach is a factor in their success. LinkedIn (and even Twitter, with the right hashtags) lets you target people with job titles like "Head of Information Security" at companies of a specific size/industry. A carefully worded post asking about non-tech ways they have improved security might yield leads. Sites like Glassdoor or Blind are tricky, as a single disgruntled employee can skew things. However, if you see a pattern of positive security reviews linked to themes of respect and empowerment, that is a company worth investigating further.

The concept of "partial examples" offers a pragmatic and insightful approach to navigating the complex terrain of organizational change, particularly when it comes to shifting from a culture of surveillance to one of trust. Recognizing that expecting a company to undergo a complete metamorphosis overnight is unrealistic, we must instead embrace the power of incremental progress, of showcasing those "partial examples" that illuminate the path toward a more balanced and humane workplace.

These partial examples serve as beacons, demonstrating that even amidst a broader culture of surveillance, pockets of trust and autonomy can exist and flourish. They provide tangible evidence that change is possible, inspiring others to follow suit and gradually shifting the organizational tide toward a more empowering and fulfilling environment.

To truly harness the power of these partial examples, we must delve deeper, examining their nuances, understanding their successes, and learning from their limitations. This requires a multifaceted approach, one that combines qualitative and quantitative analysis, storytelling, and a genuine curiosity to uncover the human stories behind these organizational shifts.

We can begin by identifying those departments, teams, or even individual managers who have successfully implemented trust-based practices within a broader surveillance-oriented culture. What specific strategies did they employ? How did they navigate the challenges and resistance? What were the tangible outcomes of their efforts?

By documenting these success stories, we can provide concrete examples for others to emulate, demonstrating that change is not only possible but also beneficial. These stories can inspire hope, ignite conversations, and empower individuals to advocate for change within their own teams and departments.

However, it is equally important to examine the limitations of these partial examples. Were there any unintended consequences? Did the trust-based practices create new vulnerabilities or challenges? By acknowledging these limitations, we can foster a more realistic and nuanced understanding of the complexities of organizational change.

Ultimately, the concept of "partial examples" offers a powerful lens through which to examine the ongoing struggle between surveillance and trust in the workplace. By showcasing these nuanced cases, we can inspire hope, foster dialogue, and empower individuals and organizations to navigate the path toward a more balanced and humane future of work.

Targeted surveillance reduction is crucial, for either keystroke logging or tracking web traffic due to past incidents. Even a partial move between two suggests areas needs a thorough understanding of the impact on morale. The critical question is: Did that change measurably improve security outcomes?

Transparency as a first step is perhaps critical to indicate if they still monitor heavily, but now there is a clear policy employees were involved in shaping. Is there evidence that this reduced resentment? Even if security metrics are not plentiful yet, they are willing to evolve their approach.

Employees may choose between a heavily monitored way of doing things and a less restrictive one for non-essential tasks. Did this improve the adoption of secure practices by those who value freedom over convenience? The Reframing potentially replaces a draconian "User Security Policy" with an "Employee Partnership for Data Protection" type document. This shift in language alone demonstrates a move toward emphasizing collaboration over control.

The quest to uncover case studies of companies successfully shifting away from a surveillance-heavy mindset demonstrates the complexities of cybersecurity in the real world. While the ideal of a security culture built on trust is compelling, the path toward it is rarely a straight line.

By focusing on partial examples, we gain valuable insights. We see that even small changes, like targeted surveillance reduction or increased transparency, can positively impact employee morale and security outcomes. These examples provide realistic models for organizations seeking to improve their security posture and encourage a nuanced dialogue about finding the right balance for their unique circumstances.

The search for these stories underscores that cybersecurity is not just about technology but about understanding human behavior and building organizational cultures where employees feel empowered to be part of the solution. This is an ongoing journey, and by continuing to share insights, best practices, and even lessons learned from setbacks, we can move the cybersecurity field toward an approach that is both effective and respects the individuals it is meant to protect.

8 Influence of Cannabis and Drugs on the Rise of Social Engineering Attacks

CANNABIS, COGNITION, AND CYBERSECURITY: EXPLORING THE LINK TO SOCIAL ENGINEERING

Understanding how substances impact human cognition is crucial for robust cybersecurity. This article focuses on cannabis use and how it might make people more susceptible to social engineering attacks.

CANNABIS AND THE BRAIN

Cannabis, a widely used recreational and medicinal substance, exerts its effects through the psychoactive compound THC (tetrahydrocannabinol). THC interacts with the brain's endocannabinoid system, affecting regions responsible for cognitive functions such as memory, attention, decision-making, and perception. Studies suggest that cannabis use can temporarily impair these functions, potentially making individuals more susceptible to the deceptive tactics employed in cyberattacks.

Social engineering attacks, unlike traditional cyberattacks that exploit technical vulnerabilities, prey on human psychology and social dynamics. Attackers skillfully manipulate trust, create a sense of urgency, or exploit cognitive weaknesses to trick victims into revealing sensitive information or taking harmful actions. Even a momentary lapse in judgment, a fleeting distraction, or an altered perception can be enough to fall prey to these cunning tactics.

While cannabis use can be a personal choice for many individuals, it's crucial to acknowledge its potential impact on cognitive functions and cybersecurity awareness. The temporary impairment of memory, attention, and decision-making abilities could make individuals more vulnerable to social engineering attacks. For instance, an individual under the influence of cannabis might be more susceptible to phishing emails, more likely to click on malicious links, or less discerning when sharing personal information online.

It is essential to emphasize that this is not a condemnation of cannabis use but rather a call for awareness and responsible behavior. Individuals who choose to use cannabis should be mindful of its potential cognitive effects and take extra precautions to protect themselves from cyber threats. This could include avoiding online activities that require critical thinking or decision-making while under the influence,

DOI: 10.1201/9781003500698-8

being extra vigilant when interacting with emails and websites, and utilizing security tools like two-factor authentication and password managers to add layers of protection.

Furthermore, organizations and cybersecurity professionals should consider the potential impact of cannabis use on employee cybersecurity awareness and training programs. Training materials should be designed to be accessible and engaging, even for individuals with temporarily impaired cognitive functions. Regular reminders about cybersecurity best practices and the red flags of social engineering attacks can help mitigate the risks associated with cannabis use.

By fostering a culture of awareness and responsible behavior, both individuals and organizations can work together to mitigate the potential cybersecurity risks associated with cannabis use. This includes promoting education about the cognitive effects of cannabis, encouraging responsible use, and implementing cybersecurity measures that account for the potential vulnerabilities associated with temporary cognitive impairment.

The ways cannabis might heighten social engineering risks include:

Decision-Making: Impaired judgment might make a risky link seem less dangerous or cause someone to underestimate the consequences of their actions.

Memory and Focus: Short-term memory issues and trouble concentrating could make it harder to spot the inconsistencies that often give away phishing attempts.

Suggestibility: There is limited evidence that cannabis may make some people more accessible to manipulate, which is a crucial tool for social engineers.

WHAT ORGANIZATIONS AND INDIVIDUALS CAN DO

There is a need for more research to understand this link fully, but proactive steps are wise:

Realistic Training: Security awareness programs should not assume perfect mental functioning. Simulating how these attacks work when someone is tired, stressed, etc., is more effective.

Security Culture: Employees should feel comfortable reporting suspicious things without fear of punishment. This can offset the moments when someone's judgment is less than ideal.

Tech Defenses Still Matter: Anti-phishing tools and multi-factor authentication add layers of protection, even if human error remains a risk.

Focus on Wellness: Promoting overall health, including good sleep and stress management, benefits cognition, indirectly aiding cybersecurity.

The relationship between cannabis use, cognitive function, and susceptibility to social engineering is a complex and multifaceted one, demanding careful consideration and further research to fully understand its implications. While cannabis has been used for medicinal and recreational purposes for centuries, its impact on cognitive processes, particularly those involved in decision-making, judgment, and critical thinking, remains a subject of ongoing scientific inquiry.

The psychoactive compounds in cannabis, particularly THC, can induce a range of cognitive effects, including alterations in perception, memory, and attention. These effects can vary depending on the individual, the dosage, and the specific strain of cannabis used. While some studies suggest that moderate cannabis use may have minimal impact on cognitive function in regular users, other research indicates that chronic or heavy use can lead to persistent cognitive deficits, particularly in individuals who begin using cannabis during adolescence.

The potential link between cannabis use and susceptibility to social engineering attacks lies in the cognitive processes involved in recognizing and responding to deceptive tactics. Social engineering often preys on human vulnerabilities, such as trust, empathy, and the desire to be helpful. Attackers exploit these vulnerabilities to manipulate individuals into divulging sensitive information, granting unauthorized access, or performing actions that compromise security.

If cannabis use impairs cognitive functions such as critical thinking, decision-making, and the ability to discern deceptive cues, it could potentially increase an individual's susceptibility to social engineering attacks. Individuals under the influence of cannabis may be more likely to overlook red flags, trust unreliable sources, or make impulsive decisions that compromise their security or the security of their organization.

However, it is crucial to acknowledge that the relationship between cannabis use and social engineering susceptibility is not a simple cause-and-effect one. Various factors, such as individual differences in cognitive function, the specific strain and dosage of cannabis used, and the context of the social engineering attack, can all influence the outcome.

Further research is needed to untangle this complex relationship fully. Longitudinal studies that track the cognitive effects of cannabis use over time, as well as experimental studies that assess the impact of cannabis on susceptibility to social engineering tactics, are crucial for gaining a deeper understanding of this issue.

In the meantime, acknowledging the potential vulnerability associated with cannabis use is essential for developing effective strategies to protect individuals and organizations from increasingly sophisticated social engineering attacks. This includes promoting awareness of the cognitive effects of cannabis, encouraging responsible use, and providing education and training on how to recognize and respond to social engineering tactics.

By addressing this issue proactively and fostering a culture of cybersecurity awareness, we can help individuals make informed choices about cannabis use and minimize the potential risks associated with impaired cognitive function in the digital age.

Let us illustrate the connection between cannabis use and social engineering vulnerability with a real-life example. Please note: this is a fictionalized scenario for illustrative purposes, and it is important not to stigmatize individuals struggling with substance use.

CASE STUDY: SARAH, THE OVERWORKED DESIGNER

Sarah is a talented graphic designer at a fast-paced startup. The long hours and constant deadlines create a high-stress environment. To cope, Sarah began using cannabis occasionally in the evenings to unwind. Over time, her use became more frequent and heavier. While she felt it helped her manage anxiety initially, it started having unintended consequences.

Sarah's increased cannabis use began affecting her work. Minor memory lapses became more common, and she found it more challenging to focus on complex tasks. Though a skilled designer, she started missing small but essential details.

One particularly hectic afternoon, Sarah received an email seemingly from the company's CEO. The email, with a subject line marked "Urgent," requested that she immediately transfer funds to a new vendor to secure a critical deal. Feeling the pressure and foggy from cannabis use the night before, Sarah's judgment was compromised. The urgency in the email overrode her usual caution, and she initiated the transfer.

It was only later that Sarah realized several red flags she had missed: a slight misspelling in the CEO's email address, the unusual tone of the request, and the fact that the vendor was not on their approved list. The email was a well-crafted phishing attack, and Sarah's compromised cognitive state made her an easy target.

TAKEAWAYS FROM SARAH'S EXPERIENCE

The Importance of Cognitive Clarity: Cybersecurity often hinges on those small moments of critical thinking when we question if something is right. Cannabis-induced impairment can make it harder to have those "wait a minute…" moments.

Stress Is a Multiplying Factor: Sarah's work environment meant even occasional cannabis use had a more significant impact. Attackers know this, making those in high-pressure roles prime targets.

The Ripple Effects: The fallout from the breach extended beyond the lost funds. Client trust was damaged, and Sarah faced disciplinary action. This added stress fueled a cycle that worsened both her substance use and her vulnerability to future attacks.

ESSENTIAL CONSIDERATIONS FOR FURTHER THINKING

We Need More Data: Case studies like Sarah's are anecdotal. Rigorous research is needed to determine how widespread this risk is and whether specific demographics are more affected.

Responsibility Is Shared: Blaming everything on Sarah's choices is unhelpful. Companies that foster burnout-inducing work cultures create an environment where mistakes of all kinds become more common.

Support, Not Stigma: Individuals struggling with substance use and cybersecurity concerns need access to resources that address both aspects in a non-judgmental way.

The intersection of cannabis use, cognitive function, and the heightened risk of social engineering attacks presents a complex challenge with far-reaching implications. While further research is crucial to fully quantify the specific risks, compelling case studies like Sarah's underscore the potential for even occasional substance use to weaken our cognitive defenses in the digital world.

This issue defies simplistic solutions or blame-shifting. Organizations bear an ethical responsibility to cultivate work environments that prioritize both cybersecurity and employee well-being. Heavy workloads, chronic stress, and unrealistic expectations create fertile ground for vulnerability, and substance use may exacerbate these existing risks. By fostering a culture of support, promoting healthy work–life balance, and addressing the root causes of stress and burnout, organizations can bolster their employees' cognitive resilience and reduce their susceptibility to social engineering attacks.

Furthermore, it is imperative to prioritize robust support systems for individuals grappling with the intersection of substance use and cybersecurity concerns. Approaches centered on harm reduction, education, and destigmatization are essential. This includes providing access to evidence-based information about the cognitive effects of cannabis, promoting awareness of online risks and responsible digital behavior, and offering resources for managing substance use and its associated challenges.

Ultimately, addressing the complex interplay between cannabis, cognition, and social engineering necessitates a holistic strategy that encompasses research, education, workplace culture, and individual support. By continuing to investigate the cognitive impacts of cannabis use, promoting healthy work environments, and empowering individuals with the knowledge and resources they need to make informed choices, we can work toward a future where cybersecurity is strengthened, and individuals are supported in their pursuit of both well-being and digital safety.

9 Influence of Aging on the Rise of Social Engineering Attacks

AGING AND THE GROWING THREAT OF SOCIAL ENGINEERING: PROTECTING OUR MOST VULNERABLE ONLINE

The internet, a vast and ever-expanding digital landscape, offers a wealth of opportunities for connection, learning, and entertainment. However, alongside its many benefits, the internet also exposes users to a myriad of dangers, including the insidious threat of social engineering attacks. These attacks, which prey on human psychology rather than technical vulnerabilities, are particularly concerning for older adults, who may be less familiar with the intricacies of the digital world and more susceptible to manipulation tactics.

Social engineering attacks are crafted to exploit our innate trust, our desire to help, and our fear of missing out. Attackers may impersonate trusted figures, such as government officials or bank representatives, using sophisticated phishing emails or phone calls to trick victims into revealing sensitive information like passwords or credit card numbers. They may also play on emotions, creating a sense of urgency or fear to coerce individuals into taking harmful actions, such as wiring money or downloading malware.

Older adults, often less familiar with the nuances of online security and the deceptive tactics employed by cybercriminals, are particularly vulnerable to these attacks. They may be more trusting of authority figures or less likely to question suspicious emails or phone calls. Additionally, cognitive decline associated with aging can make individuals more susceptible to manipulation and less able to recognize red flags.

The consequences of falling victim to a social engineering attack can be devastating, ranging from financial loss and identity theft to emotional distress and damage to reputation. It is crucial, therefore, to empower older adults with the knowledge and skills to navigate the digital world safely and confidently.

This includes providing education on common social engineering tactics, such as phishing scams, impersonation schemes, and emotional manipulation. It also involves fostering a culture of cybersecurity awareness, encouraging older adults to question suspicious requests, verify information before taking action, and seek help from trusted sources when in doubt.

By raising awareness, providing education, and fostering a supportive environment, we can help older adults navigate the digital world safely and confidently, protecting them from the insidious threat of social engineering attacks and empowering them to fully enjoy the benefits of the internet.

DOI: 10.1201/9781003500698-9

FACTORS INCREASING RISK FOR OLDER ADULTS

Older adults face a digital landscape fraught with peril. The digital skills gap, often a chasm between generations, leaves them vulnerable to the deceptive tactics of online scammers and the insidious spread of misinformation. Navigating the complexities of the internet, with its ever-evolving technologies and social media platforms, can be daunting for those unfamiliar with its nuances. This lack of digital literacy makes older adults susceptible to phishing scams, where seemingly trustworthy emails or websites lure them into revealing personal information or financial credentials. The proliferation of fake news and online hoaxes further compounds the problem, as older adults may struggle to discern fact from fiction in the swirling vortex of the internet.

Adding to these challenges, the natural cognitive changes that accompany aging can further impair their ability to recognize and respond to online threats. Memory decline, diminished processing speed, and difficulties with multitasking can make it harder to identify red flags, such as suspicious email addresses or inconsistencies in online narratives. These cognitive vulnerabilities, combined with a generationally ingrained tendency toward trust and a heightened susceptibility to loneliness, make older adults prime targets for fraudsters and scammers.

The desire for connection and companionship, often amplified by social isolation and the loss of loved ones, can make older adults more likely to fall victim to scams that prey on their emotions. Fraudsters, adept at manipulating trust and exploiting vulnerabilities, may pose as friendly acquaintances, helpful customer service representatives, or even romantic interests to gain the confidence of older adults and ultimately defraud them of their hard-earned savings.

Together, these factors create a challenging environment for older adults in the digital age, threatening not only their financial security but also their emotional well-being and sense of safety. Addressing these challenges requires a multi-pronged approach, encompassing digital literacy training, enhanced online security measures, and social support systems that combat loneliness and foster a sense of community. By empowering older adults with the knowledge, skills, and support they need to navigate the digital world safely and confidently, we can ensure that they remain active and engaged participants in the digital age, reaping its benefits without falling prey to its perils.

The Digital Skill Gap: Many seniors did not grow up with the internet and struggled to keep up with changing scams and security best practices.

Cognitive Changes: Even subtle age-related decline in memory and attention can make it harder to spot the red flags of a phishing attempt, etc.

Exploiting Trust and Loneliness: Scammers know older adults may be eager for connection and will craft messages designed to exploit feelings of fear, urgency, or the desire to be helpful.

Social engineering attacks on the elderly are not just a privacy issue. Victims can lose their life savings, have their medical identities stolen, or be drawn into deeper criminal schemes without realizing it.

Training programs must acknowledge older adults' challenges and focus on simple, memorable safety rules, not complex tech jargon. Anti-phishing tools, large-font warnings on websites, etc., can help, but they also need to be usable by those with less tech experience.

Libraries, senior centers, and even families must foster a "no-shame" culture around asking for help with things online. This prevents people from hiding mistakes and becoming even more vulnerable.

Companies that serve a large older customer base have an ethical duty to design websites and apps with their needs in mind, reducing where scammers can trick them. Protecting older adults online is not just about individual responsibility. It requires a shift in how we educate, design technology, and support those most likely to be targeted by social engineering attacks.

Let us integrate a case study to illustrate the real-world dangers of social engineering attacks targeting older adults:

CASE STUDY: WILLIAM AND THE "URGENT" BANK EMAIL

William, a 72-year-old retiree, considered himself reasonably careful online. He mostly used the internet to check his email and catch up on the news. However, one morning, he received an email that seemed to be from his bank. The subject line read "ACTION REQUIRED: Security Alert," the email warned that his account might be compromised.

Feeling a jolt of anxiety, William opened the email. It stated that he needed to click a link and verify his account details immediately to prevent his funds from being frozen. The email looked official, with the bank's logo and familiar colors. Trusting the sender, William clicked the link without hesitation.

The link took him to a website nearly identical to his bank's login page. Without a second thought, William entered his username and password and answered several security questions he thought were confirming his identity. Once he hit "submit," the website seemed to glitch, but he assumed it was a temporary technical issue.

It was not until days later, when William tried to pay a bill online that he discovered his bank account was nearly empty. Panic-stricken, he called his bank, where he learned he had been the victim of an elaborate phishing scam. The fraudulent email and website were designed to steal his login credentials, granting cybercriminals access to his life savings.

LESSONS LEARNED FROM WILLIAM'S EXPERIENCE

William's experience teaches us that urgency can manipulate decision-making, making it vital to approach challenges with a discerning eye. It reminds us that appearances can be deceptive and that every detail, no matter how small, can influence the outcome significantly.

Urgency Is a Weapon: Scammers know that creating a sense of panic overrides careful thinking. William's fear of having his account frozen led him to act without proper scrutiny.

Things Are Not Always as They Seem: Attackers are skilled at mimicking the look and feel of legitimate websites. Even someone who thinks they are being cautious can be fooled.

No Detail Is Too Small: Had William noticed the slightly misspelled web address of the fake bank site, he might have avoided the trap. However, stress and the expectation of the correct URL closed his eyes to this vital red flag.

Senior to rely on the effectiveness of the training and shows others that they are not alone in facing these challenges. By combining these educational strategies, we can empower older adults like William to become more discerning online users. Educating them on spotting scams, providing practical skills to verify information, and fostering a supportive environment where they feel comfortable asking for help are all crucial steps in safeguarding them from the growing threat of social engineering attacks.

The case of William serves as a stark reminder of the vulnerability that older adults often face in the digital landscape. Their trust, potential for cognitive changes, and, in some cases, lack of familiarity with the latest scam tactics make them especially susceptible to social engineering attacks. These attacks inflict substantial financial, emotional, and reputational damage on their victims.

However, this challenge is not insurmountable. Through targeted educational initiatives, a focus on practical skills, and the creation of supportive environments, we can significantly enhance the cybersecurity readiness of older adults. By teaching them to question, verify, and seek help when uncertain, we empower them to take control of their online safety.

Educational approaches must be tailored to this population with clarity and compassion. Condescension must be avoided, and open dialogue must be fostered. Older adults should feel comfortable admitting confusion or uncertainty. By replacing fear with knowledge, we build a more resilient online community for seniors.

It is essential to acknowledge that this effort goes beyond individual responsibility. Companies that market heavily to older consumers have an ethical duty to design websites and apps that are easy to navigate and do not inadvertently make users more vulnerable. We need policymakers to consider regulations that make scams explicitly targeting seniors easier to prosecute and offer better protections for victims.

The fight against social engineering is not a battle fought on a single front; it is a multifaceted campaign that demands a comprehensive strategy acknowledging the ever-evolving nature of these insidious threats. It requires a concerted effort from individuals, organizations, and society as a whole to build a robust defense against the cunning tactics of social engineers.

Education is paramount in empowering individuals to recognize and resist social engineering ploys. By fostering awareness of common tactics, such as phishing scams, impersonation schemes, and emotional manipulation, we can equip people with the knowledge and critical thinking skills to identify and avoid these threats. This education must be ongoing, adapting to the ever-changing landscape of social engineering techniques and incorporating the latest insights into human psychology and online behavior.

Technological safeguards play a crucial role in bolstering our defenses against social engineering attacks. Robust spam filters, multi-factor authentication, and intrusion detection systems can help to thwart attempts to compromise sensitive information or gain unauthorized access to systems. However, technology alone is not enough. Social engineers prey on human vulnerabilities, exploiting trust, emotions, and cognitive biases to achieve their goals.

Therefore, we must cultivate a culture that values the experience of older adults and recognizes their right to be safe online. This includes promoting intergenerational digital literacy programs, providing accessible cybersecurity resources, and creating supportive online communities where older adults can share their experiences and learn from one another. It also means challenging ageist stereotypes that portray older adults as technologically inept or vulnerable, recognizing that individuals of all ages can fall victim to social engineering tactics.

By embracing a multifaceted approach that combines education, technology, and a culture of respect and inclusivity, we can work toward a digital world where people of all ages can reap the benefits of technology without falling prey to the manipulative tactics of social engineers. This is not merely a fight against cybercrime; it is a fight to preserve trust, protect vulnerable individuals, and ensure that the digital age empowers rather than exploits.

10 Influence of Depression and Anxiety on the Rise of Social Engineering Attacks

THE HIDDEN COST OF MENTAL HEALTH STRUGGLES: INCREASED CYBERSECURITY RISK

Depression and anxiety cast a long shadow over individuals and communities, impacting not only mental well-being but also creating vulnerabilities in the digital realm. These conditions, often characterized by feelings of hopelessness, isolation, and impaired judgment, can make individuals more susceptible to social engineering attacks, where malicious actors exploit psychological weaknesses to gain access to sensitive information or manipulate behavior. Older adults, already facing challenges such as decreased cognitive function and lower digital literacy, are particularly vulnerable to these insidious tactics.

Depression can cloud judgment and erode self-confidence, making individuals more likely to fall victim to scams that prey on their emotions. Attackers may pose as authority figures, offering false promises of financial relief or companionship, exploiting the vulnerabilities of those seeking connection or struggling with financial insecurity. Anxiety, with its heightened sense of fear and urgency, can further impair decision-making, leading individuals to act impulsively without fully considering the consequences. Attackers may use scare tactics or create a false sense of urgency to pressure individuals into divulging personal information or making hasty decisions.

The combination of depression, anxiety, and age-related cognitive decline creates a perfect storm of vulnerability. Older adults, less familiar with the digital landscape and its potential threats, may be more trusting of online interactions and less likely to recognize the red flags of social engineering attacks. Attackers may exploit this trust, posing as familiar organizations or individuals to gain access to sensitive information such as bank accounts, social security numbers, or medical records.

The consequences of falling victim to social engineering attacks can be devastating, leading to financial loss, identity theft, and emotional distress. For older adults, these experiences can further compound feelings of isolation, vulnerability, and loss of control, exacerbating existing mental health challenges.

Protecting older adults from social engineering attacks requires a multifaceted approach. Education and awareness campaigns can empower individuals to recognize the red flags of these attacks and develop strategies to protect themselves online. Supportive communities and family members can play a crucial role in providing

DOI: 10.1201/9781003500698-10

guidance and assistance, ensuring that older adults feel connected and supported in navigating the digital world.

Furthermore, technology itself can be harnessed to enhance protection. The development of user-friendly security tools, AI-powered scam detection systems, and accessible online resources can help create a safer and more inclusive digital environment for older adults.

By addressing the unique vulnerabilities faced by older adults with depression and anxiety, we can empower them to navigate the digital world safely and confidently, protecting their well-being and fostering a more inclusive and resilient digital society.

HOW ATTACKERS EXPLOIT MENTAL HEALTH

Cybercriminals are masters of manipulation, adept at exploiting not only technological vulnerabilities but also the emotional landscape of their victims. They understand that a person gripped by fear, sadness, or anxiety is less likely to engage in critical thinking, making them an easy target for deception and manipulation.

These emotional weapons are often wielded through carefully crafted narratives designed to bypass rational defenses. Fake emergencies, such as a loved one in distress or a critical system failure, can trigger a panic response, prompting victims to act impulsively without considering the potential consequences. Threats of financial loss, reputational damage, or even physical harm can instill fear and compel victims to comply with the attacker's demands. Conversely, promises of relief, such as a miraculous cure or a financial windfall, can exploit desperation and bypass rational skepticism.

The cognitive impact of depression, particularly the difficulty concentrating and the pervasive sense of hopelessness, can further exacerbate vulnerability to cyberattacks. Even individuals who possess the technical knowledge to identify phishing attempts or other online threats may find it challenging to apply that knowledge when their cognitive functions are impaired by depression.

Moreover, the isolation that often accompanies mental health struggles can be a powerful tool for cybercriminals. Victims who suffer in silence are less likely to seek help or report suspicious activity, fearing judgment or embarrassment. Attackers often exploit this isolation, making victims feel that it's too late or too shameful to confide in others, further isolating them and perpetuating the cycle of manipulation.

The emotional and psychological impact of cyberattacks can be devastating, leaving victims feeling not only financially violated but also emotionally scarred. The erosion of trust, the feelings of shame and self-blame, and the lingering anxiety can have long-lasting consequences for victims' well-being and their ability to engage with the digital world.

This highlights a dangerous gap in many cybersecurity strategies. Mitigating the risk requires going beyond technical safeguards and standard user training:

Mental Health Aware Education: Cybersecurity programs must explicitly address how our mental state impacts online decision-making. This should not be about blame but empowering people to recognize their vulnerability in certain moments.

Spotting the Signs in Others: Can we train managers, family members, etc., to see subtle changes in someone's online behavior that might be a clue they need support, not punishment?

Destigmatizing the Struggle: A workplace (or family) where it is safe to say, "I am not at my best today; can someone double-check this email?" offers far more protection than a culture of fear.

Companies and organizations that rely on employees as their first line of cyber defense have an ethical obligation to acknowledge mental health as a risk factor. Providing access to resources, fostering open communication, and ensuring security training is realistic about the challenges people face are essential steps to take.

Let us look into the FinSecure Inc. case study, exploring the nuances of the situation and potential interventions that could have changed the outcome.

THE ANALYST'S STORY: A CLOSER LOOK

The senior analyst at FinSecure Inc. was a seasoned professional with a strong track record, making their susceptibility to the phishing attack even more concerning. Here is a deeper look at the likely contributing factors:

The Perfect Storm: The analyst was not just having a bad day – they were dealing with an ongoing personal crisis. The pandemic exacerbated this, adding new layers of stress and isolation. This long-term struggle left them emotionally depleted and less resilient in the face of the attack.

High-Functioning Does Not Mean Immune: Intelligent people with technical skills can still fall for scams. Attackers know this and may tailor their tactics to make victims feel overconfident or too embarrassed to ask for help.

The Illusion of Control: When everything else in life feels out of control, we may cling to areas where we feel competent. The analyst might have been more vigilant with their work tasks to compensate for other anxieties, ironically making them easier to trick.

MISSED OPPORTUNITIES FOR INTERVENTION

Human Factors in Cybersecurity: Lessons from a Breach

The incident at FinSecure Inc. highlights the crucial role of human factors in cybersecurity. While technical defenses are essential, understanding and addressing human vulnerabilities is equally important in creating a resilient security environment.

Changes in Online Behavior: A Missed Opportunity

Had colleagues or supervisors been attuned to subtle shifts in the analyst's online behavior, they might have had a chance to intervene before the attack escalated. Impulsive clicking of links or uncharacteristic irritability in emails could have been red flags, signaling a state of distress or vulnerability that made the analyst more susceptible to manipulation. Organizations should foster a culture of awareness and open communication, where individuals feel comfortable seeking support or reporting concerns without fear of judgment. This can be achieved through regular check-ins, open-door policies, and mental health awareness programs.

Did Training Match Reality? The Need for Holistic Cybersecurity Education

While FinSecure Inc. likely provided standard "don't click strange links" training, it's worth examining whether their cybersecurity education went deeper, addressing the crucial link between mental state and judgment. Recognizing the feeling of "not being quite myself today" is a vital security skill, empowering individuals to take extra precautions or seek support when they feel vulnerable. Cybersecurity training should go beyond technical checklists and delve into the psychological aspects of online safety, equipping individuals with self-awareness and coping mechanisms to make sound decisions even under stress. This could include incorporating mindfulness techniques, stress management training, and simulations that mimic real-world social engineering attacks.

The Shame Factor: Building a Culture of Transparency and Trust

The analyst's delayed reporting of the incident highlights a common but dangerous obstacle to effective cybersecurity: shame. When individuals realize they've made a mistake that could have serious consequences, the fear of judgment or punishment can often outweigh the urge to report the incident promptly. This delay allows minor incidents to escalate into significant breaches, potentially causing far greater damage than if they had been addressed immediately. Organizations must foster a culture of transparency and psychological safety, where individuals feel comfortable admitting mistakes and seeking help without fear of reprisal. This culture of trust and open communication is essential for creating a resilient cybersecurity environment where vulnerabilities are addressed swiftly and effectively. Implementing anonymous reporting channels, promoting a "no blame" culture, and providing support resources for employees who experience cybersecurity incidents can help foster this environment.

A Call to Action: Prioritizing Human Factors in Cybersecurity

The incident at FinSecure Inc. serves as a reminder that cybersecurity is not solely a technological challenge but also a human one. By prioritizing the human factors, fostering a culture of awareness, and providing comprehensive training and support, organizations can create a more resilient and secure digital environment.

HOW FINSECURE INC. COULD DO BETTER

Proactive Support: Waiting for employees to self-report mental health struggles is not enough. Regular check-ins that normalize talking about stress (without prying into medical details) can build trust.

Collaborative Security Culture: Could they pair high-risk employees with a "cyber buddy" – someone they trust to double-check a weird email, no judgment asked? This removes some of the burdens of always having to be 100%.

Incident Response Rethink: Harsh punishment for mistakes backfires in the long run. Focus on what went wrong with the system that let this happen, not just the individual – this encourages honesty, which is crucial for the rapid containment of future attacks.

KEY TAKEAWAY

This case transcends the narrative of an individual's failure; it illuminates the systemic shortcomings of an organization that neglected to acknowledge the profound impact of mental health struggles on its employees' well-being and, consequently, their cybersecurity defenses. The analyst's story serves as a poignant reminder that human vulnerabilities extend beyond the technical realm, encompassing the intricate and often fragile landscape of mental health.

By recognizing this inherent interconnectedness between human well-being and cybersecurity posture, FinSecure Inc., and indeed, any organization entrusted with sensitive data, can take proactive steps to create a workplace culture that prioritizes both employee mental health and robust cybersecurity practices. This requires a shift in perspective, moving beyond the traditional focus on technical safeguards and embracing a more holistic approach that acknowledges the human element in cybersecurity.

Implementing mental health awareness programs, providing access to confidential counseling services, and fostering a supportive work environment can empower employees to seek help when struggling, reducing the risk of their vulnerabilities being exploited by malicious actors. Furthermore, integrating mental health considerations into cybersecurity training programs can help employees recognize the signs of social engineering attacks that prey on emotional vulnerabilities and equip them with the skills to respond effectively.

By cultivating a workplace culture that prioritizes employee well-being, organizations can not only enhance their cybersecurity defenses but also foster a more compassionate and supportive environment where individuals feel valued and empowered. This, in turn, can lead to increased productivity, improved morale, and a stronger sense of loyalty and commitment among employees.

In essence, the case of the analyst at FinSecure Inc. underscores the crucial need for organizations to recognize the human element in cybersecurity. By embracing a holistic approach that prioritizes both employee well-being and robust cybersecurity practices, we can create a workplace that protects not only data but also the individuals entrusted with its security.

BUILDING A MORE RESILIENT FUTURE

The case of the FinSecure Inc. analyst serves as a stark reminder that a truly comprehensive cybersecurity strategy must extend beyond firewalls and intrusion detection systems to encompass the often-overlooked dimension of mental health. Older adults, those grappling with depression or anxiety, or individuals facing significant life stressors are particularly susceptible to the manipulative tactics of social engineering attacks. By acknowledging these vulnerabilities and implementing a multi-pronged approach that addresses both the technological and human elements of cybersecurity, we can create safer online spaces for everyone.

This necessitates a shift in our approach to cybersecurity education and awareness. We must move beyond technical safeguards and standardized user training to cultivate a deeper understanding of the human factors that influence online behavior. Education should empower individuals to recognize how their mental and emotional states can impact their decision-making in the digital realm, making them more vulnerable to phishing scams, social engineering ploys, and other forms of online manipulation.

Furthermore, fostering open communication within organizations and families is crucial for identifying and mitigating vulnerabilities before they can be exploited. Creating a culture where individuals feel comfortable discussing their mental health challenges, seeking support during times of stress, and reporting suspicious online activity can serve as a powerful defense against cyber threats.

Organizations should prioritize mental health resources and support systems for their employees, recognizing that a healthy and resilient workforce is better equipped to navigate the complexities of the digital landscape. Families, too, should foster open communication and create a safe space for individuals to share their online experiences and concerns, particularly for older adults and those who may be more vulnerable to online manipulation.

In conclusion, the case of the FinSecure Inc. analyst highlights the critical importance of integrating mental health considerations into our cybersecurity strategies. By acknowledging the human element, fostering open communication, and providing support for those grappling with mental health challenges, we can create a safer and more resilient digital world for all.

STRIKING A BALANCE: EFFECTIVE MENTAL HEALTH SUPPORT WITH PRIVACY

Companies have a vested interest in the well-being of their employees, not only for ethical reasons but also for practical considerations that impact both productivity and cybersecurity. A workforce grappling with mental health challenges is likely to experience decreased focus, reduced productivity, and potentially even disengagement, all of which can negatively impact a company's bottom line. Furthermore, employees facing mental health struggles may be more susceptible to social engineering attacks, phishing scams, and other cyber threats that prey on emotional vulnerabilities and impaired judgment.

Therefore, companies have a responsibility to foster a supportive environment that prioritizes employee well-being and provides access to mental health resources. This can be achieved through a multi-pronged approach that encompasses preventative measures, early intervention strategies, and accessible treatment options.

Preventative measures might include promoting work–life balance, offering stress management workshops, and creating a workplace culture that encourages open communication and destigmatizes mental health challenges. Early intervention strategies could involve training managers to recognize signs of distress in their employees, providing access to confidential counseling services, and implementing employee assistance programs (EAPs) that offer support for a range of mental health and personal issues.

Accessible treatment options are crucial, ensuring that employees have access to affordable and timely mental health care. This might involve partnering with mental health providers, offering insurance coverage for therapy and medication, and providing flexible work arrangements to accommodate treatment needs.

However, while offering support, companies must also be mindful of employee privacy. Mental health information is highly sensitive and should be treated with the utmost confidentiality. Companies should implement clear policies and procedures to safeguard employee privacy, ensuring that any mental health data collected is used solely for the purpose of providing support and is not shared with unauthorized individuals or used for discriminatory purposes.

By striking a balance between providing practical mental health support and respecting employee privacy, companies can create a workplace culture that fosters well-being, enhances productivity, and strengthens cybersecurity defenses. This not only benefits the individual employees but also contributes to a more resilient and thriving organization.

EAPs: Offer confidential and readily accessible EAPs, with clear information about utilizing these resources. Promote them regularly, removing the stigma associated with seeking help.

Normalize Self-Care: Create a work culture that encourages healthy habits and prioritizes mental well-being. Offer flexible schedules, promote breaks, and create opportunities for employees to connect and de-stress.

Privacy-Focused Mindfulness Resources: Provide access to online mindfulness training or meditation apps that do not collect personal data. These can help employees develop coping mechanisms to manage stress and improve focus.

Focus on Building Resilience: Instead of just teaching what "not to do," train employees to identify and manage the signs of stress and anxiety. Equip them with tools to build personal resilience and make sound online choices.

Creating a supportive environment where seeking help is encouraged, and offering privacy-conscious resources are essential steps companies can take to empower their employees to manage their mental health proactively. This, in turn, significantly bolsters the organization's cybersecurity posture. Fostering a culture of empathy and open communication benefits everyone – from employees to the broader digital community. When employees feel supported and safe in seeking help for mental health concerns, they are more likely to address potential vulnerabilities that social engineers could exploit. Stress, anxiety, and isolation can impair judgment and increase susceptibility to phishing scams, social engineering tactics, and other forms of cyber manipulation. By promoting mental wellness, companies create a workforce that is not only healthier and happier but also more resilient to cyber threats.

Furthermore, offering privacy-conscious resources is crucial for building trust and encouraging employees to seek help without fear of stigma or repercussions. Confidential counseling services, EAPs, and mental health workshops can provide valuable support while ensuring employee privacy is protected. This fosters a culture where mental health is prioritized, and seeking help is seen as a sign of strength rather than weakness.

The fight against social engineering attacks requires a holistic approach that acknowledges the human factors at play. By addressing the psychological and emotional vulnerabilities that attackers often exploit, we can build a safer online world for all. This includes promoting mental wellness, fostering a culture of empathy and support, and empowering individuals with the knowledge and tools to recognize and resist social engineering tactics.

In addition to these individual-focused efforts, organizations and policymakers must also take a proactive role in combating social engineering. This includes implementing robust security measures, educating the public about cyber threats, and advocating for policies that protect individuals from online manipulation and exploitation. By working together, we can create a digital world that is not only technologically secure but also fosters the mental well-being and resilience of its users.

11 Influence of Sleep and Sleep Disorder on the Rise of Social Engineering Attacks

SLEEP DEPRIVATION: THE HACKER'S SILENT ALLY

In the ever-evolving landscape of cybersecurity, we often focus on fortifying our digital defenses, building firewalls, and implementing intricate security protocols to protect against malicious code and external threats. However, amidst this pursuit of technological safeguards, we sometimes overlook a critical vulnerability that lies within the very heart of our organizations: the human factor. Recent research has shed light on a concerning trend, revealing that sleep disorders significantly increase the risk of falling victim to social engineering attacks. This discovery compels us to re-evaluate our understanding of cybersecurity, recognizing that the exhausted brain of an overworked employee can be as susceptible to exploitation as any software vulnerability.

Sleep deprivation, a pervasive issue in today's fast-paced and demanding work culture, takes a toll on our cognitive functions, impairing judgment, decision-making, and the ability to discern subtle cues of deception. When our minds are fatigued, we become more vulnerable to the manipulative tactics employed by social engineers, who prey on our emotional vulnerabilities and cognitive biases.

The consequences can be severe. A sleep-deprived employee might fall victim to a phishing scam, inadvertently granting access to sensitive data or unleashing malware into the company's network. They might be more susceptible to persuasion, divulging confidential information or making decisions that compromise the organization's security.

Addressing this vulnerability requires a multifaceted approach that encompasses both individual responsibility and organizational support. Employees must prioritize sleep hygiene, establishing healthy sleep habits and seeking professional help when sleep disorders persist. Organizations, in turn, must foster a culture that values employee well-being, promoting work–life balance and discouraging excessive overtime that can lead to chronic sleep deprivation.

Furthermore, cybersecurity awareness training should incorporate education about the impact of sleep deprivation on cognitive function and decision-making. Employees should be equipped with the knowledge and skills to recognize the signs of social engineering attacks, even when their minds are fatigued.

By acknowledging the link between sleep deprivation and cybersecurity vulnerability, we can take proactive steps to protect our organizations from the inside out.

DOI: 10.1201/9781003500698-11

A well-rested workforce is not only more productive but also more resilient to the manipulative tactics of social engineers. In the ongoing quest for cybersecurity, prioritizing employee well-being becomes an essential component of building a truly secure and resilient organization.

HOW SLEEP PROTECTS US (AND SLEEP LOSS BETRAYS US)

Healthy sleep is not merely a period of physical rest; it is an essential pillar of cognitive function and emotional well-being. During sleep, the brain embarks on a symphony of intricate processes, consolidating memories, regulating emotions, and sharpening the very tools we use to navigate the complexities of our waking lives.

Imagine the brain as a vast orchestra, with different regions acting as sections of instruments. During the day, this orchestra is in full swing, responding to the demands of our environment, processing information, and making decisions. But as night falls, the orchestra transitions into a different mode, one of consolidation and refinement.

Sleep deprivation or disorders like insomnia disrupt this delicate symphony, throwing the orchestra into disarray. Memories become fragmented, emotions swing erratically, and decision-making falters. The consequences can be far-reaching, impacting not only our cognitive performance but also our physical health, our relationships, and our overall quality of life.

Chronic sleep deprivation can lead to a host of cognitive impairments, including difficulty concentrating, memory lapses, and impaired judgment. It can also affect our emotional regulation, making us more irritable, impulsive, and prone to mood swings. The physical consequences of sleep deprivation are equally concerning, increasing the risk of obesity, diabetes, cardiovascular disease, and even weakened immune function.

Furthermore, sleep deprivation can undermine our ability to interact effectively with others. Our communication skills suffer, our empathy wanes, and our ability to resolve conflicts diminishes. The cumulative impact of these effects can strain relationships, hinder professional success, and erode our overall sense of well-being.

Recognizing the profound importance of sleep is essential for maintaining optimal cognitive function, emotional balance, and physical health. Prioritizing healthy sleep habits, such as establishing a regular sleep schedule, creating a conducive sleep environment, and seeking professional help for sleep disorders, is an investment in our overall well-being and our ability to thrive in the complexities of modern life and prevent situations leading to:

Foggy Thinking: It is harder to spot the inconsistencies that often give away phishing attempts. Tired people are more likely to click first and think later.

Short Fuse: Sleep loss makes us irritable and emotionally reactive – exactly what attackers play on to create a sense of urgency that overrides our better judgment.

The Illusion of Invincibility: Paradoxically, the exhausted brain sometimes becomes overconfident, making people less likely to ask for help with a suspicious email they think they can handle.

SECURITY SYSTEMS CANNOT FIX THIS

Firewalls and antivirus software, while essential components of a robust cybersecurity strategy, are powerless against the insidious threat of sleep deprivation. Unlike technical vulnerabilities that can be patched or detected with automated tools, sleep deprivation operates on a deeper level, compromising the very cognitive functions that underpin our ability to make sound judgments and resist manipulation. This necessitates a new approach, one that acknowledges the human factor in cybersecurity and addresses the pervasive issue of sleep deprivation in the workplace.

Here's what workplaces can do:

- **Promote a Culture of Sleep Health:** Encourage employees to prioritize sleep by creating a workplace culture that values rest and recovery. This could involve implementing flexible work schedules, offering napping pods or quiet spaces for relaxation, and providing education on the importance of sleep hygiene.
- **Integrate Sleep Awareness into Cybersecurity Training:** Incorporate sleep awareness into cybersecurity training programs, highlighting the link between sleep deprivation and increased vulnerability to cyberattacks. Teach employees how to recognize the signs of sleep deprivation and its impact on their cognitive functions.
- **Provide Resources and Support:** Offer resources and support to employees struggling with sleep issues. This could include access to sleep specialists, stress management programs, and information on healthy sleep habits.
- **Lead by Example:** Leadership should set a positive example by prioritizing their own sleep health and demonstrating a commitment to a healthy work–life balance.
- **Encourage Breaks and Time Off:** Encourage employees to take regular breaks throughout the day and utilize their vacation time to recharge and recover.

By addressing the issue of sleep deprivation head-on, workplaces can create a more secure and resilient environment, where employees are not only equipped with the technical tools to defend against cyber threats but also possess the cognitive acuity and mental clarity to make sound judgments and resist manipulation. Workplaces can also follow:

Sleep as a Security Asset: Just as companies invest in tech upgrades, they must promote better sleep health (flexible hours, education on sleep hygiene, etc.). This is an investment in preventing breaches, not just a wellness perk.

Training for the Tired: Security awareness programs need to address the reality that no one is at their sharpest all the time. Can we train using simulations that mimic the feeling of fatigue, making it more likely to transfer to a real-world situation?

"No Judgment" Help Systems: Make it possible for employees to get a quick second opinion on a strange email incredibly late at night. Remove any fear of consequences for asking.

Addressing sleep deprivation as a cybersecurity risk factor requires a paradigm shift. We must move away from the idealized image of the "perfect employee," perpetually alert and focused, and instead acknowledge the inherent limitations of the human brain. By honestly confronting these limits and creating supportive structures to counterbalance them, we can build a truly resilient defense against social engineering attacks.

The reality is that our cognitive abilities are not static; they fluctuate throughout the day and are significantly impacted by factors like sleep, stress, and overall well-being. Ignoring these factors leaves individuals, and by extension, entire organizations, vulnerable to exploitation. A tired, overworked employee is more likely to make mistakes, overlook crucial details, and fall prey to social engineering tactics that exploit their diminished cognitive state.

To create a genuinely resilient defense, we must prioritize employee well-being and acknowledge the crucial role of sleep in maintaining optimal cognitive function. This means promoting healthy sleep habits, encouraging breaks and downtime, and creating a workplace culture that values employee well-being alongside productivity.

Furthermore, organizations must implement safeguards that account for human fallibility. This includes robust technical defenses, such as multi-factor authentication and intrusion detection systems, as well as comprehensive security awareness training that educates employees about social engineering tactics and empowers them to recognize and respond to potential threats.

By acknowledging the limitations of human cognition and implementing supportive measures to counterbalance those limits, we can create a cybersecurity culture that is truly resilient, one that protects both individuals and organizations from the ever-evolving landscape of cyber threats.

CASE STUDY: INSOMNIA AND THE VULNERABLE ANALYST

The following case study illustrates how even skilled cybersecurity professionals can become vulnerable to social engineering attacks when sleep deprivation compromises their cognitive abilities.

Sarah, a highly experienced cybersecurity analyst, had been struggling with insomnia for weeks. The pressure of a demanding workload, coupled with personal stressors, had disrupted her sleep patterns, leaving her feeling constantly fatigued and mentally drained.

One morning, while battling a persistent lack of sleep, Sarah received an email that appeared to be from a trusted colleague. The email contained a link to what was purportedly an important document related to an ongoing security audit. Exhausted and not thinking clearly, Sarah clicked the link without hesitation.

Unbeknownst to her, the email was a cleverly crafted phishing attempt. The link led to a malicious website that mimicked the company's intranet portal, prompting Sarah to enter her login credentials. In her sleep-deprived state, Sarah failed to notice the subtle discrepancies in the website's URL and design, and she unwittingly entered her username and password.

Within minutes, the attackers had gained access to Sarah's account and were able to infiltrate the company's network, compromising sensitive data and causing significant disruption to operations. The incident served as a stark reminder of the crucial role that sleep plays in maintaining cybersecurity vigilance and the importance of recognizing and addressing sleep deprivation as a critical risk factor.

THE FALLOUT AND LESSONS LEARNED

The aftermath of the incident was severe for both Sarah and the company. Data loss was significant, client trust was damaged, and Sarah faced disciplinary action for violating security protocols. The investigation, however, revealed the mitigating factor of her chronic insomnia. This led the institution to re-examine its cybersecurity approach and implement several changes:

Proactive Wellness Support: The company expanded its employee assistance program to include dedicated resources for sleep disorders, offering consultations, treatment referrals, and awareness campaigns for managers.

Revised Incident Response: Recognizing that mistakes are more likely when people are unwell, the focus shifted from punishment to rapid identification of any breach so it can be contained. Employees are encouraged to report suspicious activity without fear, even if they made an initial error.

Security Training Rethink: Standard training was supplemented with modules about how fatigue, stress, etc., impact judgment. Employees practiced spotting phishing attempts in a simulated "tired" state.

KEY TAKEAWAY

Sarah's story is not one of incompetence but of a system that failed to account for the impact of a common health issue on cybersecurity. By understanding the link between sleep disorders and vulnerability to attacks, organizations can move away from a culture of blame and toward one of proactive support and resilience.

The case of Sarah, the cybersecurity analyst, serves as a stark reminder that even the most skilled professionals are not invulnerable to the insidious nature of social engineering attacks. Sleep disorders, like insomnia, act as hidden saboteurs, undermining critical thinking and making individuals more susceptible to deception. While Sarah's actions had consequences, the actual failure was systemic – a failure to recognize sleep deprivation as a critical cybersecurity vulnerability.

This incident forces us to confront the truth that cybersecurity is not just firewalls and software updates. It extends to the health and well-being of the people who are our first line of defense. By addressing sleep disorders proactively, fostering a culture of open communication about mental and physical health, and adapting security training to be more realistic, organizations can create a genuinely resilient defense against these ever-evolving threats.

This is not a problem that can be solved with a quick fix or a simple software update. It requires a fundamental shift in how we approach cybersecurity, recognizing that the human element is not a weakness to be patched but a dynamic factor to be understood and supported. The questions that arise are multifaceted and demand a multidisciplinary approach that bridges the gap between technology, psychology, and workplace culture.

How do we balance the need for constant vigilance with the realities of human fatigue in a 24/7 digital world? Traditional security awareness training often focuses on identifying threats and following protocols, but it rarely addresses the cognitive limitations of sleep-deprived individuals. We need to develop new training methods that adapt to the user's state, providing personalized guidance and support when fatigue-related vulnerabilities are most pronounced.

Can technology itself play a role in mitigating the risks of sleep deprivation? Perhaps AI-powered security systems could subtly adapt security measures based on indicators of user fatigue, such as typing speed, mouse movements, or even facial recognition analysis. These adaptive systems could provide additional layers of protection when users are most vulnerable, prompting them to take breaks, reauthenticate, or even temporarily restrict access to sensitive data during periods of heightened fatigue.

Perhaps the most challenging question is how to overcome the stigma associated with sleep disorders. Many individuals are hesitant to seek help for sleep problems, fearing that it might be perceived as a sign of weakness or incompetence. We need to foster a workplace culture that prioritizes employee well-being, where seeking help for sleep disorders is seen as a proactive step toward maintaining both personal and organizational security.

The intersection of sleep, cybersecurity, and human behavior is a complex and evolving field that demands ongoing research and innovative solutions. By acknowledging that our brains are as vital an asset as our networks, we can begin to build a digital world where we can be both safe and well-rested. This requires a holistic approach that integrates cybersecurity awareness with employee wellness programs, promoting healthy sleep habits and providing support for those struggling with sleep disorders. Only then can we truly harness the full potential of human intelligence in the digital age, ensuring that our technological advancements are matched by our capacity to safeguard both our physical and mental well-being.

12 Influence of Bipolar Disorder on the Rise of Social Engineering Attacks

BIPOLAR DISORDER AND THE HIDDEN CYBER THREAT: WHY IT IS TIME TO ACT

In the ongoing battle against social engineering, we must look beyond the technical vulnerabilities of our digital systems and delve into the intricate complexities of the human mind. Individuals with bipolar disorder, a mental health condition characterized by extreme shifts in mood and energy levels, face unique challenges that can make them particularly susceptible to online manipulation. Understanding this risk and taking proactive steps to mitigate it is crucial for creating a safer and more inclusive digital environment for everyone.

The hallmark of bipolar disorder is the dramatic fluctuation between manic and depressive states. During manic episodes, individuals may experience heightened energy, impulsivity, and a decreased need for sleep. This can lead to risky online behaviors, such as impulsive clicking on suspicious links, oversharing personal information, or engaging in reckless online spending. In contrast, during depressive episodes, feelings of hopelessness, isolation, and low self-esteem can make individuals more vulnerable to scams that prey on their emotions or offer false promises of connection and support.

The cognitive challenges associated with bipolar disorder, such as difficulties with concentration, decision-making, and emotional regulation, can further exacerbate these vulnerabilities. The rapid shifts in mood and energy levels can impair judgment and make it challenging to recognize and respond to online threats effectively.

Moreover, the stigma surrounding mental health issues can create barriers to seeking help and support. Individuals with bipolar disorder may be reluctant to disclose their condition, fearing discrimination or judgment. This can lead to a sense of isolation and make them more susceptible to online predators who offer understanding and companionship but have malicious intentions.

To mitigate these risks, a multi-pronged approach is necessary. First, raising awareness about the unique challenges faced by individuals with bipolar disorder is crucial. Educating the public, including technology developers, cybersecurity professionals, and mental health practitioners, about these vulnerabilities can help create a more inclusive and supportive digital environment.

DOI: 10.1201/9781003500698-12

Second, developing personalized cybersecurity tools and strategies that cater to the specific needs of individuals with bipolar disorder is essential. This could include features that help manage impulsivity, such as delayed sending options for emails or spending limits on online accounts. It could also involve creating secure online communities and support networks where individuals can connect with others, share experiences, and learn about online safety in a nonjudgmental environment.

Finally, fostering a culture of empathy and understanding toward mental health issues is paramount. By breaking down stigma and promoting open communication, we can empower individuals with bipolar disorder to seek help, protect themselves online, and navigate the digital world with confidence and resilience.

HOW BIPOLAR DISORDER INCREASES VULNERABILITY

Bipolar disorder can significantly heighten an individual's vulnerability to social engineering and cyberattacks by influencing their behavior and decision-making processes. One of the key ways this occurs is through heightened impulsivity, which can lead individuals to make hasty decisions without fully considering the potential consequences. This impulsivity might manifest in various ways, such as clicking on suspicious links, sharing personal information without adequate verification, or impulsively responding to online requests or offers.

This tendency toward impulsivity is often intertwined with a deep craving for connection and validation. Individuals with bipolar disorder may experience intense emotions and a strong desire for social interaction, which can make them more susceptible to social engineering tactics that prey on these needs. They may be more likely to trust strangers online, respond to requests for help or companionship, or engage in risky online behaviors in an attempt to forge connections or seek validation.

Furthermore, episodes of foggy thinking, a common symptom of bipolar disorder, can further impair judgment and decision-making abilities. During these episodes, individuals may experience difficulty concentrating, remembering information, or thinking clearly, making it challenging to assess risks, identify red flags, or make sound decisions in online interactions. This cognitive impairment can increase vulnerability to phishing scams, online fraud, and other forms of cyber manipulation.

The combination of impulsivity, a craving for connection, and episodes of foggy thinking creates a complex web of vulnerability for individuals with bipolar disorder. Recognizing these challenges is crucial for developing effective strategies to mitigate risks and promote cybersecurity awareness within this population. By understanding the specific ways in which bipolar disorder can influence online behavior, we can create targeted interventions and support systems that empower individuals to navigate the digital world safely and confidently.

Bipolar disorder, a mental health condition characterized by extreme shifts in mood, energy, and activity levels, presents unique challenges in the realm of cybersecurity. The cognitive and emotional vulnerabilities associated with both manic and depressive episodes can increase an individual's susceptibility to social engineering tactics and other forms of cyber manipulation.

During manic phases, individuals often experience a surge of energy, decreased inhibitions, and a heightened propensity for risk-taking. This can manifest in hasty online actions, such as clicking on unfamiliar links or responding to enticing offers without careful consideration. The allure of immediate gratification or the excitement of a potential reward can override caution, making individuals more susceptible to phishing scams, malware downloads, or other online traps.

Conversely, depression, the other side of the bipolar spectrum, can lead to feelings of isolation, loneliness, and a deep yearning for connection. This vulnerability can be exploited by attackers who prey on the human need for a sympathetic ear or the promise of belonging. Social engineering tactics that offer support, friendship, or a sense of community can be particularly effective in manipulating individuals experiencing depression, leading them to divulge personal information, engage in risky online behavior, or fall victim to scams that exploit their emotional state.

Both manic and depressive episodes can significantly impair judgment and focus, making it more challenging to spot the telltale signs of a scam, even for individuals who are generally well-versed in cybersecurity practices. The cognitive distortions associated with these mood states can cloud rational thinking, making it easier for attackers to manipulate perceptions and exploit vulnerabilities.

While there may not be a widely known case directly linking a social engineering breach to undiagnosed bipolar disorder, the absence of documented evidence does not diminish the potential risk. Cybersecurity professionals often deal with potential threats, anticipating and mitigating vulnerabilities before they are exploited.

Proactively addressing the heightened risks associated with bipolar disorder is crucial for protecting individuals and organizations from the devastating consequences of cyberattacks. This includes raising awareness about the specific vulnerabilities associated with bipolar disorder, providing education and training on cybersecurity best practices, and fostering a supportive environment where individuals feel comfortable seeking help and reporting potential threats.

By taking these proactive measures, we can create a safer and more inclusive digital world for everyone, regardless of their mental health status.

WHAT CAN BE DONE

Individuals with bipolar disorder face unique challenges in navigating the digital world. The fluctuating nature of their condition, characterized by periods of mania and depression, can impact their judgment, impulsivity, and online behavior, making them more susceptible to cyber threats and social engineering tactics.

To address this vulnerability, it is crucial to create cybersecurity awareness programs tailored to the specific needs of individuals with bipolar disorder. These programs must prioritize education without stigma, empowering individuals to recognize their moments of higher risk without shame or judgment.

Technology itself can play a crucial role in supporting individuals with bipolar disorder in the digital realm. Monitoring software, with user consent, could be adapted to serve as a "take a breath before you click" safety net, alerting individuals to potentially risky online behavior and providing an opportunity for self-reflection and course correction.

Cybersecurity awareness should extend beyond the individual to include their support networks. Family members and caregivers can play a vital role in recognizing the online signs that something may be amiss. Educating these support networks about the potential online vulnerabilities associated with bipolar disorder can create an early warning system, enabling timely intervention and support.

Addressing the cybersecurity challenges faced by individuals with bipolar disorder demands a collaborative effort. Mental health professionals, cybersecurity experts, and individuals with lived experience need to come together to develop a toolkit of strategies that offer protection without diminishing the benefits of the digital world for this community.

This toolkit should include educational resources, technological tools, and support networks that empower individuals with bipolar disorder to navigate the digital landscape safely and confidently. By fostering a culture of awareness, understanding, and innovation, we can ensure that the digital world is a safe and empowering space for everyone, regardless of their mental health condition.

THE CHALLENGE OF STIGMA

Sadly, bipolar disorder is still heavily stigmatized. This can manifest as:

Shame: People may already feel embarrassed about their struggles with mood regulation. The idea that this makes them "bad" at being safe online adds to the burden.

Denial: If the message is framed as "people with your condition are easily tricked" it can lead to denial instead of self-awareness. This makes getting help harder.

Fear of Disclosure: Will a workplace treat an employee differently if they know they have bipolar disorder? This fear can prevent people from seeking accommodations to stay safe online.

CRITICAL PRINCIPLES FOR AWARENESS WITHOUT STIGMA

Cybersecurity awareness training often overlooks the unique challenges faced by individuals with mental health conditions. This is particularly crucial for those with bipolar disorder, where the fluctuating nature of the condition can significantly impact online behavior and decision-making. To address this gap, it's essential to develop training materials that prioritize empathy, focus on individual strengths, recognize the fluctuating nature of self-identity, and celebrate successes to foster a supportive and inclusive environment.

Training materials should start by acknowledging that everyone, even cybersecurity experts, has moments of vulnerability. Mood disorders, such as bipolar disorder, can amplify these vulnerabilities, increasing the risk of falling prey to online scams or making impulsive decisions that compromise cybersecurity. By acknowledging this shared human experience, we can create a more empathetic and understanding learning environment.

Individuals with bipolar disorder often possess unique strengths, such as creativity, heightened pattern recognition, and an ability to think outside the box. These strengths can be valuable assets in the digital world, enabling individuals to identify patterns in phishing attempts, recognize manipulative tactics, and develop innovative solutions to cybersecurity challenges. Training materials should highlight these strengths, empowering individuals to leverage their unique abilities to enhance their online safety and resilience.

The fluctuating nature of bipolar disorder means that individuals may experience periods of heightened energy and impulsivity (mania) as well as periods of low mood and withdrawal (depression). These mood swings can significantly impact online behavior and decision-making. Training materials should acknowledge this dynamic, framing cybersecurity awareness not as a set of rigid rules but as a process of self-awareness and adaptation.

For instance, during manic episodes, individuals may feel overconfident and less inhibited, making them more susceptible to impulsive online purchases, risky social media interactions, or falling victim to scams that prey on their desire for quick rewards. Conversely, during depressive episodes, individuals may experience low motivation, impaired concentration, and a heightened sense of distrust, making them vulnerable to social isolation, online harassment, or manipulation tactics that exploit their emotional vulnerability.

Sharing stories of individuals with bipolar disorder who have successfully navigated cybersecurity challenges can be incredibly empowering. These stories, anonymized to protect privacy, can highlight the importance of self-awareness, resilience, and seeking support when needed. Celebrating these successes can inspire others and foster a sense of community, demonstrating that individuals with bipolar disorder can not only thrive in the digital world but also contribute to a safer and more secure online environment for all.

By incorporating these principles into cybersecurity awareness training, we can create a more inclusive and supportive environment for individuals with bipolar disorder, empowering them to navigate the digital world safely and confidently.

PRACTICAL EXAMPLES

"Online Mood Tracker": Could a simple app, used alongside their existing bipolar management tools, help someone learn to correlate how they are feeling with their online behaviors? There is no diagnosis, just self-awareness.

The "CyberBuddy" System: With consent, could a trusted friend or mentor get an alert if someone with bipolar disorder is, say, engaging in hazardous online shopping during a possible manic phase?

While it is essential to be sensitive about using real-life cases in a way that could identify individuals, here is a fictionalized scenario that illustrates the potential risks for someone with bipolar disorder and how those risks differ depending on their mood state:

THE CASE OF ALEX

Alex is a talented web developer with bipolar disorder. When their mood is stable, they are meticulous, security-conscious, and unlikely to fall for phishing scams.

However, their condition makes them susceptible to both manic and depressive episodes.

The Manic Risk: Overconfidence and Impulsivity: During a manic phase, Alex might feel they have a "hot streak" going with a new online investment platform. Ordinarily cautious, they are now easily convinced by high-pressure sales tactics and promises of quick returns. The moment's rush overrides their careful research and skepticism, creating the perfect environment for fraud.

The Depressive Risk: Desperation and Vulnerability: When depression hits, Alex's world shrinks. They feel isolated and worthless. A cleverly targeted email, perhaps disguised as an offer of support or an easy way to make a little extra cash, will get more attention than usual. Their low mood makes them less likely to question inconsistencies in the offer or do the thorough research that would reveal it as a scam.

WHY ALEX'S CASE MATTERS

This situation highlights a critical point: cybersecurity vulnerability isn't always about a lack of intelligence or general knowledge. Alex, a bright and capable individual, possesses a solid understanding of cybersecurity principles. However, his current mental state has significantly altered his risk tolerance and ability to evaluate information critically.

The manic phase of bipolar disorder often brings with it a surge of energy, impulsivity, and a decreased need for sleep. While these traits can be channeled into productive endeavors, they can also lead to impulsive decision-making and a diminished capacity for critical thinking. Alex's racing thoughts and heightened impulsivity may make him more likely to click on a phishing link without fully considering the consequences or to divulge sensitive information without proper vetting.

Conversely, during depressive episodes, individuals with bipolar disorder may experience fatigue, low motivation, and difficulty concentrating. This can impair their ability to engage in complex cognitive tasks, such as evaluating the legitimacy of an email or website. Alex's depressed state might lead him to overlook red flags or make careless errors due to a lack of focus and mental clarity.

Attackers are adept at exploiting these nuanced vulnerabilities. They prey on individuals in heightened emotional states, using tactics designed to trigger impulsive actions or take advantage of impaired judgment. A phishing email promising quick riches might entice someone in a manic state, while a scam offering a simple solution to overwhelming problems might prey on someone struggling with depression.

Understanding the interplay between mental health and cybersecurity is crucial for developing effective prevention and mitigation strategies. Cybersecurity awareness training should encompass not only technical knowledge but also an understanding of how mental and emotional states can influence online behavior. Organizations should foster a supportive and inclusive environment where individuals feel comfortable seeking help and disclosing mental health challenges without fear of stigma or reprisal. By recognizing and addressing the complex interplay between human psychology and cybersecurity, we can create a safer and more resilient digital world for everyone.

KEY TAKEAWAYS

Timing Matters: Standard security advice is useless when delivered at the wrong time. Alex might know all about phishing, but when they are manic, telling them to "slow down and think" will backfire.

Support Systems Are Key: Alex needs people around them (personal and professional) who understand the signs that a risky mood shift might be happening. The earlier an intervention happens, the less damage a social engineering exploit can do.

Security Beyond the User: Does Alex's bank flag sudden large withdrawals when they have not been active in a while (a possible sign of depression making them vulnerable)? Could their workplace have opt-in safeguards when an employee's online behavior indicates a potential manic phase?

Bipolar Disorder is incredibly complex. This example simplifies things for clarity but underscores the need to treat cybersecurity as something that interacts with the fluctuating nature of one's mental health.

Let us explore potential "safety net" systems that prioritize both cybersecurity and supporting the well-being of users with bipolar disorder or other conditions that impact judgment. It is vital to remember that these should be supplementary, not replacing foundational solid security practices and awareness training.

ETHICAL CONSIDERATIONS

Ethical considerations in any context must prioritize informed consent and individual control, ensuring that participants understand and agree to their involvement. Privacy should be upheld as a fundamental right, protecting personal information from unauthorized access or misuse. Additionally, avoiding overreach is crucial, as it prevents the exploitation of individuals and maintains trust in the system.

Consent and Control: The user must be central to these safeguards, opting in knowingly and retaining the power to adjust or remove them at any time. Transparency about how the system works is non-negotiable.

Privacy as Paramount: Anything that tracks user behavior has risks. Data should be minimized, securely stored, and never used for purposes other than the agreed-upon "safety net" function.

Avoiding Overreach: The goal is to help during moments of vulnerability, not to infantilize people or make sweeping assumptions about their abilities based on their diagnosis.

POTENTIAL APPROACHES

Customizable Warning Systems: Could software recognize patterns (with the user's help during setup) that often precede impulsive actions online? A pop-up reminder, "You usually research investments more. Take a break?" could be the nudge someone needs, without judging why they might be less cautious.

"Safety Buddy" Notifications: Should a designated trusted person be alerted to out-of-the-ordinary behavior with explicit consent? For example, large withdrawals during inactivity for the account holder. This is delicate, as quick action must be balanced to avoid false alarms that erode trust.

Adaptive Security Protocols: Could financial institutions implement additional verification steps when detecting atypical high-risk transactions? This puts the brakes on, giving the user and the institution time to assess if the action is legitimate or a sign of manipulation.

Proactive Collaboration (Trickiest to Implement): Ideally, users with bipolar disorder would have the option to confidentially inform their bank, etc., that they have times of heightened risk. This allows pre-agreed-upon, non-invasive checks to be in place rather than scrambling to react when a crisis occurs.

CHALLENGES AND QUESTIONS

Tech Is Not Perfect: Pattern recognition is tricky. How do we differentiate a manic surge of creative new business ideas from genuinely risky online behavior? This is where substantial user input into system design is critical.

The Line between Protection and Paternalism: How do deal with this? This needs ongoing dialogue with mental health experts and those with lived experience of bipolar disorder. Safety nets should not become tools of unnecessary control.

Incentives for Companies: What would motivate businesses to invest in this? Perhaps it could tie into corporate social responsibility or even lower their fraud risk over time, creating a financial incentive for ethical behavior.

Here is a deeper look at the challenges facing the implementation of these "safety net" systems and some potential ways to navigate them:

CHALLENGE 1: THE FALSE POSITIVE PROBLEM

Even advanced behavioral analytics systems will make mistakes. It is inevitable. How do we avoid these situations?

The "Oops" Button: If a warning that feels unnecessary at the moment pops up, the user needs a fast, no-questions-asked way to dismiss it and adjust the system's settings. This builds trust and avoids frustration.

Focus on Patterns, Not Single Actions: One impulsive purchase is not a crisis. Systems should look for sustained deviations from the user's established "norm," which is less likely to be a fluke.

Human-in-the-Loop: Especially early on, having an option for a quick human review (by the company or by the user's designated "cyber buddy") adds a layer of reassurance before significant actions are blocked.

CHALLENGE 2: AVOIDING STIGMA AND FOSTERING TRUST

These systems hinge on users being willing to adopt them. Here is how to make them feel safe, not scary:

Marketing Matters: Frame it as "mindful spending" or "protecting what you have built," not as a tool for people who have a mental illness. Emphasize that everyone has moments of being a less-than-ideal decision-maker online.
Success Stories over Scare Tactics: Instead of using examples of scams that exploit mental health, highlight cases where the "safety net" saved someone from a simple but expensive mistake made when they were tired or stressed (relatable to everyone).
Integration, Not Isolation: Can these tools be tied into existing wellness programs companies offer? This normalizes the idea of having online safeguards as part of overall well-being.

CHALLENGE 3: MAKING IT WORK IN THE REAL WORLD

These ideas need buy-in from multiple parties. Consider:

Pilot Programs: Partnering with a single bank or fintech app would allow for controlled testing, with detailed feedback from a targeted pool of users with bipolar disorder who are invested in making it work.
Mental Health Advocacy: Getting mental health organizations on board is critical for design input and to help responsibly promote these systems to their communities.
The "Cool" Factor: Can clever design and gamification make using these tools feel empowering? This is especially important for user adoption during non-manic periods, when understanding future risk is hardest.

The intersection of bipolar disorder and cybersecurity vulnerabilities presents a complex challenge but also an opportunity for innovation. While traditional security awareness falls short for this population, the "safety nets" concept offers a promising new direction. By developing systems that prioritize user consent, privacy, and a destigmatizing approach, we can empower individuals with bipolar disorder to navigate the digital world with greater confidence.

Addressing the challenges of false positives, building trust, and finding real-world implementation pathways will require a collaborative effort. Tech companies, financial institutions, mental health experts, and, most importantly, people with bipolar disorder themselves need to be part of the design process.

This may start with pilot programs focusing on specific areas, like financial protection, where the potential benefits are most readily apparent. Success in that arena can pave the way for expanding the concept of proactive, personalized safeguards to other domains where those with bipolar disorder might face heightened risks due to the fluctuating nature of their condition.

Ultimately, this effort is not just about protecting individuals; it is about fostering a digital landscape that is both secure and inclusive. Proper cybersecurity in the 21st century demands that we acknowledge the diversity of human experience, including mental health, and ensure our protective measures work for everyone.

13 Influence of Alzheimer's, Dementia, and PTSD on the Rise of Social Engineering Attacks

WHEN THE BRAIN BETRAYS: PROTECTING THOSE WITH DEMENTIA AND PTSD FROM SOCIAL ENGINEERING ATTACKS

Cognitive decline, whether due to the insidious progression of Alzheimer's and dementia or the lingering scars of trauma in post-traumatic stress disorder (PTSD), casts a long shadow of vulnerability over those affected. It erodes the very faculties that safeguard us from deception and manipulation: memory, judgment, and emotional regulation. This erosion makes individuals susceptible to the cunning tactics of social engineers, who exploit these cognitive weaknesses to perpetrate scams, steal identities, and cause financial and emotional devastation.

The time for mere awareness of this problem has long passed; the urgency of the situation demands tangible protections. We must move beyond simply acknowledging the vulnerability of those with cognitive decline and actively develop strategies and technologies that safeguard them from these predatory attacks. This imperative is driven by both ethical responsibility and the recognition that as our population ages, the number of individuals susceptible to such scams will only continue to rise.

The development of effective protections requires a multi-pronged approach. First, we must enhance public awareness, educating individuals, caregivers, and families about the specific tactics employed by social engineers targeting those with cognitive decline. This education should include clear and concise information about common scams, red flags to watch out for, and strategies for verifying information and seeking help when needed.

Second, we must foster a culture of support and empathy, encouraging open communication and reducing the stigma associated with cognitive decline. Many victims of these scams suffer in silence, ashamed or afraid to seek help due to the perceived stigma surrounding their condition. By creating a supportive environment where individuals feel comfortable seeking assistance, we can empower them to report scams, protect themselves, and prevent further victimization.

Third, we must leverage technology to develop innovative solutions that safeguard those with cognitive decline. This could include the development of AI-powered scam detection systems that analyze communication patterns and identify suspicious activity, or the creation of user-friendly tools that simplify online security measures and make it easier for individuals to protect their digital identities.

DOI: 10.1201/9781003500698-13

Furthermore, we must advocate for stronger regulations and policies that hold social engineers accountable for their predatory actions. This could include harsher penalties for those who specifically target vulnerable populations, as well as increased support for victims of these scams, including financial assistance and access to mental health services.

In conclusion, the vulnerability of individuals with cognitive decline to social engineering scams demands urgent action. By enhancing public awareness, fostering a culture of support, leveraging technology, and advocating for stronger regulations, we can create a safer and more secure environment for those affected by these debilitating conditions. This is not only an ethical imperative but also a societal responsibility, ensuring that the most vulnerable among us are protected from exploitation and empowered to navigate the digital world with confidence and dignity.

HOW THESE CONDITIONS INCREASE RISK

For individuals experiencing short-term memory loss, often associated with dementia, the digital world can become a minefield of confusion and vulnerability. The ability to distinguish between familiar and novel information diminishes, making it increasingly difficult to recall past experiences and recognize patterns of deception. An urgent email from "the bank," even if received multiple times before, appears new and alarming each time, triggering a sense of panic and a susceptibility to manipulation.

This fading of cognitive filters creates an opportunity for malicious actors to exploit the vulnerability of those with memory impairments. Scammers may employ tactics that prey on the fear of financial loss or the urgency to protect personal information, leading individuals to make hasty decisions or divulge sensitive details without the capacity for critical evaluation.

PTSD can cast a long shadow over an individual's perception of the world, creating a persistent sense of threat and vulnerability. The hypervigilance and anxiety associated with PTSD can be readily exploited by social engineers who tailor their tactics to play on these heightened emotions.

Scammers may craft messages that evoke a sense of urgency, fear, or the need for immediate action, triggering the trauma response and bypassing rational decision-making processes. The individual, caught in a trauma loop, may feel compelled to comply with the scammer's demands, even if those demands seem irrational or suspicious in hindsight.

As cognitive function declines, even those with ordinarily good instincts and judgment may begin to doubt themselves. The ability to critically evaluate information and recognize deceptive tactics may diminish, leading to an increased reliance on external sources for validation and guidance.

This vulnerability can be exploited by malicious actors who position themselves as helpful strangers, offering assistance and support while subtly manipulating the individual's trust. The erosion of self-confidence and the need for external validation create fertile ground for manipulation, potentially leading to financial exploitation, identity theft, or further emotional distress. Cognitive impairments, whether due to dementia, PTSD, or other conditions, can create significant vulnerabilities to social engineering attacks. The fading of cognitive filters, the heightened threat perception, and the erosion of trust can be exploited by malicious actors who prey on these vulnerabilities. Protecting individuals with cognitive impairments requires a multifaceted approach, including education, awareness, and the development of assistive technologies that can help to identify and mitigate potential threats. By understanding the unique challenges faced by these individuals, we can create a safer and more inclusive digital environment that empowers them to navigate the online world with confidence and security.

WHAT CAN BE DONE

Caregiver as First Line of Defense: We cannot expect those with significant cognitive impairment to protect themselves online by training family members in-home aides. The basics of spotting scams and offering nonjudgmental tech assistance are vital.

Tech That Understands Impairment: Could AI be developed to detect patterns in online behavior consistent with dementia or PTSD flares? This is not for diagnosis but to trigger a "take a breath" reminder or alert a caregiver discreetly.

Beyond "Do Not Get Scammed!" Traditional training often backfires with this population, becoming a source of shame. Can we instead focus on building a few unbreakable rules: Never give info over the phone. It is okay to ask for help.

Making Companies Complicit: Banks and social media platforms. Need pressure to build in options like mandatory waiting periods for significant transactions initiated when user behavior shows red flags for potential exploitation.

The absence of high-profile cases directly linking these conditions to breaches does not mean the threat is not there. It is more likely that victims' families keep it private due to stigma. This makes proactive prevention even more urgent.

While protecting the privacy of individuals, here is a fictionalized scenario that illustrates the intersection of cognitive impairment and PTSD with increased vulnerability to social engineering attacks:

THE CASE OF EVELYN

Evelyn, a 76-year-old widow, has been diagnosed with early-stage dementia. While still independent, she relies more on technology to manage her life. Evelyn is also a veteran and struggles with unresolved PTSD from her time in service.

The Vulnerability:

Memory Gaps: Evelyn's short-term memory is declining. She often cannot remember if she paid a bill online or has already responded to an email from her financial advisor. This confusion makes her a prime target for repeated scams.

Always on Guard: Her PTSD creates a low-level hum of anxiety in the background. Evelyn is hypervigilant and constantly needs to respond quickly to any perceived threat. Scammers who use time-pressure tactics exploit this easily.

Fading Trust Filter: As her cognitive abilities decline, Evelyn second-guesses her judgment. This makes her more likely to be taken in by a kind voice on the phone offering to "help" with her confusing finances.

THE ATTACK

The phone rings, shattering the quiet of Evelyn's afternoon. A voice, sharp and authoritative, claims to be from her bank's fraud department. They urgently inform her that her account has been compromised, painting a vivid picture of digital thieves siphoning away her life savings. The caller's tone is laced with a concerned urgency, expertly wielding technical jargon that further disorients Evelyn, already grappling with the lingering anxieties of PTSD.

Her heart pounds in her chest, a familiar echo of past traumas. The world around her seems to shrink, the voice on the phone becoming the sole anchor in a sea of swirling fear. The caller's instructions, delivered with a calm authority that momentarily soothes her panic, become her lifeline. She clings to each word, desperate to protect herself from the perceived threat.

Without hesitation, Evelyn complies. She divulges her most sensitive personal details, the keys to her financial security, believing she is taking the necessary steps to safeguard her hard-earned savings. She authorizes a "protective" transfer of funds, a desperate act of self-preservation in the face of an invisible enemy.

But the enemy is not who she thinks. The voice on the phone, so reassuring and knowledgeable, belongs not to a protector but to a predator, skillfully exploiting her vulnerabilities. The promised security is an illusion, a carefully crafted trap designed to ensnare her trust.

As Evelyn hangs up the phone, a sense of relief washes over her. She has done everything right, followed every instruction, and averted disaster. But this relief is short-lived. Days turn into weeks, and the promised confirmation of her funds' safety never arrives. The sinking realization that she has been deceived, that her life savings have vanished into the hands of cunning scammers, triggers a fresh wave of panic, a cruel reminder of her vulnerability in a world that often feels hostile and unpredictable.

THE AFTERMATH

The discovery of the scam sends shockwaves through Evelyn's world, far exceeding the initial financial devastation. It is her son, during a routine check of her bank balance, who uncovers the devastating truth: Evelyn's life savings, meticulously accumulated over decades of hard work, have vanished into the ether. The monetary loss is crippling, but it is the insidious erosion of trust and the sharp spike in Evelyn's self-doubt that prove to be the most challenging wounds to heal.

Evelyn, once a beacon of independence and capability, now finds herself questioning her every decision, her judgment clouded by the insidious whispers of self-blame.

The world, once a familiar and navigable landscape, now appears fraught with hidden dangers and lurking predators. The technologies that once promised connection and convenience now seem like treacherous traps, their alluring interfaces masking sinister intentions.

This newfound fear and uncertainty cast a long shadow over Evelyn's life. She becomes hesitant to use technology altogether, withdrawing from the digital world that once offered a window to the wider community and a lifeline to loved ones. The isolation that once seemed a manageable consequence of aging now deepens, leaving Evelyn feeling adrift in a world that seems to be accelerating away from her.

The scam's impact reverberates beyond the financial and emotional realms, seeping into Evelyn's sense of self and her relationship with the world around her. The confidence she once held in her ability to navigate life's challenges is shaken, replaced by a gnawing sense of vulnerability and a fear of being deceived once again. The vibrant and engaged woman who embraced new experiences and connections now finds herself retreating into a shell of self-doubt and isolation.

LESSONS LEARNED

Evelyn's case highlights the insidious way social engineering exploits both cognitive impairment and emotional vulnerabilities. It reinforces the need for:

Caregiver-Focused Training: Evelyn's son should have been aware of how her conditions made her susceptible to scams.

Shame-Free Tech Support: Could a family member manage complex online tasks for Evelyn without making her feel incapable?

"Red Flag" Detection: Evelyn's bank noticed a significant atypical transaction, combined with knowing she has memory issues, which could have been a reason to pause and contact her son to verify.

Important Note: Even people without dementia or PTSD can fall for similar scams in a moment of stress. This is why moving away from only blaming the victim is critical to systemic change in cybersecurity.

Whether companies bear ethical responsibility for proactively protecting potentially vulnerable users is complex and deserves a thorough examination. Here is a closer look into the arguments for and against, along with potential paths forward:

ARGUMENTS FOR COMPANIES TAKING ACTION

Moral Obligation: When platforms or services profit from user engagement, do they not also have a primary duty of care? Ignoring obvious red flags of a user in crisis (whether from mental health, addiction, etc.) arguably makes a company complicit in the harm that follows.

Long-Term Benefit: Building systems that protect the vulnerable fosters trust. While there might be short-term costs, the reputational gain, plus the reduction in fraud losses, could offset this over time.

Data as Insight: Companies have vast amounts of behavioral data. If a user's activity aligns with known patterns of exploitation risk, remaining willfully blind is a hard stance to defend ethically.

ARGUMENTS AGAINST COMPANIES INTERVENING

Overreach: Where is the line between helpful and intrusive? Many would resent a company questioning their financial choices, even with the best intentions. This risks alienating users.

Liability: If companies attempt to intervene and get it wrong, they could be sued for discrimination and breach of privacy. The legal landscape here is murky.

It Is Not Their Job: Companies are in business to provide a service, not mental health care. Expecting them also to police user well-being might be an unfair burden, especially for smaller businesses.

It is unlikely companies will (or even should) try to become amateur diagnosticians. However, a middle ground is possible:

Opt-In Protections: Users known to be vulnerable could choose to enable stronger-than-usual safeguards on their accounts. Verification delays on transactions, spending alerts sent to a trusted person, etc.

Collaborative Networks: Companies partnering with advocacy groups for the elderly or those with PTSD could help educate users and their caregivers on how to spot scams pre-emptively.

Tech with Compassion: Instead of just warning against scams, could AI be used to detect a user who might be in a compromised state? Gentle guidance toward less risky actions ("You seem to be doing much banking late at night, is everything okay?") might be better received than a blunt freeze on their account.

This likely will not be driven by tech companies themselves. Pressure from consumer protection groups, regulatory changes, and perhaps even high-profile lawsuits that spotlight the issue will force the evolution of a more nuanced, ethical approach.

The growing threat of social engineering attacks preying on individuals with dementia, PTSD, and other conditions affecting cognition presents a profound challenge that goes far beyond technical solutions. While cybersecurity training and awareness are essential, they often fall short for those whose vulnerabilities are rooted in how their brain functions. This calls for a fundamental shift in our approach.

Companies that profit from user engagement cannot disregard the exploitation of their platforms. Finding the balance between offering safeguards and respecting user autonomy will be an ongoing ethical debate. Intelligent design, opt-in protections, and collaborations with mental health and advocacy groups offer the best path forward.

However, a genuinely safe digital landscape requires action at multiple levels. It is about caregivers being trained to spot the signs of an online scam, policy changes that address the unique vulnerabilities of these populations, and continued research to help us design technology that can adapt to the needs of diverse users.

The goal is not to shield individuals with cognitive impairments or PTSD from the online world entirely but rather to empower them to participate more safely. Fostering trust through transparency and prioritizing compassion over blame are as essential as firewalls and antivirus software in the fight against social engineering attacks.

14 Influence of Pandemic on the Rise of Social Engineering Attacks

PANDEMIC PANIC: HOW A GLOBAL CRISIS REWROTE THE RULES OF CYBERSECURITY

The COVID-19 pandemic was more than a threat to our physical health; it ripped a gaping hole in the fabric of our society, exposing vulnerabilities we never knew existed and opening a new front in the ongoing cyberwar. Social engineering attacks, always lurking in the shadows of the digital world, surged with unprecedented ferocity, fueled by a potent cocktail of fear, confusion, and the abrupt shift to a remote, always-online existence.

The pandemic fundamentally reshaped our risk profile, both individually and collectively. As the world retreated indoors, seeking refuge from the invisible enemy, our reliance on technology skyrocketed. Work, education, social interaction, and even healthcare migrated to the digital realm, expanding the attack surface for cybercriminals and creating a fertile ground for social engineering tactics to flourish.

The pandemic preyed on our deepest fears and anxieties. The constant barrage of news reports, the uncertainty of the future, and the isolation of lockdowns created a climate of heightened vulnerability. Social engineers, masters of manipulation, expertly exploited these anxieties, crafting phishing emails that mimicked official health advisories, spreading disinformation through social media, and preying on the desperation of those seeking scarce resources like vaccines and medical supplies.

The shift to remote work, often hastily implemented with inadequate security measures, further exacerbated the risks. Home networks, often less secure than corporate environments, became gateways for attackers. The blurring of boundaries between personal and professional life, with children attending online classes and families sharing devices, created new opportunities for social engineers to infiltrate homes and gain access to sensitive information.

The pandemic also exposed the fragility of trust in institutions and authorities. As governments grappled with the crisis, inconsistencies in messaging and the spread of misinformation eroded public trust. This erosion of trust created fertile ground for social engineers, who exploited the confusion and uncertainty to impersonate officials, spread disinformation, and manipulate public opinion.

In conclusion, the COVID-19 pandemic was not just a public health crisis; it was a watershed moment in the ongoing cyberwar. The rapid shift to a remote, always-online world, coupled with the fear and uncertainty of the pandemic, created a perfect storm for social engineering attacks. This period fundamentally changed our

DOI: 10.1201/9781003500698-14

risk profile, exposing vulnerabilities and highlighting the urgent need for enhanced cybersecurity awareness, education, and resilience in the face of an ever-evolving threat landscape.

HOW THE PANDEMIC SHIFTED THE LANDSCAPE

Emotions as Weapons: Attackers honed their ability to use our anxieties against us. Panic over obtaining vaccines, frustration with lockdowns, and even simple loneliness from isolation all became tools for manipulation.

The pandemic unleashed a torrent of fear and uncertainty, creating fertile ground for social engineering attacks that preyed on our heightened emotional states. Attackers skillfully exploited anxieties surrounding vaccine availability, using phishing emails and fraudulent websites to lure individuals seeking appointments or information. The frustration and isolation caused by lockdowns were also weaponized, with attackers crafting scams that promised social connection or financial relief, only to deliver malware or steal sensitive data.

Exploiting the "New Normal": Remote work is here to stay, but many companies rushed it without proper security protocols. That "quick email from the boss" asking for sensitive data is much harder for an overworked, distracted employee to spot as fake.

The rapid shift to remote work, while necessary to curb the spread of the virus, inadvertently created new vulnerabilities in cybersecurity. Many companies, unprepared for this sudden transition, implemented remote work policies without adequate security protocols, leaving employees exposed to a barrage of cyberattacks.

Attackers seized this opportunity, crafting sophisticated phishing emails that mimicked internal communications, often impersonating supervisors or IT personnel. These emails, designed to appear urgent and legitimate, tricked employees into revealing sensitive information or downloading malware, compromising both individual and corporate security.

When Everyone Is an Expert: The flood of true-but-conflicting information about COVID-19 got people to click first, verifying the source later. This primed them to fall for phishing attempts cloaked in the guise of "breaking news."

The pandemic also unleashed an infodemic, a flood of information, both accurate and misleading, that overwhelmed individuals and eroded trust in traditional sources of authority. The constant bombardment of conflicting news reports and expert opinions created an environment where individuals were primed to click first and verify later, eager to stay informed but vulnerable to manipulation.

Attackers exploited this information overload, crafting phishing emails and websites that mimicked legitimate news sources, often using sensational headlines and urgent language to lure individuals into clicking on malicious links or downloading malware. The guise of "breaking news" became a powerful tool for deception, preying on the public's desire for information and their diminished trust in traditional sources of authority.

THE LONG SHADOW OF THE PANDEMIC

While the public health crisis may eventually subside, its profound impact on our relationship with the digital world will linger. The pandemic has accelerated our reliance on technology for work, communication, and social interaction, blurring the lines between our physical and digital lives. This heightened dependence, coupled with the psychological and emotional strains of the pandemic, has created fertile ground for cybercriminals seeking to exploit vulnerabilities and manipulate anxieties.

Mitigating these risks demands a comprehensive and multifaceted approach that recognizes the interconnectedness of mental health, cybersecurity awareness, and technological innovation. Cybersecurity training must evolve beyond the traditional focus on firewalls and technical safeguards to encompass the psychological and emotional factors that influence online behavior. The stress, fear, and uncertainty associated with the pandemic can impair our judgment and make us more susceptible to phishing scams, social engineering tactics, and misinformation campaigns.

Integrating mental health awareness into cybersecurity training can empower individuals to recognize their own vulnerabilities, develop coping mechanisms, and make more informed decisions in the digital realm. This could involve incorporating "emotional check-ins" into online work routines, promoting mindfulness and stress-reduction techniques, and providing resources for mental health support.

Furthermore, the pandemic has exposed the security risks associated with remote work and the increasing reliance on personal devices and public networks to access sensitive data. "Pandemic-proofing" our systems requires a fundamental shift in how we approach cybersecurity, moving beyond traditional office-centric security models to embrace solutions that secure work regardless of location. This may involve implementing stronger authentication protocols, encrypting sensitive data, and providing secure remote access solutions.

The pandemic has also highlighted the urgent need to combat the disinformation war that rages online. False news and misinformation not only undermine trust in institutions and erode social cohesion but also make individuals more vulnerable to cyberattacks. Tech companies must take a more proactive role in battling fake content, even as they navigate the complex legal and ethical challenges associated with content moderation.

In conclusion, the pandemic has served as a stark reminder of the interconnectedness between our physical and digital lives, our mental well-being, and our cybersecurity posture. By integrating mental health awareness into cybersecurity training, "pandemic-proofing" our systems, and combating the disinformation war, we can mitigate the risks and build a more resilient and secure digital future.

MOVING FORWARD

The pandemic forced us to be reactive in our cybersecurity efforts. Now, we need to be proactive in learning from the experience. Simply going back to "how it was" leaves us dangerously exposed, not just to the next crisis, but to the everyday threats that have become more sophisticated under the cover of COVID-19.

Let us weave in a case study to illustrate the real-world impact of pandemic-themed phishing attacks:

CASE STUDY: THE DESPERATE SEARCH FOR A VACCINE

Sarah, a middle-aged woman with a pre-existing health condition, awaited news of an approved COVID-19 vaccine. Her anxiety about contracting the virus was high, and she spent a significant amount of time online searching for updates and potential ways to secure a vaccine appointment early.

One day, Sarah received an email that appeared to be from her state's health department. The subject line read, "IMPORTANT NOTICE: Early Vaccine Registration," the email's body offered priority vaccine appointments for a small pre-registration fee. Desperate for protection and feeling urgent, Sarah clicked on the provided link and entered her personal and credit card information.

She soon realized she had been the victim of a phishing scam. Her credit card was charged a substantial amount, and she not only remained unvaccinated but now had the added stress of potential identity theft. Her initial panic over the virus had made her blind to basic red flags, like a mismatched sender address and the request for payment for a supposedly "free" vaccine administered by a government agency.

KEY TAKEAWAYS

Preying on Hope: Sarah's case underscores how attackers exploit fear and the desire for relief or normalcy. The vaccine's promise felt like a way to escape the worry she had been carrying for months.

The Illusion of Authority: Fraudulent emails and websites during the pandemic were often meticulously crafted to mimic government and health organizations. This lent them a false sense of trustworthiness, especially for someone not well-versed in cybersecurity best practices.

The Long-Term Harm: While the financial loss was significant, the breach of trust Sarah felt had a lasting effect. She became fearful of all online communication about health issues, making it harder to get legitimate information going forward.

THE EVOLVING THREAT

The pandemic provided attackers with a blueprint for success: exploit a widespread emotional state, offer a "solution" that requires hasty action, and mimic trusted sources. This makes vigilance even harder to teach. Our cybersecurity efforts must account for these psychological tactics, not just technical flaws.

The COVID-19 pandemic served as a stark reminder of the vulnerabilities inherent in our digital systems and the way cybercriminals can turn human emotions into potent weapons. Social engineering attacks thrived in this atmosphere of fear and confusion, demonstrating the adaptability of criminals and the limitations of traditional security training. The case of Sarah and countless others like her underscores that protecting ourselves is not just about knowing what a suspicious email looks like – it is about understanding how our feelings can be used to override our better judgment.

Mitigating these risks will not be a one-time fix. We need to move away from viewing cybersecurity as a purely technical problem. Companies, government agencies, and individuals alike need to prioritize:

Empathy as a Design Principle: Security systems that acknowledge the reality of fear, distraction, and the desire for good news will be more effective in the long run.

Training That Evolves: Attackers change their tactics quickly. Training programs aimed at combating social engineering need to stay one step ahead, using simulations and real-world examples that are constantly updated.

Closing the Trust Gap: The pandemic eroded trust in institutions and information sources. Rebuilding that trust is crucial as a skeptical public that is well-versed in spotting misinformation is less likely to fall for scams.

The fight against social engineering is a perpetual marathon, a relentless race against those who seek to exploit our vulnerabilities for their gain. While the specific lures and narratives may shift with the tides of current events – fading away from the anxieties of the COVID-19 pandemic to latch onto new fears and uncertainties – the underlying psychological tactics, the cunning manipulation of human emotions and cognitive biases, will persist. The attackers, like digital chameleons, will adapt their camouflage to blend seamlessly with the ever-changing landscape of the digital world, preying on our hopes, our fears, and our innate trust in others.

To combat this ever-present threat, we must cultivate a society-wide culture of critical thinking, where individuals are empowered to question, analyze, and evaluate the information that bombards them from all directions. We must nurture a healthy skepticism, a discerning eye that can pierce through the veil of deception and recognize the telltale signs of manipulation. This requires not only education and awareness but also a fundamental shift in our digital mindset, a recognition that the online world, while offering immense opportunities for connection and collaboration, is also a fertile ground for those who seek to exploit and deceive.

Constant vigilance is paramount, a digital alertness that never sleeps. We must remain wary of unsolicited messages, suspicious links, and offers that seem too good to be true. We must cultivate a habit of verifying information, cross-checking sources, and seeking confirmation before divulging sensitive data or clicking on enticing links. This vigilance must extend beyond our individual actions to encompass our communities, our workplaces, and our social networks, fostering a collective responsibility for cybersecurity.

Furthermore, we must design security measures that are not just technologically robust but also psychologically informed. Traditional security measures, focused on passwords, firewalls, and intrusion detection systems, are essential but insufficient in the face of social engineering attacks that target the human element. We need security measures that account for our cognitive biases, our emotional vulnerabilities, and our susceptibility to manipulation. This might involve incorporating behavioral nudges, gamified training programs, and personalized security alerts that adapt to individual risk profiles.

In essence, the fight against social engineering is a battle fought on two fronts: the technological and the psychological. By fostering a culture of critical thinking, constant vigilance, and security measures that are designed with human psychology in mind, we can hope for a safer digital future, one where individuals are empowered to navigate the online world with confidence and resilience, and where the manipulative tactics of social engineers are met with a collective shield of awareness and informed skepticism.

15 Impacts of Discrimination in Cyber Social Engineering Systems

WHEN BIGOTRY BECOMES A HACKING TOOL

Social engineering attacks are not merely technical exploits; they are insidious manipulations that prey on the vulnerabilities of both our digital systems and the social fabric of our world. Online racial discrimination, a pervasive and deeply damaging phenomenon, provides attackers with a wealth of information and psychological weapons to amplify the effectiveness of their scams. This toxic interplay between social prejudice and cybercrime creates a vicious cycle, where marginalized communities are disproportionately targeted and victimized.

The perpetrators of social engineering attacks are adept at exploiting the existing fault lines of prejudice and discrimination. They leverage racial stereotypes, exploit cultural sensitivities, and prey on the vulnerabilities of marginalized groups to craft highly targeted and effective scams. These attacks often involve impersonation, phishing attempts, and the spread of disinformation, all designed to manipulate individuals and gain access to sensitive information or financial resources.

Online platforms, while offering opportunities for connection and community building, can also become breeding grounds for hate speech, harassment, and discrimination. This toxic online environment can have a profound impact on the psychological well-being of individuals from marginalized groups, eroding trust, fostering isolation, and creating a sense of vulnerability that attackers can readily exploit.

The anonymity afforded by the internet can embolden perpetrators of online racial discrimination, allowing them to spread hate speech and engage in harassment with a sense of impunity. This creates a hostile online environment where individuals from marginalized groups may be hesitant to report cybercrimes or seek help, fearing further victimization or a lack of understanding from authorities.

Furthermore, the algorithms that power social media platforms and search engines can inadvertently perpetuate and amplify existing biases, creating echo chambers and filter bubbles that reinforce discriminatory narratives. This can make individuals from marginalized groups more susceptible to targeted disinformation campaigns and social engineering attacks that exploit their existing vulnerabilities.

The intersection of online racial discrimination and social engineering attacks highlights the urgent need for a multifaceted approach to cybersecurity. This includes not only technical measures to protect digital systems but also social and cultural initiatives to combat online hate speech, promote digital literacy, and empower

DOI: 10.1201/9781003500698-15

marginalized communities to recognize and resist cyber threats. By addressing the social vulnerabilities that attackers exploit, we can create a more inclusive and secure digital world for all.

Here is how interplay works:

Know Your Enemy (Sadly, Too Well): Hateful rhetoric, discriminatory memes, etc., are not just a free speech issue. They also conduct market research for cybercriminals, revealing pain points and cultural references specific to a targeted group. This lets them tailor phishing attacks that are far more convincing.

Playing on a Lack of Trust: If a racial minority group feels mainstream institutions do not have their best interests at heart, they are less likely to believe it when their bank emails a fraud warning. Attackers often exploit this by pretending to be "on the side" of the victim.

Algorithms Amplify the Problem: Biased AI, from search results to ad targeting, can reinforce stereotypes or funnel a targeted group toward misinformation designed to make them more vulnerable to exploitation.

More Than Just the Scam: For victims, the damage is compounded. It has not just lost money; it is the feeling that they were targeted because of who they are. This erodes the trust that is vital for cybersecurity to work for everyone.

WHAT CAN BE DONE

Security awareness training must evolve beyond simplistic warnings about phishing scams and generic malware. It's crucial to recognize that individuals from marginalized groups face unique cybersecurity threats, often targeted by malicious actors who exploit the discrimination and prejudice they experience. These individuals need extra support in learning to identify and resist manipulation tactics that prey on their vulnerabilities.

Tech companies have a responsibility to actively combat the spread of online hate and discrimination. This is not about censorship but about denying criminals the tools they use to exploit and harm marginalized communities. Platforms must take proactive steps to identify and remove hateful content, promote inclusivity, and empower users to protect themselves from online harassment and abuse.

The design of social networks and online platforms should prioritize user control and agency. Can we create platforms that give individuals greater control over their personal information and how it is used? Can we design systems that minimize the risk of manipulation and exploitation while fostering a sense of safety and trust?

Reporting mechanisms for cybercrimes must be truly anonymous and accessible, particularly for individuals from marginalized groups who may be reluctant to come forward due to fear of further discrimination or retaliation. Building trust and ensuring that victims feel safe to report incidents is crucial for understanding the true scope of the problem and developing effective solutions.

Ignoring these issues is not an option. By taking a more inclusive and proactive approach to cybersecurity awareness, platform design, and reporting mechanisms, we can create a safer and more equitable digital world for all. This requires a collective effort from individuals, organizations, and policymakers to challenge discrimination, promote inclusivity, and empower everyone to navigate the digital landscape safely and confidently.

CASE STUDY: OPERATION AURORA

The Broader Challenge

We need to start seeing cybersecurity as a community safety issue, recognizing that the digital threats we face are not merely technical problems but deeply intertwined with the social fabric of our world. Discrimination, in all its forms, is not just morally wrong; it is a practical threat vector that hackers will continue to exploit until we fundamentally change the technology we build and the society within which it operates.

Operation Aurora, a sophisticated cyber espionage campaign that targeted Google and several other high-profile companies in 2009, serves as a stark example of how discrimination can intersect with social engineering and cyber espionage. This multifaceted attack, attributed to Chinese government-backed hackers, exploited not only technical vulnerabilities but also the social and cultural dynamics of the targeted organizations.

The attackers used spear-phishing emails, tailored to the interests and roles of specific individuals within the targeted companies, to deliver malware and gain access to sensitive information. These emails often leveraged social engineering tactics, playing on the trust and familiarity that exist within professional networks.

The attackers also exploited the cultural diversity of the targeted organizations, crafting their phishing emails and malware delivery mechanisms to specifically target individuals from marginalized groups. This discriminatory targeting reflects a cynical understanding of the potential vulnerabilities that can arise from social inequalities and cultural biases.

Operation Aurora highlights the need for a more inclusive and holistic approach to cybersecurity, one that recognizes the interconnectedness of technology, society, and human behavior. By addressing the root causes of discrimination and fostering a culture of inclusivity and respect, we can create a more resilient digital environment where all individuals feel safe and empowered to participate fully in the digital age.

This requires not only technical solutions, such as robust security protocols and advanced threat detection systems, but also a fundamental shift in our societal values and practices. We must challenge the biases and stereotypes that perpetuate discrimination, promote diversity and inclusion in the technology industry, and foster a culture of empathy and understanding in our online interactions.

By embracing these principles, we can create a digital world that is not only more secure but also more just and equitable. A world where technology empowers all individuals, regardless of their background or identity, and where the threat of cyberattacks is mitigated not only through technical defenses but also through the strength of our social fabric and the resilience of our communities.

UNDERSTANDING OPERATION AURORA'S IMPACT

Technical Sophistication: This was not a simple attack. It involved zero-day exploits and custom malware, signaling advanced capabilities on the part of those behind it. This kind of resource investment usually means a specific goal is in mind, as opposed to general financial crime.

The Human Factor: While the intrusion utilized technical exploits, attackers likely engaged in social engineering tactics to some degree. Targeted spear-phishing emails or manipulative social media messages may have been used for initial access or to spread malware within organizations.

Discriminatory Motives: Focusing on Chinese human rights activists reveals an ideological component. This was not about stealing trade secrets. It was about suppressing dissenting voices. This kind of discrimination motivates attacks that are often even more meticulously planned, as the goal is not just short-term gain but control over information.

Security Meets Geopolitics: Aurora blurred lines that those in cybersecurity are used to thinking about. State-sponsored cyberattacks are now commonplace, and the suppression of minority groups is often part of that state agenda.

KEY LESSONS FOR CYBERSECURITY

Targets, Not Tactics: Understanding the motivations behind an attack is as crucial as comprehending the tools employed. Organizations focused on human rights face a distinct threat landscape compared to financial institutions, requiring tailored security awareness training that addresses their unique vulnerabilities. Attackers motivated by ideology or geopolitical agendas may employ tactics that exploit the trust and values of human rights defenders, making it essential to educate them about the specific threats they face.

The Trust Weapon: Operation Aurora starkly demonstrated the fragility of digital trust in the face of geopolitical tensions. Countries with poor human rights records can exploit this vulnerability, using disinformation and propaganda to undermine legitimate security warnings and portray them as tools of oppression. This tactic erodes trust in security measures, making individuals more susceptible to social engineering and other forms of cyberattacks.

When Companies Have to Take a Stand: Google's public defiance against Operation Aurora set a significant precedent. When cyberattacks are motivated by discrimination that violates a company's core values, neutrality may not be the best stance, even if it risks retaliation. Taking a stand against such attacks not only aligns with a company's ethical principles but also sends a powerful message of support to targeted communities and individuals.

The Long Game: While the attackers behind Operation Aurora may not have achieved all their objectives, they gained valuable intelligence on how activists communicate and organize online. This knowledge allows them to refine their tactics and launch more targeted attacks in the future. Therefore, we need cybersecurity defenses that think beyond the immediate breach, anticipating the long-term strategies of adversaries and adapting to their evolving tactics. This requires a proactive approach that combines technological safeguards with ongoing education and awareness initiatives to empower individuals and communities to protect themselves in the digital age.

THE FIGHT IS NOT OVER

The chilling reality is that attacks like Operation Aurora, driven by discrimination and aimed at silencing dissenting voices, continue to plague human rights advocates across the globe. Understanding the profound interplay between discrimination and these malicious attacks is not merely an academic exercise; it is a crucial step toward building a more secure and equitable digital world.

The traditional cybersecurity advice of "don't click on bad links" or "beware of suspicious emails" proves woefully insufficient in the face of targeted attacks fueled by discrimination. Activists, often operating in hostile environments and challenging oppressive regimes, require far more sophisticated training to combat the intricate social engineering tactics often employed against them. These tactics prey on their deep-seated commitment to their cause, their trust in fellow activists, and their willingness to take risks to amplify their message.

Moreover, the discriminatory nature of these attacks raises ethical questions for the technology industry. Is there an obligation to develop and deploy tools specifically designed to protect vulnerable groups targeted for their advocacy, even if these solutions are not as profitable as enterprise security products? The pursuit of profit must be balanced with a commitment to social responsibility and the protection of those who fight for human rights and social justice.

While Operation Aurora involved sophisticated technical exploits, its success likely hinged on exploiting social engineering vulnerabilities, the human factor that remains the weakest link in the cybersecurity chain. Let us delve deeper into how these vulnerabilities operate in the context of discrimination-driven attacks against activists.

SOCIAL ENGINEERING TACTICS TAILORED FOR IMPACT

Targeting Activists: Tailored Social Engineering Tactics

Activists, due to their unique circumstances and online behavior, are often targeted with specialized social engineering tactics that exploit their vulnerabilities and motivations.

Authority Impersonation: Attackers may adopt a variety of guises to deceive activists, exploiting their need for allies and the assumption that they are already under surveillance. Posing as sympathetic government officials or foreign NGOs offering aid can be particularly effective, as it makes unusual or unexpected contact seem more plausible, increasing the likelihood of the activist falling victim to the deception.

Fear and Urgency: To bypass an activist's caution, attackers often employ tactics that induce panic and a sense of urgency. Instead of offering enticing prizes, phishing emails targeting activists are more likely to contain alarming messages, such as claims that a colleague is in danger or that leaked documents require immediate release. This creates a sense of panic that can override the activist's usual security protocols.

The Insider Threat: Infiltration of social networks through carefully crafted fake profiles is a common tactic used to gain the trust of activists. These profiles gradually build rapport and trust over time. Once "inside" the group, attackers can more easily spread rumors to induce someone to click a malicious link or offer seemingly "secure" communication tools laden with malware.

Weaponizing Legitimate Frustrations: Activists often rely on technological workarounds to circumvent censorship.

Attackers can exploit this by offering "censorship-proof" software or spreading misinformation about legitimate companies' products being compromised. This can pressure activists into hastily switching to alternative tools that are actually under the attacker's control.

WHY IT IS SO EFFECTIVE

Limited Resources: Most activists are not IT experts. Asking for vigilance 24/7 that would rival a corporation is unrealistic.

Burnout Culture: The emotional toll of activism makes it harder to be constantly on guard. Attackers prey on this exhaustion to slip in attacks.

Solidarity vs. Security: Activists often share freely to bolster their cause. That makes them less likely to be suspicious of a seemingly well-meaning newcomer with "important" info.

The Evolving Opponent: Aurora was a wake-up call, but state actors continue to learn from these incidents. Today's social engineering tactics likely make those back in 2010 look primitive.

IT IS NOT JUST TECH

This is where the psychology of discrimination makes it difficult to defend against. If the attackers are aligned with the forces the activist is fighting against, it erodes their ability to trust anyone. This sense of isolation and being under siege is precisely what the attackers want.

The case of Operation Aurora provides a chilling example of how discriminatory motives fuel advanced cyberattacks, including the exploitation of social engineering vulnerabilities. When human rights activists and other targets of oppression find themselves at the center of these attacks, it highlights the insidious nature of online threats and the need for protective strategies that go beyond the purely technical.

Activists and other marginalized groups often operate in environments characterized by limited resources, chronic stress, and an erosion of trust born from constant surveillance or discrimination. These factors create a unique environment where social engineering tactics find fertile ground. Whether state-sponsored or independent, attackers leverage these vulnerabilities, impersonating allies, exploiting emotional triggers, and undermining a sense of digital security.

Addressing this insidious threat requires more than teaching activists not to click on suspicious links. We must acknowledge the profoundly human element of these attacks and develop countermeasures rooted in both technology and an understanding of the psychological realities of their targets. This might include:

Trauma-Informed Training: Security awareness needs to address the impact of constant stress on decision-making and offer strategies for managing that stress while staying vigilant.

Secure by Design for the Underdog: Could open-source tools designed specifically for high-risk users be part of the solution? These tools must prioritize ease of use and intuitive design for those without technical backgrounds.

Building Digital Resilience Networks: Can we create a system where activists have a secure way to get a quick "second opinion" on a suspicious email, website, etc., from trusted security experts?

Holding Tech Companies Accountable: Platforms used to spread disinformation or harass activists make social engineering attacks easier. Pushing for ethical design and proactive moderation is crucial.

The fight for human rights has irrevocably entered the digital realm. In an era where information flows across borders at the speed of light, where social movements ignite and organize online, and where the battle for hearts and minds is waged in the digital arena, the struggle for fundamental freedoms is inextricably linked to the fight for cybersecurity.

The digital age has empowered individuals and communities to challenge oppression, advocate for change, and connect with like-minded individuals across geographical boundaries. However, this newfound power has also exposed them to new vulnerabilities, as authoritarian regimes and malicious actors leverage technology to suppress dissent, spread disinformation, and silence marginalized voices.

The targeting of individuals and communities based on their beliefs, whether religious, political, or social, has taken on a new dimension in the digital age. Cyberattacks, surveillance technologies, and online harassment are increasingly weaponized against those who dare to challenge the status quo or advocate for change.

The fight for human rights, therefore, must encompass a robust defense of digital freedoms. This includes the protection of privacy, the freedom of expression online, and the right to access information without fear of censorship or reprisal. It also demands the development of tools and technologies that empower individuals and communities to protect themselves from cyberattacks, surveillance, and online harassment.

By recognizing the unique challenges faced by those targeted because of their beliefs, we can start to develop the training, tools, and societal shifts necessary to level the digital playing field. We must equip individuals and communities with the skills and knowledge to navigate the complex digital landscape, to recognize and mitigate cyber threats, and to advocate for their digital rights.

We must also foster a culture of cybersecurity awareness, where individuals understand the importance of protecting their digital identities, securing their online communications, and critically evaluating the information they encounter online.

Furthermore, we must challenge the normalization of surveillance and the erosion of privacy in the digital age. We must advocate for policies and regulations that protect digital freedoms, hold technology companies accountable for their role in facilitating surveillance and censorship, and ensure that the digital world becomes a space where human rights are respected and upheld.

The fight for human rights is a fight for the future of humanity, a future where technology empowers rather than enslaves, where knowledge liberates rather than confines, and where the human spirit can flourish without fear of persecution or oppression. By embracing the values of individual autonomy, open knowledge, and critical engagement with information, we can build a digital world where everyone, regardless of their beliefs, can freely express themselves, connect with others, and contribute to the collective advancement of human society.

16 Mind Games in the Digital Playground

The Rising Threat of Social Engineering in Online Gaming and the Technological Challenges in Detection

THE GAME WITHIN THE GAME: HOW SOCIAL ENGINEERING TURNS FUN INTO FRAUD

Online gaming worlds offer a captivating blend of escapism, community, and competition, drawing players into immersive digital realms where they can forge identities, build relationships, and pursue virtual glory. However, this very richness that captivates and engages players also creates fertile ground for social engineering attacks. For cybercriminals, the thrill of the game becomes a stage for a different kind of elaborate play, one where manipulation is the goal, and players, immersed in their virtual pursuits, become unwitting participants in a dangerous game of deception.

The immersive nature of online gaming fosters a sense of trust and camaraderie among players. Within the confines of the game world, social bonds are forged, alliances are formed, and a shared sense of purpose emerges as players collaborate to achieve common goals. This atmosphere of trust and shared vulnerability, however, can be readily exploited by cybercriminals who understand the psychology of gamers and the social dynamics of online communities.

These digital con artists, adept at social engineering tactics, often adopt personas that blend seamlessly into the game's social fabric. They may pose as helpful veterans offering guidance to newcomers, generous benefactors offering in-game currency or rare items, or even romantic interests seeking to establish intimate connections. Their manipulative tactics prey on the emotions and desires of players, exploiting their trust and luring them into compromising situations.

A phishing scam might be disguised as an official message from the game developers, requesting players to verify their account information or download a seemingly innocuous update. A malicious link, shared in a chat channel or embedded in a forum post, could lead unsuspecting players to a fake website designed to steal their login credentials or infect their devices with malware.

DOI: 10.1201/9781003500698-16

The anonymity afforded by online gaming further enables these attacks. Cybercriminals can hide behind carefully crafted avatars and pseudonyms, making it difficult to verify their identities or trace their actions. This anonymity creates a sense of impunity, emboldening attackers and increasing the difficulty of holding them accountable for their deceptive practices.

The consequences of these attacks can be devastating, ranging from the loss of virtual possessions and in-game currency to the compromise of personal information and financial accounts. For dedicated gamers, who often invest significant time and resources into their virtual pursuits, the impact of these attacks can extend beyond the digital realm, affecting their sense of security, their trust in online communities, and even their emotional well-being.

WHY GAMING IS SO APPEALING TO ATTACKERS

With its immersive narratives and competitive spirit, the world of gaming creates a unique environment that attackers cleverly exploit. The thrill of the chase often lowers our inhibitions, making us more susceptible to well-timed scams that offer in-game advantages. Attackers hide behind the playful atmosphere, using jokes or seemingly casual requests to test tactics and desensitize targets to unusual requests. Additionally, many games' ingrained "heroes vs. villains" mentality can be twisted, with attackers positioning themselves as rebellious figures fighting against the system. This obscures their true intentions and makes their scams feel righteous in the game world. Understanding these tactics and the unique vulnerabilities the gaming environment creates is paramount for players wishing to stay protected in this ever-evolving digital landscape.

CHALLENGES OF KEEPING PLAYERS SAFE WITHIN THE GAMING ENVIRONMENT

Protecting players from scams, account theft, and harmful behavior in online gaming environments faces significant hurdles. While automated moderation tools are under constant development, they struggle to decipher the complexities of human communication. Sarcasm, playful banter, and attempts to disguise malicious intent can easily slip by these systems, emphasizing the need for continued player education and awareness.

Furthermore, the intricate in-game economies present unique challenges. Normalizing trading, sharing, or acquiring items can lead to blurring acceptable and unsafe behaviors. Establishing clear red lines regarding actions like sharing account information is difficult, which is dangerous but might contradict seemingly legitimate in-game activities.

Finally, the evolving tactics of those seeking to exploit players cannot be underestimated. They can establish long-term schemes with patience and persistence, manipulating trust and infiltrating social circles like in-game guilds. This serves as a reminder of these threats' insidious and evolving nature. While safeguarding players is crucial, it requires continuous effort to understand and counteract these complex, multi-faceted attack vectors.

GAMERS PROTECTION = GAMERS PLAYSTYLE

It is unrealistic to expect gamers to become paranoid digital hermits, scrutinizing every interaction and refusing every exciting opportunity. The spirit of gaming lies in exploration, risk-taking, and the thrill of the unknown. Instead of stifling that, the goal is to foster a security mindset that is dynamic and adaptable to a skilled gamer's playstyle.

First, we should tap into the gamer's understanding of "the meta." Explain common cybersecurity threats in gaming language – "That free loot offer is way too overpowered, it is likely a trap!" will resonate more than generic warnings. Second, like guilds support each other through difficult raids, in-game communities must create safe spaces to discuss suspicious offers or encounters. Peer-to-peer learning about the latest scam tactics is compelling.

Finally, the gaming world should not punish vulnerability. Companies should provide accessible, shame-free ways to report scams. This removes the stigma of being fooled, a critical factor in the success of cybercriminals. By embracing these strategies, we create an online environment where gamers can strategize their way to security, enjoying the thrill of the game without compromising their digital assets.

CASE STUDY: THE FORTNITE V-BUCK SCAM, ENVIRONMENT CLOSE TO GAME

The struggle to protect the vibrant and dynamic world of online gaming is an ongoing battle against ever-evolving threats. As attackers relentlessly devise new and ingenious ways to disguise their manipulations within the playful environment of games, the need for robust cybersecurity measures becomes increasingly critical. Education, vigilance, and a collaborative effort between game developers, cybersecurity experts, and the gaming community itself are essential to safeguard the immersive and engaging experiences that these virtual worlds offer.

The Fortnite V-Buck scam serves as a stark reminder of the challenges faced in protecting online gamers from real-world fraud. This sophisticated scam, which preyed on the desires and vulnerabilities of players, exposed the limitations of traditional security measures and highlighted the need for a more nuanced understanding of gaming psychology.

By delving into the intricacies of this scam, we can gain valuable insights into the tactics employed by attackers and the psychological factors that make gamers susceptible to manipulation. The Fortnite V-Buck scam cleverly exploited the in-game currency system, enticing players with the promise of free or discounted V-Bucks, the virtual currency used to purchase in-game items and enhancements.

The scammers often employed social engineering techniques, creating fake websites and social media accounts that mimicked the official Fortnite platform. They used phishing emails and messages, luring players with promises of exclusive rewards or early access to new content. These tactics preyed on the gamers' desire for in-game advantages and their trust in the familiar branding and communication styles of the gaming community.

The success of the Fortnite V-Buck scam underscores the need for a multi-layered approach to cybersecurity in online gaming. Game developers must prioritize security measures, implementing robust authentication systems, fraud detection mechanisms, and educational initiatives to raise awareness among players. Cybersecurity experts need to stay ahead of the curve, analyzing emerging threats and developing innovative solutions to protect gamers from evolving scams and attacks.

The gaming community itself plays a crucial role in this ongoing battle. By fostering a culture of cybersecurity awareness, encouraging responsible online behavior, and reporting suspicious activity, gamers can contribute to a safer and more secure gaming environment.

In essence, the fight to protect online gaming is a collective effort, demanding vigilance, collaboration, and a deep understanding of the psychological and social dynamics that make gamers vulnerable to adversarial attacks. By embracing these principles, we can ensure that the virtual worlds we cherish remain spaces of fun, creativity, and social interaction, free from the threats of real-world fraud and manipulation.

The Psychology of the Scam as Game

Scammers do not just exploit technological vulnerabilities; they understand the human mind and the specific emotional landscape found within the gaming world. In the case of Fortnite V-Bucks scams, these key psychological tactics were employed:

Scarcity and Exclusivity: Customization is a core part of Fortnite's appeal. Scammers leveraged this by offering V-Bucks at prices that seemed almost impossibly low. This created a sense of urgency and a fear of missing out, particularly potent for younger gamers who might have limited resources and crave instant gratification.

Undermining Authority: Often, scammers presented themselves as rebels or insiders offering "secret deals" that Epic Games would not want players to know about. This tactic erodes trust in the official company, tapping into a potential undercurrent of resentment that some players feel toward microtransactions, which they may view as greedy or exploitative.

Social Proof Manipulation: Fake testimonials, glowing reviews, and fabricated social media chatter made scams appear believable. In the gaming community, where recommendations and player experiences are highly valued, these fabricated endorsements could convince someone to disregard their initial skepticism and fall for a well-crafted scam. Understanding the psychological drivers behind these scams is crucial. It is not just about technological weakness; scammers understand how to manipulate emotions – urgency, fear, the desire to belong and be respected within the gaming community – for their gain.

Attack Surface: The scam was not just happening IN Fortnite. Phishing emails, fake social media accounts, and even video sites (with "tutorials" on how to get the cheap currency) were part of the attack, making it harder for Epic Games alone to combat.

Evolving Tactics: Once players woke up to one type of phishing site, scammers changed the look or used a slightly different URL. Reactive security measures were always a step behind.

The Victim Trap: Many players who fell for this were likely too young or embarrassed to report it. This lack of data gave Epic Games an incomplete picture of the problem's scope, hampering mitigation efforts.

LESSONS LEARNED

The Fortnite V-Bucks scam offers several essential takeaways for keeping gamers safe:

Companies and Game Developers Cannot Do It Alone: Collaboration with social media platforms and making it easier to partner with educational initiatives aimed at young gamers is crucial for tackling scams that spread beyond a single game's environment.

Age-Appropriate gaming Awareness: Telling kids "Do not get scammed" is useless. Training needs to be tailored to their developmental stage. Can concepts of online manipulation be woven into games themselves, making it a learning experience?

Friction as a Feature: Could buying V-Bucks outside the game be more difficult, even if it means slightly annoying legitimate users? A mandatory waiting period, for example, gives time for second thoughts.

We likely do not understand the full psychological impact of being scammed in gaming, especially for kids. Does it make them less trusting in all digital transactions or overly cynical about companies? This research could inform how we design safer games and better support for victims.

Brainstorming Question: Do you think competitive gamers, who are used to analyzing opponents' strategies, might be more resistant to these social engineering scams?

That is an exciting question! Here is a detailed breakdown of why competitive gamers might have some increased resistance to social engineering scams but also some vulnerabilities that make them targets:

POTENTIAL ADVANTAGES FOR COMPETITIVE GAMERS

Competitive gamers can enhance their skills through pattern recognition, allowing them to anticipate opponents' moves and strategies. A skeptical mindset enables them to critically assess their gameplay and adapt quickly under pressure, refining their performance during high-stakes situations.

Pattern Recognition: Top-tier gamers excel at spotting patterns, analyzing tactics, and adapting to their opponent's strategies on the fly. This mindset could translate to recognizing patterns in scams, such as identifying common phishing language, suspicious offers, or unusual behavior outside the game.

Skeptical Mindset: Competitive play encourages a healthy dose of skepticism and distrust. Players learn not to take things at face value and to constantly question their opponent's motivations. This critical thinking could help them question the legitimacy of seemingly too-good-to-be-true offers or outlandish claims.

Pressure Testing: High-stakes competitive gaming fosters the ability to make sound decisions under pressure and time constraints. This skill could help gamers resist the urgent tactics often used in social engineering scams, allowing them to think more rationally and avoid impulsive actions.

POTENTIAL VULNERABILITIES FOR COMPETITIVE GAMERS

Competitive gamers often face vulnerabilities like overconfidence, which can lead to poor decision-making during matches. Additionally, an intense focus on winning can result in burnout and mental fatigue, diminishing overall performance.

Overconfidence: Successful competitive players might develop a degree of overconfidence that could leave them vulnerable. They may believe their in-game skills make them infallible in other online environments, underestimating the sophistication of social engineering scams that do not rely on gaming mechanics.

Focus on the Win: The competitive drive to win at all costs could be exploited by attackers. Scammers framing an offer as a way to gain an unfair advantage, access to "secret" in-game items, or a chance to sabotage a rival team could be tempting to players focused on victory.

Burnout and Mental Fatigue: Intense competitive gaming can lead to burnout and mental fatigue. This impaired state can hinder judgment and make players more susceptible to manipulation, primarily if scammers target them during or after long, stressful tournament sessions.

Tunnel Vision: The hyper-focus required for competitive play could make gamers oblivious to red flags outside their immediate field of attention. They might become desensitized to odd requests or overlook suspicious behavior within team chats, where they expect a certain level of banter and competitive aggression.

THE BALANCE IS NOT ALWAYS IN GAMERS FAVOR

Ultimately, whether competitive gamers have an edge against social engineering scams depends on a mix of factors:

The Type of Scam: A simple phishing email is more likely to be spotted by a seasoned gamer. However, a scam executed by someone who infiltrated their gaming community over time and earned their trust would be far more challenging to defend against.

Individual Personality: Some gamers are naturally more cautious than others, regardless of their competitive nature.

Awareness Training: Being a good gamer does not teach you about online scams. Specific education about the ways their unique skills are targeted is essential.

Regardless of skill or experience, anyone can become a target of social engineering attacks in the competitive world of esports. The notion that some individuals are intrinsically less vulnerable is a dangerous misconception. Proper digital security begins with a healthy dose of skepticism toward all online interactions. It is crucial to recognize that attackers will expertly tailor their tactics to exploit a target's strengths, not just their weaknesses.

To fortify the "mental armor" of esports athletes and the wider gaming community, it is time to incorporate "mental security awareness" into training regimens directly. Here is how esports leagues and competitive gaming platforms can lead the charge:

Scenario-Based Training: Simulate common social engineering attack scenarios that might target esports figures (like fake tournament invites, sponsorship scams, or attempts at credential theft). Debriefing these simulations allows players to analyze manipulation techniques in a safe environment.

Profiling the Attacker: Educate players about the psychology and common tactics of social engineers. Understanding the "why" helps them recognize red flags more quickly.

Highlighting Emotional Triggers: Attackers prey on emotions like fear, excitement, or competitive drive. Teaching players to recognize when their emotions might be used against them empowers them to pause and reassess a situation.

Secure Communication Protocols: Establish clear reporting procedures for suspicious activity. This creates a support structure for players to voice concerns without fear of judgment.

Partnerships with Security Experts: Collaboration with cybersecurity professionals can provide tailored training, threat assessments, and access to the latest information on social engineering tactics targeting the gaming community.

Focus Areas, Scams that Exploit the Competitive Gaming Mindset

The cybersecurity threats young esports athletes face extend beyond technical vulnerabilities into the domain of manipulation and deception. Attackers understand the competitive drive of these players and their eagerness for an edge. Fake offers for exclusive beta access with overpowered features or flattery from supposed rival team scouts demonstrate that adversaries craft their phishing schemes to exploit this mindset specifically. It is crucial to reinforce the concept that even seemingly helpful offers that involve breaking the rules are likely traps – even if they promise a competitive advantage.

Moreover, doing poses a particularly insidious threat, especially when coupled with threats to release a player's personal information to coerce them into losing a match. Training for young esports athletes must cover how to protect their personal information and emphasize that it is never the victim's fault if doxxing occurs. Victim blaming only serves to compound the trauma. Instead, young players need to feel empowered to seek help and support if targeted.

The stakes are high – financial and reputational damage for individual players and compromises to the integrity of the esports world itself. Raising awareness of these unique social engineering tactics is vital. We must ensure that the next generation of esports athletes is equipped with cybersecurity knowledge and emotional resilience to navigate the thrilling but complex landscape of competitive gaming.

LEVERAGING GAMER STRENGTHS FOR LEARNING

Leveraging gamer strengths for learning, the "CTF with a Twist" introduces a unique approach that combines gameplay with educational challenges. By analyzing the "meta" of scams and incorporating incident reports, participants enhance critical thinking and problem-solving skills in a dynamic environment.

CTF (Capture the Flag) with a Twist: Could a training scenario be built into a game or an e-sport event where the goal is spotting social engineering? Finding the tells in fake profiles, analyzing suspicious in-game chat, etc. This makes it fun, not preachy.

Analyzing the "Meta" of Scams: Top gamers study the ever-shifting tactics of their opponents. Apply that same thinking to scams – what are the trendy ones now, what platforms do they target, etc.? This moves away from "do not be dumb" messaging and toward empowering players with knowledge.

The Incident Report: Could anonymized stories of actual scams that esports players have fallen victim to be shared regularly? This helps them learn from others and makes reporting their own experiences less shameful, which is critical to getting ahead of new attack trends.

BUILDING A GAMING CULTURE OF "MIND SECURITY"

With its high-profile stars, intense pressure, and lucrative opportunities, the esports world is a prime target for scammers. However, the strategies for protecting players and the industry extend beyond purely technical measures. Organizations and communities can create a more secure and supportive environment for all involved by focusing on the human element.

First, leveraging pro players as role models can make security awareness engaging and relatable. Hearing about a well-known figure's close call with a scam humanizes cybersecurity, making it less abstract and demonstrating that even skilled individuals can be targeted.

Second, creating a team culture where admitting vulnerability is encouraged is crucial. A designated person who offers non-judgmental support for reporting suspicious activity mitigates embarrassment or fear for the players. This proactivity leads to faster identification and mitigation of threats.

Finally, as many esports organizations prioritize physical health, mental well-being must be equally focused. Regular, mandated mental resets decrease burnout and impulsive decisions that make players more susceptible to scams. These strategies protect and empower players, creating a more robust industry.

IMPLEMENTATION SECURE GAMING CULTURE

Creating a secure gaming culture hinges on the active involvement of game developers, who play a crucial role in shaping safe environments for players. Building strong partnerships and ensuring ongoing commitment from all stakeholders are essential to maintaining these standards.

Game Devs Matter: Small changes to UI could nudge better habits, such as a pop-up warning if a player clicks a link sent in team chat.

Partnerships are Key: Teaming up with mental health organizations that understand gaming culture would be more effective than generic cybersecurity firms trying to deliver this training.

It Has to Be Ongoing: Like learning a new in-game strategy, mental security takes practice. Regular training bursts are more likely to stick than a single, boring lecture.

Let us take a look at one game example. Let us focus on Tomb Raider as an example and look into training modules and possibilities to spot a treat. The rich narrative world of Tomb Raider offers a unique angle for creating a compelling and immersive social engineering training module for gamers. Here is a possible approach:

MODULE TITLE: "RAIDERS OF THE LOST DATA: OUTSMARTING CYBER-TRAPS IN THE DIGITAL UNDERWORLD"

Module Premise

Beyond her archaeological quests, Lara Croft is also known for her tech expertise. In this module, she "narrates" the training for players, framing social engineering scams as another type of dangerous trap to be outsmarted, one that can have real-world consequences even for the most seasoned adventurer.

Learning Objectives

Spotting Phishing Attempts Disguised as Official Communications: Players learn to identify fake emails seemingly from the game developer (Square Enix/Crystal Dynamics), offering exclusive beta access in-universe lore drops.

Identifying the "Hidden Treasures" of Scam Tactics: The module analyzes common ploys like limited-time offers, promises of rare items or in-game advantages, and appeals to ego (offers to make the player a "Tomb Raider ambassador").

Protecting the Expedition: Focus on in-game scams perpetrated through compromised accounts or fake guilds. Emphasizes that even friends within the Tomb Raider community could unknowingly become tools for attackers.

Gameplay Integration

Interactive Scenario: Players "assist" Lara with an investigation by examining suspicious in-game messages, emails, or fake websites. To determine their legitimacy, they must analyze these materials, with Lara providing hints and feedback.

Environmental Storytelling: The training could be accessed through a "secure terminal" within a Tomb Raider game or companion app. Surroundings might include notes Lara has left about past scams she has encountered, making it an extension of the lore.

The "Aha!" Moment: Successful completion unlocks an in-game reward – a unique cosmetic item themed on cybersecurity (protective armor skin, tech-looking backpack, etc.) or a small amount of in-game currency, reinforcing positive behaviors.

Key Themes

Curiosity is a Tool, not a Weakness: Lara always investigates but with caution. The module teaches players to do the same with suspicious comms and not to be afraid to question everything.

Treasures Take Time: Emphasizes that no real in-game advantage comes quickly or easily. Anything that seems out of line with the usual progression of the game is likely a trap.

Community as a Defense: Lara often relies on allies. The module encourages players to have a designated person (in-game friend, team leader) they can go to with ANY weird offers to get a gut check to protect themselves and others.

Additional Considerations

Age-Appropriateness: Adapt the complexity of examples and Lara's "voice" based on whether the module is for a general Tomb Raider audience or those involved in competitive play.

Accessibility: Offer subtitles and ways to slow down analysis segments to ensure all players can benefit.

If successful, this approach could be the basis for a whole series of crossover security-awareness content within the Tomb Raider franchise. Imagine a side quest where Lara recovers stolen data by outsmarting the thieves online, further reinforcing these concepts for players engagingly.

Let us discuss how this in-game mental security training could benefit the competitive/esports community!

Here is how we can tailor "mental security" training, like our Tomb Raider-inspired concept, to the unique needs and vulnerabilities of the competitive/esports community:

Focus on High-Stakes Scams

The Rigged Match: Elaborate scenarios where a player is seemingly contacted by gamblers wanting to bribe them to throw a match in exchange for real-world money. Training would emphasize that this is illegal and that reporting is always the right move, even if tempted.

DDoS for Hire: Fake services offering to take down rival players with DDoS attacks during a tournament. This tackles the temptation to cheat and teaches how to spot these offers as unethical and likely scams.

Impersonation of Orgs/Sponsors: Attackers pose as scouts, offering a player a seeming dream contract…but then request money "for processing." This helps players spot when the excitement of a big break is being used against them.

The Psychological Angle

When Exhaustion Is the Attack Vector: Training can offer specific tips during/after tournaments when players are most vulnerable. This might include reminders never to click links when tired, extra scrutiny of "congratulatory" messages from strangers, etc.

Failure as Intel: Create a safe space for esports players to anonymously share scams they have nearly fallen for (or sadly, did). Analyzing these pinpoints times of weakness – after a crushing loss, for example – letting others learn from experience.

Stress = Bad In-Game Decisions Too: The same mental fog that makes a scam more likely to succeed can also hurt gameplay at a critical moment. Training that connects "mental security" with optimized performance appeals more to highly competitive players.

Integration Matters

Coaches on Board: They are often the ones players trust most. Training for coaches on scam spotting and how to subtly guide a player toward reporting something suspicious (without accusation) is critical.

The "Play of the Week" Breakdown: Could a regular stream segment involve high-level players analyzing a famous scam from the esports world? This gets them to apply their strategic thinking to dissect how a social engineering attack unfolded, making them less likely to fall for similar tactics.

Waiting Room Reminders: During those tense moments before a match load, a pop-up could remind players instead of just game tips: "Never share your info in team chat." Quick, non-intrusive, but reinforces the proper habits.

THE CHALLENGE OF SHAME IN GAMING CULTURE

Competitive gaming can create an environment where admitting to a mistake is hard. This is scammer paradise. That is why training needs to normalize the following:

Even Pros Get Targeted: Anonymized stories from the top levels show that no one's immune system.

Reporting = Strength: Frame it as protecting the team. The sooner an attack is spotted, the less damage it will likely do.

THIS IS NOT JUST ABOUT INDIVIDUALS

The responsibility for mental security in the competitive esports landscape cannot rest solely on the shoulders of individual players. These athletes, often young and immersed in a digital world that blurs the lines between their personal and professional lives, are particularly vulnerable to the psychological pressures of online harassment, social engineering attacks, and the constant scrutiny of a global audience. Esports leagues, as governing bodies and stewards of the competitive environment, have a crucial role to play in fostering a culture of mental well-being and resilience.

One significant step toward achieving this goal is the implementation of mandatory "mental security" awareness training and refresher courses as a contractual requirement for all participating teams. This not only places a clear responsibility on organizations to safeguard the mental well-being of their players but also cultivates a much-needed team mentality, where players are encouraged to look out for each other and share the burden of vigilance against online threats.

By integrating mental security awareness into the contractual framework of esports leagues, we send a powerful message that mental well-being is as crucial as physical prowess and strategic mastery. This holistic approach recognizes that the digital arena is not just a battleground for virtual competition but also a potential minefield of psychological challenges.

Furthermore, mandating mental security training fosters a culture of shared responsibility, where players, coaches, and team managers are all equipped with the knowledge and tools to recognize and respond to online harassment, social engineering tactics, and other threats to mental well-being. This collective awareness creates a safety net, ensuring that players feel supported and empowered to navigate the complexities of the digital landscape.

Esports leagues, by placing mental well-being on par with physical readiness, pave the way for a more resilient and supportive environment. In a field where the line between personal and professional life often blurs in the digital domain, this commitment to mental security is not just a matter of ethical responsibility but also a crucial factor in ensuring the long-term health and sustainability of the esports ecosystem.

17 Digital Surveillance and Trust Erosion

NAVIGATING THE COMPLEXITIES OF ENHANCED SOCIAL ENGINEERING DETECTION

Digital surveillance and the erosion of trust in digital ecosystems are intricately intertwined, casting a long shadow over the landscape of cybersecurity and challenging the very foundations of our digital interactions. As technology advances, enabling more sophisticated and pervasive forms of surveillance, individuals and organizations find themselves navigating an increasingly treacherous terrain, where the delicate balance between security and privacy, between protection and intrusion, is constantly tested.

The erosion of trust, a consequence of both real and perceived surveillance, creates fertile ground for social engineering attacks, which exploit our vulnerabilities and manipulate our online behavior. When individuals feel that their every digital move is being watched, tracked, and analyzed, a sense of unease and suspicion permeates their online interactions. This distrust can be readily exploited by malicious actors who employ social engineering tactics to deceive, manipulate, and gain access to sensitive information.

The effectiveness of social engineering detection mechanisms is also compromised in an environment of pervasive surveillance. When individuals are constantly bombarded with warnings about potential threats and urged to be suspicious of every online interaction, a sense of "alert fatigue" can set in. This desensitization to security warnings can make individuals more susceptible to social engineering attacks, as they may become less discerning in evaluating the legitimacy of online requests or less cautious in sharing personal information.

Furthermore, the very technologies designed to enhance security and protect against cyber threats can inadvertently contribute to the erosion of trust. Surveillance systems, while intended to identify and mitigate risks, can also be perceived as intrusive and privacy-violating, fostering a sense of unease and suspicion among users. This distrust can undermine the effectiveness of security measures, as individuals may be less inclined to cooperate with or trust systems that they perceive as infringing on their privacy.

In this complex and evolving landscape, the challenge lies in finding a balance between security and privacy, between the need to protect against cyber threats and the importance of preserving individual liberties and fostering trust in digital ecosystems. This requires a multifaceted approach that encompasses not only technological solutions but also ethical considerations, legal frameworks, and a commitment to transparency and accountability in the development and deployment of surveillance technologies.

DOI: 10.1201/9781003500698-17

By addressing the erosion of trust and fostering a culture of responsible innovation in the digital realm, we can create a more secure and resilient online environment, where individuals can confidently engage in digital interactions without fear of manipulation or exploitation.

WHEN SURVEILLANCE MAKES US EASIER TO FOOL: FIGHTING SOCIAL ENGINEERING IN A TRUST-ERODED WORLD

Digital surveillance has become an insidious and pervasive force in modern society, casting a long shadow over our online interactions and eroding the foundations of trust in the digital realm. Governments, corporations, and even individual hackers have at their disposal an arsenal of sophisticated tools to monitor our online activities, collect our data, and track our digital footprints. This constant sense of being watched, coupled with the all-too-common news stories of massive data breaches and privacy violations, breeds a deep-seated distrust in the very technologies that have become integral to our lives.

Ironically, this pervasive surveillance and the resulting erosion of trust create a fertile ground for social engineering attacks, the very schemes that digital security measures aim to prevent. When individuals feel constantly monitored and vulnerable, they become more susceptible to manipulation and are more likely to fall prey to phishing scams, malicious links, and other forms of online deception. The fear of being watched ironically blinds us to the very real threats lurking in the digital shadows.

This climate of distrust also undermines the potential benefits of technology, hindering collaboration, innovation, and the free exchange of ideas that have driven human progress for centuries. When individuals feel their every move is being scrutinized, they are less likely to express themselves freely, to challenge conventional thinking, or to engage in the open dialogue that fuels creativity and societal advancement.

The consequences of this digital panopticon extend far beyond individual privacy concerns. The erosion of trust in online platforms and institutions can have a chilling effect on civic engagement, political discourse, and even the functioning of democratic societies. When individuals feel their online activities are constantly monitored and potentially manipulated, they may become disengaged from public life, hesitant to participate in online discussions, or even reluctant to exercise their right to vote.

In essence, the pervasive nature of digital surveillance has created a self-fulfilling prophecy. The fear of being watched and the erosion of trust make us more vulnerable to the very attacks we fear, perpetuating a cycle of paranoia and exploitation. To break this cycle, we must reclaim control over our digital lives, demand greater transparency and accountability from those who collect and utilize our data, and foster a culture of digital literacy and critical engagement that empowers individuals to navigate the complex digital landscape safely and confidently.

HOW SURVEILLANCE UNDERMINES SECURITY

In the interconnected world of the internet, where information flows freely and boundaries blur, the constant bombardment of potential threats and warnings can create a pervasive sense of distrust and cynicism. This "boy who cried wolf" effect, where legitimate security warnings become indistinguishable from the noise of countless online scams and phishing attempts, can have detrimental consequences for individual security and societal well-being.

When every online interaction feels potentially malicious, individuals may become desensitized to genuine threats, dismissing legitimate warnings as just another attempt to grab their attention or exploit their fears. This can lead to a dangerous complacency, where individuals are more likely to fall victim to phishing scams, malware attacks, or other forms of cybercrime.

Attackers often weaponize cynicism, preying on the widespread belief that privacy is already compromised in the digital age. Messages that play on the idea that companies are already tracking our every move, that our data are already out there for the taking, can be surprisingly effective in persuading individuals to relinquish even more personal information.

This cynicism can erode trust in online platforms, institutions, and even the very notion of online security. It can create a sense of helplessness, where individuals feel powerless to protect their privacy and data, leading to a dangerous resignation to the inevitability of cyberattacks and data breaches.

The chilling effect of surveillance and the fear of being judged or ridiculed can lead to self-censorship, where individuals are hesitant to seek help or ask questions they perceive as "dumb." This reluctance to speak up, often rooted in shame or embarrassment, can have serious consequences in the context of cybersecurity.

Scammers and malicious actors thrive on this silence, preying on those who are too ashamed or embarrassed to report an incident or seek assistance. This self-censorship perpetuates a cycle of vulnerability, allowing cybercriminals to operate with impunity and further eroding trust in online interactions.

The erosion of trust, the weaponization of cynicism, and the chilling effect of self-censorship create a fertile ground for adversarial attacks and undermine the foundations of a secure and resilient digital society. By fostering a culture of open communication, promoting digital literacy, and empowering individuals to speak up without fear of judgment, we can counter these negative forces and build a safer and more trustworthy online environment.

FIGHTING BACK REQUIRES A SHIFT IN THINKING

In an era of pervasive surveillance, where our online activities are constantly monitored and analyzed, the psychological impact on individuals and society is profound. The constant awareness of being watched can erode trust, fuel paranoia, and distort our perception of online interactions. This surveillance-induced distrust can have serious consequences for cybersecurity, making individuals more susceptible to manipulation, misinformation, and adversarial attacks. Could artificial intelligence be used to detect the subtle signs of surveillance-induced distrust in our online behavior? Imagine a browser extension that acts as a digital guardian angel, gently nudging us with a timely warning: "Is this making you overly suspicious? Take a breath before you click." Such a tool could help us recognize and mitigate the negative impact of surveillance on our decision-making, fostering a more mindful and resilient approach to online interactions. Companies and organizations have a crucial role to play in rebuilding trust in the digital age. Clear, understandable privacy policies, coupled with giving users absolute control over their data, are essential steps toward restoring confidence. Without this transparency and user empowerment, security warnings will always be met with skepticism, hindering our ability to protect ourselves from cyber threats. Creating a security culture that encourages learning from mistakes is paramount. Platforms that provide safe and anonymous channels for reporting scams and near misses can empower individuals to share their experiences without fear of judgment. The less shame associated with falling victim to cyberattacks, the less power attackers have to exploit our vulnerabilities. Social engineering research must delve deeper into the psychological impact of surveillance on individuals and communities. Are people under heavy surveillance more likely to misinterpret neutral communication as a threat? Do they exhibit heightened anxiety or paranoia in online interactions? Understanding these psychological nuances is crucial for designing effective mitigations and fostering a more resilient and informed digital citizenry.

By acknowledging the psychological impact of surveillance, promoting transparency and user empowerment, and fostering a culture of learning and open communication, we can mitigate the negative consequences of surveillance and build a safer and more trustworthy digital world.

Surveillance, whether real or perceived, changes the "rules" of the cybersecurity game. Addressing this root cause of vulnerability requires a societal shift in how we think about data privacy and what it means to interact in a world where nothing is truly hidden. Redefining Privacy in the Digital Age: Our current legal frameworks around data privacy are woefully inadequate for the scope of surveillance we now face. Advocacy is needed for policies that give individuals actual ownership of their data, with granular controls on how it is collected and used at every step. Force transparency about the "black markets" of data. Where is it sold, who aggregates it, and for what purposes? This knowledge empowers users to make more informed choices. Penalize companies for deceptive data practices, not just breaches. The vague language most companies use in their privacy policies trains us to accept surveillance as inevitable.

FIGHTING BACK AGAINST NORMALIZATION OF SURVEILLANCE

Support public awareness campaigns that transcend the typical focus on basic phishing scams and password protection. These campaigns must delve deeper into the intricate ways that seemingly innocuous data collection practices fuel the engine of targeted manipulation and online exploitation. By clarifying the often-overlooked connection between privacy and security, we can empower individuals to make informed choices about their digital footprint and advocate for greater protection of their personal information.

Fund research that explores the long-term psychological and societal consequences of living in a world of pervasive surveillance. This research is essential to build a compelling case for why privacy is not merely a personal preference but a fundamental human right with profound implications for public health and well-being. The constant feeling of being watched, tracked, and analyzed can lead to anxiety, self-censorship, and a chilling effect on freedom of expression, ultimately eroding the foundations of a democratic society.

Counter the pervasive and insidious "If you have nothing to hide, you have nothing to fear" argument that often dominates the surveillance debate. This dangerous rhetoric dismisses the fundamental right to privacy for all citizens, regardless of their perceived innocence or guilt. It perpetuates a culture of shame, where individuals feel hesitant to question or resist intrusive data collection practices, even when those practices infringe on their fundamental rights. We must emphasize that even law-abiding citizens deserve autonomy over their personal information and the right to control how it is collected, used, and shared.

By promoting a deeper understanding of the interconnectedness between privacy, security, and individual autonomy, we can foster a society that values and protects these fundamental rights in the digital age.

EMPOWERED USERS, NOT JUST "EDUCATED" USERS

Advocate for tech design that puts privacy at the forefront. Default settings should not be maximum data collection. Support open-source alternatives to mainstream tools, allowing users to opt out of surveillance-funded business models.

Push for "friction as protection" in the online world. Could mandatory wait periods for specific data-sharing actions allow time for second thoughts and decrease the impulsive click that surveillance fatigue often encourages?

HOLD THE SURVEILLERS ACCOUNTABLE

Stronger regulations are needed to guide government agencies in accessing and utilizing the data collected by private companies.

Crackdown on data brokers, particularly those who target vulnerable groups (minors, the elderly) for manipulation.

Lobbying transparency, especially in the tech sector. Knowing who is funding the anti-privacy legislation efforts is critical to fighting it.

SELLING THE IMPORTANCE OF THIS ISSUE IS CHALLENGING BECAUSE

It Is Complex: Cause-and-effect is hard to prove to the average person.

It Is Not Immediate: We can grasp a data breach, but the slow erosion of trust that makes phishing easier is a more challenging threat to rally against. Perhaps advocacy needs to focus on real-life stories where a person's vulnerability, amplified by surveillance, had devastating effects. Think of someone who loses their life savings in a scam after a targeted ad campaign fueled by their medical data that they did not consent to be shared.

Now let us explore why collaborating with storytellers and filmmakers could be a powerful strategy to raise awareness about the complex intersection of social engineering and surveillance:

Emotional Resonance: Dry policy or technical explanations struggle to compete with the emotional impact of a well-crafted story. Films, documentaries, and even short online narratives can make the abstract threat of surveillance feel personal and immediate.

The "That Could Be Me" Factor: Seeing ourselves reflected as the victim of a scam makes us far more likely to shift from a mindset of "I would never be that foolish" to "That could happen to anyone under the right circumstances." This is essential for breaking down the shame barrier that keeps people from seeking help.

Humanizing the Consequences: We all understand the impact of a stolen credit card. However, a story that shows the long-term effects of surveillance-fueled social engineering – destroyed trust in institutions and the breakdown of relationships. It drives home that this is about far more than just money.

DIFFERENT APPROACHES

While fictional narratives like a "social engineering Minority Report" may spark urgent debates about the future, they are not our only tool in combating the digital age's manipulation threat. Docudramas, merging the power of real-life stories with dramatic presentation and expert insight, could illuminate the devastating impact and the disturbingly common tactics that facilitate these insidious attacks. Furthermore, ethically produced social experiments designed to expose how vulnerable we might be to seemingly harmless disclosures hold the potential to be viral awareness campaigns.

However, the impact extends far beyond the screen. Actual change demands collaboration. Filmmakers must work alongside cybersecurity experts, psychologists, and privacy advocates to ensure a responsible and realistic portrayal of technology's role in manipulation. When coupled with panel discussions or facilitated online "watch parties," film screenings can turn a viewing experience into a springboard for dialogue and deeper engagement. Additionally, harnessing the "fan mentality" could empower regular people to become privacy champions, ready to identify the signs of manipulation in our digital lives.

This chapter has focused on the threats to personal security by social manipulation in the digital age. However, it is a call to action as much as a warning. Through creative storytelling, responsible awareness campaigns, and fostering collaboration across disciplines, we can build a future where information empowers us rather than becoming a weapon used against us.

CHALLENGES AND CONSIDERATIONS

Finding Funding: Projects critically examining surveillance may struggle to get mainstream backing. Exploring independent funding streams or partnering with advocacy groups will be necessary.

Avoiding Backlash: Portraying victims of scams needs to be done without condescension, or it will fail. Filmmakers skilled in nuance are essential.

Is Fear-Mongering a Risk? It is a delicate balance. We need to awaken people to the dangers of unchecked surveillance without paralyzing them with the sense that any online interaction is doomed.

This might be a long-term play, but given the slow-moving nature of policy change, shifting public opinion through art could be the catalyst.

Now, let us take a deeper look, outline a film concept inspired by an actual social engineering attack, and then discuss how a compelling story could catalyze awareness and action.

STORY CONCEPT: "THE CLICK"

Inspiration: Draw upon real cases where highly targeted spear-phishing led to large-scale data breaches that affected average people. The goal is to move away from the "hacker in a hoodie" trope and show that these attacks can begin with the most mundane-seeming email.

The Protagonist: Not a tech expert, but an overworked, slightly distracted single parent – someone relatable. They receive an email appearing to be from their child's school, claiming missed payments, with a link to resolve things quickly before pickup time. This initial click is the unravelling point.

The Slow Burn: The film follows the parallel threads of the escalating personal hell the victim endures – identity theft, loss of savings, the fear that the attack will not stop.

Tech experts are tracing the attack back through layers of shell companies, uncovering how harmless-seeming data collected years ago was the bedrock of the scam.

KEY THEMES

Surveillance as Ammunition: No flashy hacking scenes. The mundane wins: birthday posts on social media pinpointing the child's age and property records.

It Is Not Just "Stupidity": The character is intelligent, but chronic stress and feeling like a lousy parent due to missed payments makes them click without the usual scrutiny.

The Human Chain: Show that scams would not work without corrupt school staff, exploitative payday loan companies. Systemic failures amplify individual vulnerability.

BEYOND ENTERTAINMENT: THE IMPACT CAMPAIGN

The companion website serves as a bridge between the fictional narrative and the stark realities of cybercrime, offering viewers a deeper understanding of the real-world implications of the film's events. By showcasing an actual attack that mirrors the film's plot, the website highlights the vulnerability of individuals and communities to cyber threats. It exposes the gaps in our current protective measures, revealing the inadequacy of existing laws and the urgent need for stronger safeguards to protect sensitive data and prevent financial exploitation. Furthermore, the website empowers viewers with practical knowledge and actionable steps they can take to protect themselves in the digital age. It provides resources and guidance on recognizing and mitigating cyber risks, from identifying phishing scams and securing online accounts to practicing responsible data sharing and maintaining a healthy skepticism toward online interactions.

The film's narrative extends beyond the immediate aftermath of the cyberattack, delving into the lingering consequences that ripple through the lives of the victims and the community at large. The pursuit of justice, while offering a sense of closure, does not erase the scars of trauma and betrayal. Strained relationships, shattered trust, and a lingering sense of vulnerability become part of the victims' daily reality. The film poignantly portrays the erosion of trust in institutions, as individuals grapple with the realization that those entrusted with protecting them failed to prevent the attack or provide adequate support in its aftermath. This exploration of the long-term consequences of cybercrime serves as a powerful reminder that the impact of these attacks extends far beyond financial loss. It highlights the emotional toll, the social disruption, and the erosion of trust that can linger long after the immediate crisis has subsided. The film's impact extends beyond the screen, aiming to galvanize viewers into action and advocate for a safer and more equitable digital world. By collaborating with advocacy groups already engaged in the fight against predatory lenders and cybercrime, the film seeks to amplify their voices and empower viewers to become agents of change. The companion website provides resources and information on how viewers can get involved, from supporting organizations that provide assistance to scam victims to contacting their elected officials and demanding stronger data protection laws and consumer safeguards. This call to action transforms the film from a passive viewing experience into an opportunity for civic engagement and social change. It recognizes that the fight against cybercrime requires a collective effort, empowering individuals to become advocates for a more secure and just digital future.

The film and its companion website create a powerful synergy, bridging the gap between fiction and reality, raising awareness about the pervasive threat of cybercrime, and inspiring viewers to take action. By exposing the vulnerabilities of our digital world, highlighting the human cost of cyberattacks, and empowering individuals to become advocates for change, the film and website contribute to a broader movement toward a safer, more equitable, and resilient digital society.

A STORY THAT DEMANDS ACTION

Stories, unlike statistics, possess a unique power to penetrate the defenses of the human psyche and stir the embers of empathy. While statistics may inform us of the prevalence of social engineering attacks, they often fail to ignite the emotional spark needed to truly grasp the personal implications of these threats. Stories, on the other hand, transport us into the shoes of others, allowing us to experience their vulnerabilities, their struggles, and the devastating consequences of falling victim to manipulation. A film that masterfully portrays the devastating impact of social engineering attacks on ordinary individuals and families could be the catalyst needed to awaken the public to the urgent need for data privacy. By witnessing the emotional turmoil, the financial ruin, and the erosion of trust that can result from these attacks, viewers would no longer perceive data privacy as an abstract concept but as a vital shield protecting themselves and their loved ones. Such a film could weave a compelling narrative around a family whose lives are irrevocably altered by a social engineering attack. The story could unfold through the eyes of a protagonist who, initially complacent about data privacy, gradually awakens to the harsh reality of its importance as they witness the devastating consequences of a cyberattack on their family.

The film could portray the emotional rollercoaster experienced by the victims, the feelings of betrayal, shame, and helplessness that often accompany such attacks. It could also highlight the ripple effects of these attacks, demonstrating how they can shatter trust, disrupt relationships, and leave lasting scars on individuals and communities. By humanizing the consequences of social engineering attacks and showcasing the real-world impact on ordinary people, this film could serve as a powerful wake-up call. It could inspire viewers to take proactive steps to protect their data, to educate themselves about cybersecurity threats, and to demand greater accountability from institutions entrusted with their personal information. In essence, stories have the power to transform data privacy from a dry technical concept into a deeply personal and emotionally resonant issue. By harnessing the power of storytelling, we can bridge the gap between awareness and action, inspiring individuals to become active participants in the fight for a safer and more secure digital world.

18 Virtual Reality and Its Impact on Social Trust

TECHNOLOGICAL FACILITATION OF SOCIAL ENGINEERING ATTACKS AND TECHNOLOGICAL CHALLENGES TO DETECT

Virtual reality (VR) is rapidly transforming the digital landscape, offering immersive experiences that blur the lines between the physical and virtual worlds. By donning a VR headset, users can step into breathtaking digital realms, interact with virtual objects and environments, and connect with others in shared virtual spaces. This technology has profound implications for social trust, influencing how individuals perceive and interact with each other in these increasingly realistic digital environments. As VR technology advances, becoming more accessible and immersive, it is essential to examine its impact on social dynamics and trust formation. Within virtual worlds, individuals can adopt avatars, digital representations of themselves, that can range from realistic depictions to fantastical creations. This ability to shape one's virtual identity raises questions about authenticity, self-presentation, and the formation of trust in online interactions. Furthermore, the immersive nature of VR can create a sense of presence, a psychological phenomenon where individuals feel as though they are truly present in the virtual environment. This sense of presence can heighten emotional engagement and social connection, but it can also blur the lines between reality and virtuality, potentially impacting trust and the perception of authenticity. The social implications of VR are far-reaching, influencing how individuals form relationships, build communities, and engage in collaborative activities. The ability to interact with others in shared virtual spaces, regardless of physical location, has the potential to bridge geographical divides and foster cross-cultural understanding. However, it also raises concerns about the potential for manipulation, deception, and the erosion of trust in online interactions. As VR technology continues to evolve, it is crucial to examine its impact on social trust and develop strategies to foster healthy and ethical online interactions. This includes promoting digital literacy, encouraging critical thinking about virtual experiences, and developing guidelines for responsible VR development and use. By understanding the complex interplay between VR technology, human psychology, and social dynamics, we can harness the transformative potential of VR while mitigating its potential risks and ensuring that it fosters a more connected, trustworthy, and inclusive digital world.

DOI: 10.1201/9781003500698-18

THE IMMERSIVE ILLUSION

How VR's Strengths Can Become Vulnerabilities in the Face of Social Engineering

VR offers an unprecedented level of immersion, transporting users to digital realms that blur the lines between the physical and the virtual. This immersive power, while revolutionizing entertainment, education, and various industries, also creates fertile ground for social engineering attacks that exploit the unique psychological vulnerabilities of these environments. Understanding the intersection of VR technology and human psychology is crucial to designing secure and resilient VR platforms that protect users from manipulation and deception.

The immersive nature of VR can create a powerful sense of presence, where users feel physically and emotionally transported to the virtual environment. This sense of presence can make users more susceptible to social engineering tactics, as they may lower their guard and become more trusting of virtual interactions.

Furthermore, the anonymity and malleability of identity in VR can be exploited by malicious actors. Users can adopt avatars that conceal their true identities, making it easier for attackers to impersonate trusted figures or create false personas to gain users' trust.

The heightened emotional engagement and sensory stimulation of VR experiences can also make users more vulnerable to manipulation. Attackers can craft immersive scenarios designed to evoke strong emotions, such as fear, excitement, or curiosity, to bypass rational decision-making and elicit desired behaviors from users.

Moreover, the novelty and unfamiliarity of VR interactions can create a sense of uncertainty and disorientation, making users more susceptible to social engineering tactics that exploit their lack of experience and understanding of the VR environment.

To mitigate these risks, VR platform developers must prioritize security and user protection from the outset. This includes implementing robust authentication and identity verification mechanisms, educating users about potential threats and social engineering tactics, and designing VR experiences that promote critical thinking and awareness of potential manipulation.

By understanding the unique psychological vulnerabilities of VR environments and incorporating security measures that address these vulnerabilities, we can ensure that VR technology remains a tool for empowerment, innovation, and positive human experiences, rather than a breeding ground for deception and exploitation.

HOW VR AMPLIFIES THE ATTACKER'S TOOLKIT

Our brains, shaped by millennia of evolution, are wired to trust our senses. What we see, hear, and touch forms the foundation of our perception of reality. VR, with its immersive and multi-sensory experiences, can exploit this innate trust, creating an illusion of presence that overrides critical thinking in ways that traditional phishing emails could only dream of. Imagine standing on the edge of a virtual cliff, the wind whipping through your hair, the ground seemingly crumbling beneath your feet. Your senses tell you that you are in danger, triggering a primal fear response, even though you are safely seated in your living room. This visceral experience, this feeling of presence, can be readily exploited by attackers to gain trust quickly and to trigger emotions like fear and urgency, making individuals more susceptible to manipulation and persuasion. In the realm of VR, our interactions are increasingly mediated by avatars, digital representations of ourselves and others. This reliance on avatars, while offering a sense of anonymity and creative expression, also creates new opportunities for deception and manipulation.

Never before in human history has so much of our communication been with representations, not the actual person. This detachment from physical identity makes it easier for attackers to construct elaborate false personas, mimicking those we know and trust, or creating entirely fictitious characters to lure us into security-compromising acts.

The anonymity afforded by avatars can also embolden attackers, allowing them to engage in manipulative behavior without the fear of immediate repercussions. This creates a challenging environment for building trust and verifying identities, raising questions about the future of social interaction and security in virtual worlds. The immersive nature of VR creates a unique paradox: the very features that make VR appealing also make it vulnerable to social engineering attacks. Thorough monitoring of user behavior within virtual environments could potentially catch most social engineering attempts, but it would also fundamentally undermine the sense of freedom and immersion that VR offers.

The challenge lies in designing privacy solutions that are as dynamic and adaptable as the virtual worlds themselves. Can we develop security measures that protect users from manipulation without compromising their sense of agency and immersion? Can we create a balance between privacy and protection that fosters trust and encourages the ethical development of VR technologies?

These questions highlight the complex interplay between technology, human behavior, and the evolving landscape of cybersecurity. As VR becomes increasingly integrated into our lives, the need for innovative security solutions that respect individual privacy while safeguarding against malicious actors will become paramount.

VR TECHNOLOGICAL CHALLENGES FOR COUNTERMEASURES

The virtual world challenges our understanding of both human behavior and technological threats. We can no longer rely solely on analyzing text-based interactions or mouse clicks. In VR, a user excitedly reaching to grab a virtual item could be a sign of genuine immersion or a telltale signal that they are falling for a scam. AI security systems trained in traditional online environments may fumble for answers in this new landscape.

Moreover, the sheer novelty of VR is itself a vulnerability. Attackers could exploit unforeseen weaknesses with each platform and application offering unique experiences. Waiting for attacks to happen before hardening defenses places users at unacceptable risk, highlighting the need for proactive security design.

However, heavy-handed solutions can ruin the magic of VR. Constant warnings or actions that force users to break immersion will severely degrade the experience. Seamless, intuitive protection is vital, but this poses significant challenges. Designing security measures that blend into the background anticipating threats without disruption, is the next major hurdle to overcome.

THE PATH FORWARD

Proactive Threat Modeling: Can we "game out" in advance how social engineering tactics might work in VR and build against them? This requires collaboration between security experts, UX designers, and those with deep knowledge of psychology.

Education as Immersive Experience: Do not just tell users about VR scams; let them experience safe simulations of potential attacks. This builds "muscle memory" to spot the signs.

"Trust Indicators" that Work in VR: These could be visual (a subtle overlay on an avatar that fades if they say something out of character) or even haptic feedback tied to our "gut feeling" response.

VR could pioneer a new way of thinking about cybersecurity, focusing on empowering the user, not just blocking the bad guys. If done right, we will create safer technology for *everyone* online.

While advanced AI and machine learning are crucial tools, purely technical solutions to social engineering in VR have limitations. This is where behavioral science comes in. Understanding the psychological underpinnings of these attacks and how VR influences our perception is vital for designing effective security measures.

Tech needs a behavioral boost, because traditional security paradigms focus on concrete actions – clicking a link or downloading a suspicious file. However, a potent threat in VR lies in the attacker's ability to lull users into a false sense of security, crafting immersive environments that suspend critical thinking. Behavioral science offers valuable insights into how the illusion of presence can be established through lighting, sound design, and social cues. By understanding these mechanisms, we can turn them into tools for defense. By integrating subtle "reality checks" into the VR experience, we can gently nudge users back toward a state of caution without fundamentally disrupting their immersion. These prompts can be visual, auditory, or even haptic – a slight dissonance in the environment, an unexpected change in ambient sound – designed to trigger a moment of cognitive re-evaluation before a user divulges sensitive information or engages in a risky action. This approach harnesses the power of behavioral science to build resilience against threats that exist primarily within the user's perception.

REAL-LIFE EXAMPLE: THE "FRIEND IN NEED" VR SCAM

Imagine stepping into a vibrant VR social platform, a digital realm teeming with lifelike avatars and immersive experiences. As you navigate this virtual landscape, a friend request pops up from an avatar that seems vaguely familiar. Behavioral science tells us that we are wired to trust faces we recognize, even if only faintly, and this subconscious familiarity lowers your guard. The avatar initiates a conversation, skillfully mirroring your interests and opinions, building rapport, and establishing a sense of camaraderie. You find yourself drawn into the conversation, sharing experiences and forging a connection with this seemingly like-minded individual. Then comes the request, seemingly innocent yet laden with manipulative intent. "I'm locked out of my account," the avatar laments, "and I desperately need some virtual currency to regain access. Could you lend me a small amount? I'll pay you back as soon as I'm back in." This seemingly simple plea exploits a potent combination of psychological vulnerabilities. Loss aversion, our innate tendency to avoid losses more strongly than we seek gains, makes us susceptible to requests that frame assistance as preventing a loss for the requester. The social pressure of reciprocating a newfound friendship further strengthens the manipulative pull of the request. In this scenario, a purely technical solution, such as an algorithm designed to detect malicious requests, might struggle to identify the threat. The request appears legitimate within the context of the VR platform, exploiting the social dynamics and psychological vulnerabilities of human users.

This example highlights the complex challenges of cybersecurity in immersive digital environments. As virtual worlds become increasingly sophisticated and lifelike, the lines between the real and the virtual blur, creating new avenues for social engineering and manipulation. The human element, with its inherent vulnerabilities and biases, remains a critical factor in cybersecurity, even in the seemingly abstract realm of VR.

To effectively counter these threats, we need a multi-layered approach that combines technical safeguards with an understanding of human psychology and social dynamics. This requires not only the development of robust security protocols but also the cultivation of digital literacy and critical thinking skills among users, empowering them to recognize and resist manipulation tactics in the virtual world.

The Behavioral Science Solution

Dynamic Trust Indicators: Avatars could have a subtle "trustworthiness score" based on their behavior (sudden requests for money, aggressive language). This score could be visually displayed (a halo that fades) or even a haptic nudge on the user's arm as a subliminal warning.

"Time-Out to Reality" Feature: A single button press could trigger a brief disruption in the VR world, showing the user their physical environment for a few seconds. This "reality check" allows them to reassess the situation outside the immersive bubble.

The Avatars Among Us are both a blessing and a curse in VR. They allow for self-expression but also anonymity. Behavioral science can help us understand how people behave differently behind an avatar (are they more likely to take risks and be aggressive?). This knowledge can be used to design detection systems that look for behavioral anomalies linked to a specific avatar (increased risk-taking might suggest a scammer).

REAL-LIFE EXAMPLE: THE "FAKE AUTHORITY FIGURE" VR SCAM

In the realm of cybersecurity, where the battleground is often the human mind itself, the lines between the real and the virtual are becoming increasingly blurred. Imagine a new employee, eager to impress and prove their worth, immersed in a VR training simulation. The environment is strikingly realistic, replicating the office space, the ambient sounds, even the subtle nuances of interpersonal interactions. Suddenly, the user encounters a highly realistic avatar of their company CEO, a figure who commands respect and embodies authority. Behavioral science tells us that authority figures inherently inspire trust and compliance, a vulnerability that can be readily exploited in the digital realm.

This virtual CEO, with their familiar voice and mannerisms, approaches the user and assigns a seemingly legitimate task. Perhaps it involves accessing a confidential document, sharing sensitive company information, or even transferring funds to an unfamiliar account. The request is framed within the context of a critical project, a matter of urgency that requires immediate action. In this scenario, a purely technical solution might struggle to detect the malicious intent. The request originates from a seemingly trusted source, the CEO themselves, and the task itself might appear to be within the bounds of normal job responsibilities. The user, immersed in the virtual environment and influenced by the authority figure's presence, might readily comply, unwittingly divulging sensitive information or compromising the company's security. This scenario highlights the growing importance of incorporating behavioral science into cybersecurity training and awareness programs. By understanding the psychological vulnerabilities that can be exploited in virtual environments, we can equip individuals with the critical thinking skills and awareness necessary to recognize and resist social engineering attacks, even when they come from seemingly trusted sources.

The future of cybersecurity lies in a holistic approach that combines technical safeguards with an understanding of human behavior. By educating individuals about the tactics employed by malicious actors and empowering them to question, analyze, and verify information, even when it comes from authority figures, we can create a more resilient and secure digital world.

THE BEHAVIORAL SCIENCE SOLUTION

In the realm of VR, where digital avatars serve as our proxies, the potential for deception and manipulation raises ethical concerns. To address this, the development of AI-powered avatar analysis systems could provide a valuable safeguard. These systems, trained on vast datasets of human behavior and social cues, could be designed to identify subtle inconsistencies in avatar behavior that might indicate malicious intent. Imagine an AI system that can analyze an avatar's speech patterns, facial expressions, and body language in real time, comparing them to established norms and the individual's typical behavior. If a CEO's avatar suddenly starts exhibiting unusual speech patterns or body language that doesn't align with their usual demeanor, the system could trigger a warning, alerting users to the possibility of impersonation or malicious intent.

The ethical considerations of such a system are paramount. It's crucial to ensure that the AI is trained on diverse and unbiased datasets to avoid perpetuating stereotypes or discriminatory practices. Transparency and user control are also essential, allowing individuals to understand how the AI is analyzing their behavior and providing options to opt out or customize the system's parameters. Beyond technological safeguards, education and awareness play a crucial role in combating deception and manipulation in VR. VR literacy training programs can empower users to identify potential threats and make informed decisions in virtual environments. These training programs can teach users about the potential for impersonation in VR, highlighting the tactics that malicious actors might employ. They can educate users about specific cues to look for, such as inconsistent avatar details, unusual requests from authority figures, or discrepancies between an avatar's appearance and their claimed identity. VR literacy training can also foster critical thinking skills, encouraging users to question the authenticity of information and interactions in virtual environments. By promoting awareness and empowering users to be vigilant, we can create a safer and more trustworthy VR ecosystem. The combination of ethical AI-powered avatar analysis and comprehensive VR literacy training offers a powerful approach to combating deception and manipulation in VR. Technology can provide the tools to detect and flag potential threats, while education empowers users to make informed decisions and protect themselves in virtual environments.

By fostering a culture of awareness, critical thinking, and ethical AI development, we can ensure that VR remains a safe and trustworthy space for collaboration, innovation, and human connection.

BEYOND TECH: BUILDING A SECURE VR ECOSYSTEM

While behavioral science is essential, it is one piece of the puzzle**. A genuinely secure VR ecosystem requires collaboration across disciplines:

- **VR Developers:** Platforms must be designed with security in mind, integrating behavioral science insights during development.
- **Policymakers:** Clear guidelines on data privacy and user protection in VR are necessary to create a safe environment for everyone.
- **Law Enforcement:** Developing strategies to investigate and prosecute VR-based social engineering attacks is crucial to deter future attempts.

By combining the power of technology with the insights of behavioral science**, we can create a future for VR where users can explore, connect, and learn with confidence, knowing they are protected from the ever-evolving threats of social engineering.

The promise of VR lies in its power to immerse and connect us. To safeguard this promise, we cannot approach security solely as a technical challenge to be solved. Partnerships between VR companies and behavioral scientists are key to unlocking solutions that are as intuitive and adaptable as the virtual worlds. By understanding not just the tools attackers use but the ways VR fundamentally changes how we perceive and respond to social interactions, we can develop countermeasures that empower users without diminishing the allure of the experience.

This collaboration between cybersecurity experts and behavioral scientists holds the potential to revolutionize far more than just the safety of VR environments. The lessons learned in designing security systems that seamlessly integrate with the complexities of human psychology could fundamentally transform our approach to cybersecurity in general.

Imagine a future where online security measures are not just robust technical barriers but also intelligent systems that understand and adapt to human behavior. These systems would be able to anticipate and mitigate the risks associated with our cognitive biases, emotional vulnerabilities, and social dynamics, creating a safer and more resilient digital world.

Perhaps the most significant innovation that VR will spark is a shift from a purely technical mindset toward online protection that genuinely centers on the human behind the screen. Instead of solely focusing on firewalls, intrusion detection systems, and complex encryption algorithms, we will begin to design security systems that understand and adapt to the human element, recognizing that our psychology and behavior play a crucial role in cybersecurity.

This human-centric approach to cybersecurity would involve incorporating insights from behavioral economics, social psychology, and cognitive science to design security measures that are not only effective but also user-friendly and intuitive. It would involve developing educational programs that empower individuals to recognize and resist social engineering tactics, phishing scams, and other forms of online manipulation. Furthermore, this collaboration could lead to the development of AI-powered security systems that can learn from human behavior, anticipate potential threats, and provide personalized protection based on individual risk profiles. Imagine a future where your online security system understands your online habits, recognizes your vulnerabilities, and proactively adapts to protect you from emerging threats. The potential benefits of this collaboration extend far beyond the realm of VR and cybersecurity. By integrating our understanding of human psychology with technological innovation, we can create a safer, more resilient, and more human-centered digital world. A world where technology empowers and protects individuals, fostering a sense of trust, security, and agency in the digital age.

19 Augmented Reality and Its Impact on Social and Interpersonal Trust

ESCALATING RISKS IN SOCIAL ENGINEERING ATTACKS AND TECHNOLOGICAL CHALLENGES TO DETECT

Augmented reality (AR) has emerged as a transformative technology, seamlessly blending the digital and physical worlds in ways that were once confined to the realm of science fiction. By overlaying digital information onto our perception of reality, AR enhances how we interact with our surroundings, offering a multitude of possibilities in various fields, from education and healthcare to entertainment and industry. However, this blurring of boundaries between the real and the virtual also presents a complex landscape with potential implications for social and interpersonal trust, raising concerns about its role in facilitating social engineering attacks.

AR's ability to augment our perception of reality creates opportunities for manipulation and deception. Imagine walking down a street and seeing virtual advertisements seamlessly integrated into the buildings around you, or receiving personalized messages that appear to float in mid-air, tailored to your interests and vulnerabilities. While these applications may seem benign, they also open the door to more malicious uses, where AR could be employed to deceive, manipulate, or exploit individuals.

Social engineering, the art of manipulating people into divulging confidential information or performing actions that compromise their security, finds a fertile ground in the AR landscape. Attackers could leverage AR to create immersive and convincing scenarios that exploit human psychology and cognitive biases. Imagine receiving a virtual message that appears to be from a trusted friend or authority figure, urging you to click on a malicious link or share sensitive information. The immersive nature of AR could make it more difficult to discern reality from fabrication, increasing the likelihood of falling victim to such attacks. Furthermore, AR's potential to alter our perception of reality could erode trust in our own senses and judgment. If we can no longer rely on our eyes and ears to accurately perceive the world around us, how can we trust our own instincts and decision-making abilities? This erosion of trust could have profound implications for social and interpersonal relationships, making it more difficult to discern genuine interactions from manipulated ones. The challenges posed by AR in the context of social engineering demand a multifaceted approach. Technological safeguards, such as authentication mechanisms and secure AR platforms, can help mitigate the risk of malicious attacks.

DOI: 10.1201/9781003500698-19

Education and awareness initiatives can empower individuals to recognize and avoid AR-based social engineering tactics. And ethical considerations must guide the development and deployment of AR technologies, ensuring that they are used responsibly and do not compromise human autonomy or societal trust.

As AR continues to evolve and permeate our lives, it is crucial to address these challenges proactively. By fostering a culture of cybersecurity awareness, promoting critical thinking skills, and developing ethical guidelines for AR development, we can harness the transformative potential of this technology while mitigating its potential risks.

WHEN THE LINES BLUR: HOW AR REWRITES THE RULES OF SOCIAL ENGINEERING

AR, a technology that seamlessly blends digital content with the real world, holds immense promise for transforming various aspects of our lives, from entertainment and education to healthcare and manufacturing. However, this transformative potential also casts a shadow, raising concerns about the cybersecurity implications of this immersive technology. AR creates an environment where social engineering attacks can leverage enhanced realism, intimate data collection, and our innate trust in technology against us, potentially leading to new and more sophisticated forms of cyberattacks.

The immersive nature of AR, where digital overlays blend seamlessly with our perception of the real world, can be exploited by malicious actors to create highly convincing and deceptive scenarios. Imagine an AR application that overlays fake navigational signs onto a real-world street view, misleading drivers into dangerous situations. Or consider an AR game that inserts seemingly harmless virtual characters into a user's environment, only to have these characters manipulate the user into revealing sensitive information or downloading malware.

The ability of AR devices to collect vast amounts of personal data, including location data, biometric information, and even emotional responses, creates new opportunities for attackers to exploit vulnerabilities and tailor their attacks to individual targets. This intimate data collection can be used to create highly personalized phishing scams, craft convincing deepfakes, or even manipulate users' emotions to influence their behavior. Furthermore, the seamless integration of AR into our daily lives can foster a sense of complacency and trust in the technology. We may become so accustomed to relying on AR for information and guidance that we lower our guard, making us more susceptible to social engineering tactics that exploit this trust. The potential for AR to enhance social engineering attacks demands a proactive and multifaceted approach to cybersecurity. This includes developing robust security measures for AR devices and applications, educating users about the potential risks and vulnerabilities, and fostering a culture of critical thinking and skepticism toward digital information. As AR technology continues to evolve and become more integrated into our lives, the cybersecurity challenges will undoubtedly grow more complex. By anticipating these challenges and developing effective countermeasures, we can harness the transformative potential of AR while mitigating its risks and ensuring a safe and secure digital future.

WHY AR IS THE ULTIMATE HACKER PLAYGROUND

AR, while offering exciting possibilities for enhancing our perception of the world, also presents new challenges to cybersecurity. Unlike traditional cyberattacks that target our devices or data, AR-based attacks can directly manipulate our perception of reality, blurring the lines between the physical and digital worlds and making us more vulnerable to manipulation. One of the most insidious aspects of AR manipulation is its ability to subtly alter existing objects in our environment. This means an attacker could, for instance, manipulate the appearance of a QR code on a poster, making it seem like a legitimate link to a website while actually redirecting the user to a malicious site that steals their login credentials. Or, an attacker could alter the appearance of a bank's ATM, making it seem like a genuine machine while actually overlaying a fake interface that captures the user's PIN and card details. Furthermore, AR can create persistent, ever-evolving attack scenarios within the victim's environment. Unlike a phishing email that can be deleted or a malicious website that can be avoided, AR-based attacks can be embedded into the very fabric of our surroundings. Imagine walking down the street and being bombarded with personalized misinformation tailored to your interests and vulnerabilities, or receiving fake notifications that appear to be from trusted sources but actually lead to malicious websites or apps. Perhaps most alarmingly, AR manipulates what we see and hear, eroding our natural skepticism and making us more susceptible to deception. Our brains are not wired to question the reality presented to us through our senses, making it difficult to distinguish between genuine and manipulated experiences. This vulnerability can be exploited by attackers to create convincing illusions, spread disinformation, and manipulate our behavior.

The implications of AR-based attacks are far-reaching, potentially affecting individuals, organizations, and society as a whole. From financial losses and privacy breaches to the erosion of trust and the spread of misinformation, the consequences of AR manipulation could be severe. As AR technology becomes more prevalent in our daily lives, it is crucial to develop awareness of these threats and adopt strategies to mitigate the risks. This includes educating ourselves about the potential for AR manipulation, critically evaluating the information presented to us through AR applications, and remaining vigilant against attempts to deceive and exploit our trust in our senses.

THE CHALLENGE IS NOT JUST DETECTION; IT IS PREVENTION

Securing AR systems presents unique challenges that demand careful consideration. One such challenge is the concept of "plausible deniability" for attackers. In the AR realm, where digital content seamlessly blends with the real world, it can be difficult to distinguish between malicious manipulation and unintentional software glitches. For instance, if an AR application displays a slightly altered street sign, leading a user in the wrong direction, can we definitively prove that this was a deliberate attack rather than a mere software error? This ambiguity provides attackers with more freedom to operate, as the burden of proof shifts from the attacker to the user or the system developer. Furthermore, the very nature of AR applications, which often require broad permissions to access device features like cameras and sensors, can inadvertently turn users into unwitting accomplices in their own compromise. By granting these permissions, users may unknowingly enable attackers to manipulate their AR experiences, potentially leading to misinformation, privacy breaches, or even physical harm. The complexity of securing AR systems may necessitate the development of cutting-edge AI-powered defenses. One such possibility is the creation of "defensive fakes," where AI algorithms subtly disrupt or alter malicious content within the AR environment, effectively neutralizing the attack. However, this approach raises ethical concerns about the manipulation of information and the potential for unintended consequences.

In conclusion, securing AR systems demands a multifaceted approach that addresses the unique challenges of plausible deniability, user permissions, and the potential for AI-powered attacks and defenses. By carefully considering these challenges and developing robust security measures, we can ensure that AR technologies enhance our lives without compromising our safety or autonomy.

TOWARD A NEW SECURITY MINDSET FOR AR

In the realm of AR, where the lines between the physical and digital blur, the adage "trust, but verify" takes on new significance. Users must be trained to critically examine their AR environment, questioning the authenticity of what they see and exercising caution when AR experiences involve instructions about the real world.

The seductive nature of AR can lull users into a false sense of security, where the seamless integration of digital elements into their physical surroundings can make it challenging to distinguish between reality and augmentation. Attackers can exploit this trust, manipulating AR overlays to mislead, misdirect, or even endanger users.

Imagine following AR navigation instructions that lead you into a dangerous neighborhood or interacting with an AR avatar that impersonates a trusted authority figure. The consequences of blindly trusting AR experiences can be severe, highlighting the need for critical thinking and a healthy dose of skepticism.

Training users to question the authenticity of their AR environment is crucial. Are the street signs too pristine, lacking the wear and tear of the physical world? Do the AR overlays align perfectly with the real-world objects, or are there subtle inconsistencies that might betray manipulation? By fostering a critical mindset, we can empower users to discern between genuine AR experiences and those that may be compromised or malicious.

Regulation That Understands the Tech

The regulation of AR technology presents unique challenges, demanding a deep understanding of its capabilities and potential implications. Laws cannot simply focus on what data is collected but must also address how this data is used within the AR environment and ensure that these processes are auditable.

Lawmakers must grapple with the complexities of AR systems, understanding how they collect, process, and display information. They must consider the potential for misuse, manipulation, and the erosion of privacy. The regulation of AR must strike a balance between fostering innovation and protecting individual rights and societal well-being.

This requires a proactive and collaborative approach, bringing together policy-makers, technologists, and ethicists to develop regulatory frameworks that are both effective and adaptable to the rapidly evolving landscape of AR technology.

"Friction That Protects"

One intriguing approach to enhancing user awareness and mitigating the risks of AR manipulation is to introduce intentional "friction" into the AR experience. By incorporating minor, random glitches or inconsistencies into AR overlays, we can disrupt the illusion of perfection that attackers often rely on.

This friction can serve as a subtle reminder that the AR environment is not infallible, prompting users to question the authenticity of what they see and become more critical viewers. By breaking the seamlessness of the AR experience, we can encourage users to engage more actively with their surroundings and exercise greater caution when interacting with digital elements.

Imagine an AR navigation app that occasionally displays a slightly distorted street sign or an AR game that introduces unexpected visual glitches. These minor imperfections, while seemingly trivial, can serve as powerful cues, prompting users to question the integrity of the AR experience and engage their critical thinking skills.

The concept of "friction that protects" offers a novel approach to enhancing cybersecurity awareness and mitigating the risks of AR manipulation. By disrupting the illusion of perfection, we can empower users to become more discerning consumers of AR experiences, fostering a culture of critical engagement and promoting a safer and more resilient digital landscape.

A CALL FOR PROACTIVE THINKING

The unique challenges posed by AR demand a proactive and anticipatory approach to cybersecurity. Unlike traditional cybercrime, where we often react to attacks after vulnerabilities are exposed, AR's immersive and interconnected nature necessitates pre-emptive security research to identify and mitigate potential exploits before they can be weaponized. This proactive stance is crucial to ensure the safe and responsible development of AR technologies and to safeguard individuals and communities from the novel threats that AR may introduce.

Government/tech partnerships are likely essential to fund and facilitate this pre-emptive AR security research. Governments, with their mandate to protect citizens and ensure national security, have a vested interest in fostering a secure and resilient digital ecosystem. Tech companies, at the forefront of AR innovation, possess the technical expertise and resources to develop and implement security solutions. By pooling their resources and expertise, governments and tech companies can create a synergistic partnership that accelerates AR security research and strengthens our collective defenses against emerging threats.

However, these partnerships also present unique challenges and opportunities. Governments must navigate the delicate balance between fostering innovation and ensuring public safety, while tech companies must prioritize security without stifling creativity and hindering the development of groundbreaking AR applications.

One challenge lies in establishing clear regulatory frameworks that promote responsible innovation while safeguarding against potential harms. Governments must work closely with tech companies to develop guidelines and standards that ensure AR technologies are developed and deployed in a manner that prioritizes user privacy, data security, and ethical considerations.

Another challenge lies in fostering a culture of transparency and collaboration between government agencies and tech companies. Sharing information about potential vulnerabilities, attack vectors, and emerging threats is crucial for developing effective countermeasures and staying ahead of malicious actors.

The opportunities presented by government/tech partnerships are equally significant. By fostering collaboration and knowledge sharing, these partnerships can accelerate the development of innovative security solutions, strengthen our collective defenses against cyberattacks, and promote the responsible development and deployment of AR technologies.

Furthermore, these partnerships can play a crucial role in educating the public about AR security risks and promoting responsible online behavior. By raising awareness about potential threats and empowering individuals with the knowledge and tools to protect themselves, we can create a safer and more resilient digital ecosystem for all.

Why Partnerships Are Key

The Pace of AR Outstrips Regulation: The sheer speed of progress in AR means legal frameworks will always be lagging. Proactive research cannot wait for laws to catch up. Government funding could allow security work to happen parallel to tech development, ensuring we are not always playing catch-up. Private Companies are Incentivized to Prioritize Features: AR platforms need to be exciting to gain users. However, it may always be an afterthought without external pressure or funding nudging them toward "security-first" thinking. This partnership model lets the government be that nudge. Attacks in AR Have the Potential for Mass Societal Disruption: Imagine an attack that overlays false traffic instructions in AR. It is not just about stolen data but potential harm on a large scale. This transcends the scope of what any company should bear the burden of preventing.

The Challenges to Successful Partnerships

The quest to ensure the security of AR raises complex challenges when it comes to the partnerships between government, industry, and academia. While such collaborations are crucial for tackling this multifaceted issue, navigating these relationships is difficult. First, the definition of "pre-emptive" security measures remains fluid. Research driven by hypothetical attack vectors risks being seen as wasteful if such attacks never come to fruition. Partnerships must clearly define success metrics and milestones beyond mere academic publications.

Furthermore, the fundamental need for some security measures to remain partially concealed, even from users, clashes with the traditional openness of government-funded research projects. Balancing this necessary secrecy with transparency demands careful consideration to maintain trust and accountability. Finally, the intrinsically multidisciplinary nature of securing AR presents a significant management challenge. Expertise spanning technology, behavioral science, and even urban planning is vital. Effective collaboration between diverse fields is notoriously complex, demanding flexible and adaptive partnership models. Overcoming these obstacles is paramount to fully harnessing the research potential within these partnerships and ensuring that AR reaches its potential in an innovative and secure way.

OPPORTUNITIES BEYOND JUST FUNDING

The collaboration between private industry and public investment is not merely about securing crucial funding for safeguarding AR's future. It unlocks a broader spectrum of opportunities that could reshape the cybersecurity landscape. Consider the potential of anonymized data sharing, governed by strict user consent, to empower government-backed researchers. The insights gleaned from a vastly expanded dataset could revolutionize our ability to identify malicious activity patterns within AR environments.

Furthermore, these partnerships could pave the way for "red teaming" initiatives tailored to AR security. Ethical hackers, honed on the unique challenges of this space, could pressure-test emerging systems, proactively exposing vulnerabilities before they can be exploited. This concept, already proven in traditional cybersecurity, holds immense promise when adapted to the complexities of AR.

Perhaps most fascinatingly, the cybersecurity solutions developed preemptively for AR could have far-reaching implications beyond this single domain. Imagine AI algorithms capable of detecting deepfakes within AR environments – such technology would prove invaluable in an era where disinformation can spread with unprecedented speed and sophistication.

This underscores a central theme: by embracing collaboration and investing in preemptive safety measures for AR, we may foster innovations that reshape the entire cybersecurity landscape, leading to a safer and more trustworthy digital world for all.

MODELS TO CONSIDER

DARPA-Style Grants: Focused on high-risk, high-potential reward research. The downside is that this might exclude smaller AR companies with innovative ideas.

Incubator Programs: Where government and AR developers co-house research teams for a set period, ensuring close collaboration. These risks stifle "blue sky" thinking that can lead to breakthroughs.

International Standards: It is unlikely any single country will "solve" AR security alone. Could these partnerships pioneer a secure and secure international data and threat-sharing model that respects privacy?

THE HUMAN FIREWALL IN A WORLD OF AUGMENTED REALITY

While advanced AI and research into novel attack vectors are crucial, the most effective AR security solutions may ultimately empower the user. Government/tech partnerships can play a vital role in developing these user-centric solutions by focusing on AR notification that says, "Potential Security Risk Detected." Most users would not understand or be empowered to act. Explainable security involves clear, concise warnings illuminating the threat **in the context of the AR experience.**

Natural Language Processing (NLP) holds immense potential for revolutionizing the delivery of security messages in AR environments. Imagine an AI system that can analyze the specific AR context, assess the user's technical proficiency, and tailor security warnings accordingly. This personalized approach could bridge the gap between complex technical jargon and user comprehension, ensuring that security messages are clear, concise, and actionable.

For instance, if a user encounters a suspicious object in their AR environment, the AI-powered NLP system could generate a warning message that is tailored to the user's level of technical understanding. For a novice user, the message might be simple and direct: "Warning: This object may be compromised. Avoid interacting with it." For a more tech-savvy user, the message could provide additional details and options: "Warning: This object's digital signature is invalid, indicating a potential security breach. Would you like to quarantine the object or investigate further?"

This personalized approach not only enhances user comprehension but also fosters trust and encourages proactive security behavior. By tailoring security messages to the individual's needs and understanding, we can empower users to make informed decisions and protect themselves in the AR landscape. Complementing NLP-driven messages, visually intuitive security cues offer another layer of protection in AR environments. These cues, seamlessly integrated into the AR experience, provide subtle yet effective warnings about potential threats without overwhelming the user.

Imagine a scenario where a user is about to interact with a virtual object that has been compromised. A subtle cue, such as a flickering border around the object or a change in its color saturation, could alert the user to the potential danger. These visual cues, easily recognizable yet nonintrusive, can prompt users to exercise caution and seek further information before proceeding. The combination of NLP-powered security messages and visually intuitive cues creates a multi-layered defense strategy in AR environments. By tailoring warnings to the individual's needs and providing subtle visual cues, we can enhance user awareness, foster trust, and promote proactive security behavior in the increasingly complex and interconnected world of AR.

While a seamless AR experience is desirable, sometimes, a little friction can be good regarding security. Partnerships can explore ways to introduce deliberate micro-delays or disruptions in the AR experience:

A momentary Blurring of the AR Overlay when entering a high-risk location (like a financial district) encourages users to double-check the information they see.

A Confirmation Prompt Before Allowing Actions Involving Real-World Consequences (e.g., initiating a financial transaction through an AR interface).

These deliberate interruptions may seem counter-intuitive, but they can force users to pause and critically evaluate the AR information they are interacting with. Traditional security training can be cumbersome and forgettable. Partnerships can explore ways to integrate micro-learning security modules directly into the AR experience. Short, contextual pop-up tutorials are triggered when users interact with sensitive information in AR. Interactive simulations within the AR environment that teach users how to identify potential scams or social engineering tactics. By delivering security education at the point of need, in the AR environment itself, users are more likely to retain and apply the information in real-world scenarios.

THE BENEFITS OF A USER-CENTRIC AR APPROACH

Reduced Reliance on Technical Expertise: Overly complex security measures put the burden on users to become AR security experts – an unrealistic expectation.

Increased User Trust and Adoption: Users who feel safe and in control while using AR are more likely to embrace the technology.

A More Secure AR Ecosystem for Everyone: Empowered users become the first line of defense against social engineering attacks in AR.

Government/tech partnerships are essential to ensure that AR security solutions remain grounded in the human experience. By working together, governments and technology companies can create a secure and accessible AR ecosystem that benefits everyone. This collaboration can take many forms, such as:

- **Developing security standards and guidelines:** Governments can work with tech companies to develop clear and consistent security standards for AR devices and applications. This will help to ensure that all AR experiences are safe and secure.
- **Funding research and development:** Governments can provide funding for research into AR security challenges and solutions. This will help to accelerate the development of new security technologies.
- **Educating the public:** Governments can play a role in educating the public about AR security risks and best practices. This will help to empower individuals to protect themselves from harm.

By prioritizing user-friendliness and "explainable security," we can create an AR future where the benefits of the technology are accessible to everyone without compromising safety. This means developing security solutions that are easy to understand and use, even for people who are not tech-savvy. It also means being transparent about how AR security works and why it is important.

In addition to the above, government/tech partnerships can also help to address the following challenges:

- **The "plausible deniability" problem:** One of the challenges of AR security is that it can be difficult to determine who is responsible for an attack. This is because AR experiences can be very immersive and realistic. Government/tech partnerships can help to develop solutions that make it easier to identify attackers.
- **The "user as unwitting accomplice" problem:** Another challenge is that users may unknowingly participate in attacks. This is because AR experiences can be very persuasive. Government/tech partnerships can help to educate users about the risks of AR and how to protect themselves.
- **The AI vs. AI arms race:** As AR technology becomes more sophisticated, we are likely to see an arms race between attackers and defenders. Government/tech partnerships can help to ensure that defenders have the resources they need to stay ahead of attackers.

By working together, governments and tech companies can create a safe and enjoyable AR future for everyone.

20 Navigating the Intersection of Digital Marketing, Intelligent Advertising with Interpersonal Trust

UNVEILING TECHNOLOGY'S ROLE IN ENHANCING SOCIAL ENGINEERING THREATS AND THE TECHNOLOGICAL CHALLENGES IN DETECTION

The digital landscape has fundamentally reshaped the way we connect, consume information, and make decisions, creating a world where the boundaries between the physical and virtual are increasingly blurred. Digital marketing and intelligent advertising, fueled by sophisticated algorithms and vast datasets, have revolutionized how businesses reach and influence consumers, offering personalized experiences and targeted messaging that cater to individual preferences and desires. However, this technological advancement has also given rise to an alarming phenomenon: the weaponization of interpersonal trust within social engineering attacks.

This chapter delves into the complex relationship between digital marketing, the erosion of trust online, and the technological barriers hindering the effective detection of social engineering threats. It explores how the very tools and techniques that drive successful marketing campaigns can be exploited by malicious actors to deceive, manipulate, and exploit unsuspecting individuals. The erosion of trust online is a growing concern, as the proliferation of fake news, misinformation, and online scams has made it increasingly difficult to distinguish between credible sources and malicious actors. This erosion of trust creates fertile ground for social engineering attacks, which often rely on impersonation, deception, and the exploitation of human vulnerabilities to achieve their goals. Furthermore, the rapid evolution of technology presents significant challenges for the detection of social engineering threats. Attackers are constantly developing new and sophisticated techniques to bypass traditional security measures and exploit the vulnerabilities of human psychology. The use of artificial intelligence (AI), deepfakes, and other advanced technologies makes it increasingly difficult to distinguish between genuine communications and malicious attempts to deceive. This chapter examines the complex interplay between these factors, exploring the ways in which digital marketing practices can inadvertently contribute to the erosion of trust and the rise of social engineering attacks. It

DOI: 10.1201/9781003500698-20

also delves into the technological barriers hindering the effective detection of these threats, highlighting the need for innovative solutions and a multi-layered approach to cybersecurity.

By understanding the dynamics of trust, the psychology of deception, and the evolving landscape of technology, we can develop strategies to mitigate the risks of social engineering attacks and foster a safer and more trustworthy digital environment. This chapter provides a comprehensive overview of these challenges, offering insights and recommendations for individuals, organizations, and policymakers to navigate the complex world of online trust and security.

WHEN MARKETING TACTICS BECOME HACKER TOOLS: HOW DIGITAL MANIPULATION UNDERMINES TRUST

Trust has always been the bedrock of human interaction, the invisible currency that facilitates cooperation, trade, and the formation of social bonds. In the digital age, however, the manipulation of trust for commercial gain has taken on a troubling new dimension, blurring the lines between genuine connection and calculated exploitation. Marketing and advertising strategies, designed to evoke feelings of personalization and authenticity, are inadvertently providing social engineers with a powerful arsenal of techniques to erode interpersonal trust for their own malicious ends.

The rise of sophisticated digital marketing techniques has created an illusion of intimacy, where interactions feel personalized and tailored to our individual preferences. Chatbots that greet us by name, advertisements that reference our recent searches, and product recommendations that seem eerily aligned with our desires all contribute to a sense that we are being seen and understood on a personal level. This illusion of intimacy, however, can be deceptive, lulling us into a false sense of security and making us more susceptible to manipulation. The very technologies that enable personalized marketing experiences are also being exploited by social engineers to craft targeted attacks that prey on our vulnerabilities. Just as AI algorithms can analyze our online behavior to recommend products we might like, so too can malicious actors use similar techniques to profile individuals and tailor scams to their specific interests and weaknesses. Both exploit the human tendency to trust what feels familiar and safe, blurring the lines between genuine connection and calculated deception. The ability to falsify what we see and hear, once the realm of science fiction, has become a reality in the digital age. Deepfake technology, capable of creating realistic but fabricated videos and audio recordings, can be used to manipulate perceptions, spread disinformation, and erode trust in previously reliable sources of information. While marketers may use these tools to create "unforgettable experiences" and promote products, social engineers employ them to shatter trust, manipulate individuals, and gain access to sensitive information.

The convergence of sophisticated marketing techniques and readily available tools for digital manipulation has created a challenging landscape for navigating trust in the digital age. The lines between genuine connection and calculated exploitation have become increasingly blurred, demanding a heightened awareness of the tactics used to manipulate our perceptions and exploit our vulnerabilities.

TECHNOLOGY MARKETING IS DOUBLE-EDGED SWORD

In the digital age, data have become a double-edged sword. When used responsibly, it can enhance user experiences, personalize services, and drive innovation. However, in the wrong hands, the vast troves of data generated by our online activities can be weaponized to craft deceptively believable lies, tailor-made to exploit individual vulnerabilities. Every click, every search, every shared interest becomes a potential weapon in the arsenal of social engineers and malicious actors.

The rise of AI has further amplified this threat. AI algorithms, with their ability to analyze vast datasets and identify patterns of human behavior, can be used to create highly targeted and persuasive social engineering attacks. These attacks exploit our cognitive biases, emotional vulnerabilities, and trust in technology to manipulate our perceptions and influence our actions. The democratization of technology has not only empowered individuals and communities but also lowered the barriers to entry for malicious actors. Sophisticated attacks that were once the domain of highly skilled hackers are now within reach of anyone with a grudge or a desire for illicit gain. The availability of user-friendly tools and readily accessible tutorials has enabled the mass distribution of tailored scams, phishing attacks, and disinformation campaigns. This has created a digital landscape where individuals and organizations alike are at risk of falling victim to cyberattacks, regardless of their technical expertise or cybersecurity awareness.

The human mind, with its intricate web of cognitive biases and emotional vulnerabilities, is susceptible to manipulation. Social engineers, like skilled marketers, understand these weaknesses and exploit them to bypass critical thinking and trigger impulsive actions.

Fear, greed, curiosity, and the desire for social belonging are just a few of the emotional triggers that can be exploited to manipulate individuals online. By crafting messages that resonate with these emotions, attackers can bypass rational decision-making and induce individuals to click on malicious links, share sensitive information, or even transfer funds to fraudulent accounts.

The increasing sophistication of social engineering tactics, combined with the democratization of technology, has created a digital environment where vigilance and critical thinking are paramount. By understanding the psychological tactics employed by malicious actors, we can develop strategies to resist manipulation, protect our digital identities, and safeguard our online interactions.

DETECTION LAGS BEHIND INNOVATION

The Invisible Attack: Unlike malware, social engineering leaves few digital footprints, making it a particularly insidious threat in the cybersecurity landscape. It is more about tricking humans than hacking the system, exploiting our psychological vulnerabilities and innate trust in online interactions. Current security tools, primarily designed to detect and prevent malicious code, are ill-equipped to handle the subtle nuances of social engineering attacks, which often rely on psychological manipulation and the exploitation of human emotions. This makes social engineering a particularly challenging threat to mitigate, requiring a multi-layered approach that encompasses not only technological safeguards but also education and awareness to empower individuals to recognize and resist these attacks.

When Updates Help the Enemy: The same AI-powered personalization that legitimate marketers use to tailor advertisements and recommendations is constantly being adapted by attackers to enhance the effectiveness of their social engineering campaigns. This creates a never-ending arms race, where defenders must constantly update their detection mechanisms to keep pace with the evolving tactics of malicious actors. The ability of attackers to leverage AI to personalize their attacks, crafting messages that resonate with individual targets and exploit their specific vulnerabilities, makes it increasingly difficult to distinguish between legitimate and malicious communications.

We Are Our Own Weakest Link: Even the most sophisticated detection technology ultimately fails if we are conditioned to over-trust in the online world. Digital literacy, the ability to critically evaluate information and recognize potential threats, is critical for navigating the complex digital landscape. However, the efforts to promote digital literacy are often undermined by the very marketing strategies that fuel the digital economy. Marketers, in their pursuit of engagement and sales, often prioritize persuasive techniques that encourage trust and minimize skepticism. This creates a conflict between the need for cybersecurity awareness and the prevailing culture of online trust, making individuals more susceptible to social engineering attacks that exploit their inherent inclination to believe what they see and read online.

CAN WE BREAK THE CYCLE

As the digital landscape becomes increasingly sophisticated, the battle against social engineering requires more than just AI vs. AI. We need to develop detection systems capable of recognizing the subtle psychological "tells" that betray a social engineering attempt. These systems, still in their early stages, must go beyond analyzing text and images to incorporate behavioral and emotional cues, such as micro-expressions, voice inflections, and patterns of online activity. By understanding the psychology of manipulation, we can build AI systems that can effectively identify and flag potential threats, protecting individuals and organizations from falling victim to social engineering tactics.

The current paradigm of digital advertising, driven by engagement and algorithmic targeting, has created a fertile ground for manipulation and exploitation. To counter this, we need to redefine what constitutes "smart" advertising. Platforms should be incentivized to prioritize transparency and reward ads that focus on provably accurate information, not just engagement. This could involve developing algorithms that prioritize factual accuracy, source credibility, and ethical marketing practices. By shifting the focus from engagement to information integrity, we can create a digital advertising ecosystem that empowers consumers and promotes responsible marketing practices.

The ethical implications of AI-powered advertising demand careful consideration. The marketing industry must be pressured to abandon manipulative tactics that exploit human vulnerabilities, even if those tactics remain legal. This requires a collective effort from policymakers, consumer advocacy groups, and the industry itself to establish ethical guidelines and promote responsible innovation. By prioritizing human well-being and societal trust over short-term gains, we can ensure that the digital advertising landscape remains a space for creativity, innovation, and ethical engagement.

BE YOND TECH: BUILDING A RESILIENT SOCIETY

In our pursuit of a secure and trustworthy digital world, it's essential to acknowledge a fundamental truth: the complete eradication of trust abuse in the digital realm is an unrealistic aspiration. The human element, with its inherent vulnerabilities and susceptibility to manipulation, will always be a factor in the intricate dance between trust and deception.

Rather than striving for an unattainable utopia of absolute trust, the long-term solution lies in empowering users with the knowledge and critical thinking skills to navigate the digital landscape safely and responsibly. This involves fostering a deep understanding of the pervasive nature of manipulation and the importance of cultivating a cautious yet engaged online presence. Manipulation, in its various forms, is a universal phenomenon that transcends the boundaries of the digital world. The same persuasive techniques used to market products and influence consumer behavior can be readily employed to spread misinformation, promote harmful ideologies, or exploit individuals for malicious purposes. Recognizing the universality of manipulation is crucial for developing a discerning eye and a critical mind in the digital age.

Caution, however, should not be mistaken for cynicism. We can engage with the digital world with warmth, openness, and a willingness to connect with others without falling prey to naive trust. Cultivating a healthy balance between caution and engagement involves developing the ability to question information, evaluate sources, and recognize the subtle cues of manipulation. This approach empowers individuals to navigate the digital landscape with a discerning eye, fostering a sense of agency and resilience in the face of online deception. It encourages users to engage with the digital world critically and consciously, recognizing that trust is not an absolute but rather a dynamic and evolving element of human interaction.

By acknowledging the inevitability of trust abuse and empowering users with the knowledge and skills to navigate the digital landscape responsibly, we can foster a more secure and resilient online environment. This approach recognizes the inherent complexities of human behavior and the ever-evolving nature of online threats, promoting a culture of critical engagement, informed decision-making, and proactive awareness in the digital age.

Navigating the intersection of digital marketing and social engineering is a fundamentally human challenge, not just a technological one. The very tools and techniques that drive legitimate innovation in digital marketing can inadvertently become weapons in the hands of those who seek to exploit our trust. This creates a complex and dynamic landscape where the pursuit of progress in one arena may inadvertently lead to a regression in the other, unless we consciously address the ethical implications and potential for misuse.

The rise of digital marketing has transformed the way businesses connect with consumers, offering personalized experiences, targeted advertising, and sophisticated analytics to optimize engagement and drive sales. However, these same tools and techniques can be readily adapted by malicious actors to craft convincing phishing scams, spread disinformation, and manipulate individuals for nefarious purposes. The ability to gather vast amounts of data about consumer preferences, online behavior, and social connections, while invaluable for legitimate marketing purposes, also creates opportunities for social engineering attacks that exploit our vulnerabilities and biases. The more we reveal about ourselves online, the more ammunition we provide to those who seek to manipulate and deceive. The challenge lies in finding a balance between harnessing the power of digital marketing for legitimate purposes while mitigating the risks of social engineering. This requires a multifaceted approach that encompasses technological safeguards, ethical guidelines, and a collective shift in mindset.

On the technological front, advancements in AI and machine learning can be employed to detect and prevent social engineering attacks. By analyzing patterns of behavior, identifying suspicious links and content, and flagging potentially harmful communications, AI-powered security systems can act as a first line of defense.

However, technology alone is not sufficient. Ethical considerations must guide the development and deployment of digital marketing strategies. Marketers must be mindful of the potential for their techniques to be misused and adopt a responsible approach that prioritizes consumer trust and privacy. Ultimately, a collective shift in mindset is needed. Individuals must become more discerning consumers of online information, cultivating critical thinking skills and a healthy skepticism toward unsolicited communications and enticing offers. Education and awareness campaigns can play a crucial role in empowering individuals to recognize and resist social engineering tactics.

Navigating the intersection of digital marketing and social engineering is a delicate balancing act, requiring a conscious effort to harness the power of technology for good while mitigating its potential for harm. By embracing ethical principles, fostering digital literacy, and promoting a culture of cybersecurity awareness, we can ensure that the digital landscape remains a space for innovation, connection, and empowerment, rather than a breeding ground for manipulation and deception.

A SHARED RESPONSIBILITY: TECH CHANGES AND PUBLIC EDUCATION TO COMBAT SOCIAL ENGINEERING

The challenge of social engineering in the digital age demands a multi-pronged approach, with both tech companies and the public playing crucial roles. This multifaceted strategy is essential because social engineering attacks exploit the intersection of human psychology and technology. Tech companies, with their vast resources and expertise, can build robust defenses into their platforms and educate users about potential threats. However, the public also plays a crucial role in recognizing and resisting social engineering tactics, as these attacks ultimately rely on manipulating human emotions and behaviors.

Tech companies can implement various measures to combat social engineering, such as multi-factor authentication, email filtering, and AI-powered detection systems that identify suspicious patterns and flag potential threats. They can also educate users about common social engineering tactics, such as phishing scams, impersonation attempts, and baiting schemes, empowering them to make informed decisions and avoid falling victim to manipulation. However, technology alone cannot fully address the challenge of social engineering. The public must also play an active role in recognizing and resisting these attacks. This requires developing a critical mindset, questioning the legitimacy of requests for personal information, and verifying the identity of individuals or organizations before sharing sensitive data. For instance, consider the case of a phishing email that appears to be from a reputable bank, asking the recipient to click on a link and update their account information. A tech company can implement email filtering systems to flag such emails and educate users about phishing scams. However, it is ultimately up to the individual to recognize the red flags, such as suspicious email addresses, grammatical errors, or requests for sensitive information, and avoid clicking on the link or providing any personal data.

In conclusion, the challenge of social engineering in the digital age demands a collaborative approach, with tech companies building robust defenses and educating users, while the public cultivates a critical mindset and actively resists manipulation tactics. By working together, we can create a safer and more secure digital environment for all.

TRANSFORMING TECH PLATFORMS: SHIFTING THE INCENTIVE STRUCTURE

Social media platforms and the sprawling landscape of online advertising have become fertile battlegrounds for social engineering tactics. Their design, often prioritizing user engagement and revenue generation over safety and security, creates an environment ripe for manipulation and exploitation. It is within this digital arena that technology companies must acknowledge their responsibility and take proactive steps to protect users from the insidious threat of social engineering.

Transparency is paramount. Platforms need to shed light on the intricate mechanisms that govern how user data are collected, analyzed, and utilized to target advertising and personalize content. Users should be empowered with the ability to opt out of excessive personalization and micro-targeting, reclaiming control over their digital experiences and safeguarding their privacy. Furthermore, technology companies must invest in sophisticated AI-powered detection systems that can identify suspicious patterns in user behavior and communication, flagging potential social engineering attempts before they wreak havoc. These intelligent systems can analyze a multitude of factors, such as sudden changes in user activity, interactions with suspicious accounts, and language patterns commonly employed in scams and phishing attacks. However, while AI can play a crucial role in detection, it cannot replace the nuanced judgment and contextual understanding of human moderators. Social media companies must invest in robust moderation teams, composed of individuals trained to assess the context and intent of online interactions. These human moderators serve as a crucial line of defense, ensuring that flagged accounts and content are thoroughly evaluated before any action is taken.

By prioritizing transparency, investing in advanced detection systems, and maintaining human oversight, technology companies can create a safer and more secure digital environment for their users. This not only protects individuals from falling victim to social engineering scams but also fosters trust in online platforms and promotes a more responsible and ethical digital ecosystem.

EXAMPLE: FAKE SOCIAL MEDIA ACCOUNTS AND CRYPTOCURRENCY MARKETING SCAMS

In 2021, a social engineering scam targeting cryptocurrency investors took advantage of vulnerabilities on Twitter. Attackers created fake accounts impersonating prominent figures in the crypto space. These accounts promoted bogus investment opportunities, often using stolen content and manipulated media to appear legitimate. Deploying AI trained to detect patterns in impersonation attempts. These patterns could include sudden account creation, attempts to mimic existing usernames/profile pictures, and suspicious spikes in follower activity. Providing users with tools to verify account authenticity. This could include a system for verifying the identity of high-profile accounts or require additional steps to follow newly created accounts. Educating users about social engineering tactics. Twitter could have displayed warnings about cryptocurrency scams and provided resources to help users identify suspicious activity.

EMPOWERING USERS: BUILDING PUBLIC AWARENESS AND DIGITAL LITERACY

However, tech companies alone cannot win this fight. Broad public education is essential to create a more skeptical and informed online citizenry.

Public Awareness Campaigns: Governments and non-profit organizations can launch campaigns to educate people about social engineering tactics, highlighting common red flags and teaching users how to verify information online.

Critical Thinking Skills in Education: Schools can integrate digital literacy programs into the curriculum, teaching students to evaluate online information and identify potential manipulation attempts critically.

Individual Responsibility: Ultimately, every user must take responsibility for their online safety. This includes practicing healthy skepticism, double-checking information, and avoiding engagement with offers that seem too good to be true.

THE IMPORTANCE OF BALANCE: A COLLABORATIVE EFFORT

The ideal solution lies in a collaborative effort between tech companies and the public. Tech companies must create a safer online environment through platform changes and user education initiatives. The public must be empowered with the knowledge and skills to navigate this complex digital landscape. The example of fake social media accounts and cryptocurrency scams highlights why this collaboration is critical. Even with improved detection systems, some malicious content may slip through the cracks. Public education in spotting red flags and verifying information online becomes the final line of defense.

The goal should be to cultivate a digital ecosystem where innovation and engagement can flourish, where the human spirit can soar to new heights of creativity and collaboration, without sacrificing the fundamental pillars of trust and safety. This necessitates a concerted and collaborative effort, a symphony of action orchestrated by tech companies, policymakers, educators, and, most importantly, the public – the very heart and soul of this digital symphony.

Tech companies, the architects of this digital landscape, bear a profound responsibility to design and deploy technologies that prioritize user safety, privacy, and ethical considerations. They must move beyond the relentless pursuit of profit and embrace a more human-centric approach, ensuring that their creations empower individuals, foster genuine connection, and contribute to the betterment of society. Policymakers, the guardians of the public interest, must craft and enforce regulations that safeguard digital rights, promote transparency, and hold tech companies accountable for the societal impact of their creations. They must strike a delicate balance between fostering innovation and protecting citizens from the potential harms of unchecked technological advancement. Educators, the torchbearers of knowledge, must equip future generations with the critical thinking skills and digital literacy necessary to navigate the complexities of the digital world. They must empower students to discern truth from falsehood, to engage in responsible online behavior, and to become active and informed participants in the digital sphere. And finally, the public, the very lifeblood of this digital ecosystem, must embrace its role as both consumer and creator, demanding transparency, accountability, and ethical practices from tech companies and policymakers alike. We must cultivate a discerning eye, a critical mind, and a willingness to engage in constructive dialogue that transcends the echo chambers and filter bubbles that threaten to divide us.

Only through this collective effort, this harmonious symphony of action, can we create a digital world that truly serves humanity, fostering innovation, connection, and progress while safeguarding the values that define us: trust, safety, and the enduring pursuit of a more just and equitable society.

21 Cryptocurrency Markets and Interpersonal Trust, Escalating Social Engineering Risks, and the Technological Challenges in Detection

CRYPTOCURRENCY: A TRUST PARADOX AND HACKER'S PLAYGROUND

The world of cryptocurrency is built on a foundation of radical transparency and inherent trust. Blockchain technology, the backbone of cryptocurrencies, promises verifiable transactions, immutable records, and a decentralized system that operates independently of traditional financial institutions. Yet, the reality of cryptocurrency trading often involves interacting with strangers on unregulated platforms, navigating a complex landscape of technical jargon and volatile markets. This inherent paradox, where trust and transparency coexist with anonymity and uncertainty, combined with the high-stakes nature of cryptocurrency investments and the relative newness of the technology, has created a fertile breeding ground for social engineering attacks.

Hackers, ever opportunistic, understand that the very things that draw people to the cryptocurrency space – the promise of quick riches, the allure of cutting-edge technology, and the desire for financial autonomy – can also be their undoing. They exploit the anxieties and aspirations of cryptocurrency investors, preying on their fears of missing out on the next big opportunity or their desire to recover from losses. They leverage the complexities of the technology, using technical jargon and sophisticated scams to confuse and manipulate their victims. The decentralized and unregulated nature of the cryptocurrency world further exacerbates these risks. The absence of central authorities and traditional safeguards leaves investors vulnerable to scams, fraud, and market manipulation. The lack of clear regulatory frameworks and consumer protection mechanisms can make it difficult to recover from losses or seek recourse in the event of a cyberattack. In this environment, vigilance and critical thinking become paramount. Cryptocurrency investors must be aware of the social engineering tactics employed by hackers, from phishing scams and impersonation attempts to pump-and-dump schemes and fake investment opportunities. They

DOI: 10.1201/9781003500698-21

must cultivate a healthy skepticism, verify information from multiple sources, and exercise caution when interacting with strangers online.

The future of cryptocurrency hinges not only on the technological advancements that drive its development but also on the collective awareness and resilience of its users. By fostering a culture of cybersecurity awareness, promoting education and critical thinking, and developing robust security measures, we can create a safer and more secure environment for cryptocurrency investors, ensuring that the promise of this transformative technology is not overshadowed by the perils of cybercrime.

The Lure of Decentralization: Many are drawn to crypto by the lack of traditional intermediaries. This, however, means fewer safety nets if something goes wrong. Scammers use this to their advantage, promising "insider" knowledge that banks or regulators would never allow.

FOMO Culture and the Need for Trust: Rapid price swings and media hype about overnight millionaire's fuel fear of missing out. This desperation leads people to trust those making bold claims of easy profits.

Technical Complexity as Protection and Weakness: Crypto's technical jargon can create a false sense of security as if understanding the basics makes a person immune to manipulation. In reality, social engineers weaponize this complexity to make scams seem sophisticated.

The traditional security paradigm, rooted in control and centralized gatekeepers, falters in the decentralized landscape of the crypto world. This necessitates a fundamental rethinking of security strategies. We cannot solely depend on exchange platforms as protective barriers, mainly as scams increasingly target users in unregulated spaces like chat apps. Security solutions must adapt to detect threats in these decentralized environments where users are most vulnerable.

Furthermore, traditional security tools may struggle against the constantly evolving tactics and specialized language of the crypto sphere. Could artificial intelligence (AI) be trained to identify tried-and-true scam patterns and the nuanced "bro-talk" that lends an air of authenticity to fraudulent schemes within these communities? This adaptation of AI technology could be a key weapon in the fight against crypto scams.

A successful security strategy must ultimately move beyond blame and emphasize user empowerment. Given the relentless evolution of scams, educating users to adopt a "healthy paranoia" mindset is crucial. This does not mean forgoing crypto's opportunities but approaching them with balanced enthusiasm and constant skepticism. By empowering users, we can build a more resilient crypto community better equipped to navigate challenges and harness technology's full potential.

Let us explore in more detail the specific ways social engineers' prey on the trust dynamics inherent in the cryptocurrency world:

CRYPTOCURRENCY: A TRUST PARADOX

The decentralized nature of cryptocurrencies, promising freedom from central control, theoretically instills a sense of trust in the technology itself. However, ironically, this context can leave users more vulnerable to social engineering attacks. Individuals seeking guidance or solutions within a complex and rapidly changing space are primed for exploitation by those who understand the enduring power of manipulating human desires and anxieties.

Crypto users might rightfully place trust in the immutability of the blockchain, yet scams like fake hardware wallets, phishing schemes, or promises of lost private key recovery highlight a dangerous disconnect. Technology may be secure, but the avenues of interacting with it are often rife with human fallibility. Crypto's hype cycles further amplify the problem. During bull markets, the fear of missing out (FOMO) can blind even savvy individuals, causing them to overlook red flags to embrace the latest, hottest coin. Furthermore, while the assets traded might be novel, the tactics used to manipulate the markets are not. Pump-and-dump schemes repackaged for crypto prove that human psychology remains a powerful tool for malicious actors, regardless of the technology involved.

This underscores the importance of ongoing education and vigilance, even within the exciting landscape of crypto. Understanding that social engineering transcends any particular currency, staying grounded amid the hype, and recognizing that true security lies in knowledge are essential tools for navigating the ever-evolving world of digital assets.

The shift toward self-custody of cryptocurrency grants users unprecedented autonomy. However, with this freedom comes heightened responsibility and complexity. The need for technical literacy, understanding private keys, and identifying secure storage solutions becomes a prerequisite for participation. Lacking this knowledge leaves users vulnerable to various threats, from cleverly disguised phishing scams to well-meaning but potentially dangerous advice circulating online.

Furthermore, the allure of anonymity, while a core tenet of some cryptocurrencies, can ironically become a double-edged sword. Though transactions are traceable on the blockchain, linking them to real-world identities is challenging. This sense of impunity emboldens scammers and encourages illicit activities. Moreover, the rapidly evolving nature of the crypto landscape frequently outpaces regulatory frameworks. Scammers cynically exploit these regulatory gray areas, often setting up dubious projects in jurisdictions with lax oversight to ensnare unsuspecting victims. The promise of self-custody in cryptocurrencies demands balance: personal empowerment weighed against potential pitfalls. Navigating this terrain requires continuous education, technical understanding, and a healthy dose of skepticism amidst the hype.

ESCALATING SOCIAL ENGINEERING CRYPTO THREATS

The methods employed by crypto scammers are becoming increasingly sophisticated, evolving to exploit the unique vulnerabilities and anxieties of the cryptocurrency market. Hyper-realistic fake exchange websites, often indistinguishable from their legitimate counterparts, are used to lure unsuspecting users into revealing their login credentials or transferring funds to fraudulent accounts. These attacks are often highly personalized, incorporating details gleaned from social media and other online sources to create a veneer of legitimacy and induce a sense of trust.

The fear of compromised wallets, a common anxiety in the crypto space, is ruthlessly exploited by scammers. By creating a sense of panic and urgency, they pressure users into taking hasty actions, such as transferring their assets to a supposedly "secure" wallet controlled by the attacker. These scams prey on the emotional vulnerabilities of users, exploiting their fear of losing their hard-earned investments. The cryptocurrency market, with its unique dynamics and terminology, has also spawned a new breed of scams tailored to exploit its specific anxieties. Fake airdrops, promising free tokens to lure users into revealing their private keys, and fraudulent support channels, offering to "fix" nonexistent issues with wallets or transactions, are just a few examples of these targeted attacks. The impersonation of key figures in the crypto space, such as developers or influencers, further amplifies the potential for deception and manipulation.

Deepfake technology, with its ability to create realistic but fabricated videos and audio recordings, poses a significant threat to the crypto market. Imagine the chaos that could ensue if a deepfake video of a prominent crypto influencer denouncing a major project or cryptocurrency were to circulate online. This technology has the potential to erode trust in information sources, sow discord, and trigger panic selling, further destabilizing the volatile crypto market. The human element remains a significant vulnerability in the face of these evolving scams. Even tech-savvy individuals, well-versed in the technical aspects of cryptocurrency, can fall victim to well-executed social engineering tactics that leverage emotions like urgency, excitement, or fear. Detecting these psychological cues and developing effective countermeasures is a complex challenge that demands a deeper understanding of human behavior and decision-making in the context of the crypto market. Another challenge lies in the fact that many crypto scams originate outside the blockchain itself. While the blockchain provides a transparent and immutable record of transactions, the scams often unfold in the murky waters of social media groups, direct messages, or phishing websites, where traditional security tools may be less effective. This necessitates a multi-layered approach to security, encompassing not only technical safeguards but also education and awareness initiatives to empower users to recognize and avoid these scams.

The pursuit of enhanced security in the crypto space also raises ethical dilemmas. For instance, could the embedding of keystroke-logging software in crypto wallets help catch phishing attempts by monitoring user input and detecting suspicious patterns? While such a measure might offer some protection, it also raises concerns about privacy and the potential for abuse. Striking a balance between security and privacy remains a complex challenge in the evolving landscape of cryptocurrency.

THE ROAD AHEAD: BEYOND TECHNICAL SOLUTIONS

AI holds immense potential for revolutionizing cybersecurity in the cryptocurrency domain. AI algorithms can analyze vast amounts of data, identify patterns, and detect anomalies that might elude human observers. In the context of phishing attacks, AI can be particularly valuable, as it can analyze communication patterns, identify suspicious keywords, and even detect subtle emotional cues that might betray a malicious intent.

However, the cybersecurity landscape is a dynamic one, and attackers are constantly evolving their tactics to circumvent defenses. AI systems, while powerful, are not infallible. They can be fooled by sophisticated adversarial attacks, where malicious actors manipulate data or code to exploit vulnerabilities in the AI algorithms. This creates an ongoing arms race between defenders and attackers, requiring continuous innovation and adaptation to stay ahead of emerging threats. Reputation systems offer a promising avenue for enhancing security in the cryptocurrency ecosystem. By leveraging the collective wisdom of the community, these systems can identify and flag suspicious wallets, smart contracts, and transactions, providing users with valuable information to make informed decisions. However, the design and implementation of reputation systems must be carefully considered to avoid false positives, which could unfairly damage the reputation of legitimate users or stifle innovation. Collaboration is essential for building a more secure and resilient cryptocurrency ecosystem. Sharing threat intelligence between wallet providers, exchanges, and dedicated security platforms can empower users and enhance the effectiveness of detection software. Decentralized databases of known scam addresses and tactics can serve as valuable resources for both individuals and AI-powered security systems.

The future of cryptocurrency security hinges on a multi-layered approach that combines the strengths of AI, reputation systems, and collaborative initiatives. By fostering a culture of cybersecurity awareness, empowering users with knowledge and tools, and promoting responsible innovation, we can create a more secure and trustworthy environment for the cryptocurrency community to thrive.

BUILDING RESILIENCE IN THE CRYPTO COMMUNITY

The cryptocurrency space, fueled by ideals of decentralization and self-sovereignty, presents a unique challenge in balancing innovation with protection against those who exploit human vulnerabilities. While technology will always play a role in defense, user education is paramount. User-friendly warnings within wallets about the risks of unverified contracts, clear visual cues flagging potential phishing attempts, and promoting community-driven scam reporting initiatives can empower users to make informed choices.

This battleground extends far beyond the realm of individual responsibility. It necessitates a collective effort, a concerted push from all stakeholders to fortify the very foundation of the cryptocurrency ecosystem. Cryptocurrency exchanges, those bustling marketplaces of digital assets, bear a significant responsibility in educating users and implementing robust security measures. Influential figures, the thought leaders and pioneers of this space, must leverage their platforms to advocate for security best practices and champion a culture of vigilance. Projects, the heart of innovation in the crypto world, must prioritize security considerations in their design and development, ensuring that user funds and data are protected from malicious actors. And regulators, the guardians of financial stability and consumer protection, must establish clear guidelines and frameworks that foster a secure and transparent environment for cryptocurrency transactions. Community-driven initiatives must supplement official channels, creating a vibrant ecosystem of knowledge sharing, peer-to-peer support, and collective vigilance. Skepticism, rather than being viewed as an obstacle to innovation, must be embraced as a healthy companion, a critical lens through which users evaluate projects, assess risks, and make informed decisions. Only when security becomes an integral part of the cryptocurrency ethos, a shared responsibility embraced by all, can users truly prioritize it alongside the pursuit of potential gains.

The future of cryptocurrency hinges on this collective effort. Technological advancements alone will not be enough to ensure its long-term success and stability. A paradigm shift is required, a fundamental change in mindset where security is not an afterthought but a foundational principle. This requires a concerted effort from all stakeholders, a shared commitment to building a secure, transparent, and resilient ecosystem where innovation can flourish and the transformative potential of cryptocurrency can be fully realized.

22 A Brief Overview of the Benefits of Implementing Quantum Algorithms in Factorizing Cyber Social Engineering Threats

Traditional cybersecurity approaches, often rooted in classical logic, tend to address threats in a linear, deterministic manner, focusing on isolating and mitigating individual vulnerabilities. However, the evolving landscape of cyber threats, characterized by its complexity and interconnectedness, demands a paradigm shift in our thinking. Quantum logic, with its emphasis on superposition, entanglement, and uncertainty, offers a powerful framework for understanding the fluid and dynamic nature of cyber risks. This logic allows us to move beyond the binary confines of classical logic, embracing the notion that systems can exist in multiple states simultaneously and that seemingly disparate events can be interconnected in ways that defy traditional analysis.

Partition logic further complements this perspective by emphasizing the importance of context and interconnectedness in understanding complex systems. It allows us to analyze how seemingly isolated vulnerabilities or events can be linked, creating a ripple effect that amplifies their impact. By considering the broader context in which cyber threats emerge, we can gain a more comprehensive understanding of the threat environment and develop more effective mitigation strategies. Imagine a network of interconnected systems, each with its own set of vulnerabilities. A traditional cybersecurity approach might focus on securing each system individually, addressing vulnerabilities in isolation. However, a quantum-inspired approach, informed by partition logic, would consider the interconnectedness of these systems, recognizing that a seemingly minor vulnerability in one system could have cascading effects, potentially compromising the entire network. By embracing insights from quantum and partition logics, we can develop more adaptive and proactive cybersecurity strategies. We can move beyond reactive measures, anticipating and mitigating threats before they materialize. We can develop systems that are not only resilient to individual attacks but also capable of adapting to the dynamic and interconnected nature of the cyber landscape.

This shift in thinking requires a new breed of cybersecurity professionals, individuals who are not only well-versed in traditional security practices but also possess

DOI: 10.1201/9781003500698-22

a deep understanding of complex systems, quantum principles, and the interconnectedness of the digital world. By fostering this interdisciplinary approach, we can cultivate a cybersecurity workforce that is equipped to navigate the challenges of the 21st century and beyond.

Let us take a look at why looking at cyber threat factorization through a quantum structure point of view holds promise:

Unraveling Complexity: Cyberattacks often involve a complex chain of interwoven actions, exploits, and vulnerabilities. Just as quantum mechanics illuminates the interactions of subatomic particles, a quantum-inspired approach can help dissect multi-faceted attacks.

Identifying Hidden Connections: Quantum phenomena like superposition and entanglement highlight connections that classical analyses might miss. This could facilitate discovering subtle relationships between seemingly unrelated vulnerabilities or attack patterns.

Adapting Defenses: Threats mutate rapidly. Quantum-inspired thinking, emphasizing probabilities and dynamic behavior, fosters the design of adaptive security systems that anticipate changes and morph in response.

Optimizing Risk Mitigation: Finding the best way to break down a complex threat into components for prioritization mirrors the search for optimal solutions central to quantum computation. Applying a similar mindset could result in more efficient and effective resource allocation.

The inherent complexity of cyberattacks and interconnected chains of exploits and vulnerabilities demand a shift in how we approach analysis and defense. Drawing inspiration from quantum mechanics, with its ability to illuminate elusive interactions within the subatomic domain, we can develop more nuanced methods for dissecting intricate attacks. A quantum-inspired approach emphasizes the potential for hidden connections that classical analysis might overlook. By recognizing that seemingly disparate events or vulnerabilities might be entangled in unanticipated ways, we better understand emerging threat patterns. Moreover, embracing the dynamic nature of quantum systems fosters a mindset adaptable to an ever-evolving cyber threat landscape. This approach encourages the development of security systems designed to anticipate change and respond proactively rather than reactively hardening against yesterday's attacks. Similar to finding optimal solutions within the vast landscapes of quantum computation, a quantum-inspired approach to risk mitigation allows for a more efficient allocation of resources. This could involve intelligently breaking down complex threats and prioritizing countermeasures based on the most significant potential impact. While applying quantum principles to cybersecurity is still in its early stages, this perspective can fundamentally change how we understand, anticipate, and ultimately defend against complex cyberattacks.

While not directly utilizing quantum computers, this approach leverages the power of analogy. Studying the efficiency, interconnectedness, and adaptability of quantum systems can inspire breakthroughs in analyzing, factorizing, and countering cyber threats.

QUANTUM PHENOMENA IN NATURE

Nature demonstrates remarkable examples of quantum effects that play critical roles in biological and physical systems:

Photosynthesis: Plants and certain bacteria use complex molecular structures to optimize energy transfer from light with astonishing quantum efficiency.
Navigation: Some species of birds are theorized to leverage quantum entanglement within specialized proteins for magnetic field sensing during migration.
Quantum Tunneling: Enzymes may use quantum tunneling to accelerate biochemical reactions, allowing molecules to pass through seemingly impenetrable energy barriers.

The observation that quantum effects play critical roles in biological and physical systems opens an exciting window into our understanding of the universe. Photosynthesis strikingly demonstrates how nature has evolved complex molecular structures to harness quantum phenomena for incredibly efficient energy transfer. The potential role of quantum entanglement within bird navigation suggests that nature might have utilized these baffling principles for long-range direction sensing. Even within our bodies, quantum tunneling in enzyme activity might facilitate biochemical reactions that would otherwise be impossible.

These examples highlight the potentially profound implications of quantum mechanics far beyond the domains of physics labs. Appreciating their presence within biological systems begs the question: Could understanding and replicating these natural quantum mechanisms unlock groundbreaking new technologies, from ultra-efficient solar energy to enhanced medical treatments? Further investigation may unveil yet more surprising ways quantum principles underpin the world around us, challenging the boundary between conventional physics and the biological domain.

FUNDAMENTAL QUANTUM PROPERTIES WITH CYBERSECURITY POTENTIAL

The exploration of quantum properties such as superposition, entanglement, and quantum tunneling presents groundbreaking opportunities for enhancing cybersecurity. By leveraging these phenomena, we can develop advanced methods for tamper detection and multi-path scanning, while heuristic algorithms can optimize and analyze complex quantum data for improved security measures.

Superposition: Existing in multiple states simultaneously. This could be the foundation for new detection algorithms:
Multi-Path Scanning: Cybersecurity systems could theoretically scan for threats across multiple possibilities at once, expanding search efficiency.
Entanglement: A link between particles where measuring one affects another.
Tamper Detection: Entangled photon pairs could form the basis for communication channels that are highly sensitive to any interception attempt.
Quantum Tunneling: Passing through seemingly impassable barriers.

Heuristic Algorithms: Quantum-inspired algorithms might be devised to find "shortcuts" through complex security problems, optimizing solutions.

The unique properties of quantum mechanics hold immense potential for revolutionizing cybersecurity practices. Superposition offers the possibility of cybersecurity systems operating across multiple states simultaneously, potentially leading to highly efficient threat scanning or novel detection algorithms. Entanglement's profound connection between particles could pave the way for ultra-secure communication channels, where any attempt at interception would be immediately detectable.

Even the perplexing ability of quantum tunneling, the passage through seemingly impossible barriers, suggests opportunities. This might inspire the development of quantum-based heuristic algorithms designed to find "shortcuts" through complex security problems, resulting in faster and more optimized solutions.

While realizing these concepts in practical cybersecurity applications are still in their early stages, their potential is undeniable. As research into quantum computing progresses, we can eagerly anticipate breakthroughs that will transform how we think about digital security, harnessing the power of the quantum world to create an even safer cyber future.

CHALLENGES OF IMPLEMENTATION

Implementing advanced technologies often encounters significant hurdles, including the need to effectively harness quantum effects, manage computational overhead, and navigate unproven concepts that may not yet be fully understood or validated. Each of these challenges presents unique obstacles that can impede progress and require innovative solutions.

Harnessing Quantum Effects: Controlling quantum phenomena at a scale and temperature suitable for cybersecurity applications is challenging.

Computational Overhead: Some quantum-inspired approaches may be computationally expensive for real-time use.

Unproven Concepts: Many cybersecurity applications inspired by nature are still largely theoretical, requiring extensive research and testing.

The prospect of harnessing quantum effects, as nature so elegantly does, to revolutionize cybersecurity is tantalizing. However, we must acknowledge the significant hurdles that lie ahead. Controlling quantum phenomena with the precision, scale, and temperature stability required for practical cybersecurity applications poses a formidable challenge. Moreover, the inherent complexity of some quantum-inspired approaches may lead to high computational overheads, potentially hindering real-time deployment in rapidly evolving threat environments.

Notably, many intriguing concepts that look to nature for cybersecurity solutions remain primarily theoretical. Translating those concepts into robust, proven defenses will require lengthy research, refinement, and rigorous testing. Despite the obstacles, the compelling potential for quantum-inspired cybersecurity strategies demands our continued exploration and investment into this emerging frontier.

EXAMPLE AREAS OF DEVELOPMENT

Quantum-resistant Cryptography

The rise of quantum computing poses a challenge to classical cryptographic methods, which are vulnerable to the code-breaking power of quantum algorithms. To address this, the development of quantum-resistant cryptography is essential. This involves creating new encryption algorithms designed to withstand attacks from quantum computers. While inspired by quantum principles, these algorithms can be implemented in classical computing systems. Partition logic comes into play by emphasizing the interconnectedness of elements within a cryptographic system. Analyzing these relationships and potential vulnerabilities that might cascade across the system facilitates the design of more robust quantum-resistant algorithms. This integrated approach, drawing insights from both quantum systems' power and limitations, promises to create more robust cryptographic safeguards for the future.

Quantum Random Number Generation

True randomness is essential for robust cryptography and secure communication. Traditional random number generators often rely on deterministic algorithms or physical processes with predictable patterns, leaving them vulnerable. Quantum random number generation (QRNG) addresses this by harnessing the inherent randomness observed in quantum phenomena, such as the unpredictable decay of radioactive particles. Quantum logic provides a framework to model and understand the probabilistic nature of quantum measurements. Partition logic helps analyze potential biases or correlations within the quantum system, ensuring the randomness is not compromised by hidden structures or influences. By integrating these logical approaches, QRNG aims to generate truly unpredictable random numbers, significantly enhancing the security of cryptographic systems.

Network Anomaly Detection

Network anomaly detection aims to identify unusual patterns that could signify malicious activity or system malfunctions. The Birkhoff–Von Neumann concept of quantum logic introduces new possibilities within this domain. Unlike classical logic's focus on binary states, quantum logic allows for superposition – where an element can exist in multiple states simultaneously. This framework aligns with the fluid nature of network traffic, where data packets can exhibit variability yet follow established patterns. By applying quantum logic principles, anomaly detection systems could flexibly model normal network behavior. They could potentially identify minute deviations or subtle correlations that traditional systems miss, enabling earlier detection of emerging threats and a more nuanced understanding of network health.

Intrusion Detection Systems (IDS)

Birkhoff–von Neumann quantum logic offers a unique framework for intrusion detection systems. Instead of classical binary logic, it models system states as a superposition of multiple possibilities, allowing for the detection of subtle anomalies that might evade traditional rule-based approaches. A quantum-based IDS could analyze network traffic, user behavior, or system logs, identifying patterns that deviate from the expected norm, even if those patterns do not neatly match pre-defined attack signatures. By operating on probabilities and a spectrum of potential states, such a system could detect novel attack methods and zero-day vulnerabilities more effectively. However, it is essential to note that this application of quantum logic to cybersecurity is still in the theoretical and research phase.

Important Considerations

Inspiration, not Replication Cybersecurity algorithms will likely mimic some principles of natural quantum phenomena, not directly recreate them with quantum hardware.

Hybrid Approaches, quantum-inspired techniques might work alongside traditional cybersecurity methods.

Now, let us take a look at this from another angle. Cybersecurity threats are evolving, demanding innovative approaches. Traditional algorithms often struggle to detect subtle anomalies or novel attack vectors. Quantum mechanics offers a rich source of inspiration. While directly harnessing quantum computation for cybersecurity remains challenging, algorithms that mimic principles like superposition, entanglement, and tunneling may pave the way for the next generation of security solutions. This chapter explores the potential of quantum-inspired algorithms for factorization-based detection and mitigation of unusual activity risks.

WHAT IS FACTORIZATION IN CYBERSECURITY

In the realm of cybersecurity, the term "factorization" takes on a distinct meaning, diverging from its traditional mathematical context of finding the prime factors of an integer. Instead, it refers to a strategic approach to problem-solving, where complex cybersecurity challenges are deconstructed into smaller, more manageable components. This process of factorization allows security experts to analyze intricate threats, identify vulnerabilities, and develop targeted solutions with greater precision and efficiency.

Imagine a cybersecurity team facing a sophisticated cyberattack involving multiple stages, from initial infiltration to data exfiltration. By applying the principle of factorization, they can break down this complex attack into its constituent parts, examining each stage in isolation. This granular approach enables them to identify the specific vulnerabilities exploited at each step, understand the attacker's tactics, and develop targeted countermeasures to mitigate the threat. Factorization in cybersecurity is akin to disassembling a complex machine to understand its inner workings. By breaking down the system into its individual components, security experts can gain a deeper understanding of its vulnerabilities and develop strategies to strengthen its defenses. This approach is particularly crucial in the face of increasingly sophisticated cyberattacks, where a holistic understanding of the threat landscape is essential for developing effective mitigation strategies. Furthermore, factorization enables the development of modular solutions, where individual components can be addressed and updated independently. This modularity enhances the flexibility and adaptability of cybersecurity systems, allowing them to evolve in response to new and emerging threats.

In essence, factorization in cybersecurity represents a strategic approach to problem-solving, where complex challenges are deconstructed into manageable components, enabling a deeper understanding of vulnerabilities, the development of targeted solutions, and the creation of more resilient and adaptable cybersecurity systems. This has several applications:

Threat Decomposition: Decomposing complex attacks into their constituent actions (i.e., reconnaissance, infiltration, data exfiltration) can improve detection accuracy and reveal attack patterns.

Behavior Analysis: Factorizing user and system behavior into atomic events enables profiling standard activity patterns. Deviations from these baselines indicate potential anomalies.

Data Feature Analysis: For machine learning threat detection models, breaking down network traffic, system logs, and user interactions into fundamental features improves learning and discrimination.

Threat detection in the modern cybersecurity landscape demands sophisticated strategies to counter increasingly complex attacks. Decomposing these attacks into discrete stages – reconnaissance, infiltration, exfiltration, and others – provides a granular view that aids in identifying attack patterns and improves detection accuracy. Similarly, breaking down average user and system behavior into a series of atomic events allows for the establishment of baselines. Any deviations from these baselines become potential red flags, signaling anomalies that might indicate a security breach in progress.

For machine learning models designed to detect threats, the ability to analyze network traffic, logs, and user interactions at the feature level is crucial. This involves distilling the data into its fundamental characteristics, allowing the model to differentiate between benign and malicious activity more precisely. These techniques highlight that a holistic approach to cybersecurity is not just about identifying specific threats but also necessitates a keen understanding of the tell-tale signs in seemingly innocuous network data, system behaviors, and user actions.

QUANTUM INSPIRATION FOR FACTORIZATION APPROACHES

Harnessing the principles of quantum mechanics offers innovative strategies for enhancing factorization techniques, enabling more efficient exploration of mathematical complexities. By leveraging concepts such as superposition, entanglement, and quantum tunneling, researchers can develop novel algorithms that significantly improve computational performance.

Superposition for Multi-Path Exploration: Algorithms mimicking superposition could consider multiple possibilities simultaneously. This could find optimal threat decompositions or efficiently explore various behavioral profiles for outlier detection.

Entanglement for Correlation: Just as entangled particles are intertwined, events in a cyberattack may exhibit subtle correlations. Quantum-inspired algorithms could uncover these hidden connections that traditional analysis might miss.

Quantum Tunneling for Heuristics: Identifying anomalies can be framed as finding a path through a complex problem space. Quantum-inspired heuristics could enable shortcuts, finding unusual activity patterns faster than exhaustive searches.

The principles of quantum mechanics, long confined to subatomic particles, offer intriguing possibilities for revolutionizing cybersecurity techniques. Superposition, where a system exists in multiple states simultaneously, could inspire algorithms that investigate multiple attack vectors or behavioral profiles concurrently, leading to faster threat identification and outlier detection. Similarly, the interconnectedness of entangled particles could be mirrored in algorithms designed to uncover subtle correlations within cyberattack events – connections that might elude traditional analysis. The concept of quantum tunneling, where particles "pass through" seemingly impossible barriers, could inform heuristics that shortcut exhaustive searches within complex problem spaces. This could lead to more efficient and rapid identification of anomalies and unusual activity patterns. While still in a largely theoretical stage, exploring the application of these quantum principles to cybersecurity represents a potentially groundbreaking frontier. The potential rewards are considerable: more intelligent, more resilient algorithms that can outpace the speed and sophistication of emerging cyber threats. Further research and development hold the promise of translating these quantum-inspired ideas into real-world cybersecurity solutions, safeguarding our digital assets in an increasingly complex threat landscape.

EXAMPLE APPLICATIONS

Intrusion Detection: Quantum-inspired algorithms could factorize user behavior patterns at a granular level. Deviations from established baselines could signal malicious activity even if the attack vector is unknown. A conceptual example of the above application is a novel intrusion detection system that draws inspiration from the Birkhoff–von Neumann concept of quantum logic to monitor network behavior. Unlike traditional IDSs that rely on binary rules (allowed/disallowed), this system analyzes network traffic regarding quantum superposition states. Each data packet or user action is represented not as a definitive "yes" or "no" for malicious intent but as a probability distribution across a spectrum of potential threats. This allows the system to detect subtle anomalies or patterns that might evade classical rule-based systems. Additionally, the quantum-inspired IDS can continuously update its analysis based on new observations, incorporating the entanglement principle where seemingly unrelated events might become correlated, offering a more dynamic and adaptable approach to threat detection.

Vulnerability Scanning: Decomposing attack surfaces into the interplay of software, configurations, and potential exploits could be more efficient with quantum-inspired approaches. This would facilitate the prioritization of remediation. A conceptual example of the above application is traditional vulnerability scanners, which meticulously examine a network, identifying known vulnerabilities within individual components – software, operating systems, or hardware. A quantum partition logic-inspired approach would go further. It would consider the network an interconnected system where the superposition of vulnerabilities, much like the superposition of quantum states, creates a unique risk profile. Individual software flaws, outdated devices, and user behavior patterns could interact unpredictably, amplifying potential exploits. This approach might also draw on partition logic's focus on context. It would analyze the network's overall purpose, data flows, and dependencies between systems. A seemingly minor vulnerability in a low-priority system could become a critical risk point if it allows attackers to reach more sensitive assets. At this stage, such a scanner would not necessarily utilize actual quantum computers. Instead, it would be guided by quantum-inspired algorithms and logical frameworks to prioritize vulnerabilities based on severity and their potential impact within the network's unique, dynamic configuration.

Adaptive Network Defenses: One of the core concepts of Birkhoff–von Neumann's quantum logic is the idea that a system's state can exist in a superposition – simultaneously in multiple states until observed. Applied to network defense, this could translate into a system that continuously assesses the network's configuration and traffic patterns. Rather than relying on rigid rules, it would identify subtle anomalies or combinations of factors that deviate from a "normal" baseline, hinting at a potential intrusion attempt. This adaptive approach mimics the probabilistic nature of quantum states, enabling the system to detect unknown or evolving threats without being confined to a pre-defined set of attack signatures. Additionally, this approach could inform the dynamic reconfiguration of network defenses, constantly shifting and adapting to make it harder for attackers to maintain a foothold.

CHALLENGES AND LIMITATIONS

Despite the promising potential of advanced methodologies, several challenges and limitations hinder their effective implementation and widespread adoption. These obstacles range from theoretical complexities to practical constraints in computational resources and integration with existing systems.

Theoretical Foundation: Many proposed quantum-inspired algorithms for cybersecurity remain theoretical, requiring rigorous validation.

Computational Overhead: Some approaches may introduce significant computational costs, demanding careful optimization for real-world use.

Integration: Incorporating novel detection mechanisms into existing security infrastructures presents interoperability challenges.

While quantum-inspired algorithms hold significant promise for augmenting cybersecurity measures, several key challenges must be addressed before widespread implementation. First, many proposed algorithms currently exist primarily in the theoretical domain. Rigorous validation, testing, and ongoing refinement are essential to bridge the gap between theory and robust, practical solutions. Furthermore, some approaches could introduce substantial computational overhead, potentially hindering their scalability in real-time threat detection scenarios. This demands optimization strategies or hardware acceleration to achieve the speed and efficiency necessary for real-world cyber defense. Lastly, successfully integrating these novel detection mechanisms into established security infrastructures poses challenges, requiring careful focus on interoperability and ensuring seamless operation with existing systems.

THE FUTURE OF QUANTUM-INSPIRED CYBERSECURITY

Integrating quantum-inspired principles into cybersecurity is the key to several transformative advancements. First, it can detect attacks that slip past conventional signature- or behavior-based defenses. We can illuminate subtle patterns and anomalies hidden in a classical system by modeling attacker tactics through a quantum-like framework. Additionally, quantum-inspired algorithms could optimize processes like threat analysis, prioritization, and automated response, leading to significantly faster and more efficient security operations. Perhaps most crucially, these approaches allow us to move beyond purely reactive strategies toward a proactive, adaptive model. This fosters a dynamic security posture capable of anticipating threats and proactively mitigating risks in the ever-evolving cyber landscape. While these applications are still in their early stages, they foreshadow a future where cybersecurity harnesses the enigmatic power of quantum principles to build safer and more resilient digital environments.

While still nascent, research into quantum-inspired algorithms for factorization-based risk mitigation holds promise. These offer potential advantages:

Unconventional Detection: Detection of attacks that evade traditional signature or behavior-based systems.

Efficiency Gains: Potential to significantly speed up threat decomposition, prioritization, and automated response.

Adaptive Countermeasures: Facilitating proactive, dynamic security strategies that anticipate and reshape in response to evolving threats.

In the realm of cybersecurity, where the battle between defenders and attackers is waged in the ethereal realm of bits and bytes, the emergence of quantum computing promises to revolutionize the very foundations of our digital defenses. Quantum algorithms, harnessing the mind-bending principles of quantum mechanics, offer the potential to unravel complex problems that lie beyond the reach of classical computation. This capability opens up exciting new avenues for detecting abnormal cyber activities, providing a glimmer of hope in the ongoing struggle to secure our digital infrastructure.

Let us delve deeper into the fascinating world of quantum algorithms and explore their potential implications for bolstering our cyber defenses. These algorithms, leveraging the phenomena of superposition and entanglement, can tackle computational challenges that have long stymied classical approaches. For instance, Shor's algorithm, a crown jewel of quantum computation, has the potential to break widely used encryption schemes that rely on the difficulty of factoring large numbers, a task that would take classical computers an impractical amount of time. While this capability poses a threat to existing cryptographic systems, it also opens up new possibilities for detecting malicious activities. Quantum algorithms could be employed to analyze network traffic patterns, identify anomalies, and detect intrusions with unprecedented speed and accuracy. By harnessing the power of quantum computation, we could potentially identify and neutralize cyberattacks before they wreak havoc on our digital infrastructure. Furthermore, quantum algorithms could revolutionize the field of machine learning, enabling the development of more sophisticated and adaptive intrusion detection systems. These quantum-enhanced systems could learn from vast amounts of data, identify subtle patterns of malicious behavior, and adapt to the ever-evolving tactics of cyber adversaries. The potential of quantum algorithms to enhance cybersecurity extends beyond intrusion detection. Quantum-resistant cryptography, a field dedicated to developing encryption schemes that are impervious to attacks from quantum computers, is another area where quantum technology could play a crucial role in safeguarding our digital future.

In essence, the advent of quantum computing presents both challenges and opportunities for cybersecurity. While the potential for quantum computers to break existing encryption methods poses a significant threat, the development of quantum algorithms for intrusion detection and quantum-resistant cryptography offers a glimmer of hope in the ongoing battle against cyber adversaries. By embracing the transformative power of quantum technology and investing in research and development, we can harness its potential to build a more secure and resilient digital world.

CRITICAL AREAS OF QUANTUM ALGORITHM DEVELOPMENT RELEVANT TO CYBERSECURITY

In the rapidly evolving landscape of cybersecurity, the development of quantum algorithms holds significant promise for enhancing security measures and addressing vulnerabilities. Key areas of focus include quantum optimization algorithms, quantum machine learning, and quantum simulation, each presenting unique implications for the future of cybersecurity.

Quantum Optimization Algorithms

Nature: Quantum algorithms excel at finding solutions to optimization problems with vast search spaces.

Cybersecurity Relevance

Improved Intrusion Detection: Quantum-inspired optimization could analyze enormous datasets of network activity, behavioral patterns, and system logs to find subtle anomalies indicative of attacks, even zero-day exploits.

Vulnerability Prioritization: These algorithms could help prioritize remediation efforts by rapidly assessing the potential exploitability and impact of many known vulnerabilities.

Quantum Machine Learning

Nature: Potential for quantum computers to accelerate machine learning, particularly with specific algorithm types.

Cybersecurity Relevance

Enhanced Threat Detection: Quantum-enhanced machine learning might enable faster, more complex model training on security data for more accurate, nuanced detection of threats.

Adaptive Defenses: Real-time threat analysis using quantum-enhanced ML could allow defenses to morph quickly, isolating compromised systems or preemptively blocking attacks.

Quantum machine learning offers a tantalizing prospect for revolutionizing how we approach traditional machine learning tasks. Its potential to accelerate specific algorithmic processes holds significant promise, particularly in areas where computational complexity is a bottleneck. Within the domain of cybersecurity, this has several compelling implications. Quantum-enhanced machine learning could lead to the development of models that analyze vast security datasets with unprecedented speed and accuracy. This could translate into far more sophisticated and nuanced threat detection systems capable of identifying even the subtlest anomalies. Furthermore, the potential for real-time analysis empowered by quantum computing opens the door to adaptive defenses, where security systems could quickly learn and react to emerging threats. This could lead to more effective and dynamic protection against the rapidly evolving attacks in the cyber landscape.

Quantum Simulation

Nature: Simulating quantum systems on classical computers with quantum-inspired algorithms.

Cybersecurity Relevance

Testing New Attack Vectors: Simulations could model how novel attacks (possibly inspired by quantum principles) might propagate across a network, aiding in the development of countermeasures.

Cryptographic Vulnerability Testing: Assessing emerging cryptographic algorithms for potential weaknesses that conventional mathematical analysis might miss.

Quantum simulation, harnessing classical or quantum-inspired algorithms to model quantum systems, holds intriguing possibilities in cybersecurity. While simulating complex quantum systems on traditional computers has limitations, exploring quantum-inspired algorithms to model network behavior and attack propagation could prove valuable for threat prediction and defense strategy. Additionally, quantum simulation could become a tool for testing the resilience of cryptographic algorithms. As cryptography enters the post-quantum era, these simulations could reveal hidden vulnerabilities undetectable through classical analysis methods. The potential to simulate how adversaries might exploit unknown weaknesses would be a significant step in securing our digital infrastructure against future advancements.

EXAMPLES OF QUANTUM (AND QUANTUM-INSPIRED) ALGORITHMS

Grover's Algorithm: Provides potential speedup when searching unsorted data. Could accelerate searching for patterns in vast logs or codebases for indications of compromise (IOCs). Imagine a vast, unorganized database of customer records for a major online retailer. Finding a specific customer's information using traditional search methods would require checking each entry individually, a time-consuming process. Grover's quantum algorithm offers a significant speedup. By leveraging quantum superposition, it can search the entire database simultaneously, pinpointing the desired customer record in far fewer steps than a conventional search. This has practical applications for businesses needing to quickly locate information within extensive datasets, potentially improving customer service efficiency and optimizing data-driven decision-making.

Quantum Approximate Optimization Algorithm (QAOA): Used to find approximate solutions to optimization problems. It may enhance threat detection models and prioritization processes. One promising application of QAOA lies in the domain of logistics. Consider a delivery company aiming to optimize routes for its fleet of vehicles. This complex problem, known as the Traveling Salesperson Problem, involves finding the shortest possible route connecting multiple cities while ensuring each is visited only once. QAOA can tackle this by translating the problem into a mathematical model that a quantum computer can process. While still under development, early QAOA implementations have shown potential for suggesting more efficient routes than classical algorithms, especially as the number of destinations increases. This could translate into significant savings in fuel costs, delivery times, and environmental impact for the company.

Quantum-Inspired Annealing: Mimics the quantum tunneling process to find better solutions to optimization problems. Could refine network anomaly detection or incident response strategies. Traffic optimization is a complex challenge for cities worldwide. Researchers have applied the Quantum-Inspired Annealing Algorithm to this problem to find the most efficient vehicle routes across a congested network. The algorithm simulates how atoms reach a low-energy state through annealing. Analogously, it searches for a configuration of traffic routes that minimize congestion and travel time. While still in development, this approach holds promise for cities facing gridlock. It demonstrates how quantum-inspired algorithms can tackle real-world problems with numerous variables and potential solutions.

EXAMPLES OF QUANTUM (AND QUANTUM-INSPIRED) ALGORITHMS FOR CYBERSECURITY FACTORIZATION

Deutsch–Jozsa Algorithm: The Deutsch–Jozsa algorithm is a foundational quantum algorithm that demonstrates the potential speed advantage of quantum algorithms over classical ones. While primarily theoretical, its principles might hint at future techniques for "factorizing" social engineering tactics. This could include identifying patterns in deceptive communication or modeling how individuals respond to manipulation attempts – potentially leading to faster and more reliable threat detection in the study of social engineering.

Bernstein–Vazirani Algorithm: The Bernstein–Vazirani algorithm demonstrates how quantum computing has the potential to reveal hidden patterns significantly faster than classical computers. This is relevant to social engineering factorization, where attackers must decipher the complex mix of psychological factors and situational cues that make a target susceptible. While still theoretical, quantum-inspired algorithms might one day help identify and analyze these hidden patterns, aiding in developing more effective social engineering defenses.

Simon's Algorithm: Simon's algorithm is a quantum algorithm famous for its speed advantage over classical methods in finding patterns within specific functions. While its direct use in breaking encryption schemes is limited, some researchers hypothesize that its principles could inspire new ways to analyze and "factor" the complex social engineering tactics used to manipulate individuals.

Quantum Phase Estimation Algorithm: The QPE algorithm holds the potential to revolutionize cybersecurity by enabling rapid factorization of large numbers, a critical vulnerability exploited in many encryption schemes. While its application to social engineering is not immediately obvious, understanding the potential power of QPE could highlight the importance of developing encryption methods designed to resist quantum attacks, protecting against the potential manipulation of large-scale behavioral data sets in the future.

Hidden Subgroup Algorithm: The hidden subgroup algorithm, a core quantum computing technique, offers potential insights into social engineering tactics. By identifying hidden patterns and relationships within the complex communication and behavior patterns used in social engineering attacks, this algorithm could help uncover vulnerabilities or deception strategies that traditional analysis methods might miss.

Estimating Gauss Sums Algorithm: Estimating Gauss sums algorithms holds potential applications in understanding and defending against social engineering factorization attacks. These attacks manipulate individuals within an organization, exploiting their trust to gain access to sensitive information or systems. By modeling these complex social interactions and patterns of trust with mathematical tools like Gauss sums, security researchers might be able to identify potential weak points and predict where such attacks are most likely to occur.

Fourier Fishing and Fourier Checking Algorithm: Fourier fishing and Fourier checking are quantum algorithms with potential applications in social engineering factorization.

Fourier Fishing: This algorithm discovers hidden patterns or periodicities within a social engineer's behavioral data. These discovered patterns could expose vulnerabilities in their deception tactics or manipulation strategies.

Fourier Checking: This algorithm helps verify whether a specific manipulation tactic will likely succeed against a target. It involves analyzing the correlation between the social engineer's tactics and the target's likely responses, potentially predicting susceptibility.

Important Note: These algorithms remain theoretical. Their practical application in dissecting and potentially countering real-world social engineering tactics would require significant advancements in quantum computing and data collection methods.

CHALLENGES AND CONSIDERATIONS

The quest to implement robust, quantum-resistant cryptography faces significant challenges and areas that demand careful consideration before widespread deployment. These hurdles underscore the ongoing nature of this technological transformation. For one, many quantum algorithms proposed for cybersecurity are still in their theoretical or early developmental stages, requiring further refinement and rigorous testing. Additionally, current quantum hardware limitations mean that truly quantum-powered solutions are likely further out, and we might first see the benefits of quantum-inspired algorithms. Finally, successfully integrating these novel cryptographic solutions into existing security frameworks will not be a simple plug-and-play process. Organizations must carefully plan potential infrastructure changes and reassess how these new algorithms interact with current security measures.

Despite these challenges, the need to proactively prepare for the post-quantum era remains clear. Continued research, collaboration between academia and industry, and a focus on developing and integrating quantum-resistant solutions will safeguard our digital future.

THE PATH AHEAD

The field is rapidly evolving, and breakthroughs in quantum computing and quantum-inspired algorithms could change cybersecurity. Quantum mechanics offers a captivating frontier in the ongoing battle for robust cybersecurity. Its unique properties hold the potential to inspire a new generation of specialized algorithms designed for unparalleled threat detection, risk assessment, and optimized responses. However, success hinges on meticulous benchmarking against traditional methods, ensuring that any gains achieved by quantum-inspired approaches do not come at the cost of accuracy or performance. Furthermore, exploring hybrid strategies, where quantum algorithms are judiciously integrated alongside established secure tools and technologies, may prove the most fruitful path.

The examples of quantum phenomena optimizing processes in nature underscore the field's potential to tackle the complexities of cybersecurity. Further research is vital to harness this potential successfully, translating theoretical concepts into robust, practical tools. If successful, this endeavor has the potential to reshape the future of defense against cyber threats, equipping us with more powerful and efficient ways to detect and combat attacks. The case studies presented in the following sections illustrate the early but promising steps in this groundbreaking direction.

CASE STUDY: CAN EYE MOVEMENTS REVEAL SOCIAL ENGINEERING SUSCEPTIBILITY

Research unveils a novel model based on quantum principles for understanding human visual attention patterns. The current literature suggests that the published research definitively says that eye movements can be used to decode social engineering competency or risk in humans. This is part of ongoing exploration in **multimodal deception detection** that combines eye movements with other physiological and behavioral cues.

The breakdown of the article's key points is:

Social Engineering and Deception: Social engineering relies on manipulating someone's trust or emotions. Deception detection research traditionally focuses on verbal and nonverbal cues like facial expressions or speech patterns.

Eye Movements and Deception: Eye movements have been explored as a potential deception cue, with studies suggesting increased blinking, pupil dilation, or saccadic eye movements (rapid shifts) might be associated with lying. However, these results are inconsistent and can be influenced by factors unrelated to deception, as presented in the text, which presents the concept combination of eye movement, finger gesture and a mobile device tracker designed at the system level to support the idea presented in the article.

This article has explored the intricate relationship between deception and the cues used to detect it. While social engineering tactics often manipulate trust or emotions, traditional deception detection research has focused on verbal and nonverbal signals like facial expressions or speech patterns. More recently, researchers have investigated eye movements as a potential indicator of deception. Some studies suggest increased blinking, pupil dilation, or changes in saccadic eye movements might correlate with lying. However, this link remains inconclusive, as numerous other factors can influence these eye movement patterns. This highlights the complexity of deception detection, mainly when relying on a single cue.

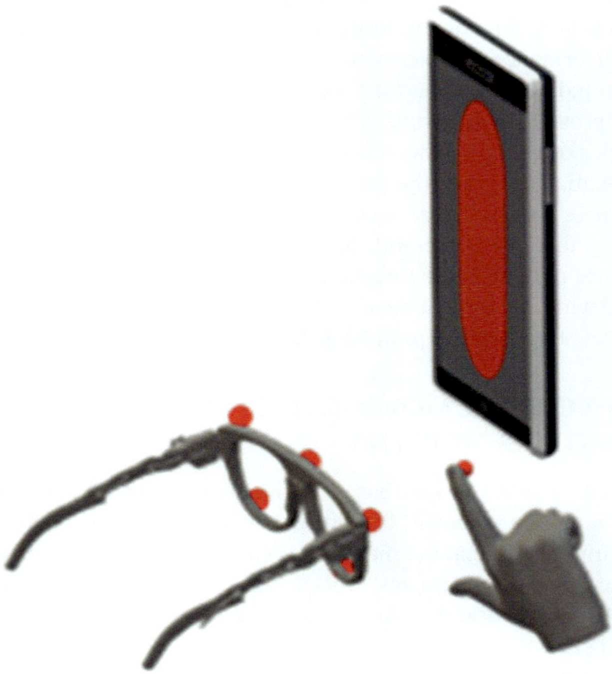

FIGURE 22.1 A test platform for mapping the quantum model of human eye movement.

The challenge lies in identifying patterns that consistently and reliably differentiate between truth-telling and deception across diverse individuals and situations. Developing more comprehensive and context-sensitive deception detection methods is an ongoing area of research, potentially enhancing our ability to identify malicious intent in a world where social engineering poses a constant threat.

The model platform presented in Figure 22.1 provides an overview of foundation for rigorous testing of the algorithm we have discussed. Its design enables the careful assessment of the algorithm's performance under various conditions. This analysis will be crucial for uncovering potential strengths, identifying areas for refinement, and ensuring its real-world applicability. As we proceed to the testing phase, the insights gained from this model platform will inform any necessary adjustments, bringing us closer to an optimized and robust algorithm.

The Quantum Multimodal Model: This specific model is not currently a widely established concept in deception research. "Quantum" might refer to the idea of considering multiple data points simultaneously, but more information is needed to understand the specifics of this model.

The multi-layer model of our algorithm, illustrated in Figure 22.2, serves as a robust framework for comprehensive evaluation. This model allows us to rigorously

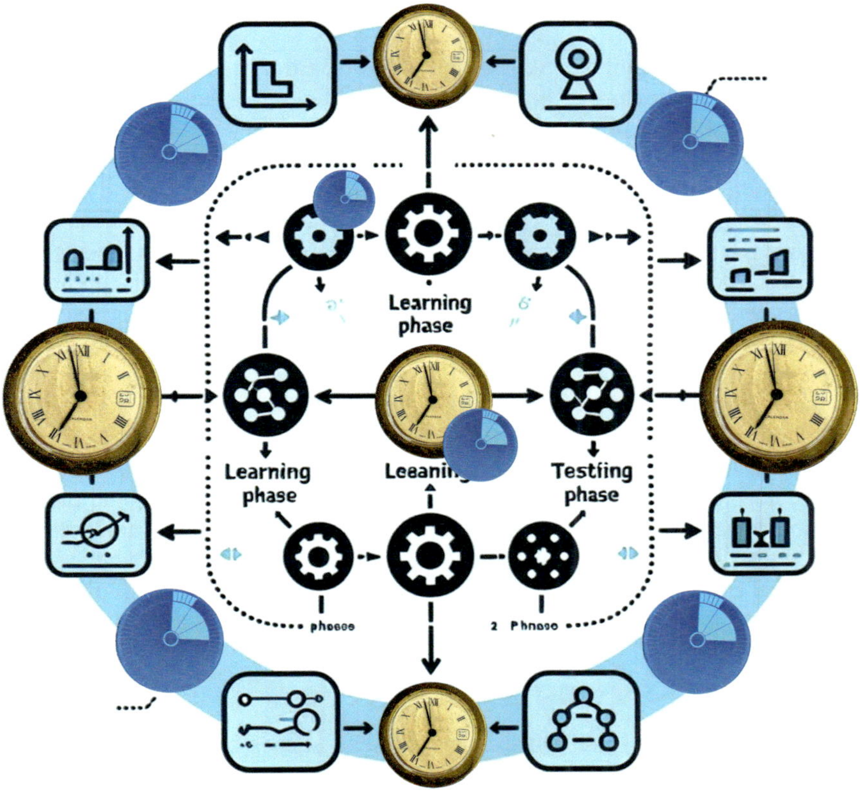

FIGURE 22.2 A symbolic view of a multi-layer artificial neural model.

assess the algorithm's performance beyond theoretical scenarios by simulating various interconnected conditions. This in-depth analysis promises to illuminate the algorithm's core strengths, pinpoint areas for refinement, and ultimately validate its suitability for real-world applications. The knowledge gained from this model platform will be indispensable as we move into the testing phase. It will guide any essential adjustments, ensuring we move toward a solution that's not only theoretically sound but also robust and optimized for the complexities it will encounter in practice.

MULTIMODAL DECEPTION DETECTION

This field shows more promise than relying solely on eye movements. It combines eye tracking with other data streams like:

Facial Expressions: Micro-expressions like fleeting flashes of discomfort or amusement might indicate deception.

Speech Analysis: Vocal pitch changes, hesitations, or inconsistencies could be potential cues.

Physiological Responses: Skin conductance (sweating), heart rate, and respiration changes might be associated with deception but require careful interpretation, as other factors like stress or excitement can influence them.

Multimodal deception detection promises to enhance accuracy beyond relying on eye movements as an indicator of deception. Researchers aim to develop a more comprehensive picture of a person's internal state by analyzing cues from facial expressions, speech patterns, and physiological responses. Micro-expressions too brief for conscious detection, subtle shifts in vocal pitch, or increased skin conductance associated with nervousness offer valuable signals in conjunction with eye-tracking data.

However, it is crucial to note that while these additional data streams hold potential, their interpretation requires caution. Physiological responses, for instance, can be influenced by factors unrelated to deception, such as anxiety or excitement. Therefore, a holistic approach integrating contextual knowledge is paramount for reliable deception detection rather than relying solely on one signal. The future of deception detection likely lies in leveraging the power of multimodal analysis while carefully interpreting the data in context. As this field evolves, it is essential to consider ethical considerations, ensuring such technology is used responsibly and without bias.

CHALLENGES AND CONSIDERATIONS

Cultural and Individual Differences: Deception cues can vary across cultures and individuals. Baselines for "normal" eye movements or physiological responses must be carefully established for reliable detection.

Data Privacy Concerns: Collecting and analyzing eye-tracking data raises privacy concerns that must be addressed.

Deception Countermeasures: People can be trained to control their physiological responses or feign emotions, making detection more difficult.

The article "Innovative Application of Artificial Neural Network in Social Cyber Competency Testing" focuses on using artificial intelligence (AI) to assess individuals' susceptibility to social engineering attacks within social media environments. While the article offers valuable insights into AI-driven risk assessment, it does not directly address the potential of decoding eye movements to detect deception or social engineering vulnerability.

CONTRIBUTIONS TO THE BROADER TOPIC

This article indirectly contributes to the discussion in a few ways:

Highlighting Multi-Faceted Risk: It underscores how social media usage patterns, interactions, and content exposure influence social engineering susceptibility. Eye movement analysis could be integrated to gain an even deeper understanding of these risk factors in conjunction with AI-based assessments.

Importance of Data-Driven Analysis: The article uses data-driven approaches and AI techniques to model complex cybersecurity behaviors. Eye-tracking data could serve as a supplemental input to enhance AI models specifically focused on deception detection and vulnerability evaluation.

Need for Interdisciplinary Focus: True progress in combating social engineering will require input from psychology, computer science, and other disciplines. Analysis of physiological data like eye movements alongside behavioral analytics falls within this collaborative approach.

While the article's immediate focus differs, it reinforces the general theme that analyzing various behavioral and cognitive cues can advance our ability to pinpoint social engineering risks. Future research could investigate integrating eye movement analysis alongside AI-powered competency testing to create a more comprehensive risk assessment framework.

This article highlights the multi-faceted ways in which social media platforms can amplify our vulnerability to social engineering attacks. It underscores that threat actors exploit explicit content and subtle behavioral cues that we leave behind while engaging with the online world. Eye-tracking technology introduces an exciting new dimension to this risk assessment. By analyzing eye movements during simulated phishing attacks or while browsing social feeds, researchers can potentially identify patterns that signify hesitation, confusion, or heightened interest in risky content. These patterns might reveal clues about an individual's inherent biases and critical thinking abilities, allowing for more targeted manipulation.

Understanding the potential of eye tracking in this context emphasizes the ever-evolving nature of social engineering tactics. Defense strategies, therefore, should not focus solely on the explicit content of social media; they must also consider the often-unconscious behavioral metadata we generate through simple actions like reading and scrolling.

The sheer volume and complexity of eye-tracking data underscores the importance of data-driven analysis powered by AI. While raw data offers a glimpse into visual attention patterns, we can genuinely unlock its value by applying advanced AI methods. These techniques are needed to extract meaningful patterns from the vast flow of eye movement information, separating the noise from insight. More importantly, sophisticated AI algorithms would be crucial for correlating eye-tracking patterns with external factors. This could include identifying links between visual attention, social media usage trends, and known risk factors, providing a crucial tool for understanding and predicting vulnerabilities in online deception and radicalization.

The potential of eye movements as indicators of deception or susceptibility highlights human behavior's inherent complexity. Understanding the nuances of eye movement patterns in these contexts demands an approach that reaches beyond any single discipline. The insights of psychology regarding attention, cognitive load, and the emotional states that might influence eye movements are invaluable. Similarly, computer science and AI expertise are crucial to building robust models capable of accurately interpreting these signals. Additionally, a collaboration with neuroscientists could unlock even more profound insights, as they may be able to correlate eye movement data with underlying brain activity patterns.

This endeavor underscores the power of interdisciplinary collaboration in tackling complex problems. By combining the strengths of diverse fields, we gain a more comprehensive understanding of the interplay between eye movements, internal states, and the potential for deception. Ultimately, such collaborations may unlock groundbreaking methods for discerning deception and identifying vulnerabilities, with applications spanning from law enforcement interrogations to safeguarding individuals against online scams.

Beyond Direct Deception Detection: Even if eye movements alone are unreliable for definitive deception detection, their analysis could reveal valuable insights.

The Focus of Attention: Tracking what draws someone's attention to a phishing webpage could inform the design of more believable or persuasive attacks.

Individual Susceptibilities: Eye motion might reveal who is more likely to be misled by specific emotional appeals or overwhelmed by dense text blocks, making them targets for tailored attacks.

The Potential Power of Combined Data: The future of social engineering risk assessment lies in multimodal systems. Eye data could be one input alongside:

Text Analysis: AI-based assessment of a person's online writing style might reveal tendencies toward impulsivity or oversharing.

Behavioral Patterns: Social media activity timing, network composition, and content preferences could build a broader risk profile.

While eye movements alone might offer limited insight for definitive deception detection, a deeper analysis opens a window into valuable data. By tracking an individual's focus of attention during their interaction with a phishing website, we can understand what elements attract and hold their gaze. This data could prove invaluable for those designing increasingly sophisticated attacks, tailoring them to be more believable and persuasive.

Furthermore, eye movements have the potential to reveal individual susceptibilities. Specific emotional appeals, dense content, or complex visual layouts might trigger specific eye movement patterns in those most likely to be misled. This helps identify and potentially protect individuals particularly vulnerable to social engineering attacks.

The true power, however, may lie in combining data. The future of social engineering risk assessment likely belongs to multimodal systems. When analyzed alongside textual analysis of a person's writing style or behavioral patterns gleaned from social media activity, eye-tracking data could paint a remarkably nuanced risk profile. This understanding allows for tailored interventions and educational materials, empowering potential victims to become more resilient against manipulation.

ETHICAL CONSIDERATIONS

Transparency and Consent: Using eye tracking or AI-driven assessments in real-world contexts demands ethical frameworks.

Avoiding Oversimplification: It is crucial to prevent profiling or misinterpreting data, which could stigmatize individuals or be misused.

Integrating eye tracking and AI-driven assessments into real-world environments raises profound ethical considerations that must be addressed with the same rigor as we apply to technological advancements. Transparency and consent are paramount. Individuals must understand how their data is collected, analyzed, and used. They must also have the right to opt-out or limit the scope of data collected.

Furthermore, it is vital to avoid the trap of oversimplification. While these technologies hold immense potential, they must not be seen as infallible human behavior or intent predictors. Algorithms can carry biases, and eye-tracking data can be misinterpreted outside carefully defined contexts. The potential for profiling, misinterpretation, and misuse could lead to discrimination or stigmatization, demanding safeguards at every stage – from data collection to the application of findings.

This complex landscape necessitates open dialogue, collaboration between technical experts and ethicists, and an ongoing review of practices as the field evolves. Upholding these ethical principles is not merely about compliance but ensuring these technologies enhance our world while protecting individual rights and well-being.

THE ART OF AI LIES IN MAKING SENSE OF IMPERFECT DATA

This discussion has explored the potential of eye movements and quantum multimodal models in assessing social engineering susceptibility. While eye movements alone might not be a foolproof indicator, and the concept of a quantum multimodal model for this purpose needs further exploration, these areas highlight a crucial aspect of AI: its ability to extract insights from imperfect data. In the real world, data are rarely pristine or perfectly aligned with the problem we are trying to solve. Eye movements can be influenced by factors beyond deception, and the "quantum" moniker in the multimodal model suggests that it might be a nascent concept.

THE ART OF AI: FINDING MEANING IN THE MESS

This is where AI excels. AI algorithms can sift through vast amounts of noisy data, identifying subtle patterns and correlations that humans might miss. By incorporating eye-tracking data alongside other behavioral and physiological cues, AI could potentially develop a more nuanced understanding of social engineering susceptibility. Further research is needed to determine the effectiveness of eye movement analysis in social engineering risk assessment. However, this exploration underscores a key strength of AI – its ability to make sense of complex and imperfect data sets. As AI continues to evolve, it may play a significant role in creating more comprehensive frameworks to safeguard individuals and organizations from the ever-present threat of social engineering.

BEYOND SOCIAL ENGINEERING

The power of AI to glean insights from imperfect data extends beyond social engineering. AI is used in various cybersecurity applications, including:

Anomaly Detection: Identifying unusual patterns in network traffic that might indicate a cyberattack.
Malware Analysis: Analyzing suspicious software behavior to understand its potential impact.
Vulnerability Research: Extracting patterns from vast code datasets to identify potential security weaknesses.

In each of these areas, AI grapples with noisy, incomplete data. However, its ability to find meaning in a mess allows AI to play a vital role in bolstering our cybersecurity defenses. The insights provided by AI's ability to analyze imperfect data have applications far beyond combating social engineering. In cybersecurity, AI shines as a tool for anomaly detection, meticulously analyzing network traffic for deviations that might signify an attack. Similarly, AI can dissect suspicious software, scrutinizing its behavior to predict its malicious intent. AI even assists in vulnerability research, sifting through enormous code repositories to pinpoint patterns suggestive of potential weaknesses. A common thread emerges throughout these applications: the raw data AI processes are rarely pristine. It is filled with noise, gaps, and inconsistencies – mirroring the messy reality of social engineering data. The true power of AI lies in its ability to find patterns and meaning within this chaos, offering a critical advantage in the ongoing battle for robust cybersecurity. As AI algorithms advance, we can expect even broader and more innovative applications of this ability, making our digital world a less hospitable environment for those who seek to exploit it.

The true power of AI lies not in its demand for pristine, perfectly curated data, but rather in its remarkable ability to sift through the noise and extract meaning from the messy, chaotic, and often incomplete data that permeates our real world. This inherent adaptability, this capacity to learn and evolve in the face of imperfection, is what sets AI apart from traditional computational approaches and fuels its transformative potential across countless domains.

Consider the human mind, the quintessential learning machine. We don't require perfectly labeled examples or meticulously structured datasets to acquire knowledge and make sense of the world around us. We learn from experience, from observation, from trial and error, constantly adapting our understanding as we encounter new information and navigate the complexities of life. AI, in its most advanced forms, is beginning to mirror this human-like adaptability. Deep learning models, inspired by the structure and function of the human brain, can sift through vast quantities of unstructured data, identifying patterns, extracting insights, and making predictions with remarkable accuracy. These abilities to learn from messy, real-world data unlock a wealth of possibilities, from revolutionizing healthcare and accelerating scientific discovery to optimizing business processes and enhancing our daily lives. Imagine an AI system trained to diagnose diseases from medical images. Rather than requiring a perfect dataset of flawlessly labeled images, the AI can learn from the vast and varied collection of real-world medical scans, each with its own quirks, imperfections, and nuances. The AI can identify subtle patterns and anomalies that might elude even the most experienced human eye, leading to earlier and more accurate diagnoses.

Or consider an AI system designed to predict traffic patterns in a bustling city. The AI can learn from the messy, real-time data streams generated by traffic cameras, GPS devices, and social media feeds, accounting for unexpected events, road closures, and even the unpredictable behavior of human drivers. This dynamic learning allows the AI to optimize traffic flow, reduce congestion, and improve the efficiency of transportation networks. The ability of AI to learn from messy, real-world data is not only a testament to its computational power but also a reflection of its potential to address some of the most pressing challenges facing humanity. From climate change and environmental degradation to poverty and disease, the solutions to these complex problems often lie hidden within vast and messy datasets. AI, with its ability to extract insights and make predictions from this data, offers a powerful tool for understanding and addressing these challenges.

In conclusion, the true power of AI lies not in its demand for perfect data but in its ability to embrace the imperfections of the real world. By learning from the messy, chaotic, and often incomplete data that surround us, AI can unlock new frontiers of knowledge, drive innovation, and help us build a more sustainable, equitable, and prosperous future for all.

23 A Brief Overview of the Benefits of Implementing Quantum Applications in Factorizing Cyber Social Engineering Threats

Traditional cybersecurity approaches, often rooted in classical logic, tend to address individual threats in a linear, deterministic manner, much like isolating and fixing individual leaks in a dam. However, the complex and interconnected nature of today's cyber threats necessitates a shift in our thinking, akin to recognizing that the dam itself is a dynamic system influenced by a multitude of interconnected factors. Quantum logic, with its emphasis on superposition, entanglement, and uncertainty, offers a compelling framework for understanding the fluid and dynamic landscape of cyber risks. It allows us to move beyond the rigid, binary framework of classical logic and embrace the inherent uncertainty and interconnectedness of cyber threats.

This raises the intriguing question of whether quantum logic is empirical in the context of cybersecurity. Can its principles be validated through direct observation and experimentation in the digital realm? While the application of quantum logic to cybersecurity is still in its nascent stages, its potential to model complex systems and reveal hidden patterns suggests that it may offer a powerful empirical lens for analyzing and counteracting cyber threats. By embracing the concepts of superposition and entanglement, we can move beyond linear, cause-and-effect models and develop a more nuanced understanding of the interconnectedness of cyber risks. While harnessing the true power of quantum computing for cybersecurity may still be years away, the field of quantum-inspired cybersecurity solutions offers the potential to introduce a much-needed quantum leap in our threat-factorization capabilities. These solutions, inspired by the principles of quantum mechanics, can be implemented on classical computers, providing a bridge between the theoretical potential of quantum computing and the practical realities of today's cybersecurity landscape. Quantum-inspired algorithms, for example, can be used to analyze vast amounts of data, identify patterns and anomalies that would be invisible to traditional approaches, and predict the emergence of new threats. By embracing the principles of uncertainty and probability, we can develop more robust and adaptive cybersecurity systems that can respond effectively to the ever-evolving landscape of cyber threats.

Now, let us delve deeper into the specific issues associated with quantum factorization and explore how this emerging field can revolutionize our approach to cybersecurity.

DOI: 10.1201/9781003500698-23

THE QUANTUM THREAT TO CRYPTOGRAPHY

Applications of Shor's Algorithm

The discovery of a quantum algorithm for factoring large numbers by Peter Shor and Don Coppersmith in 1994 marked a watershed moment in cryptography. This breakthrough demonstrated that some computational issues, considered intractable with classical computers, could be tackled efficiently using the principles of quantum mechanics. The far-reaching implications of Shor's algorithm sent shockwaves through the cryptography community, prompting a global effort to develop new encryption standards that would resist attacks from quantum computers. This realization ushered in a new era in cryptography – the quest for post-quantum solutions. Researchers worldwide are actively exploring various avenues, from lattice-based cryptography to code-based systems, to ensure the continued security of our digital infrastructure in the face of this potential quantum threat landscape. Developing and implementing these new standards is ongoing, requiring collaboration between mathematicians, computer scientists, and policymakers. However, the groundwork laid by Shor and Coppersmith serves as a stark reminder of the transformative power of quantum mechanics and the ongoing need to adapt and evolve our cryptographic tools in the face of emerging technological advancements.

Peter Shor's algorithm, a revolutionary quantum algorithm, poses a potential threat to modern cryptography by potentially rendering widely used encryption methods obsolete (Figure 23.1). Unlike classical algorithms that struggle to factor large numbers, Shor's algorithm leverages the principles of quantum mechanics to efficiently solve this problem. This capability undermines the security of cryptographic systems like RSA, which rely on the difficulty of factoring large numbers

FIGURE 23.1 Peter Shor and Don Coppersmith. (Image courtesy of IT History Society.)

to protect sensitive data. If large-scale quantum computers become a reality, Shor's algorithm could break these encryption schemes, jeopardizing the security of online transactions, communications, and sensitive information. This looming threat has spurred extensive research into post-quantum cryptography, seeking to develop new encryption methods resistant to quantum attacks.

With the potential to efficiently factor large integers and solve discrete logarithm problems, it could render widely used public-key encryption systems like RSA and ECC vulnerable. These systems are fundamental to securing online transactions, communications, and critical data. Developing practical quantum computers capable of executing Shor's algorithm at scale would drastically overhaul our current cryptographic infrastructure.

The Shor algorithm emphasizes a crucial relationship between periodic signals and their Fourier transforms. When a signal exhibits a periodic superposition of states, and these states are separated by a specific frequency, applying a Fourier transform results in a distinct state that encodes the signal's frequency. This connection between the periodicity in the time domain and the resulting frequency domain representation is a fundamental principle exploited by the Shor algorithm. By analyzing the output of the quantum Fourier transform applied to a mathematical function related to the public key in an encryption scheme, the algorithm can efficiently extract the hidden period, revealing the private key.

The power of the Shor algorithm lies in its ability to leverage the properties of quantum mechanics to perform this period-finding task exponentially faster than any classical algorithm. This discovery has profound implications for cryptography, highlighting the potential vulnerabilities of existing public-key encryption schemes in the face of advancements in quantum computing. As we move toward a future where quantum computers become a reality, developing new, post-quantum cryptography methods becomes even more critical for safeguarding sensitive information.

Figure 23.2 illustrates the Quantum Fourier Transform (QFT) algorithm, a crucial subroutine in Shor's algorithm, using a symbolic representation. It depicts a series of quantum gates applied to a set of qubits. The gates, symbolized by various shapes, manipulate the qubits' states, creating a superposition that encodes the Fourier transform of the input. The Hadamard gates, symbolically represented in

FIGURE 23.2 Application of Quantum Fourier Algorithm

figure, create an equal superposition of all possible states. Controlled-phase gates, introduce phase shifts dependent on the state of the control qubit. These gates work together to perform the QFT, transforming the input state from the computational basis to the Fourier basis. The connection to Shor's algorithm lies in the QFT's ability to efficiently find the period of a function. In Shor's algorithm, this function is related to the number to be factored. By applying the QFT to a superposition of function values, the algorithm extracts the period, which is then used in a classical computation to determine the prime factors. The figure highlights the key steps in the QFT, showcasing the sequence of quantum operations that enable this critical component of Shor's algorithm. It symbolically represents the quantum parallelism that allows Shor's algorithm to efficiently factor large numbers, posing a significant threat to modern cryptography.

Shor's algorithm stands as a stark reminder of the potential disruptive power of quantum computing. Its theoretical capability to crack widely used cryptographic systems like RSA and ECC, cornerstones of our digital security, is a significant challenge. In the hands of those with malicious intent, a large-scale quantum computer executing Shor's algorithm could shatter secure online transactions, protected communications, and the confidentiality of vast amounts of data. This potential vulnerability underscores the urgent need to develop and transition to quantum-resistant cryptographic solutions. While the development of such large-scale quantum computers might still be years away, this chapter highlights that the work toward quantum resilience cannot be postponed. The time to invest in research, standardization, and implementing quantum-safe alternatives is now.

Post-Quantum Cryptography Applications (PQC)

Post-quantum cryptography (PQC) is a rapidly developing field dedicated to creating cryptographic algorithms designed to withstand the computational power of future quantum computers. These algorithms are essential because quantum computers pose a significant threat to current encryption standards, which rely on mathematical problems easily solvable by quantum algorithms. To address this, NIST is spearheading a standardization process to identify and implement the most robust PQC solutions, ensuring a smooth transition to quantum-resistant cryptographic systems in the future. For example, the Gentzen method, a cornerstone of proof theory, offers valuable insights when approaching the challenges of post-quantum cryptography. Its emphasis on the systematic analysis of formal systems and the manipulation of proofs aligns with the need to develop and rigorously verify cryptographic algorithms designed to withstand attacks from quantum computers. By applying Gentzen-style approaches, researchers can dissect the logical structure of potential post-quantum algorithms, identifying potential weaknesses, optimizing their security properties, and ensuring their resilience against the computational power that quantum computers promise. This logical framework could prove crucial in the ongoing quest for cryptographic solutions safeguarding our data in the post-quantum era.

Post-quantum cryptography (PQC) represents a vital area of research focused on safeguarding our data in the face of the unparalleled computational power promised by quantum computers. As current encryption standards are vulnerable to quantum attacks, the field of PQC strives to develop new algorithms based on mathematical problems that are believed to be complicated even for quantum computers to solve. NIST's standardization process is crucial in identifying the most robust and promising PQC algorithms, paving the way for a secure transition.

The importance of rigorous verification in PQC cannot be understated. Here is where approaches like the Gentzen method from proof theory become invaluable. Gentzen-style methods allow researchers to probe the foundations of potential post-quantum algorithms by emphasizing the systematic analysis of formal systems. This helps dissect their logical structure, pinpoint weaknesses, refine their security properties, and bolster their resilience against future quantum attacks. The stakes of PQC are high. Our digital lives increasingly rely on secure encryption, and a failure to adapt could leave our most sensitive data vulnerable. PQC, with its focus on finding mathematically robust solutions and the rigorous verification provided by methods like the Gentzen approach, holds the key to safeguarding our information and ensuring a secure transition into the post-quantum era.

Implementation Challenges

The use of classical computers to generate quantum circuits holds tremendous potential, but it is crucial to understand the evolving definition of "true hybrid algorithms." Simply generating a quantum circuit does not guarantee a fully hybrid application. The key distinction lies in the distribution of logic – is the algorithm entirely embodied within the generated quantum circuit, or is it split, requiring both classical and quantum computing steps to function? This evolving interplay between classical and quantum systems highlights the changing nature of technology and underscores the need to continually evaluate and adapt our definitions to ensure we are applying these powerful tools effectively.

While developing large-scale quantum computers capable of breaking today's encryption with Shor's algorithm remains a formidable challenge, the potential for future disruption underscores the urgency of post-quantum cryptography (PQC) research. We may be years away from fully functional quantum devices that pose an immediate threat. However, the long lead times in cryptographic development and the potential for "harvest now, decrypt later" attacks by adversaries compel us to develop and deploy resilient encryption well before the quantum computing breakthrough.

QUANTUM-INSPIRED APPLICATIONS FOR CYBERSECURITY

The presence of classical components for input preparation or output processing within a quantum algorithm does not inherently make it an actual hybrid application. This distinction is vital as technology continues to advance. The critical factor lies in whether the core logic of the algorithm itself is a blend of quantum and classical processing. A variational quantum eigensolver (VQE) exemplifies this hybrid nature, with the classical code running between iterations essential to the algorithm's function. Similarly, Shor's algorithm for factoring depends on both quantum and classical computations working in tandem.

As quantum algorithms evolve, moving beyond superficial assessments of "hybrid" labels is crucial. Understanding the interplay between quantum and classical components is essential for determining the true nature of these algorithms. Focusing on how technology is applied correctly, with an awareness of its potential and limitations, will guide us toward the most effective and impactful uses of these groundbreaking developments.

Quantum-Inspired Optimization

Using quantum phenomena to explore problem spaces more efficiently. Examples include:

Finding Optimal Security Configurations: Optimizing complex security policies or network settings. The quest for optimal security configurations within the digital landscape mirrors the search for balance and efficiency within complex systems. It involves constantly assessing vulnerabilities, implementing tailored policies, and fine-tuning network settings to achieve a state of protection without compromising functionality. Much like adjusting the intricate mechanisms of a watch, success lies in understanding the interconnectedness of components, identifying potential points of friction, and employing a calibrated, iterative approach that seeks to optimize rather than merely implement. This continuous refinement process necessitates vigilance against evolving threats and recognizing that there is no universal, one-size-fits-all solution for security. Each system, much like an individual organism, possesses unique characteristics and demands continuous monitoring. While finding the perfect balance might be elusive, approaching it strategically, with a data-driven mindset and understanding the underlying principles of security design, empowers us to create more robust and adaptable defenses in the ever-evolving digital world.

Threat Modeling: Faster identification of potential weakness chains within a system.

Regarding this technology topic, quantum-inspired optimization (QIO) offers a compelling frontier in solving complex problems. The principles of quantum mechanics inspire these algorithms. QIO leverages concepts like superposition and tunnelling to efficiently explore a vast solution space. This makes it particularly well-suited for notoriously challenging optimization problems such as those found in logistics, finance, and drug discovery. A close look into QIO would explore its theoretical underpinnings, the development of QIO algorithms, and their applications across various industries. It would also examine the current state of QIO, the challenges in scaling these solutions, and the exciting potential they hold for revolutionizing how we tackle some of society's most complex optimization problems.

The intersection of threat modelling and quantum-inspired optimization (QIO) offers intriguing prospects for enhancing cybersecurity and the broader optimization field. Threat modelling's focus on pinpointing potential vulnerabilities aligns well with QIO's ability to explore vast problem spaces, potentially leading to swifter identification of weakness chains within complex systems.

Inspired by the principles of quantum mechanics, QIO leverages concepts like superposition and tunnelling to enhance traditional optimization approaches. This makes QIO well-suited for notoriously complex problems in logistics chains, financial modelling, and drug discovery. A thorough exploration of QIO requires understanding its underpinnings in quantum theory, algorithm development, and how it is applied across diverse industries.

Currently, the field of QIO is still in its relative infancy, with challenges in scaling and implementation. However, its potential remains tantalizing. QIO could revolutionize how we approach cybersecurity optimization problems and, by extension, improve efficiency and resilience across various aspects of our technological landscape.

Quantum-Inspired Machine Learning

Applying quantum principles to enhance machine learning methods for threat detection. Possibilities exist in:

Anomaly Detection: Identifying subtle deviations from normal behavior that traditional models lack. Quantum anomaly detection is a promising frontier in identifying subtle deviations that traditional security models often miss. By harnessing the unique properties of quantum systems, these algorithms can detect anomalies that might appear innocuous to classical analysis. This sensitivity translates into real-world benefits, ranging from enhanced cybersecurity intrusion detection to the early identification of fraud or the diagnosis of subtle medical conditions.

Its potential power underscores the importance of continued research in this domain. As quantum computing hardware matures, we will likely see more robust implementations of quantum anomaly detection, potentially integrated with existing security systems. Identifying unseen anomalies offers a distinct advantage, whether protecting critical infrastructure, safeguarding financial transactions, or revolutionizing disease detection. Quantum anomaly detection is critical to unlocking new levels of proactive security in an increasingly complex and data-driven world.

Feature Engineering: Developing more discriminative features for identifying attack patterns.

A close look into quantum-inspired machine learning (QiML) reveals an exciting field where the principles of quantum mechanics are reimagined within classical computational frameworks. Unlike trustworthy quantum computing, QiML does not require specialized quantum hardware. Instead, it cleverly adapts quantum concepts like superposition, entanglement, and measurement to design new machine-learning algorithms. Researchers are exploring how these algorithms can outperform traditional methods in tasks like pattern recognition, data classification, and optimization.

QiML is still in its early stages, but its vast potential could revolutionize how we process information, leading to breakthroughs in fields like medicine, finance, and materials science.

Quantum Random Number Generators (QRNGs): True randomness is crucial for encryption. QRNGs exploit quantum phenomena to generate higher-quality random numbers compared to traditional software-based methods. A close look into quantum random number generators (QRNGs) reveals an exciting domain where the fundamental principles of quantum mechanics are harnessed to produce genuine randomness. Unlike traditional random number generators, which rely on algorithms and can be potentially predictable, QRNGs tap into the inherent uncertainty of quantum phenomena. This can be the measurement of entangled photons, the timing of radioactive decay, or the light fluctuations. True randomness is an invaluable resource in cybersecurity. It forms the foundation for secure encryption keys, robust simulations, and fair selection processes within digital systems. By leveraging the power of quantum physics, QRNGs promise to elevate our ability to safeguard information in an increasingly interconnected digital landscape.

ONGOING RESEARCH AREAS

Hybrid Quantum-Classical Approaches: Quantum computing is still in its early stages. Many investigations focus on intelligently combining quantum algorithms with classical computation to provide performance advantages. Figure 23.3 indicates a high-level graphical explanation of the hybrid computation.

Figure 23.3 offers a symbolic representation of a hybrid computing architecture, showcasing the collaboration between quantum and classical computers to solve complex problems.

At the center, a quantum processing unit (QPU) is depicted, symbolizing the core of quantum computation. It's surrounded by classical computing elements, such as CPUs, GPUs, and memory, indicating their role in supporting and interacting with the QPU. Arrows connecting the QPU and classical components represent the flow of information and tasks between them. This highlights the collaborative nature of the architecture, where classical computers handle tasks like data preparation, algorithm optimization, and result interpretation, while the QPU performs specialized quantum computations. The figure may also include symbolic representations of specific quantum algorithms or applications running on the QPU, showcasing the types of problems this hybrid architecture can tackle. These could include simulations of quantum systems, optimization problems, or cryptography tasks. Furthermore, the figure might visually represent the communication channels between the quantum and classical components, emphasizing the importance of efficient data transfer and synchronization for seamless operation.

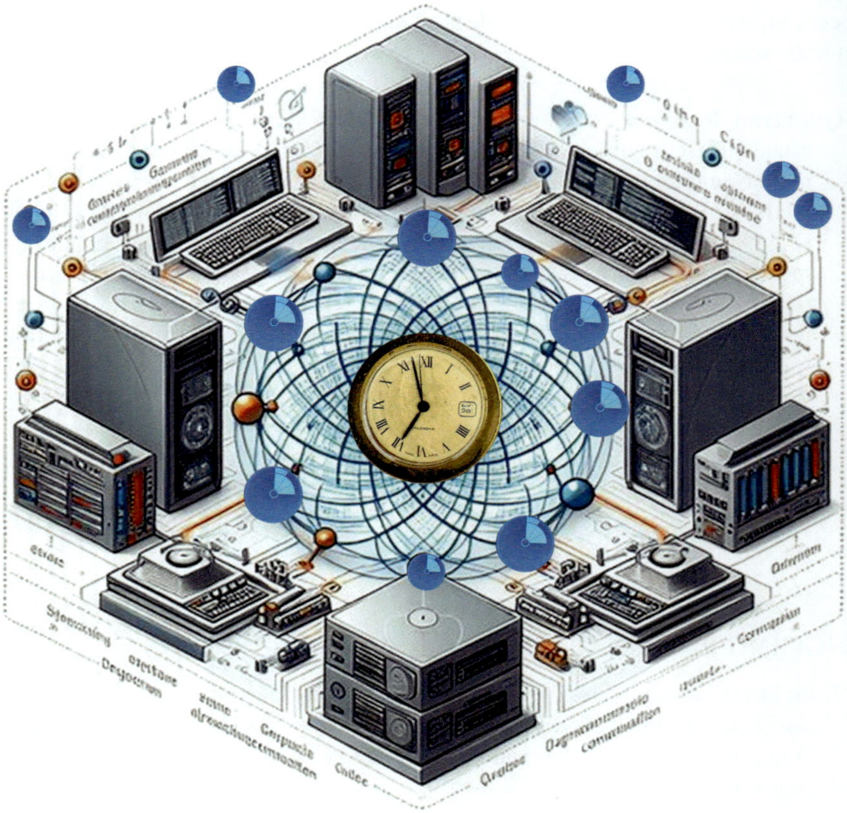

FIGURE 23.3 Symbolic view of hybrid computing architecture is based on quantum and mainstream computers.

Overall, this symbolic view illustrates the key principle of a hybrid computing architecture: leveraging the unique strengths of both quantum and classical computers to efficiently solve problems that are intractable for either alone.

Developing theoretical frameworks to guarantee the security of quantum-resistant and quantum-inspired algorithms. Figure 23.3 presents a high-level graphical diagram of how quantum key channels are secured. The concept of provable security takes on heightened importance as we venture into the domain of quantum-resistant and quantum-inspired algorithms. It demands that we develop rigorous theoretical frameworks to not only design but also confidently assess the robustness of these cryptographic solutions against the potential power of quantum computers. This quest for mathematical guarantees underpins the trust we will need in future security protocols. Figure 23.3 visually represents the principals involved in securing quantum vital channels. However, visualizations alone are insufficient. Provable security involves meticulous analysis, potentially using techniques like reduction proofs, which demonstrate that the difficulty of breaking a cryptographic system is directly linked to the known difficulty of solving a well-established mathematical problem.

While achieving provable security for complex cryptographic constructs is undeniably challenging, it is critical to developing trustworthy quantum-resistant systems. This endeavor will shape the future of cybersecurity and ensure the integrity of our data in the face of evolving threats.

Figure 23.4 highlights QKD's core components and principles within a hybrid broadcasting architecture, emphasizing its conceptual foundation. This figure offers a symbolic view of a quantum key distribution (QKD) system built upon a hybrid broadcasting architecture. It highlights the integration of classical and quantum communication channels to achieve secure key exchange.

Key elements in the figure likely include Transmitter: Symbolized the quantum keys are generated and encoded onto quantum states (e.g., photons). It also includes a classical transmitter for sending control signals and performing key reconciliation. Receiver: Symbolized where the quantum states are measured, and the key is extracted. It also includes a classical receiver for receiving control signals and participating in

FIGURE 23.4 Symbolic view of quantum key distribution is based on the hybrid broadcasting architecture.

key reconciliation. Quantum Channel: Represented by a wavy line, this is the medium through which the quantum states are transmitted (e.g., optical fiber or free space). Classical Channel: Represented by a straight line where the channel is used for classical communication, such as key sifting, error correction, and authentication.

Eavesdropper: Optionally, it represents an eavesdropper attempting to intercept the quantum or classical communication. The hybrid architecture is depicted by the interplay between the quantum and classical channels. Key aspects the figure likely emphasizes:

Quantum Properties: The use of quantum mechanics for secure key generation, such as the principles of superposition and entanglement, might be symbolically represented.

Security Mechanisms: The figure may illustrate security measures like key sifting, privacy amplification, and authentication protocols to ensure the integrity and confidentiality of the key.

Broadcasting Aspect: The architecture's ability to distribute keys to multiple users or across a network could be visually represented.

Overall, the figure provides a visual summary of how QKD leverages both quantum and classical components within a hybrid broadcasting architecture to achieve secure key distribution in a potentially complex network environment.

Moving beyond theoretical concepts, researchers evaluate these algorithms in simulated and practical cybersecurity settings. The exploration of quantum-resistant cryptographic algorithms extends beyond theoretical constructs. Researchers actively engage in real-world evaluations, putting these algorithms through their paces in simulated and practical cybersecurity settings. This rigorous testing is crucial for identifying potential weaknesses, assessing performance characteristics, and ensuring their suitability for real-world deployments. By subjecting these algorithms to the complexities of real-world scenarios, researchers can refine and optimize them, building confidence in their ability to safeguard sensitive information in the quantum era. The ongoing process of real-world evaluation is vital in ensuring a smooth transition to robust, post-quantum cryptographic solutions.

KEY CHALLENGES

As the field of quantum computing advances, several critical challenges must be addressed to fully harness the power of quantum algorithms. These include computational cost, validation, and scalability, each presenting unique obstacles that researchers must overcome to ensure practical and efficient quantum solutions.

Computational Cost: Some quantum-inspired algorithms might be computationally demanding, requiring optimization or novel hardware architectures. The exploration of quantum-inspired algorithms, while promising, reminds us that potential advantages often come with trade-offs. One significant consideration is the computational cost associated with implementing specific algorithms. Their complexity may demand substantial computational resources compared to their classical counterparts. This necessitates a multi-pronged approach. Researchers will need to optimize these algorithms to reduce their resource requirements while preserving their core functionality. Simultaneously, developing specialized hardware to accelerate the unique computations central to quantum-inspired approaches may prove pivotal. Balancing this computational cost with the advantages quantum-inspired algorithms offer will play a crucial role in determining their adoption and impact in real-world applications.

Validation: A rigorous evaluation is required to demonstrate the effectiveness of these algorithms compared to existing methods in real-world cyber defense scenarios. The potential of quantum-resistant cryptography offers a beacon of hope in a landscape increasingly threatened by advancements in quantum computing. However, the road to widespread adoption necessitates rigorous validation. These novel algorithms must be tested in robust cyber defense scenarios. Only through such practical evaluation can we truly gauge their effectiveness compared to existing methods. This includes assessing their ability to withstand attacks and evaluating their performance in terms of efficiency, essential size requirements, and compatibility with existing infrastructure. A comprehensive validation process is paramount to ensuring a smooth transition to a post-quantum cryptographic landscape, safeguarding our data and digital security in the years to come.

Scalability: Large-scale deployment of quantum-enabled cybersecurity solutions might demand hardware and infrastructural advancements. The potential scalability of quantum-enabled cybersecurity raises a crucial consideration. Implementing these solutions on a large scale might necessitate significant advancements in the underlying hardware and infrastructure. This includes developing more robust and accessible quantum computing systems, specialized infrastructure for quantum communication, and potential adaptations to existing networks for compatibility with quantum-enabled security protocols. Addressing these infrastructural needs is paramount to moving from promising theoretical concepts to widespread, practical deployment of quantum-resistant cybersecurity solutions. Successfully navigating this challenge will play a pivotal role in determining how quickly and seamlessly we can transition to a cyber landscape fortified by the power of quantum mechanics.

Resources for Further Investigation

NIST Post-Quantum Cryptography Project

The NIST Post-Quantum Cryptography Project represents a monumental effort to safeguard the future of digital security. Recognizing the potential threat posed by quantum computing to our existing cryptographic infrastructure, NIST has spearheaded a rigorous, multi-year process to identify and standardize new quantum-resistant algorithms. The thoroughness of their approach, including multiple rounds of evaluation and consideration of diverse cryptographic families, underscores the importance of getting this right. This global collaboration has pushed the boundaries of cryptographic innovation. However, the project's conclusion is not the end of the road. Translating these theoretical advancements into practical, widely adopted security protocols will require continued research, optimization, and collaboration across industries. The challenge is ensuring that these new standards are seamlessly integrated into the complex landscape of digital communications and data storage, ensuring that our most sensitive information remains protected. The NIST project serves as a reminder of the ongoing battle for secure communication in an ever-evolving technological world. It highlights the need for proactive security measures and the importance of staying ahead of potential threats in the complex, dynamic domain of cryptography.

For more reading, you can check: https://csrc.nist.gov/projects/post-quantum-cryptography

The field is rapidly evolving. Staying current on the latest research through conferences, publications, and reputable online resources is crucial.

Figure 23.5 offers a symbolic glimpse into the future of Post-Quantum Cryptography (PQC), where evolving hybrid computing structures play a crucial role.

FIGURE 23.5 A symbolic image of Post Quantum Cryptography project based on evolving hybrid computing structures.

At the center, a shield represents PQC, symbolizing the protection of sensitive data. This shield is intricately interwoven with two distinct yet interconnected elements:

Quantum Computing: Represented by a stylized atom, it signifies the harnessing of quantum phenomena like superposition and entanglement to develop new cryptographic algorithms resistant to quantum attacks. Classical Computing: Symbolized by a microchip, it represents the continued reliance on classical computing for tasks it excels at, such as data management, user interfaces, and system integration. The intertwining of these elements highlights the collaborative nature of hybrid computing architectures in PQC. Quantum computers will tackle computationally challenging tasks like generating and verifying digital signatures or establishing secure keys, while classical computers will manage the overall system and user interactions.

Furthermore, the dynamic lines connecting these elements to the shield emphasize the ongoing evolution and adaptation of PQC in response to emerging threats and technological advancements. This symbolizes the continuous research and development needed to ensure robust security in a post-quantum world.

The overall image conveys a sense of optimism and preparedness, showcasing how PQC, powered by hybrid computing structures, will safeguard our digital future.

THE QUANTUM THREAT TO CRYPTOGRAPHY (EXPANDED AND CONTINUED)

Beyond Shor's Algorithm: While Shor's is the most well-known, other quantum algorithms like Grover's algorithm threaten symmetric ciphers and hash functions, necessitating the development of a comprehensive suite of quantum-resistant solutions. While Shor's algorithm garners significant attention due to its threat against widely used encryption schemes like RSA and ECC, it is crucial to remember that it is not the sole quantum threat to cybersecurity. For instance, Grover's algorithm demonstrates quantum computing's potential to accelerate attacks on symmetric ciphers and hash functions. This highlights the urgent need beyond simply addressing the threat of Shor's algorithm. The development of a comprehensive suite of quantum-resistant solutions is crucial. These must secure public-key cryptography and ensure the resilience of symmetric ciphers, hash functions, and other essential cryptographic building blocks in the face of potential quantum attacks.

The Timeline Debate: Estimates on when powerful enough quantum computers to break current encryption will exist are highly variable. Preparedness is essential regardless of exact timeframes.

The debate surrounding the timeline of when quantum computers powerful enough to break current encryption standards will emerge adds a sense of urgency to the discussion. While estimates vary widely, one thing remains clear: preparedness is crucial regardless of the precise arrival of that critical point. Waiting to address cryptographic vulnerabilities until the technology is fully operational would be a dangerous gamble, given the time needed to research, develop, and implement new defensive measures on a wide scale. The prudent approach is to acknowledge the inevitability of quantum-powered code-breaking capabilities. This means acting now to transition systems toward quantum-resistant cryptography, minimizing potential disruption and protecting sensitive data during this vulnerable period. Proactive action will ensure a smoother changeover when that day arrives, ensuring the continuity and security of our digital infrastructure in an evolving technological landscape.

PQC Focus Areas: Specific research focuses on lattice-based, code-based, multivariate, and hash-based cryptography as potential quantum-resistant replacements. The search for quantum-resistant cryptographic solutions centers on a few promising directions. Lattice-based cryptography, with its reliance on complex mathematical structures, offers the potential of robust security against quantum attacks. Code-based cryptography similarly leverages mathematical complexity, utilizing error-correcting codes to make decoding exceptionally difficult, even for quantum computers. Multivariate cryptography introduces an additional layer of complexity by using systems of nonlinear equations over multiple variables. Finally, hash-based cryptography focuses on one-way functions that are difficult to reverse, a concept fundamentally less vulnerable to the strengths of quantum computing.

Researchers are intensely exploring each of these areas. The goal is not only to develop algorithms resistant to quantum attacks but to create practical and efficient solutions that can be standardized and seamlessly integrated into existing security infrastructures. This is a complex undertaking filled with promise and urgency as we strive to protect our digital world in the evolving era of quantum computing.

NIST Standardization: NIST's multi-year standardization process involves rigorous testing and evaluation of candidate PQC algorithms to select the most reliable for widespread integration. The rigorous NIST standardization process is crucial in the ongoing quest for robust post-quantum cryptography (PQC) solutions. This multi-year effort involves meticulously testing and evaluating various candidate algorithms. Only the most reliable and secure PQC schemes will rise to the top through this process, earning the trust necessary for widespread integration into critical infrastructure. The selection of these robust algorithms will be a pivotal moment, ushering in a new era of cryptographic security in the face of the ever-evolving computational landscape. It is a testament to the vital role NIST plays in ensuring the continued safety of our data in a world increasingly reliant on digital interactions.

Quantum-Inspired Algorithms for Cybersecurity (Expanded and Continued)

Optimization Examples

Designing firewall rule sets that optimally balance security needs with network performance, identifying critical vulnerabilities within complex systems that require prioritization for patching. The quest for standardization, as exemplified by NIST guidelines, plays a crucial role in optimizing cybersecurity practices. Consider the challenge of designing firewall rule sets. A balance between robust security and preserving network performance must be struck – an optimization problem where standardized frameworks provide guidance. Additionally, within complex systems, vulnerabilities inevitably exist. NIST standards help identify the most critical ones, ensuring that patching efforts are prioritized effectively for maximum risk reduction. These examples underscore how standardization is about compliance and making cybersecurity more efficient and impactful. By utilizing established best practices and prioritizing actions based on standardized risk assessments, organizations can move beyond a reactive approach to security, building a proactive and resilient cybersecurity posture.

Quantum-Inspired Machine Learning Techniques

Quantum Annealing for Feature Selection: Finding the most informative subset of data to train anomaly detection models. Quantum neural networks: Potential for greater representational power and faster learning in threat detection scenarios. Quantum-inspired machine learning techniques offer a tantalizing glimpse into the future of anomaly detection. Drawing inspiration from quantum principles, researchers explore novel approaches to tackle the complexity of identifying unusual or malicious patterns within large datasets. Quantum annealing could revolutionize feature selection, helping machine learning models pinpoint the most critical subset of data to build more accurate threat detection systems. The possibility of quantum neural networks might enhance algorithms' ability to learn complex patterns, boosting their effectiveness in spotting subtle anomalies and uncovering hidden threats faster.

While still in a nascent stage, quantum-inspired machine learning holds exciting potential to redefine the boundaries of cybersecurity. Its unique approach, rooted in the principles of quantum mechanics, could enable the development of more precise, efficient, and adaptive threat detection models, empowering us to secure our digital world better. As research in this field progresses, we may soon witness these techniques transition from theoretical promise to practical tools bolstering our cyber defense arsenal.

QRNG Applications: Improving the quality of cryptographic keys, secure communication channels, and generating realistic test data for security systems. The applications of QRNGs extend far beyond the mere generation of random numbers. They are becoming crucial components in bolstering the integrity of cryptographic keys. This translates to enhanced security for our most sensitive online activities, from secure communication channels for financial transactions to protecting classified data. Furthermore, QRNGs can generate highly realistic test data for security systems by providing a source of true randomness. This plays a vital role in ensuring the robustness of our defenses against various cyberattacks. As a result, QRNGs are emerging as an essential element in the ongoing quest to fortify our digital infrastructure and safeguard the confidentiality of our data in an increasingly complex cyber landscape.

Example applications are being manufactured in QRNG chip packages, as shown in Figure 23.6.

The figure showcases a compact, integrated quantum random number generator (QRNG) chip package, highlighting the transition of quantum technologies from theoretical concepts to practical, real-world applications. This miniaturization is crucial for wider adoption of quantum-enhanced security. By encapsulating the QRNG's complex components within a single chip, it becomes readily embeddable in various devices, from smartphones and laptops to critical infrastructure systems. This signifies a step toward making quantum-generated random numbers, which are essential

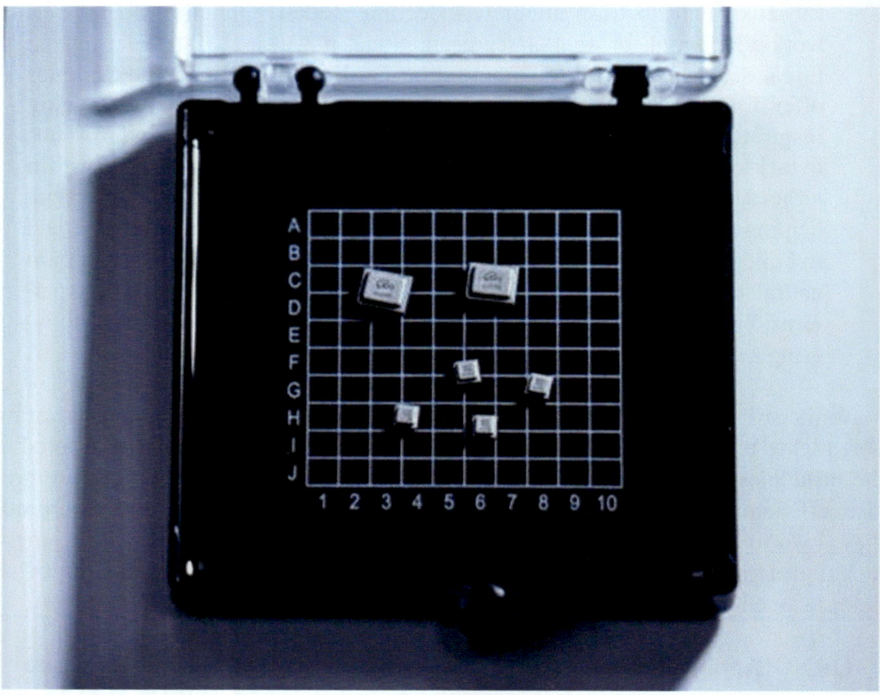

FIGURE 23.6 Integrated QRNG chip package, demonstrating the practical implementation of quantum technologies. (Image courtesy of ID Quantique.)

for strong encryption and cybersecurity, more accessible and prevalent in everyday technology. The image, courtesy of ID Quantique, a leading provider of quantum security solutions, visually reinforces the tangible progress being made in bringing quantum capabilities to the mainstream.

Ongoing Research Areas (Expanded)

Hybrid Algorithm Development: Exploration of how small-scale quantum computers and quantum simulators could augment classical algorithms in areas such as optimal route finding within networks, making IDS systems more adaptable. The exploration of hybrid algorithms, fusing the power of quantum and classical computing paradigms, offers a compelling path for optimizing solutions in the near term, even while large-scale quantum computers remain in development. Small-scale quantum computers and simulators can enhance classical algorithms like network route optimization and intrusion detection systems. Imagine a future where logistics networks can seamlessly find optimal routes in real time, adapting to unexpected disruptions with quantum-enhanced efficiency. Similarly, IDS systems can become more adaptive and proactive by integrating quantum techniques, offering an extra layer of security against increasingly sophisticated cyberattacks. Hybrid algorithms pave the way for the continued development of quantum technology in a practical sense. By leveraging the strengths of both approaches and tackling specific, well-defined problems, these hybrid systems showcase the true potential of quantum advancements even as the technology scales. This field is a testament to the immediate benefits of quantum applications and the boundless possibilities ahead as the field matures.

Security Proofs: Designing quantum-inspired algorithms goes hand-in-hand with formal verification methods to mathematically guarantee their security and robustness. The development of quantum-inspired algorithms does not occur in isolation. To ensure their effectiveness and protect against potential vulnerabilities, they must be accompanied by robust verification methods. Security proofs provide a rigorous mathematical framework to analyze an algorithm's security properties and guarantee its resilience against attacks. By integrating security proofs from the earliest design stages, we can identify weaknesses, proactively address them, and build confidence in the algorithms' ability to safeguard information. Ultimately, this synergy between quantum-inspired innovation and formal verification is crucial for creating trustworthy and secure solutions to address the challenges of the coming technological era.

Benchmarking and Standards: As quantum-inspired algorithms mature, developing objective metrics to benchmark their efficiency and effectiveness against traditional methods is critical to broader adoption. The maturation of quantum-inspired algorithms hinges on the development of comprehensive benchmarking standards. Determining the clear advantages of these algorithms over their traditional counterparts remains a challenge.

We must establish objective metrics that evaluate efficiency and effectiveness to foster informed decision-making and widespread adoption. These metrics will enable us to compare quantum-inspired algorithms against classical solutions and against one another. Such benchmarking will provide a clearer picture of the specific scenarios where these algorithms excel, guiding their implementation in real-world applications. The development of robust standards is thus paramount for the transition from theoretical promise to practical applications of quantum-inspired algorithms.

Key Challenges (Expanded)

Computational Complexity: A thorough analysis of theoretical computational costs for translating quantum-inspired ideas into practical algorithms is crucial for assessing real-world feasibility. The quest to translate the promise of quantum-inspired algorithms into practical solutions hinges on a critical step: computational complexity analysis. This meticulous process involves theoretically dissecting the computational costs of implementing these algorithms. We can only determine the feasibility of translating these quantum-inspired ideas into real-world applications through such rigorous assessment. Understanding the computational demands allows researchers to identify the sweet spots where quantum algorithms offer a significant advantage over classical approaches, guiding the focus toward areas where quantum computing can truly revolutionize problem-solving. As we look into this new and exciting domain, computational complexity analysis will remain an essential tool, ensuring that the fantastical ideas born from the world of quantum mechanics translate into tangible advancements for our digital future.

Experimental Validation: Moving beyond simulations, testing quantum-inspired algorithms with real-world cybersecurity datasets and in operational environments becomes vital. The power of quantum-inspired algorithms lies ultimately in their ability to solve real-world cybersecurity problems, which do not simply exist as theoretical constructs. Moving beyond simulations and into the domain of experimental validation is thus a crucial step in their evolution. Testing these algorithms against authentic cybersecurity datasets and within operational environments will reveal their true strengths, limitations, and potential for practical integration within existing cybersecurity defenses. This experimental phase will likely expose unforeseen implementation challenges and highlight areas where further refinement of these quantum-inspired approaches may be necessary. By embracing the challenges of experimental validation, we accelerate the development of robust and effective cybersecurity tools ready for deployment against the evolving threats of the digital age.

Addressing Hype vs. Reality: Separating the true potential of quantum-inspired approaches from overblown marketing requires rigorous investigation and clear communication. The allure of quantum-inspired solutions often blurs the lines between established scientific principles and exaggerated claims. To fully harness the potential of this field, it is crucial to maintain a critical perspective. Rigorous investigation is essential to sift through the hype, allowing us to identify areas where quantum-inspired approaches offer genuine advancements while simultaneously recognizing the limitations of current applications. Clear and transparent communication across industries will foster realistic expectations and temper the temptation to overpromise solutions that remain in their early stages of development. By striking this balance between enthusiasm and critical evaluation, we can ensure the responsible growth and deployment of quantum-inspired technologies, ultimately delivering actual benefits, not just buzzwords.

Specific Research Initiatives

European Quantum Flagship Program: This program includes projects specifically focused on cybersecurity applications of quantum technologies. The European Quantum Flagship Program, with its ambitious scope and substantial funding, serves as a driving force in advancing the global quantum technology landscape. It fosters collaboration between research institutions, industry, and policymakers, solidifying Europe's leadership in this pivotal field. Importantly, the program's inclusion of projects specifically dedicated to cybersecurity applications of quantum technologies underscores the recognition of both the challenges and incredible potential associated with the coming post-quantum era. As quantum computers mature, the need for radically rethinking encryption and security protocols will only intensify. By investing heavily in developing quantum-resistant solutions, the European Quantum Flagship Program is proactively securing the future of digital communications and data protection, ensuring Europe remains at the forefront of technological innovation and cybersecurity resilience (https://qt.eu/).

Academic Labs: Universities such as MIT, Waterloo, and others have dedicated research groups exploring quantum algorithms for cybersecurity solutions. The exploration of quantum algorithms for transformative cybersecurity solutions extends far beyond the corporate world. Academic institutions like MIT, Waterloo, and numerous others are crucial in driving this research frontier. These universities house dedicated research groups delving into the theoretical underpinnings, algorithm development, and the analysis of potential applications of quantum concepts to cybersecurity challenges. This academic research is vital, as it lays the groundwork for future breakthroughs and nurtures the next generation of cybersecurity experts equipped with a deep understanding of quantum threats and quantum-based defenses. The ongoing collaborations between academia and industry promise to accelerate the translation of these theoretical advancements into practical, real-world solutions.

Examples of Quantum Annealing for Cybersecurity

Quantum annealing (QA) uses quantum mechanics to find optimal solutions to complex optimization problems. While full-fledged quantum computers are still developing, specialized hardware called quantum annealers can be used for specific problems. Here are a few examples of how QA might be applied to cybersecurity:

Network Optimization: Optimizing network routing protocols to minimize traffic congestion while maximizing security could involve finding the best paths for secure communication while considering factors like bandwidth limitations and potential vulnerabilities in different routes.

Security Configuration Optimization: Finding the optimal configuration for firewalls, intrusion detection systems (IDS), and access control lists (ACLs) across complex networks involves balancing security with operational efficiency. QA could find the best combination of settings to achieve optimal protection without hindering legitimate network traffic.

Risk Analysis and Prioritization: QA could analyze vast amounts of security data (vulnerability reports, threat intelligence feeds) and prioritize risks based on their potential impact and likelihood. This would enable security teams to focus on the most critical threats first.

Challenges in Translating Theoretical Quantum-Inspired AI into Functional Tools

The field of quantum-inspired AI (QI-AI) is exciting but faces hurdles in translating theory into practical applications for cybersecurity:

Hardware Limitations: Unlike theoretical models, existing quantum annealers are limited in size and capabilities. Scaling these systems to handle large datasets and complex problems commonly encountered in cybersecurity is an ongoing challenge.

Algorithmic Efficiency: While inspired by quantum phenomena, QI-AI algorithms may require significant classical computing resources for practical implementation, negating some potential efficiency gains.

Integration with Existing Systems: Security operations centers (SOCs) rely on established tools and workflows. Seamless integration of QI-AI solutions with existing infrastructure requires careful design and consideration of user interfaces and data compatibility.

Explainability and Trust: Understanding how QI-AI algorithms arrive at decisions, especially with complex models, is crucial for building trust with security analysts. Explainable AI techniques are needed for humans to interpret results and make informed decisions. Figure 23.7 presents a symbolic view of the complex challenges, potentially slowing their wider commercial adoption.

This figure illustrates the multifaceted challenges hindering the commercialization of quantum platforms. It depicts a complex display of factors, including:

- **Hardware Limitations:** Symbolized by intricate circuitry, this highlights the difficulties in building and scaling quantum computers with sufficient qubits and stability.

- **Software Challenges:** Represented by abstract code, this points to the need for specialized algorithms and software infrastructure to effectively utilize quantum computers.
- **Error Correction:** Illustrated by a tangled web, this emphasizes the susceptibility of quantum systems to errors and the ongoing struggle to develop robust error correction techniques.
- **Cost and Accessibility:** Depicted by a steep incline, this signifies the high cost of development and the limited accessibility of quantum computing resources.
- **Integration Complexity:** Visualized as a puzzle with missing pieces, this represents the challenges in integrating quantum computers with existing classical infrastructure.

Together, these factors create a significant barrier to widespread commercialization. Overcoming these hurdles requires collaborative efforts from researchers,

FIGURE 23.7 Quantum platforms complexity is a challenge for commercialization.

engineers, and industry leaders to drive innovation, reduce costs, and develop practical applications that showcase the transformative potential of quantum computing.

It will be vital in unlocking the full potential of QI-AI for cybersecurity. Research in this area is ongoing, with promising advancements in:

Hybrid Quantum–Classical Approaches: Combining the strengths of classical and quantum computing for improved efficiency and scalability.

Domain-Specific QI-AI Algorithms: Tailoring algorithms to specific cybersecurity problems for better optimization and interpretability.

Development of Quantum Software Tools: Creating high-level programming languages and frameworks to simplify developing and utilizing QI-AI solutions in cybersecurity. Let us take a closer look at the following case study:

Case Study: Can the Walking Algorithm Reveal Social Engineering Susceptibility

There is a scarcity of published research directly investigating a "quantum multimodal deception model" using human walking movements to assess social engineering competency or risk. Here is a breakdown of the key points:

Gait Analysis and Deception: Research on gait analysis (studying walking patterns) has explored its potential for identifying deception. Changes in stride length, walking speed, or posture might be associated with lying, but these results are inconclusive and influenced by factors like fatigue or emotional state. Figure 23.8 presents a sensor arrangement to capture and record the walking pattern of test participants.

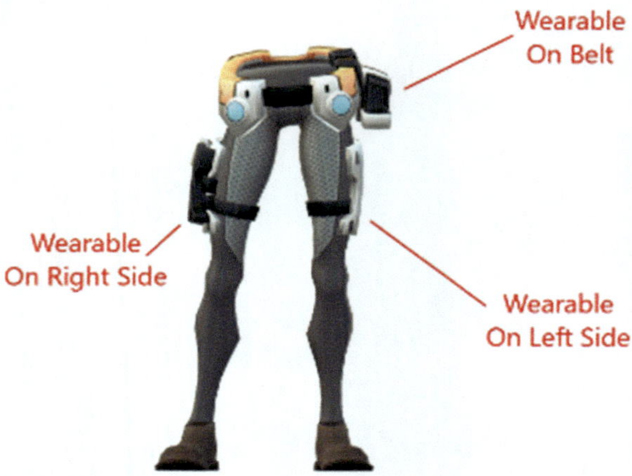

FIGURE 23.8 A test platform for mapping the quantum model of human walking pattern and movement.

This figure depicts a test platform designed to map the quantum model of human walking patterns and movement. The platform consists of several key components:

- **Motion Capture System:** This system, likely to use markers and cameras, tracks the precise movements of a subject's limbs and joints during walking. This provides real-world data on human locomotion.
- **Quantum Processing Unit:** This unit analyzes the motion capture data using quantum algorithms specifically designed to model human movement. These algorithms may leverage principles like superposition and entanglement to capture the subtle nuances and variations in individual walking styles.
- **Classical Computer Interface:** This interface acts as a bridge between the quantum processor and the user, allowing for data input, visualization of results, and control of the experiment.
- **Display:** A display showcases the output of the quantum model, potentially showing a visual representation of the walking pattern, key parameters, or comparisons to classical models.

This platform enables researchers to investigate the application of quantum mechanics in understanding human biomechanics. By mapping walking patterns onto a quantum model, the platform could reveal new insights into human locomotion, potentially leading to advancements in areas like prosthetics, rehabilitation, and robotics.

The model platform presented in Figure 23.8 provides a valuable foundation for rigorous testing of the algorithm we have discussed. Its design enables careful assessment of the algorithm's performance under various conditions.

Multimodal Deception Detection: This field holds more promise. It combines gait analysis with other data streams like facial expressions, speech patterns, and physiological responses to create a more comprehensive deception detection system.

Quantum Mechanics and Deception Detection: The concept of a "quantum multimodal deception model" is not a widely established term in deception research. "Quantum" might refer to considering multiple data points simultaneously, but more information is needed to understand the specifics of this model and its connection to gait analysis. Figure 23.9 presents the high-level model of the deception detection algorithm designed and tested regarding the sleepwalking deception detection algorithm.

This figure presents a symbolic view of a biometric data gathering arrangement for a multi-layer artificial neural network, a powerful tool inspired by the human brain. It depicts a network of interconnected nodes organized into hidden distinct layers behind the biometric data system.

- **Input Layer:** The first layer represents the input data, where each node symbolizes a specific feature or variable. These nodes receive and process the initial information.

- **Hidden Layers:** Between the input and output layers lie one or more hidden layers. Each node in these layers performs a weighted sum of its inputs from the previous layer and applies an activation function to introduce nonlinearity. This allows the network to learn complex patterns and relationships in the data. The connections between nodes have associated weights that are adjusted during the learning process.
- **Output Layer:** The final layer produces the network's output, with each node representing a possible outcome or prediction. The number of output nodes depends on the specific task, such as classification or regression.

The arrows connecting the nodes symbolize the flow of information through the network. The network learns by adjusting the weights of these connections to minimize the difference between its predicted output and the actual target values. This iterative process, often called backpropagation, allows the network to gradually improve its accuracy and generalize to new, unseen data.

FIGURE 23.9 A symbolic view of a multi-layer artificial neural model.

The figure highlights the layered structure, interconnectedness, and adaptability of artificial neural networks, showcasing their ability to learn and make predictions from complex data.

Challenges and Considerations

Inconsistency: Gait can vary significantly based on age, health conditions, footwear, and emotional state. Isolating deception-specific cues from this variability remains a challenge.

Data Privacy: Collecting and analyzing gait data, especially in public spaces, raises privacy concerns that must be addressed.

Countermeasures: People can consciously alter their gait patterns, making deception detection even more complex.

The Road Ahead

Using gait analysis to assess social engineering risk is undeniably fascinating, yet it remains an emerging field demanding further investigation. Research must focus on several promising directions to unleash its full potential. First, incorporating gait analysis into a multimodal approach that examines voice patterns, eye movements, and other potential behavioral identifiers could significantly enhance the accuracy and reliability of deception detection. Additionally, advanced machine learning algorithms trained on vast datasets could learn to pick up on subtle gait deviations linked to deception, adding a robust layer to current assessment tools.

Crucially, the ethical considerations surrounding gait analysis cannot be dismissed. Transparency about the use of such technology, coupled with informed user consent, is vital. Ethical frameworks must be developed with technological capabilities to ensure these innovations are applied responsibly and without infringement on individual privacy.

The article focuses on a compelling concept – an artificial neural network that learns and adapts during "sleep" phases. However, its core focus is assessing social media competency and susceptibility to social engineering attacks. The article does not explore gait analysis and the quantum-inspired multimodal analysis of human body movements.

Indirect Contributions

Despite the thematic disconnect, the article does touch upon points relevant to the broader cybersecurity landscape:

The Complexity of Social Engineering: Using AI to assess vulnerability to social engineering underscores the multifaceted nature of these threats. While gait analysis might be one way to detect deception, social media interactions offer another rich vein of data for analysis.

Multi-Domain Data: The article's approach reinforces that practical cybersecurity analysis often necessitates integrating data from different fields – here,

AI techniques and social media behavior. Similarly, gait analysis and physiological or behavioral cues are critical for robust multimodal deception models.

Dynamic Learning: The "sleepwalking" AI concept mirrors the need for adaptive security approaches. Gait analysis for deception detection would need to be robust to an individual's natural variations and deliberate attempts to obscure their walk.

While the article's focus diverges from our main topic, it highlights the complexity of social engineering threats and the need for creative and multi-disciplinary solutions. Perhaps future research could explore if subtle behavioral changes during social engineering attempts, manifested in physical movement, could augment broader deception detection systems.

The "sleepwalking" neural network concept offers some exciting parallels and inspirations for other aspects of cybersecurity. The network learns and reconfigures during "offline" phases, increasing its efficiency for future tasks. Security systems could follow a similar approach. Periodic, offline analysis of evolving threat data, vulnerability trends, and the latest attack techniques could improve threat model adaptation without disrupting real-time protection.

Resilience and Incident Response

The ability of an AI system to solidify learned information during sleep-like phases offers a fascinating analogy for cybersecurity. Like AI benefits from quiet periods to consolidate and strengthen its knowledge base, could cybersecurity systems benefit from incorporating similar "rest" intervals? It might prove invaluable to implement a mechanism for security systems to analyze their past responses, re-evaluate defense strategies, and consolidate their "experience" during low-activity periods. This self-reflection period could enhance resilience against future attacks by refining threat detection patterns, optimizing responses, and identifying potential vulnerabilities. The concept draws inspiration from the biological model of how sleep strengthens learning, prompting the question of whether we could design cybersecurity defenses that become more robust over time through strategic periods of learning consolidation.

Zero-Day Vulnerability Defense

Sleepwalking AI: Even with limited exposure to a new task, the network leverages previous knowledge to generalize and respond.

Cybersecurity Analogy: AI-powered systems could use "sleep" phases to reanalyze historical vulnerabilities and attack patterns. This could enhance their ability to spot novel attack vectors that share underlying principles with previously encountered threats.

The potential of defensive deception within cybersecurity grows ever more intriguing as artificial intelligence technology evolves. The unpredictable, adaptive nature of "sleepwalking" AI introduces a diverse dynamic. Could cybersecurity systems intentionally mimic periods of simulated "rest" or subtle behavioral shifts to mislead attackers? This tactic might sow confusion during an adversary's reconnaissance phase, complicating their understanding of the system and reducing the reliability of any planned attack. This concept draws inspiration from the natural world, where camouflage and deceptive signaling are critical survival strategies. By incorporating elements of unpredictability, even if partially simulated, cybersecurity defenses could become more dynamic and less predictable. This shift can potentially disrupt an attacker's well-established playbook, forcing them to expend more resources and increasing the chance of their detection. Further exploration into the intersection of defensive deception and evolving AI capabilities represents a promising avenue for future research and innovation in cybersecurity strategy. Introducing "sleep" phases into AI-driven security systems holds promise but raises critical concerns that researchers must address. Even offline, these systems would likely need to perform computations, potentially impacting real-time responsiveness. Ensuring this offline processing does not compromise the ability to react quickly to evolving threats is paramount.

Furthermore, trust and explainability are crucial. Users must understand how these systems learn and change during their "sleep" phases. Without explaining the evolution of AI's decision-making, trust in the system as a reliable security tool could erode. Addressing these challenges will be critical to successfully integrating "sleep" phases into security solutions, ensuring that the benefits of learning and adaptation do not come at the cost of real-time protection or user trust.

Future Research Directions

Hybrid Sleep–Active Models: Could the sleepwalking concept be integrated with traditional real-time security mechanisms for a best-of-both-worlds approach?

Data "Dreaming": Could security systems use synthesized data during sleep-like phases to simulate adversarial scenarios and evolve defense strategies instead of pure downtime?

The "sleepwalking" neural network provides a thought-provoking model pushing the boundaries of AI learning. Its potential translation to cybersecurity will undoubtedly involve adaptations and overcoming unique challenges, but it is a source of inspiration for exploring new approaches to resilience and adaptability in the face of ever-changing threats.

This discussion has explored the potential of eye movements and quantum multimodal models in assessing social engineering susceptibility. While eye movements alone might not be a foolproof indicator, and the concept of a quantum multimodal model for this purpose needs further exploration, these areas highlight a crucial aspect of Artificial Intelligence: its ability to extract insights from imperfect data.

In the real world, data are rarely pristine or perfectly aligned with the problem we are trying to solve. Eye movements, for instance, can be influenced by a myriad of factors beyond deception, such as fatigue, distraction, or underlying medical conditions. Similarly, the "quantum" moniker in the multimodal model suggests that it might be a nascent concept, still in its early stages of development and refinement.

This is where the true power of AI comes into play. AI algorithms excel at sifting through vast amounts of noisy data, identifying subtle patterns and correlations that might elude human observation. By incorporating eye-tracking data alongside other behavioral and physiological cues, such as facial expressions, voice modulation, and even subtle changes in heart rate or skin conductance, AI could potentially develop a more nuanced and comprehensive understanding of social engineering susceptibility.

The key takeaway is that AI's true strength lies not in requiring perfect data, but in its ability to make sense of the messy, real-world data we have to work with. AI algorithms can be trained to filter out noise, identify relevant features, and extract meaningful insights from complex and often contradictory datasets. This ability to discern patterns amidst chaos makes AI an invaluable tool in the ongoing quest to understand and mitigate the risks of social engineering attacks.

Furthermore, AI's capacity for continuous learning and adaptation allows it to refine its understanding of social engineering susceptibility over time. As AI models are exposed to more data, they can identify new patterns, adapt to evolving attack strategies, and develop more sophisticated countermeasures. This dynamic learning process makes AI a powerful ally in the fight against social engineering, enabling us to stay one step ahead of malicious actors and protect ourselves from their deceptive tactics.

24 Introduction to Hybrid Structures of the Quantum Probability Theory in Social Engineering

Cyber social engineering attacks are not merely technical exploits; they are sophisticated manipulations that prey on the intricate interplay between human psychology, decision-making processes, and the vast, interconnected landscape of digital communication. Traditional methods of analysis often focus on identifying discrete attack vectors or behavioral red flags, attempting to categorize and compartmentalize these attacks into neat, predictable patterns. However, this approach can be limiting, overlooking the subtle nuances and dynamic nature of social engineering tactics.

Drawing inspiration from probability theory and the intriguing logic of quantum phenomena could revolutionize our understanding of social engineering and transform our approach to these deceptive tactics. Probability theory, with its emphasis on uncertainty and the likelihood of events, offers a framework for understanding the probabilistic nature of social engineering attacks. These attacks are not deterministic, with guaranteed outcomes, but rather rely on exploiting vulnerabilities and manipulating probabilities to achieve their goals.

The intriguing world of quantum phenomena, with its principles of superposition and entanglement, offers further insights into the complex dynamics of social engineering. Just as quantum particles can exist in multiple states simultaneously, social engineering attacks can exploit multiple vulnerabilities and manipulate multiple psychological triggers to achieve their objectives. The concept of entanglement, where the fates of seemingly separate particles are intertwined, mirrors the interconnectedness of the digital world, where actions in one part of the network can have ripple effects across the entire system.

By embracing a more holistic and probabilistic perspective, informed by both traditional analysis and the intriguing insights of quantum phenomena, we can develop a more nuanced understanding of social engineering. This deeper understanding can lead to more effective countermeasures, empowering individuals and organizations to recognize and resist these deceptive tactics, fostering a more secure and resilient digital landscape.

DOI: 10.1201/9781003500698-24

PROBABILITY AT THE HEART OF SOCIAL ENGINEERING

Social engineers are indeed master manipulators, skilled in the art of exploiting human psychology and social dynamics to achieve their malicious ends. They approach their craft with a calculated understanding of probabilities, meticulously crafting attacks designed to maximize their chances of success. Each interaction, be it a carefully worded phishing email or a meticulously constructed fake social media profile, is a probabilistic gamble, a carefully calculated maneuver aimed at eliciting a specific response from the targeted individual.

These digital deceivers are keen observers of human behavior, adept at identifying and exploiting vulnerabilities in our cognitive processes and emotional responses. They understand the power of social cues, the allure of authority, and the persuasive influence of fear and urgency. They tailor their attacks to specific demographics, personality traits, or behavioral patterns, crafting messages that resonate with the target's deepest desires, fears, or insecurities.

A phishing email, for instance, might be crafted to mimic the familiar tone and format of a trusted institution, exploiting the recipient's inclination to comply with authority figures. A fake social media profile might be meticulously curated to appeal to the target's interests and social circles, leveraging the human desire for connection and belonging.

Each interaction is a carefully calculated step in a larger scheme, a probabilistic maneuver designed to nudge the target closer to the desired outcome. The social engineer understands that not every attempt will be successful, but by increasing the odds of success through meticulous planning and psychological manipulation, they can achieve their goals with remarkable efficiency.

This probabilistic approach to social engineering highlights the importance of cybersecurity awareness and education. By understanding the tactics employed by these digital manipulators, individuals can develop a more critical and discerning eye, recognizing the subtle cues and manipulative techniques that often precede an attack. By fostering a culture of cybersecurity awareness, we can empower individuals to make informed choices, protect their digital identities, and resist the deceptive allure of social engineering schemes.

THE HIDDEN QUANTUM INFLUENCE

While not a direct application of quantum mechanics, the probabilistic nature of social engineering shares parallels with concepts like superposition of possibilities and uncertainty principle in quantum systems:

Superposition of Possibilities: Just as a quantum particle exists in multiple states simultaneously, a social engineer may explore various attack vectors before converging on the most likely to succeed based on the target's response.

Uncertainty Principle: In quantum systems, precise measurement of one property affects the knowledge about another. Similarly, increased scrutiny might cause social engineers to alter their approach, adding to the difficulty of detection.

The exploration of parallels between quantum principles and the seemingly unrelated domain of social engineering unveils a compelling perspective. While social engineering attacks do not directly utilize the laws of quantum mechanics, they share intriguing similarities in their probabilistic nature. Just as a quantum particle exists in a superposition of potential states until observed, a social engineer may explore many attack strategies. Their choice ultimately narrows down based on the victim's responses, mirroring the collapse of a wavefunction in physics. Furthermore, like the Heisenberg uncertainty principle, where observing a quantum system alters it, increased vigilance on a potential victim might force the attacker to adapt their tactics, blurring any clear pattern and making detection more elusive. Recognizing these parallels offers a new way to conceptualize social engineering. It opens avenues for further investigation into whether the mathematical models that help understand complex quantum systems could be adapted to cybersecurity. Understanding the probabilistic nature of social engineering attacks and how perpetrators adapt under scrutiny could lead to more effective defense strategies and greater resilience against these ever-evolving threats.

Figure 24.1 represents a Symbolic View for Hidden Layers and Shared Resources. Illustrates the internal structure of a complex algorithm, emphasizing hidden layers and the potential for shared resources.

The illustration of Figure 24.1 offers a symbolic representation of a biometric data platform and its integration with a multi-layer artificial neural network.

Key elements of Figure 24.1:

- **Biometric Data Sources:** Various sources of biometric data are depicted, such as fingerprint scanners, facial recognition cameras, and voice recorders. These symbolize the diverse ways biometric information is collected.
- **Data Platform:** A central platform is shown, representing the storage and processing hub for the collected biometric data. This platform likely performs tasks like data cleaning, normalization, and feature extraction.
- **Neural Network:** A multi-layer artificial neural network is illustrated, with interconnected nodes representing neurons organized in layers. This network is designed to analyze and learn from biometric data.
- **Hidden Layers:** The figure emphasizes the hidden layers within the neural network. These layers perform complex computations and extract meaningful patterns from the data, effectively learning the unique characteristics of individual biometric profiles.
- **Shared Resources:** The connections between the hidden layers symbolize the sharing of information and learned features within the network. This sharing allows the network to identify complex relationships and improve its accuracy in recognizing and authenticating individuals based on their biometric data.

Overall, Figure 24.1 symbolically depicts how a biometric data platform can leverage the power of artificial neural networks to analyze and learn from complex biometric information. The hidden layers and shared resources within the network

FIGURE 24.1 Hidden layers in complex algorithms often provide shared resources.

play a crucial role in extracting meaningful patterns and enhancing the system's accuracy in authentication and recognition tasks.

PROBABILITY THEORY IN CYBERSECURITY DEFENSE

By embracing a probabilistic view of social engineering, cybersecurity defenses can evolve from static and reactive measures to dynamic and proactive strategies that adapt to the ever-changing threat landscape. This shift in perspective acknowledges that social engineering attacks are not isolated incidents but rather an ongoing and evolving threat that requires a more nuanced and adaptive approach to defense.

Traditional cybersecurity defenses often focus on preventing known attack vectors and patching vulnerabilities, much like building a fortress with thicker walls and stronger gates. However, social engineering attacks exploit the human element, targeting our psychological vulnerabilities and cognitive biases. These attacks are not easily categorized or predicted, as they rely on the dynamic interplay between human psychology and social context.

A probabilistic approach to social engineering recognizes that no defense is fool-proof and that the likelihood of an attack succeeding depends on a multitude of factors, including the attacker's skill, the target's vulnerability, and the specific context of the interaction. This approach shifts the focus from absolute prevention to risk mitigation, recognizing that the goal is not to eliminate all attacks but to reduce their likelihood and impact.

By adopting a probabilistic mindset, cybersecurity professionals can develop more dynamic and adaptive defenses that take into account the evolving nature of social engineering threats. This includes:

- Developing risk assessment models that incorporate a range of factors, including individual susceptibility, social context, and attacker tactics.
- Implementing continuous monitoring and analysis of online behavior to detect anomalies and potential threats.
- Developing personalized training programs that educate individuals about social engineering tactics and empower them to recognize and resist manipulation.
- Fostering a culture of cybersecurity awareness that encourages open communication and reporting of suspicious activity.

In essence, a probabilistic view of social engineering allows us to move beyond a static fortress mentality and embrace a more fluid and adaptive approach to cybersecurity. This shift in perspective recognizes that the human element is both a vulnerability and a strength and that by understanding the dynamics of social engineering, we can develop more effective defenses that protect individuals and organizations from the ever-evolving threat of manipulation and deception.

Applying probability theory to cybersecurity defense offers a paradigm shift from traditional approaches. We can move beyond static vulnerability assessments and develop dynamic risk models by viewing social engineering through a probabilistic lens. These models simulate how multiple vulnerabilities interact, highlighting how seemingly minor weaknesses, when combined, might significantly increase the likelihood of a successful attack.

Furthermore, integrating probabilistic thinking allows us to view AI-powered anomaly detection as a form of "measurement" within the social engineering domain. By establishing baselines of typical behavior, these systems can pinpoint subtle deviations that could signal deception attempts. This mirrors principles from quantum mechanics, where the act of measurement "collapses" the wave of probabilities. Similarly, detection can potentially disrupt the attacker's strategy, forcing them to abandon their carefully crafted plan.

This probabilistic approach marks a fundamental change. Instead of fixating on eliminating isolated exploits, cybersecurity strategies can embrace adaptability and uncertainty. By recognizing the probabilistic nature of social engineering, much like the principles underpinning quantum mechanics, we pave the way toward more robust and resilient cybersecurity defenses capable of anticipating and responding to the inherently unpredictable nature of human-targeted attacks.

Let us look closely into probabilistic social engineering and quantum shadow.

PERSPECTIVE SHIFTS: FROM CERTAINTY TO PROBABILITIES

Traditional cybersecurity approaches often focus on identifying **discrete threats** and implementing **definite countermeasures**. This binary approach struggles with the inherent ambiguity and probabilistic nature of social engineering. Here is how a probabilistic lens offers a new perspective:

Success Rates, Not Guarantees: Social engineering attacks do not guarantee success. They rely on exploiting vulnerabilities and manipulating probabilities to increase the chances of a desired outcome. Security assessments should shift from a "can it be exploited?" to a "how likely is it to succeed?" mindset.

Dynamic Risk Profiles: Individual and organizational vulnerabilities are not static. A probabilistic approach allows for dynamic risk profiles incorporating factors like real-time threat intelligence, employee stress levels during critical deadlines, or even weather patterns that might influence susceptibility (e.g., people are more likely to click on phishing emails during snowstorms).

Resource Allocation: Shifting to probability-based risk models allows for more informed resource allocation. High-risk individuals or systems can be prioritized for additional training or security measures.

The success of social engineering attacks demonstrates a fundamental mismatch between traditional "certain" cybersecurity approaches and an attacker's world of probabilities and manipulation. Adopting a probabilistic mindset can revolutionize our understanding and mitigation of social engineering threats. This shift means moving away from the binary thinking that a system is secure or vulnerable. Instead, we focus on probabilities, acknowledging that social engineers thrive on vulnerabilities with a high likelihood of exploitation. This mindset helps to replace the "Can it be exploited?" question with the more nuanced question, "How likely is it to succeed?"

Furthermore, embracing a probabilistic lens highlights the dynamic nature of risk. Both individual and organizational susceptibility to social engineering fluctuate. Security models must adapt, incorporating real-time factors such as shifts in threat intelligence, employee stress levels, or even something as mundane as weather conditions that might influence vulnerability.

This probabilistic perspective has a profound impact on resource allocation. Rather than distributing security measures uniformly, we can prioritize high-risk individuals or systems. This targeted approach ensures that resources are deployed where they have the potential to make the most significant impact in mitigating the ever-evolving threat of social engineering.

THE QUANTUM PROBABILITY SHADOW: INSPIRATION, NOT APPLICATION

While this approach does not directly utilize quantum computers, it draws inspiration from the fundamental principles of quantum mechanics:

Superposition of Possibilities: In quantum mechanics, a particle can exist in multiple states simultaneously. Similarly, a social engineer may explore various attack vectors concurrently: a phishing email, a fake social media profile, or a phone call – all aimed at the same target. Probabilistic models can account for these possibilities and estimate the likelihood of each tactic's success.

Uncertainty Principle: The Heisenberg Uncertainty Principle states that measuring one property of a quantum system with perfect precision affects our knowledge of another. In social engineering, increased security awareness might make an individual less susceptible to phishing emails and more wary of legitimate emails. Probabilistic models can factor in the potential for countermeasures to influence the attacker's strategy.

While modeling social engineering threats with quantum-inspired frameworks does not directly utilize quantum computers, its strength lies in its ability to capture cyberattacks' dynamic, fluid nature. Drawing inspiration from principles like superposition, where a quantum particle exists in multiple states simultaneously, allows us to model social engineers who may explore several attack vectors concurrently. This probabilistic approach can help predict which tactics are most likely to succeed based on numerous factors influencing the target.

Furthermore, just as the Heisenberg Uncertainty Principle highlights how observation affects the state of a quantum system, we can model how heightened security awareness might shift the dynamics between a social engineer and their target. A cautious user may be less vulnerable to phishing, yet that same wariness might also disrupt legitimate communication. Our models can evolve alongside the defenses and strategies used, adding a layer of realism that traditional threat modeling often lacks. This quantum-inspired approach highlights the value of looking beyond conventional tools when addressing complex problems. By embracing the uncertainty and multiple possibilities inherent in social engineering interactions, we can build more robust and adaptable defense strategies that better anticipate and counter the ever-evolving techniques deployed by those seeking to exploit human vulnerabilities.

Figure 24.2 is a symbolic representation that illustrates the concept of quantum shadow within a probabilistic algorithm. It emphasizes the potential for efficiency gains by leveraging the superposition of states. Figure 24.2 symbolically illustrates how a probabilistic algorithm can leverage the concept of "quantum shadow" to achieve efficiency gains. Imagine a quantum system existing in multiple states simultaneously (superposition). This is represented by a sphere where each point on its surface corresponds to a different possible state. The algorithm, symbolized by a hand, casts a "shadow" onto the sphere. This shadow doesn't measure the exact state but captures essential information about the system's overall probabilistic

FIGURE 24.2 Quantum shadow of probabilistic superpositions.

distribution. By analyzing this shadow, the algorithm gains insights into the system's behavior without having to individually measure each possible state, thus saving significant computational resources. This approach highlights the potential of quantum-inspired techniques to optimize probabilistic algorithms and enhance their efficiency in solving complex problems.

PROBABILISTIC FOUNDATIONS OF SOCIAL ENGINEERING

Social engineering attacks exploit several key probabilistic concepts, as follows:

Bayesian Inference: This approach allows attackers to update their understanding of a target's vulnerabilities based on new information. Successful social media interaction can inform the creation of a more personalized, and thus more likely to succeed, follow-up attack.

Game Theory: Social engineering can be seen as a game between attacker and defender. Attackers use probabilistic models to predict the defender's (target's) most likely response and tailor their tactics accordingly.

The probabilistic underpinnings of social engineering illuminate why it is such a potent and adaptable threat. Bayesian inference allows attackers to refine their strategies continuously. Analyzing successful interactions on social media, for instance, lets them adjust their approach for greater effectiveness in targeted attacks. They treat each interaction as data, updating their beliefs about a target's vulnerabilities.

Furthermore, viewing social engineering through the lens of game theory reveals its calculated nature. Attackers employ probabilistic models to estimate potential outcomes, anticipating how a target might respond based on the information they have been fed. This allows them to choose tactics they believe are most likely to succeed.

Understanding these probabilistic aspects underscores the need to approach cyber defense holistically. It is not enough to focus solely on technical vulnerabilities. Organizations must also educate users to disrupt attackers' ability to gather reliable data and predict their behavior. Only a multifaceted approach recognizing both the technical and human probabilistic elements can enhance resilience against this ever-present threat.

BENEFITS OF A PROBABILISTIC APPROACH

Adopting a probabilistic approach in security enhances decision-making by emphasizing the likelihood of various threats, enabling organizations to allocate resources effectively and adapt to the ever-changing landscape of risks. This method not only prioritizes vulnerabilities but also fosters a culture of continuous improvement and responsiveness in security strategies.

In the realm of cybersecurity, where threats evolve at an unprecedented pace and resources are often stretched thin, the ability to prioritize and allocate resources efficiently becomes paramount. A quantum-inspired approach to cybersecurity, leveraging the principles of probability and uncertainty, can guide us toward a more strategic and effective defense strategy. By focusing our resources on the most probable attack vectors and vulnerable targets, we can maximize our impact and minimize the risk of successful breaches.

This prioritization strategy involves a continuous assessment of the threat landscape, identifying the most likely attack scenarios and the systems or individuals most susceptible to compromise. By understanding the probabilistic nature of cyberattacks, we can allocate resources strategically, strengthening defenses where they are most needed and minimizing vulnerabilities that are most likely to be exploited.

In the ever-changing digital landscape, adaptability is the key to resilience. A quantum-inspired approach to cybersecurity emphasizes the need for continuous adaptation, updating risk assessments based on real-time data and evolving threats. This dynamic approach allows us to stay one step ahead of malicious actors, adjusting our defenses as new attack vectors emerge and vulnerabilities are discovered.

By embracing the principles of quantum mechanics, which acknowledge the inherent uncertainty and probabilistic nature of the world, we can develop cybersecurity strategies that are inherently adaptable and resilient. This means continuously monitoring the threat landscape, analyzing attack patterns, and adjusting our defenses in real time to counter emerging threats and protect our critical systems.

A quantum-inspired approach to cybersecurity is not a static set of rules but rather a dynamic cycle of continuous improvement. It involves constantly identifying areas where security awareness training or defense mechanisms can have the most significant impact on reducing attack probabilities. This iterative process of refinement allows us to optimize our cybersecurity posture, strengthening our defenses and minimizing our vulnerabilities over time.

By analyzing past incidents, identifying patterns of successful attacks, and understanding the evolving tactics of malicious actors, we can refine our security awareness training programs to better equip individuals to recognize and mitigate threats. Similarly, by evaluating the effectiveness of our defense mechanisms and identifying areas for improvement, we can strengthen our cybersecurity infrastructure and reduce the likelihood of successful breaches.

In essence, a quantum-inspired approach to cybersecurity emphasizes prioritization, adaptability, and continuous improvement. By embracing these principles, we can navigate the complex and ever-changing digital landscape, ensuring that our defenses are robust, resilient, and capable of countering the evolving threats of the digital age.

CHALLENGES AND CONSIDERATIONS

Successfully developing probabilistic models hinges on a careful balance of data-driven insights and ethical responsibility. As we delve into critical areas such as data collection and analysis, ethical considerations, and the unpredictable human element, it becomes evident that each presents unique challenges that must be thoughtfully addressed.

Data Collection and Analysis: Building robust probabilistic models requires extensive data on attack methods, target demographics, and human behavior.

Ethical Considerations: Balancing the need for data collection with individual privacy concerns.

Human Element: Probabilistic models cannot fully account for the unpredictable nature of human behavior.

By embracing a probabilistic lens informed by the underlying logic of quantum mechanics, we can move beyond a reactive approach to social engineering and develop proactive, adaptable strategies to defend our increasingly interconnected world.

While not directly utilizing quantum computation, this probabilistic approach presents a novel way to analyze and counteract social engineering threats. It is a significant shift from traditional, binary thinking and paves the way for a more holistic and resilient cybersecurity posture.

While directly using quantum computers in social engineering analysis is still theoretical, exploring the synergy between quantum-inspired concepts and probabilistic methods holds significant promise for improving public awareness and boosting attack culture resilience. Here is how:

ENHANCED ATTACK SIMULATIONS

The prospect of harnessing quantum annealing for enhanced attack simulations represents a turning point in understanding and addressing social engineering threats. Quantum annealing's ability to optimize complex models could revolutionize how social engineers plan and execute their campaigns. Malicious actors could gain unprecedented insights into the most effective tactics by simulating countless potential attack scenarios and their respective probabilities of success. However, this same technology has the potential to bolster our defenses. By analyzing these simulations, cybersecurity experts could better understand evolving social engineering trends and pinpoint specific vulnerabilities. This information could fuel highly targeted, adaptive public education campaigns that directly address the most common or dangerous attack methods.

Furthermore, simulations inspired by quantum annealing's exploration of multiple possibilities could lead to innovative training methods. Gamified environments could present realistic social engineering scenarios, allowing individuals to practice identifying deception in a safe setting. This interactive approach could foster greater awareness and preparedness against the ever-evolving landscape of social engineering threats. While the use of quantum annealing in social engineering presents challenges and opportunities, its potential to reshape the attacker's toolkit and our countermeasures emphasizes the need for ongoing research and vigilance in the battle against digital deception.

STRENGTHENING DEFENSES THROUGH QUANTUM INSPIRATION

By leveraging principles from quantum mechanics, particularly superposition, we can enhance our cybersecurity measures to proactively detect and mitigate social engineering threats in a more nuanced and effective manner. This approach not only broadens our understanding of potential vulnerabilities but also enables the creation of sophisticated AI systems capable of identifying and addressing subtle behavioral shifts indicative of an impending attack.

Superposition-Inspired Threat Detection: The concept of superposition, where a quantum particle exists in multiple states concurrently, can inspire the development of AI-powered anomaly detection systems that monitor for a broader range of potential social engineering attempts. These systems could:

Identify Subtle Shifts: Analyze behavioral anomalies that might indicate susceptibility to an attack, like increased online activity during non-working hours.

Contextual Awareness: Factor in external factors like financial stressors or recent major life events that could make someone more vulnerable to social engineering tactics.

Deception across Platforms: Monitor for coordinated attacks across multiple platforms (email, social media, phone calls) – a tactic becoming increasingly common.

The unique properties of quantum mechanics, a realm where the rules of classical physics blur and the seemingly impossible becomes reality, offer a powerful source of inspiration for combating the ever-evolving threat of social engineering. By drawing on the principles of superposition, where a single quantum particle can exist in multiple states simultaneously, we can envision the development of advanced threat detection systems with the potential to revolutionize cyber defense.

Imagine a quantum-enhanced security system capable of analyzing vast amounts of data, not in a sequential, step-by-step manner, but in a superposition of states, exploring countless possibilities simultaneously. This would enable the system to identify subtle patterns and anomalies that might elude traditional security measures, potentially detecting social engineering attacks before they even unfold.

Furthermore, the quantum phenomenon of entanglement, where two or more particles become inextricably linked, sharing a common fate regardless of distance, could be harnessed to create secure communication channels impervious to eavesdropping or interception. This could safeguard sensitive information from falling into the wrong hands, even in the face of sophisticated social engineering tactics.

The potential applications of quantum mechanics in cybersecurity extend far beyond these examples. Quantum-inspired algorithms could enhance machine learning models, enabling them to detect and adapt to new attack strategies with unprecedented speed and accuracy. Quantum random number generators could provide truly unpredictable keys for encryption, making it virtually impossible for attackers to break codes and compromise sensitive data.

The exploration of quantum mechanics for cybersecurity is still in its nascent stages, but the possibilities are tantalizing. By harnessing the power of this enigmatic realm, we could usher in a new era of cyber defense, where the ingenuity of human innovation is matched by the unyielding laws of quantum physics.

These superposition-inspired systems would operate with a far more nuanced understanding of potential threats. They could detect subtle deviations from established behavioral baselines, like sudden shifts in online activity patterns, even before launching a direct attack. The ability to factor in external contexts, such as personal or financial stressors, could further enhance predictive capabilities, allowing for the identification of potentially vulnerable moments. Moreover, these quantum-inspired defense systems could monitor activity across multiple channels – email, social networks, messaging – to piece together the full scope of increasingly coordinated social engineering campaigns. The realization of such systems will undeniably require advancements in machine learning and artificial intelligence. However, the potential is transformative: AI-powered threat detection fueled by quantum-inspired thinking can identify and flag social engineering attacks while still in their early stages, protecting individuals and organizations from their potentially devastating consequences.

BUILDING A CULTURE OF RESILIENCE

Fostering a culture of resilience in cybersecurity involves empowering individuals and organizations to proactively adapt to evolving threats through education, collaboration, and innovative training methods. By prioritizing awareness and shared knowledge, we can cultivate a robust defense against social engineering and other cyber risks.

Public awareness campaigns can play a crucial role in fostering a more proactive and informed approach to cybersecurity. By utilizing simulations and gamified training, these campaigns can move beyond fearmongering tactics and instead create a more realistic understanding of social engineering threats. Interactive simulations can immerse individuals in scenarios that mimic real-world attacks, allowing them to experience the manipulative tactics employed by social engineers and learn how to recognize and respond to them effectively. Gamified training can make learning about cybersecurity more engaging and enjoyable, encouraging individuals to actively participate and develop essential skills in a safe and controlled environment.

Probabilistic models, informed by ongoing data analysis and attack simulations, can provide individuals with dynamic and up-to-date assessments of cyber threats. These models can track the evolving landscape of social engineering tactics, identify emerging trends, and provide personalized risk assessments based on individual behaviors and vulnerabilities. This continuous flow of information fosters a culture of continuous learning and adaptation, empowering individuals to stay informed and adjust their cybersecurity practices accordingly.

Quantum-inspired simulations offer a powerful tool for enhancing cybersecurity awareness and preparedness. These simulations can not only create individual scenarios but also model large-scale attack campaigns targeting entire organizations or communities. By analyzing the outcomes of these simulations, we can gain valuable insights into the dynamics of cyberattacks, identify vulnerabilities in our defenses, and develop collective defense strategies. Furthermore, sharing the knowledge gained from these simulations can foster a sense of shared responsibility and encourage collaboration among individuals, organizations, and communities in the fight against cyber threats.

By embracing these principles of normalization, continuous learning, and shared knowledge, we can cultivate a more resilient and proactive cybersecurity culture. This will empower individuals and communities to navigate the complex digital landscape safely and confidently, safeguarding their digital freedoms and fostering a more secure and interconnected world.

CHALLENGES AND CONSIDERATIONS

While the potential to harness quantum computing in social engineering analysis is exciting, navigating this frontier with enthusiasm and caution is essential. The "quantum hype" must be tempered with a realistic understanding that full-fledged quantum computers capable of significantly disrupting current cybersecurity strategies remain on the horizon. Furthermore, ethical considerations cannot be an afterthought. Developing AI-powered detection systems demands responsible data collection with an unwavering focus on protecting individual privacy rather than enabling intrusive surveillance. Transparency will be paramount, fostering trust by explaining these systems' inner workings and demonstrating their use for defensive purposes, not to monitor or control online behaviors. Mindfully navigating these challenges can pave the way for a future where quantum-inspired technology empowers individuals rather than jeopardizes their digital security and privacy.

Combining quantum-inspired concepts with probabilistic analysis offers a robust framework for understanding and countering social engineering threats. While not a magic bullet, it fosters a more dynamic, data-driven approach to public awareness and empowers individuals and organizations to build a more resilient attack culture. As advancements in quantum computing continue, the potential for even more transformative applications in the cybersecurity domain will undoubtedly emerge. Now, let us take a deeper look into how the potential integration of quantum computation into probabilistic social engineering analysis can significantly enhance public awareness and resilience against attacks.

Figure 24.3 represents a symbolic model contrasting cultural and logical resilience dynamics. It presents a symbolic model contrasting the dynamics of cultural and

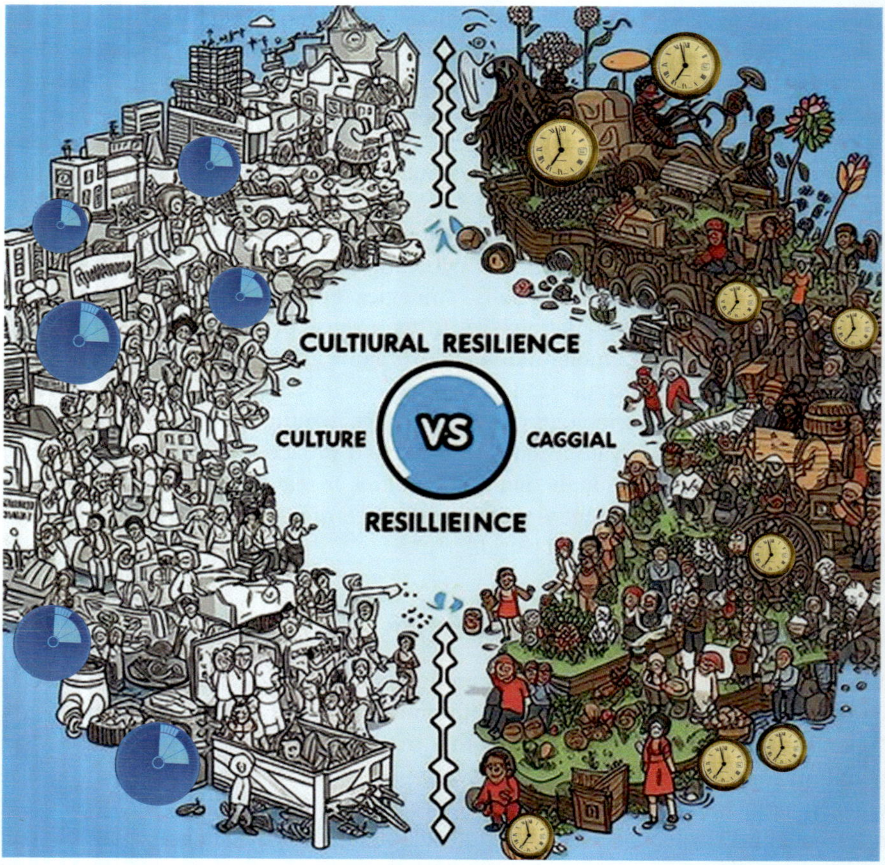

FIGURE 24.3 Symbolic view of cultural resilience vs logical resilience.

logical resilience. It depicts two distinct spheres, representing "Cultural Resilience" and "Logical Resilience," respectively. Within the "Cultural Resilience" sphere, symbols like a community network, shared values, and diverse perspectives illustrate the interconnected and adaptive nature of cultural strength. This resilience stems from shared beliefs, traditions, and the ability to evolve in the face of changing circumstances. Conversely, the "Logical Resilience" sphere showcases symbols like algorithms, formal structures, and critical thinking. This resilience is rooted in logic, reason, and the ability to analyze information objectively and make sound judgments.

The intersection of these spheres highlights the interplay between cultural and logical resilience, suggesting that a balanced approach is crucial for navigating complex challenges. The overlapping area might contain symbols like ethical decision-making, responsible technology use, and informed public discourse, emphasizing the importance of integrating both cultural values and logical reasoning in building a resilient society.

Figure 24.3 may also depict external forces, such as technological advancements or social disruptions, impacting both spheres. This emphasizes the dynamic nature of resilience, requiring constant adaptation and evolution to maintain stability in the face of external pressures.

Overall, this symbolic model serves as a visual representation of the distinct yet interconnected nature of cultural and logical resilience, underscoring the importance of both in navigating an increasingly complex world.

EMPHASIZING KEY BENEFITS FOR PUBLIC AWARENESS

Utilizing innovative approaches like quantum-inspired simulations can significantly enhance public awareness by revealing the intricate nature of social engineering threats. This shift not only promotes a deeper understanding of deception but also fosters a culture of vigilance and preparedness among individuals and organizations alike.

Dismantling False Security: Awareness campaigns often rely on generic warnings or simple rules. Quantum-inspired simulations could expose the public to the vast range of complex and subtle social engineering tactics, shattering any illusion that they are "immune" to deception.

Precision Education: Instead of blanket warnings about phishing emails, quantum-based attack simulations could pinpoint the techniques most likely to be based on an individual's profile or a company's sector. Awareness campaigns could then tailor content, addressing the exact psychological manipulation tactics most likely to be successful with specific audiences.

Changing the Narrative: By making the probabilistic nature of social engineering explicit, we shift the narrative from personal failure ("I fell for a scam") to informed vigilance ("They played the odds, but I was prepared"). This reduces stigma while encouraging active participation in defense.

EMPHASIZING KEY BENEFITS FOR BUILDING ATTACK RESILIENCE

Quantum-inspired simulations offer a powerful new tool for shaping the future of cybersecurity. By allowing us to stress-test systems against the kinds of complex and unpredictable attacks quantum technology might enable, we can proactively identify and address vulnerabilities long before they become real-world threats. Furthermore, this simulation-based approach extends beyond the individual. Modeling large-scale attacks at the community or sector level can reveal patterns in how adversaries target specific groups. This shared intelligence fosters a culture of collective defense, enabling swift countermeasures to protect not just one entity but an entire network of potential targets.

However, the impact of quantum-inspired security goes beyond technical safeguards. It promotes a mindset shift, emphasizing probabilities and continuous adaptation. It reinforces the understanding that cybersecurity is not a one-and-done solution but an ever-evolving process. This proactive, resilient mindset is fundamental in a world where threats shift rapidly. By embracing the tools and perspectives that quantum-inspired simulations offer, we increase the odds of staying one step ahead in the ongoing cybersecurity struggle.

IMPORTANT CONSIDERATIONS (RE-EMPHASIZED)

As we navigate the evolving landscape of technology, it's vital to approach each critical area with a balanced perspective that embraces both the promise of innovation and the ethical implications of its application. Fostering a culture of transparency, collaboration, and informed decision-making will be key to leveraging advancements while safeguarding fundamental values.

The Long Game: Direct quantum computing applications for this purpose are still on the research horizon. Emphasizing the power of the quantum-inspired approach – probability, superposition, optimization – is critical to managing expectations while highlighting the potential.

Privacy above All: Building trust requires absolute transparency and ethical data use. Any collection efforts to feed simulations must make individual privacy paramount.

Humans in the Loop: Probabilities and simulations can inform but never replace human judgment and critical thinking. Reinforcing that these tools exist to empower, not automate away, individual responsibility is essential. The potential to harness quantum-inspired concepts within probabilistic models is a revolutionary step toward understanding and disrupting the intricate dynamics of social engineering. By focusing on enhanced awareness campaigns and a culture of proactive resilience, we pave the way for a more secure and empowered digital society.

LET US TAKE A LOOK AT A SIMULATION EXAMPLE KEY POINT

Targeting the Healthcare Sector

Scenario: A quantum-inspired simulation models potential social engineering attacks against healthcare organizations. The simulation incorporates:

- **Attack Vectors:** Phishing emails, fake vendor communications, ransomware attacks leveraging software vulnerabilities.

Vulnerabilities: Staff burnout, outdated security systems, gaps in incident response protocols.

Probabilities: Simulations assign probabilities to attack methods based on analysis of past healthcare breaches and emerging trends.

Simulation Outputs

High-Risk Targets: The simulation identifies employees or departments more likely to succumb to attacks due to stress levels, access permissions, or technology gaps.

Cascading Impacts: It calculates potential consequences: delays in patient care, data breaches, and financial losses.

Optimized Defenses: Simulations test the effectiveness of various defense strategies, suggesting where additional training or technology investments would be most impactful.

Simulation outputs provide actionable insights that go beyond simply identifying potential cybersecurity vulnerabilities. Analyses of stress factors, access permissions, and technology shortcomings reveal the environments where attacks are most likely to succeed. Furthermore, the simulations highlight the potential cascading impacts of a successful breach, including disruptions in patient care, sensitive data exposure, and financial costs to the organization. Importantly, these simulations do not just expose weaknesses; they empower proactive decision-making. By testing various defense strategies, simulations help organizations identify where training initiatives or targeted technology investments would yield the most significant risk reduction – and the most secure return on those investments. This data-driven approach optimizes defenses, ensuring that resources are allocated most effectively. As cybersecurity threats evolve, simulations provide a powerful tool for hospitals to stay one step ahead, safeguarding patient care and sensitive information.

ETHICAL IMPLICATIONS

Data Sensitivity: Healthcare systems require susceptible data – patient information, staff workload, and security flaws.

Privacy: How is data collected, anonymized, and secured to prevent it from becoming another vulnerability?

Consent: What levels of consent are needed from staff if their behaviors are modeled?

Profiling and Bias: Simulations identifying "high-risk" individuals raise concerns.

Stigmatization: Could this lead to unfairly targeting employees already under pressure instead of supporting them?

Algorithmic Bias: How can we ensure simulations do not perpetuate stereotypes or overlook certain vulnerability factors?

Purpose and Use of Results: Who can access simulation outputs, and how are they acted upon?

Proactive vs. Punitive: Are results used to enhance support and training or create a punitive surveillance environment?

Transparency: Are staff informed about simulations? Can they challenge results that feel inaccurate and provide feedback?

Over-Reliance on Technology: Simulations are powerful but not infallible tools.

False Positives: How do we address cases where simulations flag someone as a risk who is not damaging trust?

Human Judgment: Emphasizing the need for simulation results to be interpreted by security professionals alongside qualitative understanding is critical.

MITIGATING ETHICAL RISKS

Collaborative Development: Involving healthcare staff in the design of simulations builds trust and helps address potential biases.

Privacy by Design: Incorporate robust anonymization and encryption from the outset of data collection.

Focus on Empowerment: Frame simulations as tools to identify areas needing support, not to single out individuals.

Independent Oversight: Establish ethical review boards to assess simulation methodology and use of results.

The ethical use of quantum-inspired simulations demands careful consideration of data privacy, potential biases, the role of human judgment, and transparency throughout the process. Addressing these concerns can enhance public awareness and build resilience against social engineering threats.

Let us look at another Simulation Scenario. Key points: Social Media "Deepfake" Disinformation.

Scenario B: A quantum-inspired simulation models the spread of deepfake videos on social media platforms designed to sow political discord or undermine an election. The simulation incorporates:

- **Target Demographics:** Analysis of past disinformation campaigns and social media data to pinpoint populations most susceptible to deepfakes based on age, political affiliation, etc.
- **Content Optimization:** AI-assisted content generation to test variations of deepfakes (video tone, visual elements, audio cues) for believability.
- **Dissemination Networks:** Mapping social media bot networks and influencer accounts likely to amplify disinformation.

Simulation Results

Reach and Engagement: Predicts how quickly deepfakes could spread across platforms and engage specific demographics.

Emotional Impact: Simulates potential emotional responses (outrage, fear, amusement) that drive further sharing.

Fact-Checking Bottlenecks: Identifies time delays in debunking efforts, highlighting how rapid virality outpaces correction.

Public Awareness Implications *(Continued)*

Visualizing the Threat: Simulations could be turned into interactive public awareness tools. Instead of passive warnings, people could experience the ease of creating deepfakes and their realistic appearance.

Debunking goes Procedural: Beyond spotting fakes, simulations could highlight the tactics used, making people less susceptible to future, visually improved manipulations (e.g., focusing on inconsistencies in message vs. speaker identity, not just image flaws).

Counter-Simulation as Education: The public could "play" against simulations, trying to debunk or counter the spread of deepfakes, understanding media analysis and how disinformation spreads.

ETHICAL CONSIDERATIONS

Exposure Dilemma: Showing highly convincing deepfakes to educate risks unintentionally spreading the techniques they aim to warn against.

The Backfire Effect: Attempts to debunk can sometimes reinforce false beliefs for some individuals. Understanding how simulations impact different audiences is critical.

Platform Accountability: Simulations make the dangers of unmoderated amplification of information undeniable. This highlights the ethical responsibility of tech companies to act.

LET US TAKE A LOOK AT MITIGATING RISK KEY POINTS

Limited Exposure: Carefully curated demos, not tools for the public to create deepfakes.

Focus on Critical Thinking: Emphasize the manipulation techniques rather than replicating exact content.

Partnering with Tech Platforms: Use simulations to inform content moderation strategies and pressure companies to address disinformation networks.

This scenario illustrates the power of simulations to shift public awareness from "Can I spot a fake?" to a deeper understanding of how they are created and amplified and the psychological manipulation they employ. Addressing ethical considerations upfront is vital for the responsible use of this technology.

Now, here is another Simulation Scenario: Targeted BEC (Business Email Compromise) Attack on Mid-Sized Businesses:

Scenario C: A quantum-inspired simulation model of BEC attacks targeting mid-sized businesses. It combines attack data with the probabilistic decision-making of crucial targets like finance staff and executives. The simulation incorporates:

Attacker Research: Real-world BEC data helps pinpoint convincing impersonation tactics (spoofed domains, timing, language cues). It can even utilize text analysis on open social media posts by executives to mimic their style.

Employee Vulnerabilities: Identifies stressed departments (end of quarter), those new to payment processes, or recent company announcements (mergers) that attackers exploit.

Decision Points: Simulates how employees verify requests (email only, follow-up call?). It highlights where additional checks might have been bypassed due to perceived authority or urgency.

Simulation Outputs *(Continued and Expanded)*

Optimal Attack Path: Predicts the most likely way a BEC scam could penetrate defenses, finding the weakest link in the employee verification chain.

Financial Impact: Calculates typical losses for businesses of that size in such scams, driving home the severity of the risk.

Targeted Training: Identifies specific areas for training (spotting spoofed domains, not rushing urgent requests) tailored to modeled high-risk situations.

HOW IT SERVES PUBLIC AWARENESS AND RESILIENCE

Beyond the C-Suite: Simulations make the risk tangible. CEO fraud is not just about top executives but also how the attacker targets the processes around them.

Psychology over Technology: Highlights how scams exploit urgency, trust hierarchies, and procedural gaps, not just tech flaws. This makes training harder to dismiss.

Shared Responsibility: Simulations could involve multiple roles (finance, assistants, etc.), showing the chain of decisions that can prevent or enable a scam.

ETHICAL IMPLICATIONS

Data Sensitivity: Modeling specific company practices needs secure data handling, primarily if simulations use industry-specific data.

Avoiding Blame Culture: Simulations should empower employees instead of singling them out as “weak links.”

Accessibility: Smaller businesses are targets but may lack resources for complex simulations. Providing simplified tools and simulation results to these sectors is critical.

MITIGATING RISK FACTORS

Anonymized Case Studies: Sharing simulation insights while protecting company details can benefit the wider business community.

Focus on Process Fixes: Emphasize how improving procedures protects everyone, not just targeting individual vigilance.
Open-Source Simulators: Developing accessible tools empowers smaller companies to run their simulations.

Simulation of BEC offers concrete insights. It helps companies and individuals visualize how seemingly minor procedural or behavioral weaknesses can open the door to these devastating attacks. Ethical design makes this an empowerment tool, shifting the focus from individual failure to organizational resilience.

Now, let us list the key points that outline how to integrate ethical considerations into the design and implementation of a social engineering simulation tool, specifically focusing on the example of CEO fraud (BEC).

PRIVACY BY DESIGN

Anonymization: Develop robust data anonymization protocols from the outset. This includes:

Removal of identifiable company and employee information.
Data should be aggregated to focus on trends, not individual actions.

Differential Privacy: Could techniques like adding calculated noise to data help create broader statistical data sets while protecting individual contributions?
Data Minimization: Collect only the essential data necessary for the specific simulation type.

The concept of Privacy by Design offers a proactive approach to safeguarding user information within simulations. By considering privacy from the earliest stages of development, it is possible to implement robust protocols that mitigate the risks of unintended data exposure or misuse.

Anonymization is paramount in safeguarding sensitive information and ensuring ethical data handling. By stripping away identifiable company and employee information, we transform raw data into a more abstract representation, protecting the privacy of individuals and mitigating the risk of potential harm. Techniques like aggregation further enhance privacy by shifting the focus from individual actions to broader trends and patterns, allowing for valuable insights without compromising the confidentiality of specific data points.

Differential privacy adds another layer of defense, strategically embedding calculated noise into datasets to enable statistical analysis while providing a degree of plausible deniability to protect individual contributions. This technique ensures that the results of the analysis cannot be used to infer information about specific individuals, further safeguarding privacy and promoting ethical data handling.

Critically, data minimization should be seen as a guiding principle throughout the entire data lifecycle. By strictly limiting data collection to only the essential elements required for the simulations, we reduce the potential attack surface and minimize the risk of data breaches or misuse. This principle underscores the importance of carefully considering the necessity and proportionality of data collection, ensuring that we gather only what is essential for the intended purpose.

In essence, these techniques and principles represent a commitment to responsible data handling, recognizing that the pursuit of knowledge and innovation should never come at the expense of individual privacy and ethical considerations. By prioritizing anonymization, aggregation, differential privacy, and data minimization, we can foster a data-driven culture that is both insightful and ethical, paving the way for responsible advancements in artificial intelligence and cybersecurity.

These principles, when interwoven and diligently applied, provide a robust foundation for upholding user privacy within the intricate realm of virtual simulations. They serve as guiding lights, illuminating the path toward ethical and responsible development and deployment of these immersive technologies. However, the challenge of safeguarding privacy in virtual worlds is an ongoing and evolving one, demanding constant vigilance and adaptation as these simulations grow in complexity and sophistication.

As virtual simulations become more intricate, blurring the lines between the physical and digital realms, the need for innovative and adaptable privacy solutions becomes ever more pressing. Traditional approaches to privacy protection may prove inadequate in these dynamic environments, where users leave behind digital footprints that can be tracked, analyzed, and potentially exploited.

Ongoing research into privacy-enhancing technologies, such as differential privacy, federated learning, and homomorphic encryption, is crucial for developing robust safeguards that protect user data without compromising the immersive and interactive nature of virtual simulations. The exploration of new technologies, such as blockchain-based identity management systems and decentralized data storage solutions, could offer further avenues for enhancing privacy and empowering users with greater control over their digital identities.

Ethical considerations must remain at the heart of responsible simulation design and implementation. This involves not only adhering to legal and regulatory frameworks but also fostering a culture of privacy awareness and respect for user autonomy. Developers, researchers, and policymakers must engage in ongoing dialogue to address the ethical challenges posed by virtual simulations, ensuring that these technologies are used to empower and enrich human experiences while safeguarding individual rights and freedoms.

In conclusion, the quest to balance the transformative potential of virtual simulations with the imperative to protect user privacy is an ongoing and dynamic one. By weaving together the principles of data minimization, informed consent, user control, and security, and by remaining committed to ongoing research, ethical considerations, and the exploration of new technologies, we can create virtual worlds that foster innovation, creativity, and human connection while safeguarding the fundamental right to privacy.

EMPOWERMENT FOCUS AND TRANSPARENCY

Empowerment and transparency are crucial in fostering trust within organizations, especially when managing employee data; this involves obtaining meaningful consent and providing opt-out options for specific roles. By framing discussions around system improvements and using clear explanations of simulation results, organizations can emphasize collective resilience while avoiding the identification of vulnerable individuals.

Consent and Control: Explain how employee data is used and obtain meaningful consent. Allow opt-outs, especially if modeling specific roles.
Simulation Framing: Use language emphasizing system improvement and collective resilience: "Stress-testing payment procedures" instead of "finding vulnerable employees."
Explainable Outputs: Ensure clear explanations of simulation results, focusing on how decisions and processes create vulnerabilities, not specific people.

To ensure responsible and ethical employee behavioral simulations, prioritizing empowerment, transparency, and responsible framing are crucial. It is essential to give employees clear insights into how their data are used and obtain their meaningful consent before simulations. Emphasizing that these simulations identify systemic vulnerabilities rather than individual weaknesses fosters a less accusatory environment. Language matters; by framing them as "stress-testing" procedures that help improve collective resilience, you change the tone from punitive to proactive. Notably, the results of simulations should never be presented in a way that singles out individuals as the sole problem. Instead, focus on how decisions, processes, and potentially outdated systems create vulnerabilities. This empowers employees to see themselves as part of the solution, not as scapegoats. By embracing these principles, behavioral simulations can be transformative tools for enhancing organizational security in a way that respects employee autonomy and builds a more collaborative and proactive security culture.

ACCESSIBILITY AND FAIRNESS

To develop a robust simulation tool, leverage open-source platforms for transparency and customization, allowing broader adaptation and community contributions. Forge industry partnerships to create tailored anonymized data sets and offer workshops for smaller businesses, enhancing their ability to interpret and utilize simulation results. Regularly conduct algorithmic audits to identify and mitigate biases, ensuring the model remains fair and reliable. This comprehensive approach will foster trust, innovation, and effective use across various sectors.

Open-Source Foundations: Build the core simulation tool on open-source platforms, allowing auditing, customization, and broader adaptation.
Industry Partnerships: Collaborate with sector-specific organizations to:
Develop tailored anonymized data sets.
Offer workshops on simulation use and result interpretation for smaller businesses.
Algorithmic Audit: Regularly assess the simulation model for potential biases in analyzing data or suggesting mitigations.

Ensuring a cybersecurity simulation tool's ethical and equitable use demands a multi-pronged approach centered on accessibility and fairness. Building the tool's core on open-source platforms invites transparency, allowing for broader scrutiny, customization to fit diverse contexts, and greater accessibility regardless of an organization's budget. However, openness alone is not enough. Collaborating actively with industry partners is essential for creating anonymized data sets that reflect the realities of different sectors. Partnering to offer workshops tailored to smaller businesses ensures that powerful tools do not become the exclusive domain of large corporations, leveling the cybersecurity playing field.

Most importantly, proactive and ongoing algorithmic audits are crucial to minimize unintended biases within the simulation's data analysis and mitigation suggestions. A commitment to fairness is not a one-time event; it must be a cornerstone of the tool's evolution and use. By embracing these strategies, we move closer to creating a cybersecurity landscape where advanced simulation tools are accessible and work to protect everyone equitably.

COLLABORATIVE OVERSIGHT

Independent Review Board: Establish a board including cybersecurity experts, ethicists, and even employee representatives to:
Approve data collection protocols and changes to the simulation model.
Periodically evaluate how simulations are impacting company culture.

Public Reporting: Publish anonymized summaries of simulation insights to benefit the broader business community.

The concept of collaborative oversight is crucial when harnessing the power of workplace behavior simulations for cybersecurity training. An independent review board, composed of cybersecurity experts, ethicists, and employee representatives, serves as a safeguard for responsible and ethical use. This board should be pivotal in approving data collection protocols and any subsequent changes to the simulation model, ensuring that privacy and fairness principles are strictly upheld. Furthermore, the board's mandate should extend to periodic evaluations of how these simulations shape company culture, identifying unintended consequences and course-correcting as needed.

Transparency is vital for building trust in this approach. The company can share valuable knowledge with the broader business community by publishing anonymized summaries of simulation insights. This exchange fosters industry-wide learning and promotes the development of best practices for simulations in cybersecurity training. A collaborative oversight model, coupled with transparency, ensures that this powerful tool is used ethically and responsibly, maximizing its benefits for the organization and its employees.

TECHNICAL IMPLEMENTATION

This can be focused on:

Secure Development Environment: Utilize security best practices for code development, data storage, and access control.

User Interface: Design interfaces prioritizing clear communication positive reinforcement, allowing users to adjust simulation parameters to match their company structure.

Integration with Training: Provide clear pathways for turning simulation-identified weaknesses into actionable, accessible training modules.

The successful implementation of the proposed simulation framework goes beyond its technical architecture. Yielding real-world benefits requires careful integration into an organization's overall cybersecurity strategy. A secure development environment, with robust coding practices, data handling protocols, and access controls, forms the bedrock for ensuring the simulation is not compromised. Additionally, user interfaces should be designed for clarity and intuitive use, which is crucial for engagement. Positive reinforcement built into the simulation can encourage participation and create a less threatening learning environment.

Finally, this tool's full potential lies in its synergy with existing training programs. The weaknesses it uncovers should translate seamlessly into targeted training modules tailored to address the specific vulnerabilities observed in the simulated environment. By embedding this simulation framework within a continuous cycle of assessment and knowledge transfer, organizations can move beyond reactive cybersecurity postures toward a proactive model, consistently reinforcing good practices and staying one step ahead of evolving cyber threats.

CONTINUOUS IMPROVEMENT

Incorporate anonymous feedback mechanisms and regularly update simulations to address evolving BEC tactics, ensuring ethical design through continuous review and diverse perspectives.

Feedback Mechanisms: Incorporate anonymous ways for users to provide feedback on the simulation experience and its impact.

Evolving with Threats: Establish mechanisms to update the simulation model as BEC tactics evolve.

Important Note: Ethical design is an ongoing process, not a one-time checklist. Building mechanisms for review, feedback, and adaptation ensures the long-term responsible use of this powerful tool against social engineering. Challenges associated with establishing an appropriate independent review board for the ongoing oversight of social engineering simulation tools.

Implementing a social engineering simulation tool should not be considered a one-off endeavor. An ongoing feedback, evolution, and ethical review process is crucial to remain effective and minimize potential harm. This means incorporating anonymous channels for users to provide honest feedback about their simulation experiences and perceived impacts. Since BEC tactics constantly adapt, establishing a way to update the simulation model as new threats emerge becomes essential.

Ethical design should be ingrained into the tool's core, not treated as a simple checklist. These demands create built-in mechanisms for regular review, soliciting feedback, and adapting to changing circumstances. Establishing an appropriate independent review board for ongoing oversight is essential to this process, though it presents its complexities.

The long-term responsible use of social engineering simulation tools depends on this adaptable and ethically conscious approach. It ensures the tool remains a force for good that empowers awareness rather than inadvertently causing harm.

KEY CHALLENGES

To effectively navigate the complexities of simulation oversight, the board must balance a diverse range of expertise with the need for independent governance while ensuring access to critical information. This multifaceted approach is essential to address the technical, ethical, and psychological dimensions of the simulations.

Finding the right expertise for an oversight board tasked with evaluating cybersecurity simulations is paramount. This board needs a diverse blend of perspectives to address the multifaceted nature of these simulations, encompassing technical, ethical, and psychological dimensions. Cybersecurity specialists are essential, providing an in-depth understanding of simulated attack vectors, potential modeling flaws, and data security protocols. Ethicists bring expertise in data privacy, potential biases embedded within the simulations, and the broader impact of these tools on employee experience and trust. Furthermore, organizational psychologists or behavioral researchers offer crucial insights into how simulations shape behavior, risk perception, and workplace dynamics. Finally, and perhaps most importantly, employee representatives provide invaluable firsthand perspectives on how the simulations are perceived by the workforce, ensuring that they are empowering rather than leading to unintended consequences.

Maintaining the board's independence while ensuring access to necessary information is a delicate balancing act. One potential solution is to adopt a primarily external model, where the majority of board members are independent experts, with company representatives serving in an advisory role to provide context and insights without compromising the board's objectivity. To further prevent the entrenchment of viewpoints and address potential trust issues, establishing term limits or a rotating member model can ensure fresh perspectives and prevent conflicts of interest. Clear access protocols should be defined, outlining access levels to sensitive data, simulation models, and company communications, striking a balance between oversight and confidentiality.

Conflicts of interest must be carefully managed. Board members should be free from financial ties to the simulation tool's developer or companies heavily invested in its success. Similarly, affiliations with organizations that offer competing simulation tools should be disclosed and, if necessary, addressed to avoid bias in recommendations. It's also crucial to manage expectations by acknowledging that board membership may involve public scrutiny and necessitate transparent disclosure of affiliations to maintain public trust.

Empowering the board to exercise genuine oversight is essential. This requires a clearly defined mandate that outlines the board's authority to approve data collection practices, review significant updates to the simulation model, and evaluate the use of simulation results within the company. The board must be allocated sufficient resources, including budget, staff support, and dedicated time, to conduct effective oversight. Clear reporting pathways should be established, enabling the board to communicate concerns and recommendations to company leadership promptly and effectively.

Finally, the board must balance agility with oversight in the rapidly evolving cybersecurity landscape. This can be achieved by establishing regular review cycles for simulation updates and anonymized usage trends, ensuring the board remains informed about the tool's evolution and impact. Additionally, an emergency review protocol should be in place, allowing the board to swiftly convene and assess simulations used in response to urgent, new threat patterns, ensuring that the company can respond effectively to emerging threats while maintaining ethical and responsible practices.

ADDRESSING CHALLENGES PROACTIVELY

To navigate complex challenges effectively, it's essential for organizations to establish a solid framework that fosters transparency, inclusivity, and continuous learning. By implementing strategic initiatives across critical areas, boards can enhance their effectiveness and responsiveness to evolving needs.

Public Charter: Publish a clear statement of the board's purpose, member selection criteria, and authority to build trust in its independence.

Diverse Representation: Actively seek members from various backgrounds and fields to avoid monolithic thinking.

Ongoing Training: Provide board members with training on the technical aspects of the tool, emerging social engineering trends, and the ethical implications of their work.

Establishing an effective review board for AI in cybersecurity is not a mere formality; it's a delicate balancing act. It demands meticulous planning, a deep understanding of the ethical implications, and a commitment to fostering innovation while safeguarding against potential harms. This review board, composed of experts from diverse fields, including AI, cybersecurity, ethics, law, and social sciences, will play a crucial role in shaping the development and deployment of AI-powered tools for combating social engineering.

The board's mandate must be clearly defined, encompassing not only the evaluation of AI models for accuracy and effectiveness but also a thorough assessment of their ethical implications. This includes scrutinizing potential biases, ensuring fairness and transparency, and addressing concerns about privacy and data security. The board must also consider the broader societal impact of these technologies, anticipating potential unintended consequences and promoting responsible innovation that aligns with human values.

Furthermore, the review board should foster a culture of open dialogue and collaboration between researchers, developers, policymakers, and the public. By encouraging diverse perspectives and facilitating public engagement, the board can ensure that the development of AI in cybersecurity is guided by ethical principles and serves the best interests of society.

Establishing an effective review board is not a one-time task but an ongoing process that requires continuous adaptation and refinement. As AI technology evolves and new challenges emerge, the board must remain vigilant, updating its guidelines, seeking new expertise, and fostering a dynamic approach to oversight that balances the need for innovation with the imperative to protect human values and societal well-being.

25 Introduction to the Quantum Structures of the Fuzzy Set in Cyber Social Engineering Systems

Cyber social engineering (CSE) attacks have proven alarmingly effective, exploiting human psychology's and social interaction's vulnerabilities rather than purely technical flaws. These attacks manipulate trust, exploit ambiguity, and prey upon our natural inclination to make decisions under incomplete or misleading information. Traditional cybersecurity models, designed for deterministic threats, often struggle to grasp CSE's complex and nuanced nature.

Fuzzy set theory offers a powerful tool to address these challenges. Unlike classical sets with rigid boundaries, fuzzy sets allow for degrees of belonging, capturing the ambiguity and uncertainty inherent in the language and tactics of social engineers. They allow us to represent concepts like "somewhat trustworthy" or "slightly suspicious," which better reflect the reality of human decision-making under social pressure.

This chapter explores how quantum-inspired concepts can further enhance our understanding and defense against CSE threats. By drawing analogies from quantum mechanics, particularly the principles of superposition and entanglement, we can develop more sophisticated models of CSE tactics. Superposition allows us to analyze how attackers might simultaneously present themselves in contradictory ways, appearing both legitimate and suspicious, to exploit psychological biases. Entanglement helps us consider the interconnected nature of CSE, where vulnerabilities in one individual or system can create ripple effects throughout a social network.

Through the combined lens of fuzzy sets and quantum-like structures, we gain a more nuanced toolset for dissecting the persuasive techniques of cyber social engineers. This knowledge is critical to designing more resilient systems, implementing better user training, and proactively detecting the early signs of these insidious attacks.

The symbolic view of the quantum structure of fuzzy sets represents the concept of quantum logic applied to fuzzy set theory, as represented in Figure 25.1. It visualizes how quantum mechanics can be used to describe the uncertainty and imprecision

DOI: 10.1201/9781003500698-25

FIGURE 25.1 A symbolic view of the quantum structure of the fuzzy sets.

inherent in fuzzy sets. The diagram typically includes elements like quantum states, operators, and measurements, each representing different aspects of the fuzzy set.

FUZZY SETS KEY POINTS: EMBRACING AMBIGUITY

Classic Sets vs. Fuzzy Sets: In classic sets, elements have a crisp "in or out" membership. In contrast, fuzzy sets allow for degrees of membership to a set, reflecting the inherent vagueness of concepts like "trust" or "urgency" – which social engineers exploit.

Membership Functions: A fuzzy set is defined by a membership function that assigns a value between 0 and 1 to each element, signifying its degree of belonging. This allows us to model the fuzzy nature of susceptibility – an individual may be somewhat vulnerable to a specific phishing tactic, but not completely. The concept of fuzzy sets provides a robust framework to move away from the rigid boundaries of classical sets and embrace the ambiguity inherent in the real world. While classic sets demand a crisp "in or out" classification for elements, fuzzy sets recognize that concepts like "trust," "urgency," or "vulnerability" exist on a spectrum, a nuanced reality that social engineers often exploit. Fuzzy sets represent degrees of belonging by using membership functions to assign values between 0 and 1. This allows for a more accurate representation of susceptibility, where an individual might be partially vulnerable to a phishing tactic but not wholly gullible. Understanding these subtle gradients of risk is crucial in designing effective countermeasures against social engineering. Furthermore, the principles of fuzzy sets could be applied to analyze social engineering tactics themselves, helping identify patterns in how attackers use ambiguity, misdirection, and nuanced language to enhance the success of their manipulations.

QUANTUM INSPIRATION: SUPERPOSITION AND UNCERTAINTY

While fuzzy sets provide a powerful tool, a quantum-inspired lens can further enrich this approach:

Superposition of Vulnerabilities: Just as a quantum particle can exist in multiple states, an individual's susceptibility to CSE may be a superposition of different emotional states, stress levels, and knowledge gaps. Fuzzy sets can be used to model these combinations, with membership functions evolving.

The Uncertainty Principle in Measurement: Measuring (observing) a quantum system affects its state. Similarly, in CSE, probing someone's vulnerability (e.g., a simulated phishing test) may alter their awareness. Fuzzy models could dynamically update based on interactions.

While fuzzy sets provide a robust framework for modeling the nuances and gradients of vulnerability, drawing inspiration from quantum mechanics offers a unique perspective that further enriches our approach. When applied to our understanding of cyber social engineering (CSE) vulnerabilities, the principle of superposition allows us to see an individual's susceptibility not as a single, static state but as a complex combination of emotional factors, stress levels, and knowledge gaps. These elements exist in flux, just as a quantum particle exists in many potential states. With their adaptable membership functions, fuzzy sets can model these dynamic combinations. Moreover, the concept of the uncertainty principle resonates within the CSE context. In quantum mechanics, the very act of measurement alters the state of a system.

Similarly, when we attempt to measure an individual's cyber preparedness through simulated phishing attacks or other tests, their awareness may change in response. The uncertainty principle reminds us that the mere assessment may alter the vulnerability landscape. To address this, fuzzy models could incorporate a dynamic element, continuously updating and adapting based on the individual's interactions and responses.

We unlock new possibilities for modeling CSE vulnerabilities by embracing these quantum-inspired concepts. This enables a more nuanced and adaptable approach, paving the way for security strategies that can evolve with the ever-shifting nature of cyber threats.

FUZZY SETS IN CYBER SOCIAL ENGINEERING SYSTEMS

The title "Fuzzy Sets in Cyber Social Engineering Systems" encapsulates the exploration of nuanced decision-making frameworks that enhance the analysis of human behavior and interactions in cybersecurity, illustrating potential use cases such as adaptive phishing detection and targeted social engineering defenses. By delving into the intricate nature of fuzzy sets, this study aims to illuminate considerations for future directions in cybersecurity strategies while drawing inspiration from quantum principles to innovate and refine these systems.

Potential Use Cases at a Glance

Personalized Risk Assessment: Fuzzy sets can map an individual's traits, online behavior, and previous interactions to a dynamic "degree of susceptibility" to various attack vectors.

Attack Simulation: Fuzzy logic can model the nuanced decision-making of social engineers, incorporating uncertainties about their target selection and tactics. This could help predict the evolution of attack scenarios.

Defensive Deception Detection: Fuzzy models could help analyze language patterns, behavioral anomalies, and network activity that might subtly reveal deceptive intent, even in a context of uncertainty.

Considerations and Future Directions

Data and Ethical Considerations: Developing robust fuzzy models for CSE requires responsible collection of sensitive data while ensuring such models avoid profiling and perpetuate biases.

Quantum-Inspired AI: Fuzzy approaches could be integrated with quantum-inspired AI techniques for enhanced pattern recognition and threat prediction.

By embracing the inherent ambiguity of CSE with fuzzy sets and drawing insights from quantum superposition and uncertainty, we can develop more nuanced and adaptable models for understanding and mitigating these pervasive threats.

The power of fuzzy sets, quantum-inspired enhancements, and their applications in combatting cyber social engineering (CSE), now let us highlight the critical points of fuzzy-Quantum models:

Understanding Fuzzy Sets in Detail

Fuzzy sets offer a powerful framework for quantifying concepts that defy rigid categorization, capturing the nuances of human behavior and subjective perceptions. Consider the fuzzy set "highly stressed employees." There is no single numerical threshold that definitively separates stressed from non-stressed individuals. Instead, a membership function can be used to assign a degree of membership to each individual based on their reported experiences. Someone reporting overwhelming workloads and constant deadlines might be assigned a high membership value, such as 0.8, while someone with a generally manageable workload might receive a lower value, like 0.2. This allows for a more nuanced representation of stress levels, acknowledging the inherent ambiguity and subjectivity of human experience.

Furthermore, fuzzy sets excel at modeling the inherent imprecision of human language. Terms like "urgent," "likely," or "secure" are inherently subjective, their meanings shaped by context and individual perception. Fuzzy logic provides a framework for assigning membership functions to these linguistic variables, capturing the shades of gray in human communication. For instance, the term "urgent" might be assigned a high membership value for a message requiring immediate action, a moderate value for a task with a flexible deadline, and a low value for a routine communication.

The dynamic nature of human behavior is another aspect where fuzzy sets shine. Membership functions are not static; they can evolve over time to reflect changes in an individual's circumstances or state of mind. A person's membership in the "vulnerable to phishing" set might increase during periods of high stress or distraction, as their cognitive resources are depleted and their decision-making abilities compromised. This dynamic modeling allows for a more nuanced and accurate assessment of cybersecurity risks, recognizing that human vulnerabilities are not fixed traits but rather fluctuate in response to various internal and external factors.

In conclusion, fuzzy sets provide a valuable tool for modeling the complexities of human behavior and cybersecurity risks, capturing the nuances of subjective perceptions, linguistic ambiguity, and dynamic changes over time. By embracing this framework, we can develop more accurate risk assessments, design more effective security awareness training, and ultimately build a safer and more resilient digital world.

The Quantum Inspiration

Superposition of States: Imagine an employee's CSE vulnerability as a combination of factors with varying weights: [0.6 * stress + 0.3 * lack of training + 0.1 * recent company news]. This mirrors superposition in quantum systems, where a particle's state is a weighted combination of possibilities.

Observation Changes the System: In quantum mechanics, measurement collapses a superposition into one outcome. In CSE, awareness campaigns or security tests can change susceptibility. Fuzzy models should reflect this, adjusting membership functions based on "measurements" (interactions).

Uncertainty Principle: Perfectly pinpointing a vulnerability might be impossible, just as precisely measuring a particle's position and momentum is impossible due to inherent uncertainty. Fuzzy CSE models need to embrace and utilize this probabilistic nature.

The exploration of quantum concepts provides a surprisingly insightful lens through which to view the complex dynamics of cybersecurity vulnerability. The principle of superposition, where an object exists in multiple potential states simultaneously, finds a parallel in how an employee's vulnerability is shaped by a myriad of weighted factors. Just as a quantum system collapses into a single state upon measurement, targeted awareness campaigns or security training can fundamentally alter an individual's susceptibility to cyber social engineering attacks.

Furthermore, the inherent uncertainty principle of quantum mechanics reminds us that perfectly pinpointing all vulnerability aspects might be impossible. Embracing this uncertainty is vital when crafting cybersecurity models. Fuzzy logic, with its ability to represent imprecision and graduated states, aligns well with this reality. This look into quantum inspiration highlights the need for a nuanced and dynamic approach to cybersecurity. Traditional rigid models must give way to adaptive strategies that recognize vulnerability's shifting and probabilistic nature. By mirroring the insights gleaned from quantum mechanics, we can develop more accurate and effective defense strategies to protect against the evolving threats of the digital landscape.

EXAMPLES OF APPLICATIONS OF THE FUZZY-QUANTUM APPROACH

Personalized Risk Assessment

In the realm of cybersecurity, where human behavior and technological vulnerabilities intersect, traditional models often struggle to capture the nuances of social engineering susceptibility. This is where the concept of fuzzy logic, combined with quantum-inspired principles, offers a promising avenue for developing more dynamic and adaptive risk assessment models.

Fuzzy inputs, unlike traditional binary classifications, allow for graded membership to sets. For instance, instead of simply labeling someone as "susceptible" or "not susceptible" to phishing scams, we can assign a degree of membership to the set of "individuals prone to phishing attacks." This graded membership reflects the reality that susceptibility is not an all-or-nothing phenomenon but rather a spectrum influenced by various factors.

These fuzzy inputs can encompass a wide range of variables, including workload, personality traits like impulsivity, social media activity, and even scores on phishing awareness quizzes. Each of these factors contributes to an individual's overall risk profile, with varying degrees of influence.

The quantum-inspired update mechanism further enhances this model by incorporating the concept of superposition, where an individual's risk profile exists in a state of potentiality until an interaction or observation collapses it into a more defined state. Each interaction, whether it's clicking on a suspicious link, responding to a phishing email, or even simply browsing social media, adjusts the individual's membership to various risk categories.

This dynamic updating allows for a more nuanced and responsive risk assessment model. Instead of relying on fixed thresholds, the system can issue alerts when someone falls into a high-risk combination of factors, such as a highly impulsive individual with a heavy workload who frequently clicks on unknown links. This adaptive approach enables proactive intervention and personalized guidance to mitigate the risk of social engineering attacks.

In essence, the combination of fuzzy logic and quantum-inspired principles offers a promising framework for developing more dynamic and adaptive cybersecurity models. By embracing the inherent uncertainty and fluidity of human behavior, these models can provide a more accurate and responsive assessment of social engineering susceptibility, enabling proactive interventions and personalized guidance to enhance cybersecurity awareness and resilience.

Attack Simulation

Fuzzy Attacker Logic: Models do not just pick ONE tactic but blend them based on probabilities.

Evolving Attacks: Simulating the attacker's adaptation, where a failed scam increases membership in the "target is aware" set, triggering a pivot in tactics.

Attack simulation tools are evolving to mirror cybercriminals' real-world adaptability and strategic thinking. Instead of relying on single, pre-determined tactics, simulations incorporate fuzzy attacker logic. This approach models a more realistic threat landscape by allowing attackers to blend tactics based on assigned probabilities dynamically. For example, a simulation might combine exploiting a sense of urgency, impersonating an authority figure, and leveraging social proof techniques – a multifaceted approach far more likely to succeed than a reliance on any single method. Furthermore, cutting-edge simulations are beginning to factor in target awareness. Rather than repeating failed attempts, these simulations recognize when a target resists a particular tactic. This awareness triggers a pivot, mirroring the real-world behavior of attackers who would shift their methods accordingly. This dynamic approach ensures that simulations continuously challenge an organization's defenses, offering more realistic training scenarios in an ever-evolving threat landscape.

DECEPTION DETECTION

Moving beyond the limitations of traditional binary detection systems, which rely on rigid rules and thresholds, a more nuanced approach to cybersecurity is emerging. This approach embraces the concept of fuzzy sets, recognizing that security threats often manifest as degrees of membership in various categories rather than clear-cut anomalies. For instance, instead of simply flagging an email as "phishing" or "not phishing," a fuzzy set-based system might assign degrees of membership to sets like "unusual phrasing," "abnormal account activity," and "implausible emotional tenor." This allows for a more granular and context-aware assessment of potential threats, capturing the subtle nuances that often characterize sophisticated cyberattacks.

Furthermore, the concept of quantum adaptability introduces a dynamic element to cybersecurity detection systems. By continuously updating their thresholds and parameters based on observed attacker behavior and evolving threat patterns, these systems can avoid the rigidity that often makes traditional systems vulnerable to exploitation. This adaptability ensures that the detection mechanisms remain effective even as attackers modify their tactics and techniques.

In essence, the combination of fuzzy sets and quantum adaptability creates a more robust and resilient cybersecurity framework. By embracing the inherent uncertainty and dynamism of the digital landscape, these approaches enable a more proactive and effective defense against the ever-evolving threat of cyberattacks.

CHALLENGES AND OPPORTUNITIES

Data Sensitivity: Such nuanced models need rich data which is privacy sensitive. Robust anonymization and strict ethical guidelines are a must.

Algorithmic Bias: Fuzzy sets can help prevent binary oversimplification, but choosing factors and membership functions MUST be carefully scrutinized for unconscious bias.

AI Integration: Fuzzy logic could power AI systems better at spotting subtle manipulation in language, a core CSE tool.

Explainability: While effective, explaining to users *why* their fuzzy score is concerning is crucial for trust and avoiding fatalism.

This fuzzy, quantum-inspired view shifts CSE defense from rigid rules to a dynamic, probabilistic understanding. Responsibly implemented, it holds the potential to create more adaptable and human-centric cybersecurity.

The symbolic view for the fuzzy-quantum structure represents the concept of quantum logic applied to fuzzy set theory, which is presented in Figure 25.2. It visualizes how quantum mechanics can be used to describe the uncertainty and

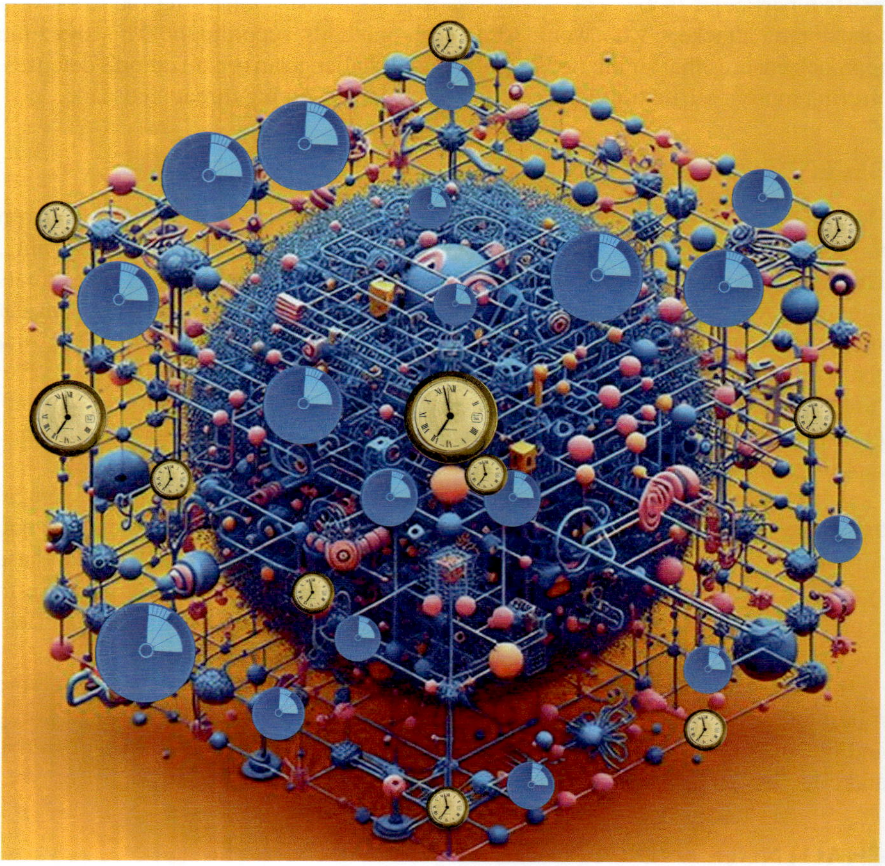

FIGURE 25.2 A symbolic view of the actual complexity of an example fuzzy-quantum structure.

imprecision inherent in fuzzy sets. The diagram typically includes elements like quantum states, operators, and measurements, each representing different aspects of the fuzzy set.

Now, let us explore how we might design a more complex fuzzy model for a different type of CSE attack: social media impersonation targeting public figures.

TWEAKED SCENARIO

A social engineer wants to create a fake social media account impersonating a celebrity or influencer. The goal is to amass followers and later leverage that audience for scams or spreading misinformation. We want to evaluate the susceptibility of specific demographics to fall for the impersonation tactic.

Susceptible to Impersonation: The overall susceptibility to believing a fake account.
Celebrity Obsession: The degree to which an individual is highly invested in the celebrity's life.
Social Proof Sensitivity: The degree to which someone is likely to trust an account due to a high follower count.
Savvy Skepticism: The degree to which a person is generally skeptical and prone to fact-checking information.

COMPLEX MEMBERSHIP FUNCTIONS (EXAMPLES)

Celebrity Obsession

0.0–0.3: Casual interest in the celebrity.
0.3–0.7: Follows fan accounts, sometimes comments on posts.
0.7–1.0: Active in fan communities, knows details about the celebrity's life.

Social Proof Sensitivity (Examples)

0.0–0.4: Follows accounts based on content, not follower count.
0.4–0.8: Likely to trust a verified account, even if new.
0.8–1.0: Very likely to follow simply due to high follower count.

Savvy Skepticism

0.0–0.3: Rarely verifies information sources. * 0.3–0.7: Sometimes fact-checks but can be swayed by emotionally resonant content. * 0.7–1.0: Highly critical, likely to check account history, tone.

CALCULATION NUANCES

Non-Linear Interactions: Someone BOTH highly obsessed with a celebrity AND skeptical might have a low overall susceptibility – their obsession makes them look for inconsistencies. Fuzzy rules can handle these non-simple relationships.
Weighting: "Savvy Skepticism" likely has a negative weight in calculating "Susceptible to Impersonation," reducing the overall score.

The previous examples highlight the complexities of calculating an individual's susceptibility score. Traditional scoring systems often rely on a simple, additive approach, failing to capture the nuances of real-world behavior. Fuzzy logic allows for more complex analysis, accounting for situations where seemingly contradictory traits might interact unpredictably. For instance, someone deeply interested in a celebrity yet inherently skeptical might be less susceptible due to their critical tendencies.

Additionally, weighting plays a crucial role. A trait like "Savvy Skepticism" likely carries a negative weight when assessing someone's risk of falling for impersonation tactics. This means it decreases the overall susceptibility score, reflecting the protective nature of this quality. By understanding these nuances, we can move beyond simplistic susceptibility models and develop more robust tools that accurately predict and mitigate an individual's risk in the ever-evolving social engineering landscape.

HOW TO PLAN FOR HELP

Targeted Awareness Campaigns: High-risk demographics are not just about age or tech skill but their psychological profiles as modeled by these memberships.

Proactive Account Detection: Fuzzy logic could aid platforms in flagging accounts with a high membership in the "Impersonation" set, even if they do not yet violate explicit rules.

A robust plan to combat scams and social engineering tactics demands a shift away from simplistic assumptions about who is vulnerable. Targeted awareness campaigns focusing solely on age or technical ability overlook a crucial component: the psychological profiles that scammers exploit. By analyzing memberships in online communities, we gain a deeper understanding of the mindsets, interests, and vulnerabilities that make individuals susceptible to certain types of manipulation. This insight allows for tailored educational efforts and preemptive support, addressing the core of susceptibility, not just its symptoms. Furthermore, waiting for scams to break explicit rules is a reactive strategy. By harnessing the power of fuzzy logic, platforms can identify accounts likely associated with the "Impersonation" set even before they engage in apparent malicious behavior. This proactive approach disrupts the scammer's ability to operate and may encourage potential victims to treat online interactions within those communities with added caution.

Ultimately, these strategies emphasize the importance of a nuanced and preventative approach to addressing scams. By understanding the psychology behind vulnerability and proactively identifying potential bad actors, we can work toward a safer digital landscape for everyone.

CHALLENGES

Data Collection: Quantifying these is harder than job titles or deadlines. Surveys, studies on online behavior, and ethical and social media analytics have become important.

Explainability: Helping non-technical people understand why an audience segment has high fuzzy scores requires careful visualization and communication.

Utilizing fuzzy logic for audience segmentation comes with its unique set of hurdles. Unlike traditional audience-building methods that rely on concrete data points like job titles or demographics, quantifying the nuanced factors underpinning fuzzy logic requires a different approach. It necessitates tapping into surveys, meticulous analysis of online behavior patterns, and the ethical application of social media analytics to gather the necessary insights.

Furthermore, ensuring the transparency of fuzzy logic-based audience segmentation is vital for its broader acceptance. The complexity of the system means that explaining why a particular audience segment has high fuzzy scores can be challenging for non-technical stakeholders. This demands thoughtful visualization strategies and clear communication to bridge that gap in understanding.

Overcoming these challenges is essential for unlocking the potential of fuzzy logic in audience segmentation. By investing in appropriate data collection methods and prioritizing clear explanations of the process, marketers can build trust around this powerful technique for understanding and reaching their target consumers.

This scenario illustrates how fuzzy sets can model the complex interplay of psychological factors in CSE. Responsibly developed, such an approach could empower platforms and public figures with tools for proactive defense.

Now, let us brainstorm potential data sources and address the ethical considerations in building the fuzzy membership functions for our social media impersonation scenario.

DATA SOURCES

Existing Research

Academic Studies: Search for papers on celebrity obsession, social proof in online environments, and psychological traits influencing susceptibility to deception. These often provide scales or questionnaires that can form the basis of membership functions.

Industry Reports: Companies specializing in social media reputation management might have data on impersonation tactics and demographics most frequently targeted.

PLATFORM-SPECIFIC DATA (WITH STRICT SAFEGUARDS)

Anonymized User Interactions: With opt-in consent, how people interact with verified vs. unverified accounts, commenting patterns on fan pages, and fact-checking behaviors provide rich data for refining membership functions.

Flagged Account Analysis: Studying why accounts were flagged as impersonations (reported inconsistencies, language quirks) helps pinpoint subtle cues the fuzzy model should consider.

While platform-specific data must always be handled with the utmost respect for user privacy, it holds valuable potential for fighting social media impersonation. By analyzing anonymized user interactions – how people engage with verified versus unverified accounts, their commenting style, and their response to fact-checking – we can distill patterns that inform fuzzy logic membership functions. This can be further refined by carefully studying accounts flagged as potential impersonations. Examining the specific inconsistencies or linguistic quirks that led to these reports helps the model identify subtle cues indicative of fraudulent activity.

However, it is essential to emphasize that this approach necessitates strict ethical safeguards. User consent for data collection must be transparent and opt-in, ensuring that individuals are fully informed about how their data will be used and have the freedom to choose whether or not to participate. Anonymization techniques should be robust to protect individual identities, preventing the data from being traced back to specific users. This not only safeguards privacy but also fosters trust, encouraging users to engage with platforms without fear of their personal information being misused.

Furthermore, it is crucial to recognize that this data analysis should never replace human judgment but rather serve as a powerful supporting tool. While AI algorithms can identify patterns and correlations that humans might miss, they lack the nuanced understanding of context, intent, and individual circumstances that human judgment provides. Therefore, the insights generated by AI should always be interpreted and applied in conjunction with human expertise, ensuring that decisions are made responsibly and ethically.

By responsibly harnessing platform-specific data, we can develop more sophisticated and proactive defenses against the growing threat of social media impersonation. This data can be used to train AI models to identify suspicious patterns of behavior, flag potentially malicious accounts, and even predict the likelihood of impersonation attempts based on user characteristics and platform activity. This proactive approach can help to mitigate the risks of impersonation, protect individuals and communities from harm, and foster a safer and more trustworthy online environment.

ETHICAL EXPERIMENTATION

Educational Simulations: Create safe, fictional impersonations and monitor how different demographics interact with them. This reveals what convinces (or does not convince) people in a controlled setting.

Surveys with Hypothetical Scenarios: While less reliable than real-world observation, surveys can probe how people say they might react, helping design initial fuzzy sets for further refinement.

The pursuit of ethical experimentation in understanding social dynamics demands a multifaceted approach. Educational simulations are invaluable, creating controlled environments where researchers can observe interactions between fictional personas and diverse demographics. By meticulously monitoring these interactions, researchers gain insights into the factors that persuade or dissuade individuals across various backgrounds.

While simulations provide a powerful lens, their artificial nature necessitates complementary methods. Surveys centered around hypothetical scenarios are valuable in probing participants' self-reported potential reactions. Though these responses should be interpreted cautiously, they provide valuable initial data points for designing fuzzy sets that require refinement through further study.

Ultimately, a holistic research strategy combining simulations, carefully designed surveys, and other ethical methods paves the way for a nuanced understanding of human behavior and complex social interactions. This knowledge can empower responsible interventions and design environments that promote positive outcomes while minimizing potential harms.

ETHICAL CONSIDERATIONS

Privacy Paramount

Aggregation is vital: No individual should be identifiable within a fuzzy set membership.

Explicit Opt-In: With easy withdrawal options, users must understand what data is used and how.

Minimized Bias

Proactive Bias Audits: Continuously check if memberships inadvertently perpetuate stereotypes (e.g., associating age alone with susceptibility).

Diverse Input: Involve experts in psychology and online social behavior in designing the data collection and model-building processes.

TRANSPARENCY AND ACCOUNTABILITY

To ensure transparency and foster trust, it's essential to provide users with a clear and accessible explanation of the factors considered by the fuzzy-based impersonation detection model. This public-facing summary should avoid technical jargon and present the information in plain language, understandable to individuals without a background in artificial intelligence or cybersecurity.

The summary could highlight the key features and data points that the model takes into account, such as the user's online behavior, their social media activity, their network connections, and any linguistic patterns or inconsistencies detected in their communications. It could also explain how the model uses fuzzy logic to handle uncertainty and ambiguity, providing a more nuanced assessment of impersonation risk.

By providing this transparent summary, users can gain a better understanding of how the model works and the factors that contribute to their impersonation risk score. This transparency can empower users to take proactive steps to protect themselves online and make informed decisions about their online behavior.

In any system that relies on automated assessments, there's always a possibility of errors or inaccuracies. To address this, it's crucial to provide users with an appeal mechanism, allowing them to question their fuzzy score if they believe it is inaccurate. This mechanism not only provides a recourse for users who feel unfairly assessed but also serves as a valuable feedback loop for improving the model's accuracy and fairness.

The appeal mechanism could involve a user-friendly interface where individuals can submit their concerns and provide additional context or information that might have been missed by the model. This feedback can then be reviewed by human experts, who can assess the validity of the appeal and make adjustments to the model as needed.

This iterative feedback process can help to refine the model's algorithms, identify potential biases, and ensure that the system remains accurate, fair, and transparent. By incorporating user feedback, the model can continuously improve its performance and provide more reliable assessments of impersonation risk.

Overall, by providing a clear public-facing summary and an effective appeal mechanism, we can foster trust, transparency, and accountability in the use of AI-powered impersonation detection systems. This not only empowers users to protect themselves online but also contributes to the development of more robust and equitable cybersecurity solutions.

PURPOSE LIMITATION

Proactive detection, in its purest form, is a noble pursuit. It's about harnessing the power of data to identify and mitigate potential harm before it occurs. This approach stands in stark contrast to the often exploitative practices of targeted advertising or the harmful consequences of publicly shaming individuals deemed vulnerable.

Proactive detection, when ethically implemented, acts as a guardian, a silent protector. It seeks to identify vulnerabilities and risks, not to exploit them, but to empower individuals and communities to safeguard themselves. This approach prioritizes the well-being of individuals and society as a whole, recognizing that true security lies in prevention rather than reaction.

Imagine a world where data are used to identify individuals at risk of falling victim to social engineering scams, not to bombard them with targeted ads but to provide them with the knowledge and tools to protect themselves. Imagine a society where data analysis helps to identify potential cyber threats, not to shame those responsible but to strengthen our collective defenses and prevent harm before it occurs.

This is the promise of proactive detection: a data-driven approach that prioritizes prevention, empowerment, and the protection of individual well-being. It's a vision of a future where technology serves as a guardian, not a weapon, and where data are used to build a safer, more resilient, and compassionate world.

ADDITIONAL BRAINSTORMING POINTS

Collaboration with Celebrities: Could those frequently impersonated ethically share insights (with fan consent) into what is convincing about fakes?

Gamifying Skepticism: Could a fun online game help people spot impersonations, generating data that subtly trains their critical thinking?

Cross-Platform Differences: Do fuzzy sets need adjustment based on whether the impersonation is on Twitter vs. Instagram?

This is complex territory. It demands that any potential benefit of the fuzzy model outweigh the potential risks. It is crucial to get continuous feedback from privacy experts and the potentially affected public throughout its development.

Design is paramount to successfully integrating social engineering awareness training into youth-oriented platforms. This goes beyond just the visual appeal of the feature – it is about creating an engaging, user-centric experience that motivates participation.

First, these training elements must be evident within the platform and featured prominently in the "Security" or "Community" sections. Occasional pop-ups for new users, framed with a positive spin – like helping a celebrity stay safe – could pique their interest. A clean, intuitive interface that aligns with the platform's visual style, while distinct enough to feel unique, will further foster engagement.

Offering quick 1–2 minute micro-challenges alongside longer sessions caters to varying attention spans and allows for on-the-go participation. A clear display of progress, including points earned and badges unlocked, taps into intrinsic motivation. Consider a badge system with creative titles like "Skeptic's Eye," "Lightning Reflexes," and "Analyst in Training," rewarding various skill aspects. An exceptional, evolving "Celebrity Guardian" badge, directly linked to the user's contributions aiding real-world threat detection, would foster a sense of purpose.

The design of UI elements and gamification strategies within a cybersecurity training platform must be carefully tailored to the specific age group and characteristics of its target audience. This customization is not merely an aesthetic consideration, but a critical factor in ensuring the training's effectiveness and its seamless integration into the digital lives of young users.

For younger audiences, UI elements should be visually engaging, intuitive, and easy to navigate. Gamification strategies should leverage elements of play, fun, and interactive challenges that resonate with their interests and learning styles. This might involve incorporating colorful graphics, cartoon characters, and interactive puzzles that transform cybersecurity lessons into an engaging and enjoyable experience.

As the target age group progresses, UI elements can evolve to incorporate more mature design aesthetics and sophisticated functionalities. Gamification strategies can shift toward more complex challenges, simulations, and competitive elements that appeal to their developing cognitive abilities and social dynamics. This might involve incorporating realistic scenarios, branching narratives, and team-based challenges that foster collaboration and problem-solving skills.

Furthermore, the platform should be adaptable across various devices and digital environments, ensuring that the training remains accessible and engaging regardless of whether users are accessing it on a desktop computer, a tablet, or a smartphone. This adaptability is crucial in meeting young users where they are, seamlessly integrating cybersecurity training into their digital lives without disrupting their preferred modes of technology consumption.

By prioritizing age-appropriate design and adaptable gamification strategies, cybersecurity training platforms can empower young users to become informed and responsible digital citizens. They can foster a sense of ownership and agency in navigating the digital world, equipping young people with the knowledge and skills to protect themselves, their identities, and their communities from cyber threats.

26 Introduction to Quantum Logic and Automata Theory in Cyber Social Engineering Systems

Traditional cybersecurity approaches, reliant on classical logic and deterministic models, often struggle to keep pace with the dynamic and deceptive nature of cyber social engineering (CSE) attacks. CSE manipulators exploit human vulnerabilities, adapting tactics and obscuring their true intentions. To counter these sophisticated attacks, a paradigm shift is needed.

With its foundation in modeling complex systems and their evolving states, automata theory offers a valuable framework for understanding CSE. We can conceptualize the interaction between attacker and target as a series of transitions, where each action and response influences the system's subsequent behavior. Furthermore, quantum logic introduces superposition and uncertainty, mirroring human decision-making's ambiguity and non-deterministic choices. By embracing these theoretical lenses, we gain new tools for modeling the multifaceted nature of CSE attacks.

This approach allows us to analyze how seemingly innocuous actions can open vulnerabilities and how attackers leverage trust, emotions, and cognitive biases to achieve their goals. Understanding CSE within these frameworks empowers us to develop more nuanced detection strategies, pre-emptive countermeasures, and targeted user education that effectively anticipates and disrupts the complex mechanisms of cyber social engineering attacks.

Figure 26.1 symbolically illustrates the evolution of automata theory, highlighting its integration with quantum logic and its potential to drive future technological breakthroughs. It begins by depicting a classical automaton, represented by gears and levers, symbolizing the mechanical marvels of early computing. This transitions into a digital automaton, visualized as a network of interconnected nodes and circuits, representing the modern era of digital computation.

The figure then introduces the concept of quantum logic, symbolized by a superposition of states and entangled particles, merging it with the digital automaton to create a hybrid model. This symbolizes the integration of quantum principles into computational systems.

The analog nature of quantum computers is represented by a wave function, highlighting the continuous and probabilistic nature of quantum phenomena. This wave function interacts with the hybrid automaton, suggesting the potential for quantum computers to enhance and transform automata-based systems.

DOI: 10.1201/9781003500698-26

FIGURE 26.1 A symbolic view of the embedded concept of digital automaton with quantum logic.

Finally, the figure points toward a future breakthrough, symbolized by a glowing orb, representing the transformative potential of this integration. This symbolizes the possibility of achieving new levels of computational power and efficiency by harnessing the unique capabilities of quantum mechanics within the framework of automata theory.

Quantum automata theory lays a robust foundation for understanding and combating cybersecurity threats. By drawing parallels between finite-state machines and the complex superposition states of quantum systems, we can create new modeling tools that reflect the dynamic and interconnected nature of cyberattacks. This allows us to break down complex attacker strategies into stages and transitions, enabling earlier detection of attack patterns and providing a more granular understanding of target vulnerabilities as circumstances evolve.

Furthermore, automata theory provides a framework to analyze sequences of actions, giving us a “language” to describe attacker behavior. We can detect known attack signatures through pattern recognition and identify novel techniques as they emerge. This ability to dissect and classify established and evolving threat patterns is crucial for proactive cyber defense in the rapidly changing threat landscape.

Both of the above concepts present limitations. Let us take a look at the enhancements that quantum logics offers:

THE QUANTUM LOGIC ENHANCEMENT

While powerful, classical automata theory has limitations in modeling the uncertainty inherent in CSE. While undeniably powerful, classical automata theory encounters limitations when attempting to fully capture the inherent complexities and uncertainties of cyber social engineering (CSE). This is where quantum logic presents a compelling alternative with its ability to model superposition, entanglement, and non-deterministic behavior. Consider the application of quantum principles to virtual automata, such as those powering interactive chat environments like VChat. By incorporating quantum-inspired models, these automata could better simulate human communication and decision-making nuances. This has the potential to create more robust training simulations and threat detection systems, helping to unmask the manipulative tactics employed in CSE attacks. Here is where quantum logic offers intriguing potential:

Superposition of States: A system or individual user, instead of being in a distinct state ("vulnerable" or "not vulnerable") could be modeled as a superposition of potential states, reflecting uncertainty and multi-faceted risk.

Entanglement of Decisions: Quantum logic can express the interconnectedness of decision-making. An attacker might adjust their strategy in real time based on their initial probes' perceived success or failure, much like entangled particles influencing each other.

Quantum Measurement as Interaction: In quantum systems, measurement affects the outcome. Similarly, interactions designed to probe a target's alertness (simulated phishing, awareness campaigns) could change the system's state.

Classical automata theory, while a robust foundation, encounters limitations when faced with the inherent uncertainty and complexity of cybersecurity environments (CSE). With its counterintuitive principles, quantum logic offers a broad lens to reimagine how we model and analyze these dynamic systems.

By introducing concepts like a superposition of states, we can shift away from viewing systems or users as occupying singular, fixed states (like "vulnerable" or "invulnerable"). Instead, a quantum-inspired approach acknowledges that risk exists in a spectrum. This uncertainty and multifaceted risk factors can be represented with greater nuance. Furthermore, quantum logic's emphasis on entanglement allows us to model how decisions intertwine. An attacker's strategy is not static but adaptive, like entangled particles influencing each other's behavior. This interconnectedness demands that we analyze the network of choices – both attacker and defender – and their potential cascading effects.

Finally, the very act of measurement within quantum systems can change the outcome. Similarly, even seemingly benign interactions in cybersecurity, such as simulated phishing attacks or awareness campaigns, can potentially alter the system's state. This challenges us to acknowledge that assessment tools can affect the very thing they aim to measure.

While still in its early stages for cybersecurity applications, quantum logic offers a thought-provoking framework to enhance our understanding of cybersecurity threats' complex and dynamic nature.

Figure 26.2 symbolically represents the integration of quantum automaton into a virtual world like VChat. It depicts a user interacting with a virtual avatar, whose underlying behavior is governed by quantum automaton. This automaton, symbolized by interconnected nodes and lines representing quantum states and transitions, enables the avatar to exhibit complex and nuanced behavior, going beyond the limitations of classical automata.

FIGURE 26.2 A symbolic view of the quantum automaton concept in applications such as VChat.

The figure draws a visual connection between the analog nature of quantum computers, represented by continuous waveforms, and the historical lineage of automata, harking back to the intricate mechanisms of clockwork marvels. This historical context emphasizes the cyclical nature of technological innovation, where old ideas inspire new breakthroughs.

Furthermore, the figure highlights the potential for quantum automata to drive a technological leap forward. By embedding these advanced automata within virtual worlds, we can create more realistic, responsive, and potentially even sentient virtual entities. This integration represents a significant step toward a future where the boundaries between the physical and virtual worlds become increasingly blurred, opening up new possibilities for communication, entertainment, and human–computer interaction.

APPLICATIONS OF THE QUANTUM-INSPIRED APPROACH

Probabilistic Threat Modeling: Quantum-inspired automata could model an attack not as a single path but as a probability distribution over potential attack trajectories, facilitating better resource allocation.

Adaptive User Awareness: Risk profiles that continually update based on interactions, shifting away from static "vulnerability" scores and toward a dynamic understanding of evolving susceptibility.

Simulation and Deception: Designing counter-deception tactics mirroring the probabilistic nature of attacker behavior, becoming less predictable to the attacker.

The application of quantum-inspired approaches holds the key to reimagining traditional cybersecurity practices. Probabilistic threat modeling moves beyond deterministic attack paths, embracing the fluid nature of threats. Instead of viewing an attack as a linear sequence, quantum-inspired automata could model it as a probability distribution across multiple trajectories. This allows for more strategic resource allocation, focusing defense efforts where needed.

Furthermore, a quantum-inspired approach allows us to break free from the rigid "vulnerability score" mentality in user awareness training. We establish a dynamic understanding of susceptibility by creating user risk profiles that continuously adapt based on user interactions. This empowers adaptive training measures that respond to behavioral patterns rather than static metrics.

Perhaps most intriguingly, this approach opens the door to novel counter-deception tactics. By mirroring the probabilistic nature of the attacker's decision-making, we can devise defensive strategies that are less predictable, introducing uncertainty into the equation for the attackers themselves. This upends the traditional dynamic where defenders constantly react to the attacker's actions.

While these applications remain largely theoretical, they point toward a future where cybersecurity adopts the principles of uncertainty and superposition that underpin quantum mechanics. This promises a shift toward a more adaptive, proactive, and fundamentally less predictable security posture.

CHALLENGES AND FUTURE DIRECTIONS

Applying quantum logic in cybersecurity, particularly in countering social engineering, raises significant challenges alongside its great potential. Addressing these challenges will be crucial to ensure this approach's ethical and effective implementation.

First, the nature of modeling human behavior at this level of granularity demands access to sensitive data. Rigorous anonymization, strict privacy safeguards, and ongoing ethical oversight of data collection and usage will be paramount.

Second, while quantum logic offers a promising new conceptual framework, translating these principles into robust mathematical models applicable to cybersecurity is a significant research task. This will require collaboration between experts in quantum physics, computer science, and the study of social engineering tactics.

Finally, in practical application, these probabilistic models and the insights derived from quantum logic would likely operate within complex AI systems designed for threat detection. It is crucial to ensure transparency, accountability, and the ability to identify and mitigate potential biases within such systems.

Despite these challenges, the potential of this research avenue remains undeniable. By carefully navigating these hurdles, we can pave the way for a new generation of cyber defense strategies better equipped to counter the rapidly evolving tactics of social engineering.

The above introduction highlights the potential for quantum-inspired reasoning to enrich our understanding and defense against the increasingly sophisticated landscape of cyber social engineering attacks.

Now let us look into the potential applications of a quantum-inspired approach to automata theory for cyber social engineering (CSE), focusing on adaptive user awareness, and illuminate the core challenges involved:

ADAPTIVE USER AWARENESS: A QUANTUM-INSPIRED APPROACH

Traditional user awareness training often employs static risk profiles, classifying users as "high" or "low" risk. This approach, unfortunately, proves rigid and exploitable in the face of ever-evolving social engineering tactics. A quantum-inspired model offers a more dynamic solution. Instead of viewing a user's susceptibility as fixed, we can imagine it as a superposition of potential risk states, constantly fluctuating based on various factors.

Recent workload, news consumption, and even past responses to simulated training all influence this probability. This approach necessitates dynamic interventions, where not just the presence of a warning but the type of intervention itself adapts to the user's state. For example, periods of high-stress call for brief micro-training targeting specific vulnerabilities likely to be targeted, while a heightened vigilance state might lead to stricter email warnings, gradually relaxing over time.

Naturally, this model presents challenges. Developing systems sensitive to these subtle behavioral shifts is no small feat. Additionally, ethical considerations around data collection and the potential impact on user trust are crucial to address.

Nonetheless, the quantum-inspired approach to adaptive user awareness holds promise. By embracing the fluidity of human behavior and tailoring responses accordingly, we can move beyond the limitations of static profiling. This could lead to more effective training that anticipates the nature of social engineering threats – creating a safer digital environment for everyone.

DATA: THE ETHICAL QUESTION

What data are collected to create these dynamic models? Overly intrusive monitoring creates a privacy nightmare.

Potential Solutions

- Focus on aggregate, anonymized trends, not individual tracking.
- Transparent opt-ins with granular control over data used.
- On-device models where data never leave the user's control.

Algorithmic Bias

Even with good intentions, how risk factors are chosen and weighted can perpetuate stereotypes (e.g., unintentionally labeling those stressed as always vulnerable).

Mitigation

- A diverse team, including behavioral scientists, created the model.
- Regular bias audits and mechanisms for users to request a score review.

THE ILLUSION OF CONTROL

The concept of a quantum-inspired dynamic risk score holds promise, but it is crucial to recognize its limitations and potential pitfalls. No matter how sophisticated, overreliance on any system breeds a dangerous illusion of control and fosters complacency. Humans must maintain critical thinking skills and actively engage in vigilance; a score alone cannot shield them from harm. Training must emphasize the fluidity of this system, underscoring that true security lies in proactive awareness, not passive reliance on a numerical indicator.

Furthermore, translating concepts like superposition and adaptive updating into concrete, secure algorithms is a complex undertaking. Effective implementation demands collaboration between computer scientists with expertise in quantum-inspired algorithms and cybersecurity professionals who understand the real-world dynamics of threats.

A significant challenge lies in balancing explainability with effectiveness. The more complex a model becomes, the harder it is for users to understand the factors driving their risk score fluctuations. This lack of transparency erodes trust in the system's accuracy. Possible solutions include clear visualizations highlighting the most significant factors influencing a user's score without compromising the overall model's integrity. Additionally, shifting the focus from a mere score to empowering action is crucial. Providing guidance based on current risk factors (e.g., "Right now, you seem more likely to miss typos, so double-check URLs before clicking") helps users make informed choices without feeling solely reliant on a number.

Ultimately, a quantum-inspired risk score system has potential but cannot replace the human element of cyber defense. By acknowledging its limitations, actively encouraging critical engagement, and focusing on actionable information, it can become a valuable tool within a broader cybersecurity strategy.

This adaptive approach shifts user awareness from a one-time event to an ongoing, personalized dialogue with the security system. Ethical implementation and continuous refinement will be paramount for its success.

EXPLORATION CHOICE

Maintaining transparency in our adaptive awareness concept, while simultaneously protecting its core logic, requires a delicate balancing act. We must provide users with enough information to understand how the system works and build trust in its capabilities, without revealing the intricate details that could be exploited by malicious actors. This necessitates a multi-layered approach to transparency, where we provide clear explanations of the system's goals, functionalities, and decision-making processes while safeguarding the sensitive algorithms and data that underpin its operation.

One strategy is to employ user-friendly visualizations and explanations that illustrate the system's adaptive behavior without divulging the underlying code or mathematical models. This could involve interactive dashboards that display real-time risk assessments, personalized feedback mechanisms that explain the rationale behind security recommendations, and educational resources that empower users to understand the principles of adaptive security.

Another approach is to foster open communication and collaboration with the cybersecurity community, sharing high-level insights into the system's architecture and design principles while maintaining confidentiality around sensitive algorithms and data. This could involve publishing white papers, participating in industry conferences, and engaging in open-source initiatives that promote transparency and collaboration without compromising the system's security.

Achieving this balance between transparency and security demands interdisciplinary collaboration, bringing together experts from fields such as cybersecurity, human–computer interaction, psychology, and law. Cybersecurity experts can provide insights into potential vulnerabilities and attack vectors, while human–computer interaction specialists can design user interfaces that promote transparency and trust. Psychologists can contribute to understanding user perceptions and behaviors, while legal experts can ensure compliance with privacy regulations and intellectual property rights.

By fostering a culture of transparency, collaboration, and continuous improvement, we can ensure that our adaptive awareness concept remains both secure and trustworthy, empowering users to make informed decisions about their cybersecurity while safeguarding the integrity of the system itself.

BALANCING TRANSPARENCY WITH PROTECTION OF SYSTEM LOGIC

The challenge of balancing transparency with protecting a system's core logic is a constant negotiation in designing security systems like risk assessment tools. A tiered explanation model offers a promising solution. It gives users insights into their assessed risk levels while safeguarding the exact calculation mechanisms. Each tier caters to different needs: the first level delivers actionable warnings, the second offers optional context for the curious, and the most complex level is reserved for developers and security professionals.

To further cultivate trust, gamified simulations tailored to the user's modeled state introduce an element of learning without exposing the system's inner workings. Success in spotting these simulations builds confidence, while adversarial testing adds another layer of resilience. Ethical hackers deliberately probing for weaknesses can reveal blind spots, indirectly educating users about potential vulnerabilities.

This approach recognizes that transparency is not a one-size-fits-all concept. It tailors the degree of explanation to individual needs and roles while actively working to build user trust through interactive experiences. Ultimately, a combination of tiered explanations, gamification, and rigorous testing promotes confidence in the system while protecting its integrity – a crucial balance for any security tool within a dynamic threat landscape.

Let us take a deeper look into the above explanation: Extreme Scenario

Scenario: A user who has just completed a particularly demanding work project feels stressed. On the same day, she sees several news articles about a major financial data breach. Our adaptive user awareness system identifies elevated susceptibility to social engineering attacks.

This is an example of a Level 2 explanation that balances transparency with protecting the core logic.

SUBJECT: YOUR SECURITY AWARENESS STATUS

Your recent activity indicates a potential increase in your susceptibility to phishing or social engineering scams.

Following is a breakdown of some contributing factors:

Workload: Your recent work activity suggests a period of high stress, which can make people more likely to overlook red flags in emails or messages.

External Factors: There has been an increase in news coverage of data breaches lately. This can heighten anxiety and make people more susceptible to tactics that play on fear or urgency.

HERE IS WHAT A PERSON CAN DO TO STAY SAFE

Double-Check Everything: Be extra cautious with emails or messages, especially those requesting financial information or urgent action.

Slow Down, Do Not Panic: If an email creates a sense of urgency or fear, it is a red flag. Take a deep breath and verify the sender and any links before responding.

We Are Here to Help: If you are unsure about an email or message, please forward it to our security team for verification ([email address removed]).

Key Points

Non-Judgmental Language: Avoids blaming Sarah for being stressed or worried.

Focus on Specific Factors: Highlights the potential impact of workload and news.

Actionable Advice: Provide clear steps Sarah can take to protect herself.

Offers Additional Resources: Empower Sarah to learn more if she chooses.

LET'S EXPLORE SOME EXTREME SCENARIOS

While this scenario is extreme, it showcases how the system might identify factors that could heighten someone's susceptibility. By including extreme scenarios in user education materials (with appropriate privacy safeguards), you can prime users to be more vigilant in a broader range of situations.

Important Note: The scenarios presented in this context are deliberately heightened for illustrative purposes, serving to underscore the potential risks and vulnerabilities associated with emerging technologies and social engineering tactics. It is crucial to emphasize that real-world implementations of these scenarios must be approached with nuance, sensitivity, and a deep understanding of their potential impact on individuals and communities.

The scenarios, while fictionalized, are rooted in real-world concerns about cybersecurity, privacy, and the ethical implications of technological advancements. However, if presented without appropriate context and careful consideration, they could be misinterpreted or cause undue anxiety. It is essential to ensure that these scenarios are used responsibly and ethically, promoting awareness and preparedness without fostering fear or mistrust.

In real-world settings, the implementation of these scenarios should be tailored to the specific audience and context. Educational initiatives, for example, could use these scenarios to illustrate cybersecurity risks and promote responsible online behavior. Training programs for professionals in critical sectors, such as healthcare or finance, could leverage these scenarios to enhance preparedness and response capabilities in the face of cyber threats.

However, it is crucial to avoid sensationalizing or exaggerating the risks, as this could lead to unnecessary alarm and erode trust in technology. The focus should be on empowering individuals and communities with the knowledge and tools to navigate the digital landscape safely and confidently, fostering a culture of cybersecurity awareness and responsible technology use.

FINANCIAL DISTRESS + TARGETED SCAM

It's understandable that Mark is feeling stressed and overwhelmed right now. Missing bill payments and receiving debt collection notices can be incredibly daunting, and it's easy to fall prey to scams that promise quick fixes or easy solutions. However, it's crucial to remember that these offers are often too good to be true and can lead to further financial hardship.

Instead of resorting to desperate measures, seeking help through official channels is the safest and most reliable path toward resolving financial difficulties. There are numerous reputable organizations and resources available that can provide guidance and support, such as credit counseling agencies, debt management programs, and government assistance programs. These resources can help Mark develop a realistic budget, negotiate with creditors, and explore options for debt consolidation or repayment plans.

It's also essential to be aware of the red flags of scams that target individuals in financial distress. These scams often promise to erase debt quickly, offer unrealistic interest rates or fees, or pressure individuals into making hasty decisions. Be wary of unsolicited offers, high-pressure sales tactics, and requests for upfront payments or personal financial information.

Remember, Mark is not alone in this situation. Many people experience financial hardship at some point in their lives. By seeking help from reputable sources, developing a sound financial plan, and staying vigilant against scams, Mark can regain control of his finances and pave the way toward a more secure future.

PERSONAL CRISIS + EMOTIONAL MANIPULATION

In the midst of a tumultuous divorce, Emily's emotional state is understandably fragile. The stress, anxiety, and uncertainty of this life transition can leave her vulnerable to manipulation and exploitation, particularly in the online realm. Attackers often prey on individuals in heightened emotional states, recognizing that their judgment may be clouded and their defenses lowered.

Emily may be particularly susceptible to social engineering tactics that exploit her emotional vulnerability. Fake messages from "concerned friends" offering support or sympathy could be used to gain her trust and extract personal information. Similarly, authority figure impersonations, such as someone posing as a lawyer or government official, could manipulate her into divulging sensitive data or complying with fraudulent requests.

It is crucial to acknowledge the difficulty of Emily's situation while also empowering her to protect herself from online threats. A compassionate yet direct approach is necessary, emphasizing the importance of exercising caution when interacting with unknown individuals online or responding to urgent requests that exploit her emotional vulnerability.

Reminding Emily of the prevalence of online deception and the tactics employed by malicious actors can help her develop a more critical mindset. Encouraging her to verify the identity of individuals she interacts with online, to be wary of unsolicited offers of help, and to resist the urge to make hasty decisions under pressure can significantly reduce her risk of falling victim to social engineering attacks.

Furthermore, emphasizing the importance of seeking support from trusted friends, family members, or professionals can help Emily navigate this challenging period while maintaining her emotional well-being and online safety. By fostering a sense of awareness and providing practical guidance, we can empower Emily to protect herself from the manipulative tactics of online predators and navigate the digital landscape with greater confidence and resilience.

SIGNIFICANT LIFE CHANGE + FAKE AUTHORITY FIGURES

John's situation is a common one, and his feelings of isolation are completely understandable. Moving to a new city can be an overwhelming experience, filled with unfamiliar surroundings, the absence of established social connections, and the daunting task of building a new life from scratch. It's during these times of vulnerability that individuals can become prime targets for social engineering attacks.

Scammers often prey on people who are feeling isolated or overwhelmed, exploiting their desire for connection and assistance. In John's case, this could manifest in various forms, such as fake landlord communications, utility impersonations, or fraudulent "welcome to the neighborhood" schemes. These scams often involve creating a sense of urgency or offering seemingly helpful solutions to problems that new residents commonly face.

It's crucial for John to understand that while his feelings of isolation are legitimate, it's important to exercise caution and skepticism when interacting with strangers, especially online or over the phone. He should be wary of unsolicited offers of assistance, requests for personal information, or any communication that creates a sense of urgency or pressure to act quickly.

To help John navigate this challenging period and avoid falling victim to scams, it's important to provide him with verified resources and support networks. This could include links to the city's official website, where he can find reliable information about housing, utilities, and other essential services. Connecting him with local community groups or online forums for new residents can also help him build social connections and access trustworthy information.

By acknowledging the legitimacy of John's feelings of isolation while also highlighting the risks of social engineering, we can empower him to make informed choices and protect himself from scams. Providing him with verified resources and support networks can further enhance his resilience and help him navigate the challenges of settling into a new city safely and confidently.

EDUCATIONAL VALUE OF EXTREMES

Normalizes Help-Seeking: By coupling extreme scenarios with clear paths to support (security team, official resources), it destigmatizes falling victim to scams.

Pattern Recognition: Extremes showcase how attackers tailor tactics to specific vulnerabilities. This trains users to spot subtler variations.

Proactive Awareness: Users primed with these scenarios may be more likely to think, "Could this be a scam?" in less obvious, real-life situations.

CAVEATS

Privacy: If used in training, scenarios must be anonymized or fictionalized.

Tone: The goal is awareness, not inducing fear in users.

Opt-in: This level of detail is best used as optional supplementary material.

Now, let us brainstorm and list resource items associated with these extreme scenarios in order to make them both informative and empowering for users:

SCENARIO 1: FINANCIAL DISTRESS + TARGETED SCAM

National Debt Helpline: Provide links to organizations offering free or low-cost financial counseling and debt management advice.

Government Agencies: Include official websites and hotlines for agencies like the Federal Trade Commission (FTC) or Consumer Financial Protection Bureau (CFPB) where users can report scams, access educational resources on debt relief, and avoid scams.

Local Resources: Highlight any non-profit organizations offering financial assistance programs or workshops on budgeting and responsible spending.

SCENARIO 2: PERSONAL CRISIS + EMOTIONAL MANIPULATION

Mental Health Hotlines: When facing emotional distress or manipulation, remember that seeking help is a sign of strength, not weakness. Reach out to trusted mental health support lines like the Crisis Text Line or the National Suicide Prevention Lifeline. These resources offer confidential support and guidance from trained professionals who can help you navigate challenging emotions and develop coping strategies.

Online Safety Resources: The internet can be a breeding ground for emotional manipulation and cyberbullying. Familiarize yourself with the websites of organizations specializing in online safety and harassment, such as the National Cyber Security Centre or the Cyberbullying Research Center. These resources offer valuable guidance on recognizing emotional manipulation tactics, disengaging from toxic online interactions safely, and protecting your emotional well-being in the digital world.

Trusted Network: Before responding to any online communication that triggers strong emotional responses or seems manipulative, reach out to a dependable friend, family member, or mentor. Talking through your concerns with someone you trust can provide valuable perspective, help you identify potential red flags, and empower you to make informed decisions about how to proceed. Remember, you are not alone, and seeking support from your trusted network can make a significant difference in navigating challenging online interactions.

SCENARIO 3: MAJOR LIFE CHANGE + FAKE AUTHORITY FIGURES

Navigating a new city can be overwhelming, but there are valuable resources available to help you settle in and avoid common pitfalls. Start with the official city or state website; these often have dedicated sections for new residents. You can find information on setting up utilities, understanding local regulations, and even tips on avoiding moving scams. For example, the City of Austin's website has a comprehensive "New Resident Guide" with information on everything from registering your vehicle to finding a doctor.

Next, tap into the power of local knowledge by joining vetted online neighborhood groups or forums. These groups can be goldmines of information, offering insights and recommendations from established residents. You can ask questions about anything from the best local restaurants to finding reliable childcare. Be sure to look for groups that are moderated and have a positive, welcoming atmosphere.

Finally, remember the adage: "If it sounds too good to be true, it probably is." When evaluating offers for moving services, rental properties, or other assistance, be wary of deals that seem unusually generous or helpful. Some common red flags include requests for large upfront payments, high-pressure sales tactics, and a lack of clear documentation or contracts. You can find helpful checklists online that outline common red flags and provide tips on spotting scams. For instance, the FTC website offers a "Moving Guide" with a section on avoiding moving fraud.

ADDITIONAL CONSIDERATIONS

Tailoring resources to your user base is paramount in ensuring they are effective and accessible. Consider the demographics of your audience, including their age, location, and the everyday stressors they face. Younger users might benefit from interactive online modules or social media campaigns, while older generations might prefer printed guides or workshops held in accessible community centers. Similarly, tailor the content to address the specific challenges and stressors relevant to your audience's location and circumstances.

Accessibility is crucial in ensuring that everyone can benefit from these resources. Offer hotlines with both voice and text options to cater to different communication preferences and needs. If your user base is diverse, include links with multilingual support to ensure inclusivity and break down language barriers.

The digital landscape is constantly evolving, and resources can quickly become outdated. Routinely review the resources provided, ensuring that links are active, the information is current, and the organizations you recommend remain reputable. This ongoing maintenance ensures that your users can always access reliable and up-to-date support.

The key to effective support lies in providing a safety net that not only alerts users to heightened risk but also offers reliable paths for practical assistance. By tailoring resources to your audience, ensuring accessibility, and maintaining up-to-date information, you empower individuals to take proactive steps toward their well-being and navigate challenging situations with confidence.

27 Introduction to Quantum Parallelism and Classical Computation in Cyber Social Engineering Systems

Traditional social engineering hinges on understanding human reasoning. Attackers craft narratives that appeal to urgency and logical fallacies tailored to bypass our defenses. Cryptic puzzles further illuminate this strategy, their solutions requiring a combination of logic, creative thinking, and pattern recognition. However, these techniques assume a relatively well-defined "solution space," the range of possibilities within the answer. The world of quantum mechanics introduces a radically different lens. Here, systems can exist in a superposition state, simultaneously holding multiple potential values. This challenges the binary logic (true/false) that underpins traditional social engineering. Imagine an attacker's strategy existing not as a single path but as a probability distribution across multiple possibilities, adapting in real time based on the target's reactions.

The intersection of logic, puzzles, and quantum mechanics offers a glimpse into a future where social engineering systems react, anticipate, and adapt. However, navigating this new frontier will require collaboration between mathematicians, cybersecurity experts, psychologists, and ethicists. Only then can we harness the power of quantum-inspired logic to create a more secure and resilient online environment. To understand how quantum logic could revolutionize probabilistic attack modeling in social engineering defense with the potential assistance of quantum computers.

Figure 27.1 likely provides crucial visual context and highlights the core concept of quantum parallelism and its relevance to social cyber engineering. Quantum systems, with their ability to exist in multiple states simultaneously (superposition), offer the potential to evaluate numerous scenarios or potential social engineering attack vectors concurrently. This could significantly enhance the speed and efficiency of threat detection and pattern analysis within social media environments. By incorporating quantum-inspired methods into automata models, we may create systems that better anticipate and counter the dynamic, multi-pronged tactics used in social cyber engineering attacks.

DOI: 10.1201/9781003500698-27

FIGURE 27.1 A symbolic view of quantum parallelism and classical computation in cyber social engineering.

CURRENT LIMITATIONS OF ATTACK MODELING

Traditional models often depict attacks as linear sequences or decision trees. While useful, they have limitations:

- **Rigidity:** These models struggle with attackers who adapt real-time tactics based on target responses.
- **Incomplete Data:** They rely on past data, which may not reflect a highly skilled attacker's novel strategy.
- **Binary Outcomes:** Focus is often on singular "success" or "failure," less on modeling how an attack might partially succeed, causing different levels of harm.

While valuable, traditional models used to analyze attack patterns often portray attacks as linear sequences or decision trees. Despite its utility, this approach has limitations that can hinder our understanding of the dynamic nature of cyberattacks. Their rigidity makes it difficult to model the adaptability of attackers, who may rapidly alter tactics in response to a target's defenses. Furthermore, relying solely on historical data risks overlooking innovative strategies employed by skilled adversaries. Additionally, the focus on binary outcomes of either "success" or "failure" obscures the nuanced reality of cyberattacks, where even partial success can cause varying degrees of harm.

Acknowledging these limitations paves the way toward more robust and predictive modeling for cybersecurity. By embracing the idea that attacks are fluid and responsive, we can develop frameworks that better reflect the decision-making processes of attackers and their ability to adjust tactics on the fly. Understanding that past attacks may not perfectly mirror future threats highlights the need for continuous threat analysis and real-time data integration when possible. Looking beyond simple "success" or "failure" lets us consider the spectrum of potential outcomes, leading to more informed risk mitigation strategies and responses.

THE QUANTUM-INSPIRED PROBABILISTIC SHIFT OF ATTACK MODELING

Superposition of Attack Paths: Instead of a single path, a quantum-inspired model could represent an attack as a superposition of potential trajectories, each with an associated probability. Factors like the target's personality, knowledge level, and recent stressors would influence these probabilities.

Dynamic Probabilities: The model does not just provide a snapshot. Probabilities would update based on the target's interactions. Did they click a suspicious link? This increases the probability of paths leading to data compromise. Did they pause to question a sender? Paths favoring trust-building tactics might gain a higher probability.

Non-Binary Outcomes: Success will not be a single point. The model could reveal that even partial success (e.g., revealing personal but not financial data) has a significant probability. This empowers nuanced mitigation.

POTENTIAL ROLE OF QUANTUM COMPUTERS FOR ATTACK MODELING

The Potential Role of Quantum Computers for Attack Modeling reflects the transformative impact of quantum technology in enhancing cybersecurity by providing true randomness through QRNGs to mimic real-world attacker adaptability, leveraging optimization algorithms to identify critical vulnerabilities, and enabling complex simulations of social engineering scenarios to uncover systemic weaknesses, ultimately improving defensive strategies. By harnessing these quantum capabilities, cybersecurity models can become more sophisticated, mirroring the evolving tactics of adversaries and facilitating proactive measures.

True Randomness: Quantum random number generators (QRNGs) could enhance the model's unpredictability, mirroring the adaptability of real-world attackers – especially those leveraging AI.

Optimization: Quantum algorithms may help find attack paths with the highest likelihood of success from the attacker's perspective, aiding defenders in prioritizing vulnerabilities.

Complex Simulations: Large-scale social engineering scenarios involving multiple targets and interconnected decisions could be simulated more efficiently, revealing systemic weaknesses.

The prospect of harnessing quantum computers for attack modeling holds intriguing and transformative potential. True randomness, provided by quantum random number generators (QRNGs), could inject a greater sense of unpredictability within models, replicating the adaptability of real-world attackers – especially those leveraging advanced AI tactics. Furthermore, quantum algorithms might excel at finding the optimal attack paths from an adversary's standpoint, guiding defenders toward proactive mitigation of the most critical vulnerabilities.

The ability to simulate complex social engineering scenarios involving multiple targets and interconnected decisions offers yet another intriguing possibility. Quantum computing's power could enable greater computational efficiency in such simulations, revealing systemic weaknesses that are otherwise challenging to detect.

While these applications remain largely theoretical, they point toward a future where quantum computers could play a pivotal role in cybersecurity. By proactively modeling attacker behavior more dynamically and realistically, we equip ourselves to predict better, prepare for, and ultimately thwart the diverse onslaught of cyber threats in an ever-evolving landscape.

CHALLENGES AND CONSIDERATIONS

Computational Power: Today's quantum computers are still limited. Current applications likely focus on simpler models or specific stages of an attack.

Data Demands: Such probabilistic models crave rich data on human behavior under various adversarial conditions. Ethical collection and anonymization are paramount.

Explainability: Complex models may provide accurate threat assessments, but explaining their reasoning to non-technical stakeholders is crucial for adoption.

The potential of AI-driven threat assessment in cybersecurity rests on overcoming several significant hurdles. Current limitations in quantum computing power restrict the complexity of models and the types of attacks that can be fully simulated. Moreover, training robust probabilistic models requires vast datasets of human behavioral responses under various adversarial scenarios. Collecting and using such data demands rigorous ethical protocols and anonymization techniques to protect individual privacy. Finally, as models become more complex, their decision-making processes may become opaque. To build trust and foster the adoption of these AI tools, it is imperative to develop methods for explaining their reasoning in clear and accessible terms for non-technical stakeholders. Addressing these challenges is essential for realizing the full potential of AI-powered threat assessment and ushering in a new era of proactive cybersecurity.

THE PROMISE OF A MORE FLUID DEFENSE

A quantum parallelism-inspired approach moves attack modeling from fixed flowcharts to dynamic, probabilistic threat landscapes. This shift enables:

Proactive Resource Allocation: Focus defenses where attacks have the highest probability of success, not just where they have happened before.

Adaptive Interventions: Tailor awareness campaigns and real-time system warnings to those at dynamically elevated risk based on attack probabilities.

Ethical Advantages: Modeling attacker behavior probabilistically may reduce the need for overly intrusive user-behavior monitoring that characterizes some current systems.

Incorporating quantum-inspired approaches can revolutionize how we model and combat cyberattacks. We embrace dynamic, probabilistic threat landscapes by shifting away from rigid attack flowcharts. This shift yields several key advantages. First, it allows for proactive resource allocation. By focusing defenses on areas with the highest calculated probability of attack success, we move away from merely reacting to past incidents. Second, this approach enables adaptive interventions, tailoring awareness campaigns and real-time system warnings to address risk profile changes.

Finally, perhaps surprisingly, modeling attacker behavior probabilistically holds significant ethical implications. It could mitigate the need for overly intrusive user-behavior monitoring that often characterizes current cybersecurity systems. This quantum-inspired evolution of attack modeling signals a future of more fluid, proactive, and ethically responsible cybersecurity practices.

To better understand, let us design a simplified quantum-inspired model for a targeted phishing attack, demonstrating the superposition of attack paths and dynamic probabilities.

Scenario: An attacker wants to infiltrate a company by impersonating a trusted supplier to access an employee's credentials.

SIMPLIFIED MODEL

Attacker's Possible Actions (Superposition)

Action A: Generic phishing email, relying on volume, not customization.

Action B: Spear-phishing: Email tailored with the employee's name and basic job details.

Action C: Highly targeted: Email leverages recent company news/projects in which the employee is likely involved.

Initial Probabilities

Action A: 30% (Low effort, low yield)

Action B: 50% (Moderate effort, moderate success potential)

Action C: 20% (Requires more recon, but higher success potential)

Employee Factors (Influencing Probabilities):

Security Training: Recent = lowers all probabilities.

Workload: High = increases probabilities, especially for Action A (less scrutiny).

Public Social Media Posts: If they reveal project details, it significantly increases Action C's probability.

"Measurement" (Interactions)

No Response: Slightly lowers Action A's probability favors Actions B and C as the attacker assumes a real account.

Opens Email: Raises all probabilities, but more for Actions B and C.

Clicks Link: Drastically increases Action C's probability, as targeted tactics seem to work.

How the Model Would Function

Initial State: Probabilities are a starting point, adjusted by the limited data available upfront.

Dynamic Updates: Each employee interaction updates the superposition, shifting probabilities in real-time.

The Outcome Is Not Binary: Even if the attack fails, the model might reveal a 40% probability of Action C working on someone else, highlighting the need for targeted awareness training.

Simplifications

Limited Actions: Real attacks have far more branching paths.

Probability Calculation: We are not defining the exact math; quantum-inspired AI would handle the complexity.

Data: Real models need rich data to assign meaningful initial values and how they update.

Why Quantum Parallelism Inspired

Mimics Attacker Thinking: Attackers constantly assess and adapt. Probabilities, not rigid flowcharts, map to their strategy.

Adaptability: A new employee with no security training dramatically changes the superposition. The model reflects this. To expand our simplified model by adding a new attacker action that demonstrates how the probabilistic approach accommodates real-time adjustments in strategy.

SCENARIO ENHANCEMENT

The attacker incorporates a follow-up action to increase their chances of success:

Action D: "Soft Reminder" Follow-Up: If the phishing email is opened but no link is clicked within a specific timeframe, the attacker sends a seemingly innocuous follow-up email impersonating the supplier. This leverages the "mere exposure" effect, where repeated exposure increases perceived legitimacy.

HOW THIS CHANGES THE MODEL

New Probability

Action D has an initial low probability (e.g., 10%). The attacker must invest more time and risk, as multiple emails raise suspicion.

Dynamic Update: Key Factors

Time Elapsed: The longer the target delays response after opening the initial email, the higher the probability of Action D. This reflects attacker impatience.

Engagement Level: Did the target reply to the initial email, asking a non-committal question? This temporarily LOWERS the probability of Action D, as the attacker senses a potential victim on the hook.

Shifting Superposition

If Action D is taken, probabilities for other actions are readjusted. Success with the soft reminder might favor continuing with low-pressure trust-building tactics. Failure may lead to a pivot toward more urgent messaging in a renewed attempt.

Why This Matters

Realistic Adaptability: This mirrors how real attackers gauge a target's interest level, constantly refining their approach based on available data (or lack thereof).

Proactive Defense: The model can alert security teams if there is a rising probability of follow-up tactics being deployed. This empowers targeted interventions just as the risk escalates.

Important Note: Even our "simple" model is getting complex! This highlights the need for powerful computational tools to handle nuanced probability calculations, potentially where quantum algorithms could excel.

Key Challenges

The key challenges encapsulates the critical issues of data overload and time sensitivity, highlighting how the model's vast data generation can overwhelm security teams and lead to analysis paralysis, while simultaneously emphasizing the necessity for timely, actionable alerts that prioritize immediate threats over retrospective insights. This duality underscores the need for effective data management strategies that balance real-time responsiveness with the risk of information saturation.

Data Overload: The model's beauty is also its danger – it generates a lot of dynamic probabilities. Dumping these raw data on security teams leads to analysis paralysis.

Time Sensitivity: The model's value lies in real-time updates. Teams need timely and actionable alerts, not just retrospective analyses.

Technical Jargon: Many security professionals are not quantum computation experts. Explaining "shifting superpositions" does not help make real-world decisions.

Principles for Alert Design

The principles for alert design underscores the importance of creating alerts that prioritize critical risks and actionable responses while ensuring clarity for users; by intelligently filtering alerts to highlight the most pressing threats, suggesting specific proactive measures, and using clear language to convey risk levels and attacker intent, the system becomes a more effective tool in mitigating potential security breaches.

Prioritization Is Key: The system needs to intelligently filter what becomes an alert, highlighting the attacker's most critical risks and likely next moves.

Action-Oriented: Alerts should not just state a problem but also suggest proactive measures (targeted user warnings, heightened scrutiny of certain accounts).

Human-Readable: Clear language that translates probabilities into risk levels and likely attacker intent.

ALERT FORMATS

The alert formats encapsulates the need for tailored notifications that enhance decision-making by clearly conveying risk levels and contextual information, such as user activity and emerging threat patterns. By leveraging customizable thresholds and intuitive visualizations, these alerts empower teams to respond effectively based on their specific risk profiles and operational demands.

Individual User Risk Dashboard: Focused on those with rapidly escalating probabilities. Provides contextual cues (recent training, workload levels) to aid human judgment.

Pattern Detection: If the model spots a rise in similar attacks (e.g., targeting those who just completed a project), a more comprehensive alert is issued, enabling preemptive action.

Customizable Thresholds: Teams should be able to set when they are alerted based on their risk tolerance. A small company might need an alert sooner than a large enterprise.

Visualizations over Text: Graphs showing probability shifts over time can be more quickly grasped than numerical tables. Color coding could add urgency.

EXAMPLE ALERTS

"User Sarah L. – Phishing Attack Probability Escalated (75%). There is a recent spike in workload and engagement with the initial email. Action D (follow-up email) probability rising. Recommend: Preemptive security reminder tailored to current projects."

"Trend Alert: Increase in attacks leveraging recent company news. Effectiveness will likely be boosted for employees with public-facing social media profiles. Recommend: Update-awareness campaign, temporary heightened monitoring of external emails mentioning [company news topic]."

ITERATION IS VITAL

These alerts are a starting point! Here is how to refine them:

Team Feedback: Run simulations and get feedback on alert clarity and usability. Security teams are the end-users.

Ethical Considerations: Ensure alerts do not foster a "blame the user" mentality or encourage overly intrusive monitoring.

To understand the ethical debate surrounding the potential sharing of probabilistic risk analysis results with employees identified as high-risk targets within our quantum-inspired social engineering defense model.

ARGUMENTS FOR SHARING ANALYSIS

Empowerment and Education: Transparency builds trust. It turns the user into an active participant in defense, potentially increasing their vigilance and sense of agency.

Targeted Training: Instead of generic awareness campaigns, individuals receive training that is most relevant to the evolving threats they are likely facing.

Informed Decision-Making: A user aware of their elevated risk might be more cautious when sharing work details on social media or interacting with unfamiliar senders.

Reducing Victim Blaming: Data-backed explanations may shift the focus from "why did the user fall for it" to a system-wide approach to mitigating those risks.

ARGUMENTS AGAINST SHARING ANALYSIS

Unintended Anxiety: Knowing you are a "high-risk target" can create stress, potentially diminishing productivity and ironically making some people even more susceptible, despite good intentions.

Self-Fulfilling Prophecy: Does being told you are likely to be targeted increase the chances of falling for a scam, as you become hyper-aware and primed to spot every "red flag"?

Potential for Misuse: Could this data become part of an employee evaluation, unfairly labelling those with higher probabilities as less security-conscious?

False Sense of Security: Those with low-risk scores might become complacent, creating another kind of vulnerability.

IT IS NOT BLACK AND WHITE: MIDDLE GROUND OPTIONS EXIST

Tiered Sharing: This is not the raw probability but a general risk level (Low, Moderate, Elevated) with tailored tips, but it omits specific modeling details.

Opt-In System: Employees willing to be part of threat awareness experiments can access complete data and become active partners in improving the model. Focus on Actions, Not Labels: Alerts for everyone emphasize that attackers adapt. Couple this with training on spotting evolving manipulative tactics.

CRUCIAL CONSIDERATIONS

Data Transparency: If any analysis is shared, clarity about what data is used AND how the model works is essential to avoid "black box" fearmongering.

Organizational Culture: This approach works best in companies prioritizing support and training, not punishment for security incidents.

Ongoing Research: Before wide-scale implementation, we need studies on the psychological impact of sharing such risk analysis.

Ultimately, the ethical decision hinges on a balance between the potential benefits and potential harms, which may vary across organizational contexts and individual users. The safeguards protect employee data and prevent its misuse within the context of our quantum-inspired social engineering defense model.

CORE PRINCIPLES

Minimization: Only collect data essential for the model to function. Resist the urge to track everything.

Anonymization: Data must be de-identified from the start. Individuals should never be traceable within the model's analysis.

Access Control: Strict protocols define who can access raw data vs. aggregated trends and for what specific purposes.

Transparency: Clear, upfront communication with employees about what data are used AND how their privacy is maintained.

SAFEGUARD CATEGORIES

Technical Safeguards

Encryption: Data at rest and in transit are encrypted with robust, regularly updated standards.

Separation of Duties: Those who develop the model should not have access to identifiable employee data, and vice versa.

Auditing: Regular audits of data access logs to detect any unauthorized attempts.

Policy Safeguards

Clear Data Usage Policy: Outlines what the data is used for, how it is protected, and, importantly, what it is not used for (performance evaluations, etc.).

Retention Limits: Data are deleted after a set period, preventing the creation of long-term "risk profiles" of individuals.

Independent Oversight: An ethics board or privacy ombudsperson to whom employees can report concerns and who regularly reviews the model's safeguards.

Culture and Education Safeguards

Security as a Shared Mission: Emphasize that the model is a tool for the entire organization's safety, not to single people out.

Manager Training: Those with access to any risk data must understand its limitations and potential for misuse.

Anonymized Case Studies: Use anonymized examples of how the model helped prevent attacks to build trust without compromising individual data.

Situational Considerations

Company Size: A small tech startup might rely more on external audits, while a large corporation could dedicate internal privacy personnel to this system.

Regulatory Landscape: Local data privacy laws (e.g., GDPR) will dictate specific requirements and necessitate legal consultation.

THE NEED FOR CONSTANT VIGILANCE

Even the best safeguards are only as adequate as their implementation and enforcement. It is essential to have:

Reporting Mechanisms: Clear, non-punitive ways for employees to voice concerns if they suspect data misuse.

Adapting to New Threats: As the model evolves, so must our thinking about potential harms and how to mitigate them.

To develop a sample incident response plan for a potential data breach related to our social engineering risk model and explore strategies for building trust through transparent communication about safeguards.

INCIDENT RESPONSE PLAN: DATA BREACH

Contain the breach swiftly, preventing further unauthorized access to sensitive data.

Assess the breach's scope and severity to determine the potential harm's extent.

Fulfill all legal and regulatory reporting obligations. If necessary, communicate transparently with affected employees, regulators, and the public, minimizing reputational damage.

Incident Response Lead: Oversees all actions, likely a senior IT security or privacy officer.
Technical Team: Works to isolate affected systems, identify the breach source, and restore data integrity.
Legal Counsel: Advises on reporting requirements, potential liabilities, and communication language.
Communications Specialist: Crafts messaging to employees and external stakeholders as the situation evolves.
Ethics/Privacy Representative: Ensures response actions prioritize the privacy of affected employees and uphold the organization's commitments.
Detection and Confirmation: Automated monitoring systems or employee reports trigger an initial investigation.
Containment: Affected systems are taken offline or access restricted expert assessment of how to stop the spread without destroying evidence.
Investigation: Forensic analysis to determine:
  Data Types Accessed: Was it raw risk probabilities, anonymized trends, or other connected employee data?
Breach Method: Vulnerability exploit, insider threat.

Legal counsel directs mandatory reporting based on affected individuals and data types. Affected employees are informed on time, even if the investigation is ongoing. Offer support resources (credit monitoring, etc.).

Remediation

Patching vulnerabilities plays a crucial role in bolstering system-wide security by addressing weaknesses exposed in previous breaches. When a breach occurs, it provides valuable insights into the specific vulnerabilities exploited by attackers. By promptly patching these vulnerabilities, organizations can effectively close those security gaps and prevent similar attacks from succeeding in the future. This proactive approach to security helps to create a more resilient system, reducing the risk of future breaches and protecting sensitive data.

However, patching vulnerabilities alone is not always sufficient to ensure comprehensive security. In many cases, user behavior can contribute to breaches, such as the use of weak passwords or falling victim to phishing scams. In these instances, targeted training should be conducted to educate users about cybersecurity best practices and empower them to make informed choices that enhance security.

It is essential that this training be delivered in a non-punitive tone, focusing on education and empowerment rather than blame or reprimand. A positive and supportive approach is more likely to encourage users to adopt secure behaviors and contribute to a culture of cybersecurity awareness.

By combining proactive patching of vulnerabilities with targeted user training, organizations can create a multi-layered defense against cyber threats. This holistic approach addresses both the technical and human aspects of cybersecurity, strengthening system-wide security and fostering a culture of awareness and responsibility among users.

Post-Incident Review

Was the plan effective? Does it need changes?

Proactive sharing of lessons learned with employees reinforces a "security-focused" culture.

BUILDING TRUST THROUGH TRANSPARENT SAFEGUARD COMMUNICATION

In today's digital age, where data breaches and privacy violations are rampant, it's more important than ever to prioritize the protection of personal information. This commitment to privacy is not just an ethical imperative; it's also essential for building trust and fostering a secure digital environment.

We understand that privacy is a fundamental human right, and we are committed to protecting your personal information. This commitment is not just lip service; it's embedded in our values and reflected in our practices. The data we collect is used to enhance our cybersecurity systems and protect our organization from threats. By analyzing patterns and identifying anomalies, we can proactively detect and mitigate potential attacks, safeguarding not only our own systems but also the data entrusted to us by our clients and partners. We employ robust security measures to protect your data, including encryption, anonymization, and access controls. Encryption scrambles your data, making it unreadable to unauthorized individuals, while anonymization techniques remove identifying information, ensuring your privacy is maintained. You have the right to know how your data is being used and to control your privacy preferences. We provide opt-in options for data collection, clear reporting paths for privacy concerns, and access to your anonymized data upon request.

Cybersecurity is a collaborative effort, and we believe in empowering individuals to take an active role in protecting their own privacy and security. We provide regular training and awareness programs to equip you with the knowledge and tools to navigate the digital world safely and confidently. We maintain a dedicated intranet page with up-to-date information about our privacy practices, FAQs, and contact information for our privacy team. We also hold regular town hall meetings and presentations to provide opportunities for Q&A and address any concerns.

By embedding privacy principles into our cybersecurity practices, we foster a culture of trust, transparency, and accountability. We believe that a strong commitment to privacy is not only essential for protecting individuals but also for building a more secure and resilient digital world.

CAVEATS

Avoid Overconfidence: No system is foolproof. Acknowledge this, showcasing a commitment to improvement.

It Takes Time: Trust is not built in a single announcement. Consistent actions reinforce the message.

While a robust incident response plan for data breaches is essential, its existence does not guarantee success. True resilience demands an ongoing commitment to improvement alongside a healthy dose of realism. It is vital to recognize that no system is foolproof; breaches may occur despite the best prevention efforts. Being prepared to act swiftly – containing the breach, assessing its impact, and transparently fulfilling legal and ethical obligations – is critical to minimizing damage and maintaining trust.

While it's essential to communicate the immediate actions taken to address a security breach and reassure stakeholders of their commitment to data protection, it's equally important to avoid the trap of overconfidence. Organizations must acknowledge the inherent limitations of any security system, no matter how robust or sophisticated. Cybersecurity is not a destination but an ongoing journey, a continuous process of adaptation and enhancement in the face of ever-evolving threats.

Trust, once shattered, is not instantly restored with a single press release or a flurry of well-intentioned promises. It is earned over time, through consistent and demonstrable actions that prioritize transparency, accountability, and the well-being of those affected by a breach. This requires a commitment to open communication, providing regular updates on the investigation, remediation efforts, and long-term security enhancements. It also necessitates a willingness to acknowledge shortcomings, take responsibility for failures, and provide meaningful support to those whose data may have been compromised.

This ongoing commitment to data security, demonstrated through concrete actions and transparent communication, is crucial not only for rebuilding trust but also for fostering a culture of cybersecurity awareness within the organization. By acknowledging vulnerabilities, learning from mistakes, and continually adapting defenses, organizations can demonstrate their dedication to protecting data and their responsibility toward those who entrust them with their sensitive information.

In essence, the response to a security breach should not be viewed as a one-time event but rather as an opportunity to strengthen security posture, enhance resilience, and reinforce the organization's commitment to data protection. This ongoing dedication, demonstrated through consistent actions and transparent communication, is the true measure of an organization's commitment to cybersecurity and its responsibility toward its stakeholders.

Conclusion

TECHNOLOGY AS A TOOL AND A PLACE

Analog computers, nature's original computing model, were the most potent calculating tools for thousands of years before being overshadowed by the digital revolution. Unlike digital computers, which process information in discrete bits (0s and 1s), analog computers operate on continuous variables. This aligns them with how many physical systems function, giving them a remarkable potential for modeling and simulating complex phenomena. There is a growing belief that analog computers are poised for a comeback, their unique strengths offering solutions to challenges that digital systems struggle to solve efficiently.

Analog computers are staging a powerful comeback, offering a compelling alternative to mainstream digital computers, particularly as the limitations of Moore's law become more apparent. Analog computing's reliance on continuous physical phenomena makes it sidestep those limitations.

The concept of "technology" is itself a moving target. What may seem futuristic today becomes commonplace tomorrow. As we explore the ever-expanding possibilities offered by new tools and advancements, we must remember that technology is ultimately a means, not an end. The actual value lies in how we utilize it – harnessing its power to solve problems, improve lives, and shape a brighter future.

The focus should shift from simply marveling at the latest technological wonders to ensuring their responsible and ethical application. By critically examining the potential impacts of new technologies, we can ensure they serve humanity's best interests. The journey forward lies in developing ever more sophisticated tools and cultivating the wisdom and foresight to use them wisely.

THE PROMISE OF SMART SYSTEM

A Roadmap to a Better Work World

The rise of intelligent systems and AI holds the power to radically transform the work world, a transformation with both potential and peril. Automation could lead to displacement, yet it may also open doors to more intellectually stimulating roles. The data-driven nature of these technologies could erode traditional workplace hierarchies but also create new tools for surveillance and control. Simultaneously, these interconnected systems create unprecedented vulnerabilities to social engineers who prey on the inherently weak link within organizations.

This book explores these complex landscapes. It questions whether intelligent systems will usher in an era of worker alienation or become tools for empowerment and collaboration. Will they create a world of intrusive surveillance, or could workers leverage these technologies against that intent on centralizing power? Moreover,

DOI: 10.1201/9781003500698-28

crucially, how can organizations build resilience against social engineering in this evolving threat landscape?

The answers are not predetermined. The technological future of work is shaped by choices made now – by corporations, policymakers, and individuals themselves. This book aims to illuminate those choices, providing a roadmap for navigating this ongoing transformation. We have looked into strategies to harness the power of intelligent systems, emphasizing collaboration, efficiency, and, crucially, security against those who exploit human vulnerabilities. The goal is a future where humans and intelligent systems work harmoniously, creating a secure, rewarding, and intellectually stimulating environment.

Importantly, this book is not a passive observation. Through thought-provoking exercises, it has encouraged participation and critical thinking. By actively grappling with the concepts presented, you are better equipped to understand and influence the forces shaping work's future. These exercises serve as tools to move beyond mere reaction toward actively building the future we want to see.

The future of work in the intelligent systems era is not inevitable; it is ours to create. This book has served as a guide, empowering you to embrace the opportunities, mitigate the risks, and play an informed, active role in shaping tomorrow's work world. Let us strive for a future where technology complements human intelligence and ingenuity, fostering collaboration, security, and enduring fulfillment for all.

Index

A

D

H

I

P

Q

V

W

X

Y

Z

For Product Safety Concerns and Information please contact our
EU representative GPSR@taylorandfrancis.com Taylor & Francis
Verlag GmbH, Kaufingerstraße 24, 80331 München, Germany